HRSB
Dartmouth Teachers'
Centre

Atlantic Canada
IN THE GLOBAL COMMUNITY

JAMES CREWE
RUSSELL MCLEAN
WILLIAM BUTT
ROBERT KENYON
DEIRDRE KESSLER
DENNIS MINTY
ELMA SCHEMENAUER

BREAKWATER/PRENTICE HALL GINN

Atlantic Canada in the Global Community was developed as a project of the Breakwater Educational Consortium.

BREAKWATER
100 Water Street
P.O. Box 2188
St. John's, NF
A1C 6E6

PRENTICE HALL GINN CANADA
1870 Birchmount Road
Scarborough, ON
M1P 2J7

Canadian Cataloguing in Publication Data
Main entry under title:
Atlantic Canada in the global community
Co-published by Breakwater Books.
Includes index.
ISBN 0-13-727876-4
1. Atlantic Provinces. I. Crewe, James.
FC2005.A84 1997   971.5   C97-931107-1
F1035.8.A768 1997

Copyright ©1998 Breakwater Books Ltd./Prentice-Hall Ginn Canada Inc.

ALL RIGHTS RESERVED. No part of this work covered by copyright hereon may be reproduced or used in any form or by any means without the prior written permission of the publisher. This applies to classroom usage as well.

ISBN 0-13-727876-4

Publishers: Clyde Rose, Breakwater Books Ltd./
Anita Borovilos, Prentice Hall Ginn Canada Inc.
Project coordinator: Carla Kean
Project development: Carol Stokes
Editor: Elynor Kagan
Copy editor: Patti Giovannini
Contributing editors: Helen Mason, Margaret Hoogeveen
Art direction: Alex Li
Design: Alex Li, Zena Denchik
Page layout: Zena Denchik
Production coordinator: Julie Preston
Permissions and photo research: Rebecca Rose
Maps: Deborah Crowle
Illustrations: Kevin Cheng, David Cheung, VictoR GAD, Renée Mansfield/Three in a Box Inc., Allan Moon, Russ Willms/Three in a Box Inc.
Cover design: David Cheung

Cover photographs: Top left: NASA. Top right: Greg Locke. Centre Left: Tourism New Brunswick. Centre right: ©Barrett & MacKay photo. Bottom: Sky-Shots Aerial Photography.

Printed and bound in Canada
1 2 3 4 5   01 00 99 98 97

Contents

PREFACE	v
ACKNOWLEDGEMENTS	vi

UNIT 1 PHYSICAL SETTING 1

CHAPTER 1 Finding Your Way 2
Finding Location Using Latitude and Longitude 3
Finding Location with the Global Positioning System 5
Finding Places from the Air 8
Finding Your Way with a Topographic Map 10
Finding Your Way Downtown 12
CASE STUDY: Finding a Sunken Ship 14

CHAPTER 2 Our Natural Environment 18
Atlantic Canada as a Region 19
How Large Is Atlantic Canada? 20
Distance and Time 22
Landforms in Atlantic Canada 24
Water Forms in Atlantic Canada 26
People in Their Environment 30

CHAPTER 3 The Changing Weather 33
What Is a Snowstorm? 34
Factors Affecting the Climate of Atlantic Canada 37
Examining Weather 43
CASE STUDY: The Flight of a Radiosonde 46

CHAPTER 4 A Place to Live 49
Population Patterns 50
CASE STUDY: The Growth of Fredericton 53
Roots of Our Population 55
Aboriginal Peoples 55
Early European Settlement 57
African-Canadian Communities 61
Immigration in the Twentieth Century 63

UNIT 2 CULTURE 65

CHAPTER 5 What Is Culture? 66
Defining Culture 67
Meeting Our Needs 70
Material and Non-material Culture 71
Traditional Culture, Popular Culture, and the Global Connection 72
The Many Agents of Socialization 74
Mainstream and Contributing Cultures 78

CHAPTER 6 Our Cultural Mosaic 80
Cultures Change 81
Celebrating Cultural Diversity 82
What Is Racism? 86
Combatting Racism 89
CASE STUDY: Educating Against Racism 90

CHAPTER 7 Expressions of Atlantic Culture 93
Traditional Music Meets Popular Culture 94
Storytelling as Entertainment 96
Literature and the Making of an Industry 100
A Focus on Fine Art 102
A Focus on Fashion 104
CASE STUDY: The Acadian Renaissance 105

CHAPTER 8 Occupation and Lifestyle 108
Why Do We Work? 109
CASE STUDY: The Labrador Inuit 112
CASE STUDY: The Lebanese Community of Prince Edward Island 115
CASE STUDY: Developing an Economy in Lunenburg 118

CHAPTER 9 Culture and Politics 123
What Is Politics? 124
Government in Our Lives 124
The Power of the Vote 127
CASE STUDY: Wayne Adams: Representing the People 130
Democracy in Action 133
CASE STUDY: Janet Conners: Profile of a Political Activist 135
CASE STUDY: Labour Unions: The Politics of the Workplace 136

UNIT 3 ECONOMICS 139

CHAPTER 10 Economics: Close to Home 140
What Is Economics? 141
The Laws of Supply and Demand 144
The Hidden Market 146

Economic Thinking and Your Personal
   Finances   147
It's a Matter of Interest   150
CASE STUDY: A Financial Fable   152

CHAPTER 11   The Atlantic Economy   156
Sectors of Our Economy   157
Primary Industry   159
CASE STUDY: Mining at Voisey's Bay   164
CASE STUDY: Potato Farming in Prince
   Edward Island   166
Secondary Industry   169
CASE STUDY: Processing Potatoes: Have a
   French Fry!   170
Tertiary and Quaternary Industries   172
CASE STUDY: The Prince Edward Island
   Food Technology Centre   173
The New Economy   174

CHAPTER 12   Our Economic Outlook   179
Sabian Cymbals: An International Success
   Story   180
The Prosperity of Our Region   183
Quality of Life   183
Atlantic Canada: Looking for Solutions   187
The Importance of Trade   188
CASE STUDY: Atlantic-Allstar Genetics   190
CASE STUDY: Blue Mussels, Prince Edward
   Island   191
CASE STUDY: Instrumar Limited   192
CASE STUDY: The Aerospace Industry
   Association and IMP Aerospace   193

UNIT 4   TECHNOLOGY   195

CHAPTER 13   Technology: Past to Present   196
What Is Technology?   197
Technology and Change   198
Technology in Everyday Life: Then
   and Now   200
CASE STUDY: Technology of Water
   Transportation: A Comparative Study   202
Technology: A Double-Edged Sword?   209

CHAPTER 14   Technological Links   213
Transportation in Atlantic Canada   214
CASE STUDY: Transportation Links:
   Confederation Bridge   216
Communications: Reshaping Our World   218

The Information Age   220
CASE STUDY: On-Line Services   222

CHAPTER 15   Technology and Resources   226
Technology and the Northern Cod   227
Technology and Resource Use   230
Technology Below Ground   232
Technology and the Forest   234
Technology on the Farm   237

CHAPTER 16   Technology at Work   240
Businesses in the New Economy   241
Workers in the New Economy   246
Changes in Manufacturing and Marketing   250
CASE STUDY: Making a CD   252

UNIT 5   INTERDEPENDENCE   255

CHAPTER 17   Our Views of the World   256
Global Citizens   257
Developing a View of the World   259
A Global World-View   262
CASE STUDY: The Pugwash Conferences   265
CASE STUDY: A Place of Refuge   266
Becoming a Contributing Member of the
   Global Community   268

CHAPTER 18   Our Global Connections   270
A Vision of the Future   271
Our Environmental Connections   272
CASE STUDY: Raising the *Irving Whale*   273
Our Cultural Connections   274
Our Political Connections   277
CASE STUDY: The Coady International
   Institute   278
Our Economic Connections   279
Our Technological Connections   282
Conclusion: A Personal Vision   285

APPENDIX 1: New Brunswick   287
APPENDIX 2: Nova Scotia   288
APPENDIX 3: Prince Edward Island   289
APPENDIX 4: Newfoundland and Labrador   290
GLOSSARY   291
INDEX   295
CREDITS   298

Preface

Atlantic Canada in the Global Community is an innovative program that has drawn on the combined effort of all four Atlantic provinces. The program was started by the Department of Education in Newfoundland and Labrador but, under the umbrella of the Atlantic Provinces Education Foundation (APEF), it evolved to reflect the perspectives and curriculum goals of all the partner provinces.

The text is designed to involve you in examining and reflecting on the major issues that affect you as individuals, as Atlantic Canadians, and as global citizens. In the five units, you will explore and appreciate the unique physical features of this region; the diverse cultural, ethnic, and historical backgrounds of the people who live here; the economic issues and challenges we all face; the role of technology in your past, present, and future; and the importance of effective global citizenship.

SPECIAL FEATURES

Chapter Openers: Each chapter in the book introduces the main topic from a student's perspective, before placing it in an Atlantic and global context. As a result, you will be aware of your personal connections to each of the themes examined.

Rich Resources: Chapters feature a wide variety of resources, including extracts and quotes, interviews, maps, tables and graphs, photographs, artwork, and cartoons. You are encouraged to analyze these materials through questions in captions or "Focus" boxes.

"Did You Know…?" Boxes: These sidebars provide added interest and extension of topics.

Case Studies: These allow you to explore selected topics in greater depth, and to apply general understanding to issues of particular concern to Atlantic Canada.

Focus on an Issue: Some chapters include an examination of a featured issue. You are encouraged to analyze, evaluate, and think critically, to suggest solutions.

Career Focus: Many chapters include a career focus that demonstrates the practical value of chapter topics and their possible application in everyday life.

Explorations: These activities appear at the end of each major section and are grouped into several levels: "Reviewing the Ideas," "Applying Your Skills," "Analyzing and Reflecting," and "Connecting and Extending." Each chapter ends with an extended activity called "Seeing the Big Picture" which draws together the themes of the chapter and makes connections with global themes.

Map Appendix: The book includes an appendix of four detailed full-page maps — one for each province — that can be used for reference.

Glossary and Index: The book concludes with a glossary of key terms, which have been highlighted in the text. An index is also included.

The five themes of this text are interrelated and we hope that you will draw on the links among units wherever possible. We also encourage you to draw on current events, issues, and examples to apply and extend what you learn from the text. In addition, we hope you will use technology throughout this program as a means of connecting with other students, doing research, and preparing for the future.

Acknowledgements

Many organizations and individuals have helped in the development of this resource, within a very challenging schedule. We would like to acknowledge, above all, the contributions of Avis Fitton, Smita Joshi, Sue LeBel, Rick MacDonald, and Willard Moase. Together with APEF coordinators Deborah McLean, Glenn Davis, and Laurie Alexander, these consultants devoted considerable time and energy to developing the text, all with a remarkable spirit of cooperation and common interest.

We would like to thank all those who reviewed the text, supplying suggestions for improvements and additional information. Our thanks go, in particular, to the following people:

Harry Baglole	Basil Favaro	Maud McCarty
Genette Baldwin	Peter Fleming	Peter Neary
William Barbour	Wanda Garrett	Doug Oldford
Tim Borlase	Claire Gossen	Sylvia Parris
Peter Bowyer	William Hamilton	David Perley
Patrick Brannon	David Hughes	Jim Petrie
Frank Cramm	Albert Jones	Wanda Whitlock
Leslie Dawes	Heather MacLellan	Ed Woodrow

We acknowledge, with thanks, the following teachers and their students, who worked with the early drafts of the manuscript. Their comments helped to direct the process of revision and the development of the finished text.

Leo Abbass	Maurice Lewis	Gary Pyke
James Camsell	Basil Ludlow	Jim Scott
Lester Capstick	Marie MacLeod	Brenda Sisson
Donnie Craig	Maud McCarty	Carma Smith
Leonard Cusack	Clarence Mercer	Gary Sparkes
Danny Eddy	J. Patrick Milligan	Valerie Sullivan
Enos House	George Mitchell	Ross Tilley
Jamie Jennings	Sandra Mitchell	
J. Paul LaLande	David Power	

We would also like to thank the many Atlantic Canadians who graciously agreed to be interviewed for the text or to provide materials that have been included. Their contributions reflect the spirit of cooperation that underlies this project and the vision it projects for the future.

UNIT 1
Physical Setting

CHAPTER 1 *Finding Your Way*

How can we locate the Atlantic provinces within Canada, North America, and the world?

CHAPTER 2 *Our Natural Environment*

How big is Atlantic Canada, and what are its main land and water forms?

How do people in the region interact with their natural environment?

CHAPTER 3 *The Changing Weather*

What are the basic weather and climate patterns of Atlantic Canada?

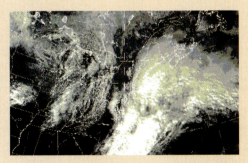

CHAPTER 4 *A Place to Live*

Which main groups of people have lived in Atlantic Canada over the centuries?

Where have people in the region settled, and why have they gone to these locations?

CHAPTER 1
Finding Your Way

Figure 1.1 The *Amphion*, an ore carrier about two football fields in length, was carrying a load of steel from Germany to Philadelphia, USA, when it encountered high winds and heavy seas east of Newfoundland. The captain sent out a distress signal that was picked up by satellite and beamed all over the world.

Figure 1.2 Rescue centres in Falmouth, England, and New York, USA, relayed the location of the *Amphion* to the Halifax Rescue Coordination Centre. The officers and crew of the vessel were rescued, in a race against time, by the Canadian fisheries patrol vessel the *Leonard J. Cowley* (foreground).

You are a Coast Guard officer stationed at the Halifax Rescue Coordination Centre on January 10, 1996. You have just received a distress signal regarding the *Amphion*, a bulk carrier adrift in an ocean with three-storey-high waves. The lives of the 24 crew members are at risk, unless a rescue crew can reach them soon. The nearest port is St. John's, Newfoundland, 900 km away.

- How will you tell rescue vessels where to find the *Amphion*?
- What methods could they use to locate the vessel?

PHYSICAL SETTING

Finding Location Using Latitude and Longitude

The *Amphion* sent out its distress signal using the universal language of location: latitude and longitude. Many of the ways that we use to find places are based on these imaginary lines on the surface of the earth. On maps and globes, **lines of latitude** are drawn east-west to show distances north or south of the equator (0°). The greatest distances are to the North Pole (90°N) or to the South Pole (90°S). Each line of latitude runs parallel to the equator, all around the world.

Lines of longitude are drawn north-south from pole to pole to show distances east or west of the Prime Meridian (0°), which passes through Greenwich, England. The greatest distance is on the opposite side of the globe, in the mid-Pacific, at 180°, travelling either east or west from the Prime Meridian. Every line of longitude runs straight from the North Pole to the South Pole.

The Prime Meridian (0°) and the 180° line of longitude divide the globe into two halves, the Eastern Hemisphere and the Western Hemisphere. The equator divides the globe into the Northern Hemisphere and the Southern Hemisphere.

Each degree of longitude or latitude consists of exactly 60 minutes ('). However, one degree of latitude equals approximately 111 km on the earth's surface, while the distance covered by one degree of longitude varies depending on the distance north or south from the equator.

Latitude and longitude lines intersect to make up a set of **coordinates** to indicate the **absolute location** of any point on the earth's surface. For example, the absolute location of the rescue centre in St. John's, Newfoundland, from which the *Leonard J. Cowley* set sail, is 47°35'N, 52°40'W. By using these coordinates you can find the precise location on the map in Figure 1.8. The **relative location** of a place is not as precise, but it gives you a good idea of the general area in which a place is located. Relative location is usually described in terms of distance or direction from another place. Halifax, for example, is a Canadian port city centrally located on the Atlantic coast of Nova Scotia.

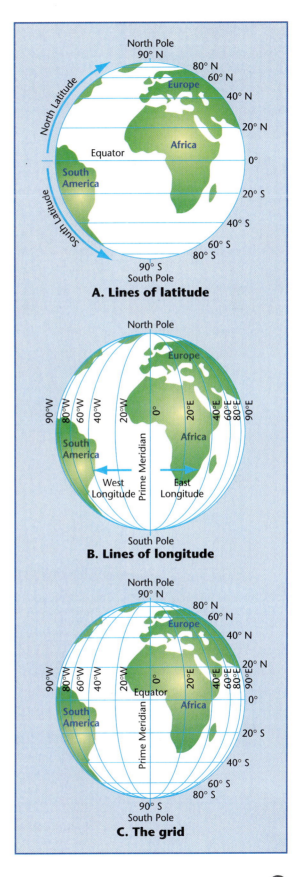

Figure 1.3 Lines of latitude and longitude

A. Lines of latitude

B. Lines of longitude

C. The grid

Finding Your Way 3

Figure 1.4
Charlottetown, capital of Prince Edward Island

FOCUS ON FIGURE 1.8

1. Identify the lines of latitude and longitude on this map. Between which two lines of latitude and which two lines of longitude is Atlantic Canada located?
2. Describe the relative location of each of the four Atlantic capitals.
3. Record the absolute location of each of the capitals.

Figure 1.5
Fredericton, capital of New Brunswick

Figure 1.6
Halifax, capital of Nova Scotia

Figure 1.7
St. John's, capital of Newfoundland and Labrador

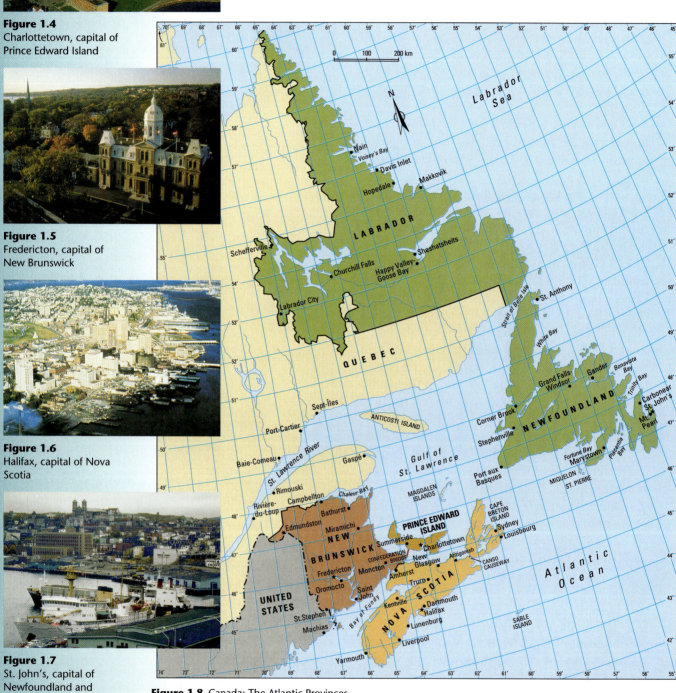

Figure 1.8 Canada: The Atlantic Provinces

4 PHYSICAL SETTING

Finding Location with the Global Positioning System

Traditionally, mariners calculated their latitude by measuring, in degrees, the height of the North Star above the horizon. To find longitude, they first calculated the local time by observing the sun's position. They then compared the local time with Greenwich time (at the Prime Meridian), which they had recorded on a timepiece called a chronometer.

Today, navigators use various technologies, including the **Global Positioning System (GPS)** to find their location. GPS consists of a fleet of satellites that orbit the earth twice a day to give the precise time and location of any place on the earth. A ship can use GPS to determine its latitude and longitude quickly and accurately.

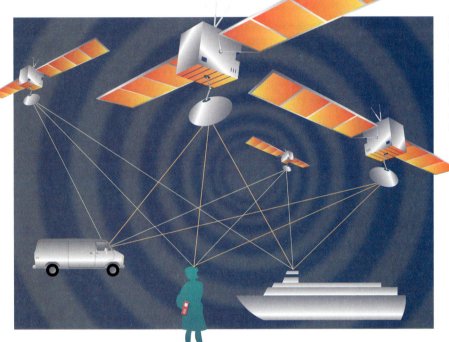

Figure 1.9 The GPS receiver on a ship, aircraft, car, or person receives a signal from at least three satellites. The receiver is programmed to calculate the distance to each satellite automatically. It then uses the distances to calculate the absolute location of the object, place, or person.

DID YOU KNOW...?

GPS has a wide variety of uses. For example, the system was used in the construction of the Confederation Bridge between New Brunswick and Prince Edward Island. It allowed construction crews to position the pier supports in the Northumberland Strait accurately, within 1 cm of the planned location. GPS is also used by some transportation companies to track their trucks, and some long-distance hikers use GPS to give them precise location for setting a course through unfamiliar terrain. In addition, GPS can be used by people who are visually challenged to "navigate" through unfamiliar neighbourhoods. The individual carries a small computer pack that has the locations for street intersections in a specific city stored in its memory. The device receives signals from three satellites to calculate the position of the individual as he or she stands at an intersection. The computer then matches this position with one of the positions stored in its memory and communicates the match as a voice message.

Career Focus: Meet a Coast Guard Captain

Captain Rosemary Lundrigan was born in Nova Scotia. As a superintendent of planning with the Operational Services Directorate in St. John's, Newfoundland, she is responsible for organizing the yearly operations of Coast Guard vessels.

Figure 1.10 Captain Lundrigan

Canadian Coast Guard Officer Training Program

Entrance Requirements

English, mathematics, physics, French, chemistry, medical and eyesight exam, Canadian citizenship or landed immigrant status

Training for Navigation Officer Cadets Courses include:

- computer
- seamanship
- signals
- chartwork and pilotage
- meteorology
- nautical astronomy
- navigation instruments
- navigation safety
- radar simulation
- French

Q: How well did your education prepare you for your job?

A: The program at the Coast Guard College provided the necessary knowledge, but it was only the beginning. When you are first hired, you start with a low certificate level. While at sea, you get practical experience to qualify you to write examinations for other certificates. It can take up to ten years to acquire the Master Mariner level.

Q: Did you always want to have a career related to the sea?

A: I first became interested back in high school. During Career Days someone from the Coast Guard College came to the school to talk about their work and the three-year program of study in Navigation and Engineering at the College in Sydney. I wanted to do something different, so I applied to the Coast Guard College.

Q: What are your main duties with the Coast Guard?

A: As a superintendent of planning I help to deploy our fleet vessels each year, making crew arrangements, assessing costs, and confirming the work that crew members have to do. I miss the work on board the vessels. I came ashore to have my family (I have two little girls). But I'd go back now if I ever had the opportunity.

Q: Is it necessary to speak a second language in the Coast Guard?

A: It is a requirement that Canadian primary search and rescue vessels have a percentage of French-speaking people on board. I studied French at Coast Guard College, and I'm now bilingual. It has been useful at times in communicating with ships that have French-speaking crews.

Q: Does the Coast Guard use the Global Positioning System (GPS)?

A: Oh yes, it does. Everybody uses GPS, although we use the Loran C system as well. Loran stands for **Lo**ng-**ran**ge navigation. It's a system for determining location using signals from radio transmitters.

Q: Are people surprised when they find out that you are with the Coast Guard?

A: Yes. I'm still surprised at that, even though I've been in the Coast Guard for 20 years. There are a fair number of women in the Coast Guard, but we're so few over all. Attitudes are changing, but very slowly.

Q: Are there any experiences that stand out in your mind?
A: There are quite a few. I remember one severe storm off Newfoundland's west coast when ice began to build up on the upper part of the ship. I was Chief Officer at the time, and I was down below having a cup of tea after having been relieved from the bridge by the captain. The rough water sent dishes flying down in the galley. We were on our way to search for a fishing boat that had disappeared. We did recover some of the bodies, which made me feel very bad.

Once I was the commanding officer of the *Harp*, a primary Search and Rescue vessel based in St. Anthony. It was the first time in Newfoundland and Labrador that a woman in the Coast Guard was a commanding officer. Sometimes when I had to take a vessel in tow, those on the other boat would ask questions to test me. But I could always convince them that I was the commanding officer and prove that I knew my stuff.

Q: Would you recommend this job to other people?
A: I'd recommend it, but not to the weak-hearted by any means. It's not a job you do for eight hours a day and go home and forget about. But if you want something challenging, something that will take you to many areas of our great country, and something in a marine way of life, the Coast Guard is the way to go.

EXPLORATIONS

APPLYING YOUR SKILLS

1. **a)** You are the radio operator aboard the *Amphion*. According to Figure 1.1, what coordinates for your absolute location would you give Search-and-Rescue in Halifax?

   b) How would you describe the relative location of the *Amphion*?

   c) From which of the following ports would you hope that a Search-and-Rescue vessel would be available: Saint John, New Brunswick; Halifax, Nova Scotia; or St. John's, Newfoundland? Explain.

2. On February 3, 1996, an ocean-going tug towed the *Amphion* into a port at 44°40′N, 63°30′W. Identify this port.

3. Using a globe or atlas, describe the location of Atlantic Canada with respect to the four hemispheres.

ANALYZING AND REFLECTING

4. Do you agree with the following statement? "Technology was key to the rescue of the crew of the *Amphion*." Give reasons for your view.

5. Operations such as the rescue of the *Amphion's* crew are very expensive. Who do you think should pay: ship owners, taxpayers in the closest country, or international agencies?

   a) Discuss your ideas in class.

   b) Make a short speech or write a "letter to the editor" giving your views.

6. **a)** What skills and personal qualities do you think helped Captain Lundrigan become successful in her job?

   b) Which aspects of a Coast Guard career might interest you? Explain.

7. What steps do you think could be taken to encourage more women to join the Coast Guard? Discuss your ideas in a group.

CONNECTING AND EXTENDING

8. In groups, role play the Rescue Centre response to the *Amphion's* distress signal. Assign appropriate roles (e.g., shift supervisor, communications officers, response coordinators, etc.) to analyze the problem and set a course of action. Follow these steps:

   a) Summarize available information.

   b) Determine what additional data you need to respond effectively.

   c) Determine the urgency of the situation.

   d) Propose a course of action.

FINDING PLACES FROM THE AIR

Most of us will never have to pinpoint a ship's location in thousands of square kilometres of open sea. For a variety of reasons, however, we all need to know how to find our way around our own region or community. There are many ways to find location, using everything from a satellite image of a whole province to a street map.

With satellite technology, it is possible to obtain pictures of enormous regions of the earth. Satellites orbiting the earth about every 103 minutes at an altitude of 700 to 920 km can photograph an area measuring 185 km^2. In a satellite image, we can distinguish both physical and cultural features of an area. **Physical features**, such as river valleys, occur as a result of natural forces. **Cultural features** are either made by humans or show the imprint of human activity. Examples of cultural features include farming and settlement patterns, highways, bridges, or buildings.

Figure 1.12 shows a satellite image of the Chignecto Bay area in New Brunswick and Nova Scotia. The exercises below will help you examine this image.

EXPLORATIONS

APPLYING YOUR SKILLS

1. Construct a map of the area shown in the satellite image in Figure 1.12.

   a) Draw a grid that you can use to indicate locations on the map. Use a ruler to divide the left and right edges into five equal segments; assign a letter from A to E to identify each segment. Then divide the top and bottom edges into five equal segments; assign numerals 1 to 5 to identify the segments.

   b) Use the colour key to interpret the satellite image. On your map, sketch and label physical features such as forested areas, hills, rivers, bays, and peninsulas; and cultural features such as farmland, roads, and communities.

   c) On the map, find and label the following cities or towns: Moncton, Dorchester, Sackville, and Amherst.

2. The following chart identifies features on the satellite image. Indicate whether each is a physical or cultural feature and, where possible, find its absolute location according to your grid. Use an atlas, if necessary.

Feature	Physical	Cultural	Absolute Location
Moncton	___	___	___
Amherst	___	___	___
Hopewell Cape	___	___	___
NS/NB border	___	___	___
Petitcodiac River	___	___	___
A cultivated area	___	___	___
A highway	___	___	___
An airport	___	___	___

3. A service centre is a community that provides goods and services for communities in its surrounding area. It is usually larger than other communities and has transportation links with them.

   a) Identify a service centre on the satellite image.

   b) What is its relative location in terms of another nearby community?

   c) What services do you think this centre would offer? Consider retail and trade, financial (e.g., banks), administrative (e.g., government offices), health, and any other services.

Figure 1.11 Location of Chignecto Bay

Legend:
- rocky outcrops
- reclaimed marsh soils
- cultivated land
- forest and vegetation
- deep water in bay areas
- rivers and shallow water at the heads of bays
- towns and cities

Figure 1.12 A view of the Chignecto Bay area from approximately 900 km in space.

Figure 1.13 Tantramar Marsh, among others, was drained for cultivation by settlers to the Chignecto Isthmus during the eighteenth and nineteenth centuries.

Finding Your Way with a Topographic Map

You have decided to vacation in Prince Edward Island and would like to rent a cottage near the Prince Edward Island National Park. You want to get a detailed look at the area in order to make a decision, so you use a **topographic map**. Find examples of the following features on Figure 1.14:

- Physical features, such as vegetation, lakes, rivers, marsh, hills and valleys. The map key explains how symbols and colours are used to do this; for example, wooded areas are in green and water features in blue.

- Cultural features, such as highways, bridges, sports tracks, buildings, and built-up areas. Again, the map key shows the symbols used for this purpose; for example, a tent indicates a campsite; a skiing figure indicates a ski area.

- The elevation, or height of the land, through the use of numbered contour lines. These are imaginary lines that connect points at the same height above sea level.

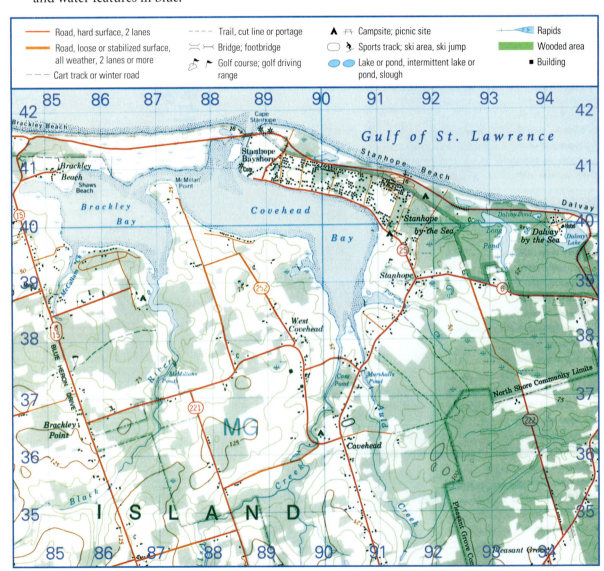

Figure 1.14 A topographic map of the Brackley-Stanhope Beach area, Prince Edward Island. The Prince Edward Island National Park, which extends 40 km along the island's northern shore, was established to protect a wide variety of physical features: sand dunes, red cliffs, marshes, ponds, and saltwater beaches, as well as various types of vegetation.

Figure 1.15 Dalvay-by-the-Sea, Prince Edward Island. What physical and cultural features can you see?

Pinpointing Locations on a Topographic Map

Features are not always located conveniently where two grid lines intersect on a topographic map. The bridge at Cape Stanhope, for example, is in the block to the right of line 88 and above line 41. How do we pinpoint the exact location? First, we mentally divide the distance between the grid lines into tenths and estimate the location. Thus, because the bridge is about seven-tenths of a grid space beyond 88, we designate the east-west location as 88.7. Because the bridge is about six-tenths of a grid space beyond 41, we designate the north-south location as 41.6. We then simplify the two location indicators to "887" and "416," respectively. We put these location indicators together into a convenient six-digit location code that always indicates the east-west location first and the north-south location second. In this case, the grid reference for the bridge is 887416.

◆ Location through use of a grid consisting of numbered blue lines.

◆ Direction through use of the same grid. The horizontal lines run west-east and the vertical lines run north-south.

EXPLORATIONS

APPLYING YOUR SKILLS

1. Name or describe the physical feature at each of the following locations.
   - **a)** 900400
   - **b)** 920377
   - **c)** 873405
   - **d)** 884413

2. Name or describe the cultural feature at each of the following locations.
   - **a)** 944399
   - **b)** 912393
   - **c)** 904364
   - **d)** 867388

3. **a)** You are travelling by road from the crossroads at 903363 to Stanhope Beach at 923406. In which general direction would you travel?

   b) Describe the physical and cultural features that you would see when taking the shortest journey.

   c) What is the name of the body of water beyond Stanhope Beach?

   d) Where would the nearest campsite on the beach be located?

4. With a partner, consider the following situation. You work at a Prince Edward Island Tourist Information Centre. List the kinds of information about the Brackley-Stanhope Beach area you would provide to:

   a) a tourist from Halifax who visited the Brackley-Stanhope area several years ago

   b) a tourist from British Columbia who has been to the Atlantic coast before, but never to the Brackley-Stanhope beach area

   c) a tourist from Tokyo, Japan, who is visiting Canada for the first time

Finding Your Way Downtown

To find our way around built-up or urban areas we use street maps which are usually drawn on a very large scale compared to other maps. To remember the difference between large- and small-scale maps, think of the amount of detail. A **small-scale** map, such as a provincial road map, shows a **small** amount of detail and a **large-scale** map, such as a city road map, shows a **large** amount of detail.

Figure 1.16 is a street map of downtown Fredericton, New Brunswick. Figure 1.17, a photograph of part of downtown Fredericton, was taken from a hot-air balloon. The following exercises will allow you to practise using a street map to locate different sites in a downtown area. Street maps are usually drawn so that the top of the map points north.

Legend

- **A** Fredericton Exhibition Grounds
- **B** Fredericton Small Craft Aquatic Centre
- **C** Lord Beaverbrook Art Gallery
- **D** Old Government House
- **E** Christ Church Cathedral
- **F** University of New Brunswick
- **G** Carriage House Inn
- **H** UNB Tourist Hotel (seasonal use of student residence)
- **?** Tourist Information Centre
- Parks & Walking Trails
- Arenas
- Sports Fields

Figure 1.16 Street map of downtown Fredericton

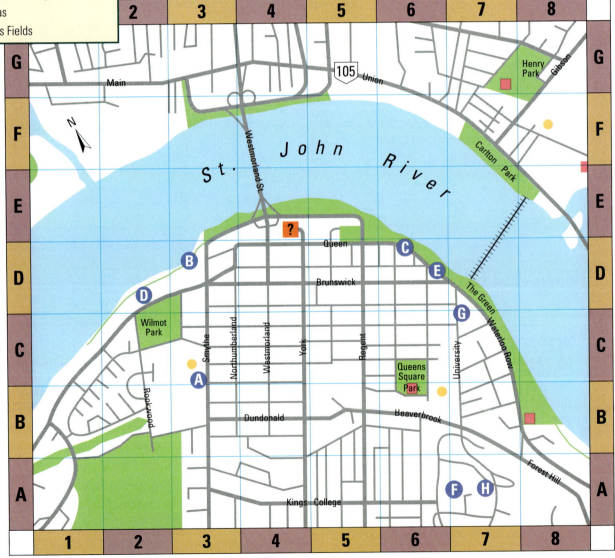

12 PHYSICAL SETTING

Figure 1.17
Photograph of downtown Fredericton. Locate this section of the city on the map. What clues did you use to identify the location? In the photograph, find evidence of an old bridge that does not show on the map.

EXPLORATIONS

APPLYING YOUR SKILLS

1. **a)** You are staying at the University of New Brunswick Tourist Hotel. According to the street map, what is the grid location (grid reference) for this hotel?

   b) Write a statement to describe the relative location of this hotel.

2. **a)** You are meeting a friend who is staying at the Carriage House Inn. Which street would you take to get to this hotel?

   b) You wish to relax on "The Green" for an hour or so at street map grid reference 7D. Where is this location on "The Green" relative to the Carriage House Inn and the St. John River?

   c) If you were to look north across the river from this point, which park would you see?

3. **a)** You then walk to the building designated on the street map by "C". What is the name of this flat-roofed building?

   b) Find this building on the photograph. What is the grid location on the photograph?

4. From here you get a cab and go south to Brunswick Street and then take a left towards the church at grid reference 14F in the photograph.

   a) What is the name of this church?

   b) What is the grid location on the street map?

   c) You then proceed towards Waterloo Row. What is the grid reference on the street map of the railway bridge on the photograph?

   d) The cab then takes a right on University to take you to your hotel. In which direction are you travelling now?

5. From evidence in the photograph, how has the river influenced the location and growth of Fredericton?

CASE STUDY

Finding a Sunken Ship

On April 10, 1912, the *RMS Titanic* set sail on its maiden voyage from Southampton, England. The *Titanic* was considered the supreme symbol of human and technological progress. Its launch was hailed as an event of international significance.

At 269.2 m long, 28.2 m wide, and 18.2 m deep, the *Titanic* was the largest vessel ever put to sea. The engines propelled the 46 000-tonne ship at a speed of 22 knots (one knot equals 1.85 km per hour). For safety, its thick double-plated steel hull was fitted with 16 "watertight" compartments. It was equipped with the latest in communications technology, the Marconi Telegraph.

Figure 1.18 The majestic *Titanic* before its launch. The ship was described as a "floating palace." It was believed to be unsinkable.

Time Line of the Sinking

11:40 PM — Lookout sees an iceberg straight ahead, radios the bridge.

12:15 AM — Lighthouse keeper at Cape Race, Newfoundland, hears *Titanic* giving position 41°44′N, 50°24′W.

12:25 AM — Call received from *Titanic* by *Carpathia*. *Titanic* says, "Come at once. We have struck a berg. Position 41°46′N, 50°14′W."

12:30 AM — *Titanic* gives position to *Frankfurt* and says, "Tell your captain to come to our help. We are on the ice."

1:45 AM — Last signals heard from *Titanic* by *Carpathia*, "Engine room full up to the boilers."

After leaving Southampton, the *Titanic* called in at Cherbourg, France, proceeded to Cobh, Ireland, and then headed westward into the Atlantic Ocean en route for New York City.

Just before midnight on April 14, the *Titanic* collided with an iceberg that tore a 90-m gash in the hull below the waterline.

The Titanic

And out there in the starlight, with no trace
Upon it of its deed but the last wave
From the Titanic fretting at its base,
Silent, composed, ringed by its icy broods,
The grey shape with the Paleolithic face
Was still the master of the longitudes.

Excerpt from "The Titanic" by Newfoundland poet E.J. Pratt. The *Titanic* tragedy had a major impact on the people of Atlantic Canada. What do you think "it" in line 2 refers to?

Location of *Titanic*'s Deathbed Placed by Canadian Marine Official

HALIFAX, April 15, 1912 — The 'deathbed' of the ten-million-dollar steamer *Titanic*, and of probably many who must have been dragged down with her, is two miles (3.2 km), at least, below the surface of the sea.

The calculation was made by an official of the Government Marine Department, who finds it on the chart at a point about 500 miles (800 km) from Halifax and about 70 miles (112 km) south of the Grand Banks, where he believes the *Titanic* went down.

Source: The New York Times, April 16, 1912.

Figure 1.19 A message in a bottle that washed ashore after the *Titanic* disaster.

Our Ship is lost. All hope of being saved is abandoned. John Steward, Ill-fated Titanic

Figure 1.20 Location on board and survival rate

Numbers of passengers

Class	Gender: Male	Gender: Female	Total
1st	180	145	325
2nd	179	106	285
3rd	510	196	706

100
80
60
40
20
0
Percentage (%) of passengers saved
Men
Women
Children
1st
2nd
3rd
Class

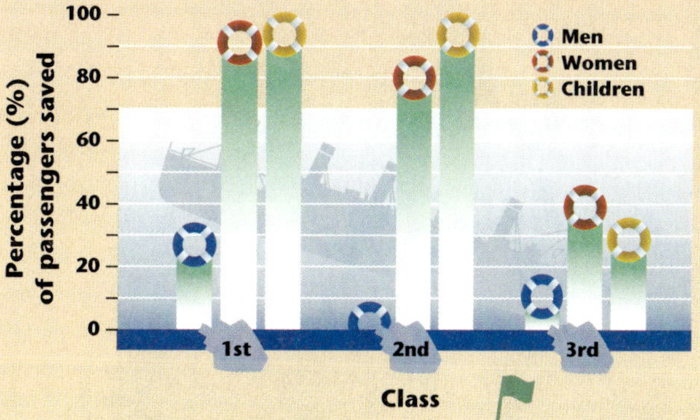

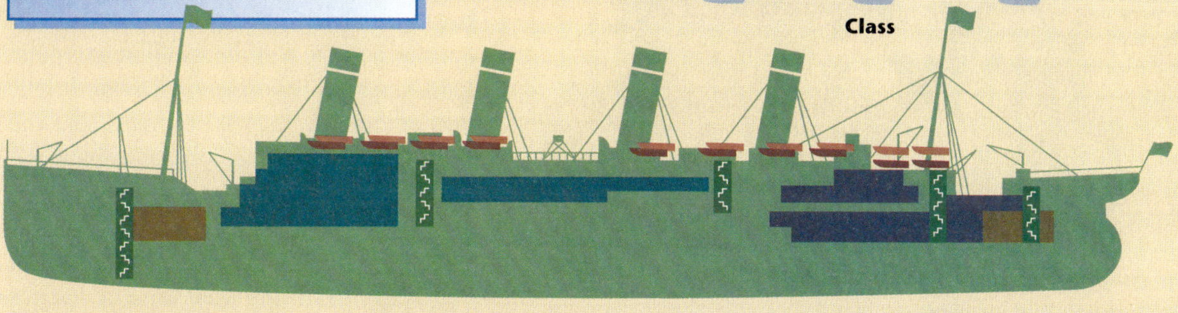

First-class rooms (aristocracy, business tycoons, very successful professionals)
Second-class rooms (business and professional people)
Third-class rooms (workers, immigrants)
Stairwells
Lifeboats

Location and Survival Rate

The *Titanic* was equipped with only 20 lifeboats; more than 50 would have been required to hold all the passengers and crew. Some of the lifeboats were rowed away half-full. Over 1500 people lost their lives.

The *Titanic* tragedy was the central news item in the media for weeks. Throughout the month of April, ships out of Halifax and St. John's continued with the grim task of recovering bodies. Those bodies not claimed were buried in the Fairview Cemetery in Halifax.

International Team Finds the *Titanic*

The search for the *Titanic* did not end with the rescue of the survivors and the recovery of the deceased. Many books and movies have recorded the disaster. In 1991, in one of the most exciting underwater explorations ever undertaken, Canadian, American, and Soviet scientists and a film crew explored the *Titanic's* grave, which had first been discovered in 1985. Their submersible, the Soviet-built MIR (meaning "Peace"), could dive to depths of 4000 m and withstand deep-sea pressures as high as 560 kg/cm^2. Under the leadership of its chief scientist, Nova Scotian Steve Blasco, the team recovered samples from the ship for scientific analysis.

To locate the wreck, the team used GPS and "acoustic photographs." These "photographs" are underwater images traced by sound waves. Separate images can be placed next to each other to make an accurate map of the ocean floor. The team also used new lights that allowed expedition members to see clearly up to 20 m. "These techniques have

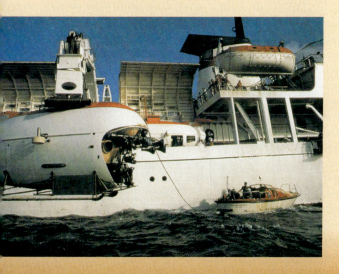

Figure 1.21 Submersible MIR 1 is launched off the *Akademik Keldysch*, the world's largest research vessel, with over 30 laboratories on board.

Figure 1.22 Some of the 130 Canadian, American, and Soviet expedition participants, including scientists, submersible pilots, technicians, ship's crew, and film production personnel. Steve Blasco points to the importance of teamwork: "Environmental problems are not individual problems; you have to work as a team to solve them."

revolutionized our work," says Steve Blasco. "Before, even if you found a wreck on the ocean floor, you wouldn't necessarily be able to find it again. And the most you would be able to see on the ocean floor was three to five metres."

Not only was the expedition a landmark in scientific exploration; it also marked a new attitude toward the funding of scientific projects. Blasco approached the commercial film company IMAX, which was shooting a documentary of the *Titanic*. He proposed that the scientific research mission accompany the film crew. "Anybody who wants to become involved in science in the future will have to become an entrepreneur," insists Blasco. "You have to decide what kind of science you want to do, and then go out and sell it, whether to a research agency or a client."

EXPLORATIONS

REVIEWING THE IDEAS

1. What part did technology play in the story of the *Titanic*? Explain with reference to:

    a) the construction of the ship

    b) the location and exploration of the wreck

APPLYING YOUR SKILLS

2. On an outline map of the North Atlantic:

    a) Draw the route that the *Titanic* took from Southampton to Cherbourg, to Cobh, and then west across the Atlantic.

    b) Indicate on your map roughly where the *Titanic* collided with an iceberg, using the 1912 newspaper article as a guide.

3. **a)** Describe the relative location of first-, second-, and third-class passengers with respect to the location of lifeboats and stairwells.

    b) Construct a bar graph showing the percentages of first-, second-, and third-class passengers, using the numbers in Figure 1.20. Use a computer graphing program, if possible.

    c) Does the pattern of your graph match the pattern of the graph showing percentage of passengers saved? What conclusions can you draw?

    d) Do you think the location of the first-, second-, and third-class cabins had any bearing on survival rates? Support your answer with evidence from Figure 1.20.

4. It is April 15, 1912. You are a journalist. Write the newsflash that will appear in the next edition of the newspaper to report the sinking of the *Titanic*. If possible, use a computer to prepare your report. Alternatively, prepare a newsflash that will be read on the radio. If possible make a tape recording of your report.

ANALYZING AND REFLECTING

5. a) Assume you have the opportunity to interview Steve Blasco, chief scientist of the *Titanic* expedition. What questions would you ask? Work with a partner to prepare your interview.

b) Role play the interview, answering as many questions as you can with information from the text. If possible, make a tape or video recording of your interview.

6. In 1996, an unsuccessful attempt was made to raise part of the *Titanic*.

a) In a group, discuss reasons for and against raising the ship.

b) In a short speech, essay, or "letter to the editor," argue your own point of view: Should the *Titanic* be raised or should it be left as it is?

7. Re-read the excerpt from the poem "The Titanic," on page 14.

a) Poets use images to convey what they have to say. Give an example of the visual imagery the poet used in this verse.

b) Do you think that Pratt would say the sinking of the *Titanic* offers a lesson for those who think that technology can conquer the forces of nature? Explain.

CONNECTING AND EXTENDING

8. a) Identify the places referred to and the nationalities of the people involved in the *Amphion* and *Titanic* dramas.

b) Use a globe to find the places identified.

c) Draw a world map or use an outline. Map the places you located in (b).

d) How would you describe the relative location of Atlantic Canada with respect to these countries?

e) How have advances in location technology affected the ability of countries to cooperate in responding to disasters at sea?

9. a) Research the attempts that have been made to raise the *Titanic*. Who were the organizers? Who funded these attempts? What technology was used? What were the results?

b) Prepare a report or make a display of your findings.

SEEING THE BIG PICTURE

Work individually or in a group.

1. With the help of your teacher, try to locate a satellite image that includes your area. Identify important physical and cultural features.

2. Obtain a topographic map that includes your community.

a) Give the absolute and relative locations of your community.

b) List the main physical and cultural features of your local area.

3. Obtain a street map of your area. Use four or five photographs to create a display of some of the features shown on the street map.

4. Draw a map that shows the route you take to school. Your map should be at a larger scale than the street map of your whole area. Follow these steps:

a) Draw a rough sketch map before making a good copy.

b) Indicate north.

c) Label major features such as parks, shopping centres, or schools.

d) Include a legend to explain features such as major streets and minor streets, one-way streets, traffic lights, etc.

e) Give your map a title.

f) Add a scale to your map.

CHAPTER 2
Our Natural Environment

Figure 2.1 What land and water forms are evident in these photographs? How are the forms of human activity shown related to the environment?

Your school is participating in an international student exchange program. A student from New Zealand will be spending the summer and fall term with a family in Atlantic Canada. Your principal has asked you to work with several other students to put together a kit about the physical environment of Atlantic Canada as useful information for the exchange student.
- What features of the natural environment would you consider to be of interest to the exchange student?
- In what ways can you show how people in Atlantic Canada interact with their physical environment?

Atlantic Canada as a Region

Canada, with its area of 9 970 610 km², is the second largest country in the world. In a country so large, people in one area may have little contact with those who live in another. As a result, people often identify most closely with those who live in a region close to their local community.

Geographers define a **region** as an area that shares common features that make it different from other areas. These features may include language, ways of making a living, cultural expressions, physical environment, climate, or location. Many of these features are covered in later chapters of this text. This chapter will focus on features of the natural environment.

New Brunswick, Nova Scotia, Prince Edward Island, and Newfoundland and Labrador make up Atlantic Canada. They are known as the Atlantic provinces because their shores border on the Atlantic Ocean. These provinces are also grouped together because they are located next to each other and can be identified by certain physical features.

Figure 2.2 Physical features of Atlantic Canada. A map that shows the features of the land's surface is known as a relief map.

Our Natural Environment

EXPLORATIONS

REVIEWING THE IDEAS

1. Survey the different kinds of maps provided in this unit, and describe the following:
   - **a)** a topographic map
   - **b)** a street map
   - **c)** a locator map
   - **d)** a relief map
   - **e)** a political map

APPLYING YOUR SKILLS

2. Determine the approximate location of your community on Figure 2.2. What information does the map give about the physical features of your community?

3. Physical features such as mountains, rivers, swamps, and oceans may serve as natural boundaries to define one area from another. A political boundary between two areas is decided on for administrative or political reasons, and it might follow one or more of these physical features.

   a) Using Figure 2.2, examine the physical features of the political boundary between Quebec and New Brunswick. Which natural features help determine the location of this boundary?

   b) With a partner, decide which of the following statements are correct. Rewrite the incorrect statements to make them correct.

   i) The political boundary between Atlantic Canada and the United States was drawn with little reference to water forms.

   ii) The ocean determines the eastern extent of much of Atlantic Canada.

   iii) The location of the boundary between Labrador and Quebec is largely determined by physical features.

ANALYZING AND REFLECTING

4. Conduct a class survey to investigate different views of what it means to be an Atlantic Canadian. What features of the region as a whole make it different from other regions? Which shared features of your local area make it distinct from other areas?

How Large Is Atlantic Canada?

One way to describe the size of a region is to compare it with the size of other places. Figure 2.3, for example, compares the area of the Atlantic provinces with that of other regions in Canada. This comparison, however, may not help someone from another country appreciate the size of Atlantic Canada. It would be more meaningful to use that person's country as a standard for comparison. For example, if you were to tell the exchange student from New Zealand that Atlantic Canada is more than twice the size of her home country, she would see that the region covers a large area (see Figure 2.4).

Finding Distances on the Ground

Because maps cover large areas, they use a **scale** to help determine the distance between two places on the earth's surface. Figure 2.2, for example, uses a line scale to relate distance between two points on a map and the actual distance on the ground. Scale may also be stated verbally (e.g., 1 cm represents 100 km), or expressed as a representative fraction (e.g., 1:10 000 000 cm).

Figure 2.3 Area of Canada's provinces and territories

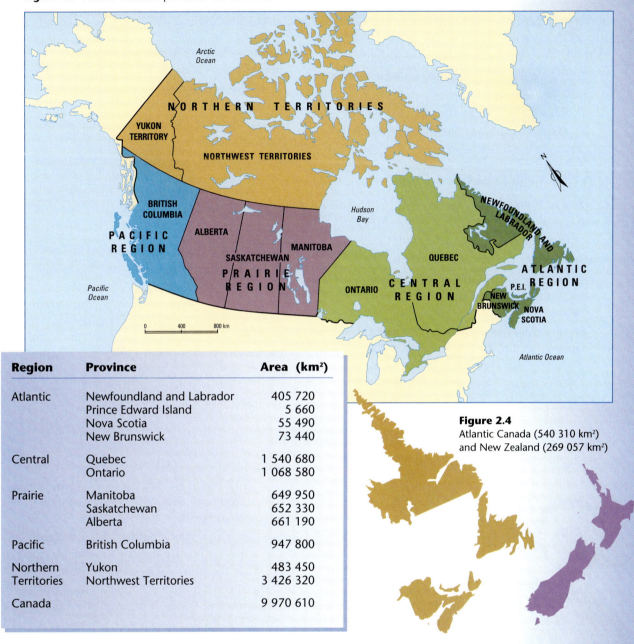

Region	Province	Area (km²)
Atlantic	Newfoundland and Labrador	405 720
	Prince Edward Island	5 660
	Nova Scotia	55 490
	New Brunswick	73 440
Central	Quebec	1 540 680
	Ontario	1 068 580
Prairie	Manitoba	649 950
	Saskatchewan	652 330
	Alberta	661 190
Pacific	British Columbia	947 800
Northern Territories	Yukon	483 450
	Northwest Territories	3 426 320
Canada		9 970 610

Figure 2.4
Atlantic Canada (540 310 km²) and New Zealand (269 057 km²)

The line scale drawn on the map in Figure 2.2 may be used to find the distance between selected points in Atlantic Canada. To find the distance between St. John's and Port aux Basques, for example, you could use the following steps: Construct a paper-strip ruler by placing a strip of paper along the scale line. Make a pencil mark at the 0, 100 km and 200 km points. Next, place the 200 km mark you have just made at 0 on the line scale and mark off another 200 km in 100 km intervals. Repeat this until you have covered the map distance from St. John's to Port aux Basques. Add all the 100 km intervals you have marked off on the strip of paper. About how far is it from St. John's to Port aux Basques? The measured distance between two points is referred to as **physical distance**.

OUR NATURAL ENVIRONMENT

Explorations

REVIEWING THE IDEAS

1. Assume you have a map on which 1 cm represents 5 km.

   a) Draw a line scale for the map.

   b) Express the scale as a representative fraction.

APPLYING YOUR SKILLS

2. Refer to Figure 2.3.

   a) Estimate which of the *regions* (not provinces) is the largest and which is the smallest.

   b) Calculate the size of each region.

   c) Rank the regions from the largest to the smallest. How accurate was your initial estimate?

   d) How does the area of Atlantic Canada compare with that of the other regions of Canada?

3. **a)** Using Figure 2.3, measure the distance between:

   i) the northernmost and southernmost points of your province

   ii) the most easterly and westerly points of your province

   b) Make a chart or diagram to record the distances.

CONNECTING AND EXTENDING

4. Use a graph to indicate size.

   a) Using an atlas, print or CD-ROM encyclopedia, or the Internet, identify the five largest countries in the world.

   b) Draw a bar graph, or make one on a computer, to show the sizes of these countries. Remember to label both axes of the graph and the bars. Give your graph a title.

DISTANCE AND TIME

For many years, communities across the world set their clocks according to the sun. When the sun was at its highest point, it was 12 noon. During the mid-1800s, time differences began to pose a problem as communications improved. **Time distance**, or the time it takes to get between given points, was shrinking. Undersea cables and overland telegraph lines made it possible for Atlantic Canadians to communicate with others in different parts of the region, in different parts of North America, and in Europe. They had little way of knowing, however, what the time was in other communities. The Intercolonial Railway increased the speed of travel within Atlantic Canada and points west. Its schedules, however, had to deal with five different local times between Halifax and Toronto. To help deal with such situations, special watches were manufactured, with as many as seven dials, to show time in different cities.

A Canadian surveyor, engineer, and scientist proposed a solution. In 1879, Sir Sandford Fleming suggested that the globe be divided into 24 **time zones**, one for each 15 degrees of longitude. Time zones to the East are one hour ahead, and time zones to the West are one hour behind. Fleming's plan was adopted at the 1884 International Prime Meridian Conference in Washington, D.C.

Figure 2.5 Watches such as this one were used to show different local times.

PHYSICAL SETTING

DID YOU KNOW ...?

Newfoundland Time is one-half hour later than Atlantic Time. When 25 countries agreed at the Prime Meridian Conference to adopt standard time, Newfoundland had two obvious choices. It could have adopted Atlantic Time (4 hours behind Greenwich Time) or it could have adopted Greenland Time (3 hours behind Greenwich Time). Rather than adopting either of these choices, Newfoundlanders decided to set their clocks 3 hours and 30 minutes behind Greenwich Time. In fact, St. John's is exactly 3 hours and 31 minutes behind Greenwich.

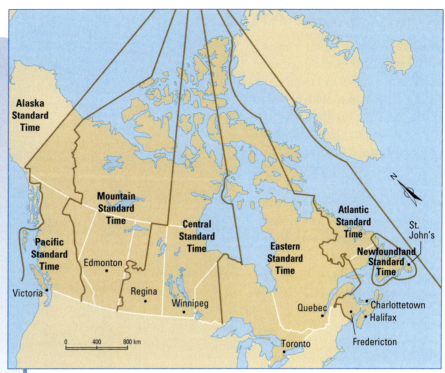

Figure 2.6 Time zones in Canada. Note that Newfoundland Standard Time extends into southern Labrador, although most of Labrador is on Atlantic Standard Time. In which time zone do you live?

EXPLORATIONS

REVIEWING THE IDEAS

1. Make a simple cause and effect chart to show how developments in the mid-1800s created a need for standard time zones.

APPLYING YOUR SKILLS

2. Team Canada is playing Team USA in a hockey match in Edmonton. Live coverage of the game is due to start at 7:00 p.m. Edmonton time. At what time will the game start on television in your community?

3. **a)** According to Figure 2.6, if you were to travel from Halifax to Toronto, how many times would you adjust your watch?

    b) A business person is flying from Moncton to Gander, a trip that will take 2 hours. If the flight leaves Moncton at 11:00 p.m., when will the person arrive in Gander?

ANALYZING AND REFLECTING

4. All provinces in Canada, except for Saskatchewan, move their clocks forward by one hour in the spring. This adjustment is known as "daylight saving." In a small group, brainstorm the advantages of daylight saving. Why do you think daylight saving is not considered practical in Saskatchewan?

CONNECTING AND EXTENDING

5. Do some research to find out why the 180° line of longitude is called the International Date Line. Check atlases and encyclopedias.

Landforms in Atlantic Canada

Much of Atlantic Canada is known for its rugged terrain, dotted with thousands of lakes and ponds, and its coastline, broken with bays and inlets. Nevertheless, the region has a wide variety of physical features, as you can see in Figure 2.2.

In northern New Brunswick, much of the land, with its mountains and hills, is high. A **mountain** can be defined as a mass of land that is significantly higher than the surrounding area. Although it is difficult to use one height to distinguish all mountains from hills, a mountain is often considered to be a mass of land with an elevation of 600 m or more. The highest land in Nova Scotia is found on Cape Breton Island, but other parts, such as the Springhill to Stellarton and Annapolis Royal to Windsor areas, are also hilly. In Prince Edward Island, the highest land is found in the hills of the central region, while gently rolling hills are found in the east and west. The most striking physical feature on the island of Newfoundland is the Long Range Mountains which run along its western side. East of these mountains, much of the island is formed by an upland area with rolling hills and valleys, lakes, ponds, and bogs. An upland area generally has an elevation of 100 m to 400 m.

The mountain and upland systems of Newfoundland are part of the Appalachian Mountains, which extend across the rest of the

Figure 2.7 A view of Woody Point, Newfoundland, with the Long Range Mountains in the background

Atlantic region and into the United States as far south as the state of Georgia. These mountains were formed by **folding** — a bending of the earth's crust. They were once high and jagged, but erosion over their 300-million-year history has reduced them to low mountains and rolling hills separated by wide valleys.

In Labrador, however, the land is an extension of the Canadian Shield, a vast area of rock that stretches across central Canada. Although the mountains in Labrador have been heavily eroded by glaciers, some are rugged and high.

Table 2.1 Atlantic Canada: Principal elevations by province

Province	Mountain/Hill	Elevation	Absolute Location
Newfoundland and Labrador	Lewis Hills	806 m	48°50'N 58°29'W
	Mount Caubvick	1652 m	58°43'N 63°43'W
Nova Scotia	Cape Breton Highlands	532 m	46°62'N 60°36'W
New Brunswick	Mount Carleton	817 m	47°23'N 66°53'W
Prince Edward Island	Queen's County	142 m	46°20'N 63°25'W

The Power of a Glacier

A **fiord** is a long, narrow inlet of the sea, bordered by steep mountain slopes. All fiords were once river valleys. During the last ice age, glaciers scoured these valleys, making them deeper and the sides steeper. This action changed the V-shape of the valley to a U-shape. Once the ice melted, the sea "drowned" the valley, creating the fiord. Fiords are found along the coast of Labrador.

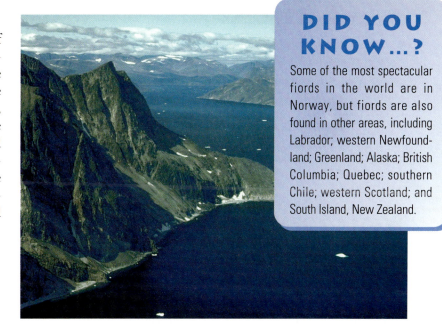

DID YOU KNOW...?

Some of the most spectacular fiords in the world are in Norway, but fiords are also found in other areas, including Labrador; western Newfoundland; Greenland; Alaska; British Columbia; Quebec; southern Chile; western Scotland; and South Island, New Zealand.

Figure 2.8 Nachvak Fiord, in northern Labrador. Fiords are considered to be one of the most dramatic of landforms. Explain why with reference to this photograph.

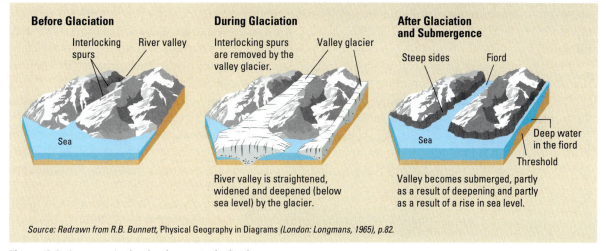

Figure 2.9 Sequence in the development of a fiord

EXPLORATIONS

REVIEWING THE IDEAS

1. Why are the Appalachian Mountains generally rounded in appearance?

APPLYING YOUR SKILLS

2. a) According to Table 2.1, which province has the highest point of land?

b) Using the absolute location given in Table 2.1, locate this point on the map in Figure 2.2. Describe its relative location.

3. Refer to Figure 2.2.

a) Lowlands are large low-lying areas of flat or gently rolling land. Describe the relative location of such an area in New Brunswick and Nova Scotia.

b) Which province in Atlantic Canada has the largest share of its area in the form of lowlands?

c) What is the elevation of the highest point of land in this province? (Refer to Table 2.1.)

CONNECTING AND EXTENDING

4. Do an experiment to demonstrate how fold mountains, such as the Appalachians, are formed.

   a) Take three different coloured strips of plasticene and stack them on top of each other.

   b) Put the stack on a firm surface. Place your hands on either side of the stack and slowly push the ends towards each other.

   c) What changes do you observe in the layers?

   d) Make a diagram to record your observations.

5. On a world map, locate the countries in which fiords are found. If necessary, look at separate relief maps of each of these countries. What do the locations of fiords have in common?

Water Forms in Atlantic Canada

With the aid of satellite imaging technology, it has been determined that Atlantic Canada has more than 295 000 inland lakes, ponds, and rivers. A **river** can be defined as a long, narrow body of water that flows in a channel from high to low land and empties into a body of water such as an ocean or a lake. A **lake** can be defined as a body of water completely surrounded by land. A **pond** is a fairly small body of still water.

The type of water forms found in an area depends upon underlying rock structure. Areas with igneous bedrock (rock formed from magma, after volcanic activity) overlain with thin soils tend to have numerous lakes and ponds. Such areas include Newfoundland and Labrador, New Brunswick, southwestern and the eastern shore of Nova Scotia, and northern Cape Breton. Areas with sedimentary bedrock (rock formed by the build up of layers of rock particles) overlain with thick soils tend to have more rivers and streams. Such areas include the St. John River valley and much of Prince Edward Island.

Some areas are waterlogged; that is, they are neither solid ground nor open water. Such areas are known as **wetlands**. Wetlands may take the form of bogs, fens, swamps, or marshes. **Bogs** are composed mainly of peat, a thick mass of decomposing plants, formed over thousands of years. Mosses, low shrubs, and sparse black spruce or tamarack grow in bogs. The water table in a bog is near the surface in the spring but lower during the rest of the year. Bogs are fed only by rain or snow. **Fens** are also composed of peat and share the same type of vegetation as bogs. Unlike bogs, however, they are fed by streams. As a result, the water table is usually at or above the surface of the peatland. **Swamps** occur where water collects in pools. In forested areas, swamps contain mature trees such as the black spruce. In thicketed areas, swamps contain tall shrubs such as the alder and willow. **Marshes** are areas that are either permanently or seasonally covered by water. Stands of sedges, grasses, and rushes are divided by channels that carry off water very slowly. Cattails and water lilies are typical marsh plants.

Figure 2.10 The Margaree River as it empties into the Gulf of St. Lawrence

Focus on an Issue

Our Fragile Wetlands

If you have ever visited any wetlands, you know that they present a unique landscape and provide habitat for numerous plants and animals. Wetlands are also considered to be nature's kidneys. Plant-filled channels in the wetlands filter slow-moving water, trapping sediments and contaminants. The water that drains from a wetland is clear and clean.

Wetlands, however, have not always been valued. Many have been drained in the construction of roads or buildings. Others have been used as garbage dumps. Some wetlands have been drained to provide rich land for agriculture, and peat has been mined from bogs or fens to be used for growing plants elsewhere or for burning. Wetlands are very fragile, and even human feet can do damage, crushing the top layer of plants and splitting the roots below. Heavy all-terrain vehicles that sometimes cross wetlands during the building of a road or other development cause extensive damage.

Many environmentalists believe all wetlands should be protected, as they are in national parks such as New Brunswick's Kouchibouguac. Others maintain that we can continue to use wetlands, as long as we do so responsibly. The key, they argue, is to use them in a limited way that will allow these areas to renew themselves.

Source: Adapted from D. Minty et al., Finding the Balance (St. John's: Breakwater Books, 1993).

Figure 2.11 Classify this wetland as a bog, fen, swamp, or marsh. Give reasons for your choice. Identify wetlands in your local area. How do residents of the area use these wetlands?

ANALYZING THE ISSUE

Work in a small group.

1. Assume that a new road is planned to pass through wetlands not far from your community. Would you support or oppose the plan? Why? What alternatives to the plan might you be able to propose?

2. As an opponent to the plan, what steps could you take to encourage protection of the wetland? Try to reach a consensus on a course of action with your group.

3. Present your ideas to the class.

The major bodies of water that influence Atlantic Canada are the Atlantic **Ocean** and the Gulf of St. Lawrence. A **gulf** can be defined as a very large area of the sea that is partially enclosed by the land. There are, however, a variety of other smaller features. During the last ice age, the Atlantic region, along with much of North America, was covered by a large ice sheet. The weight of the ice "pressed" down coastal areas, and river valleys were flooded by the sea once the ice sheet melted. Much of the eastern edge of Atlantic Canada, along the Atlantic Ocean, became a "drowned coastline" — very irregular, broken with deep bays, and dotted with offshore islands. A **bay** can be defined as a partially enclosed body of water that has an opening to the sea.

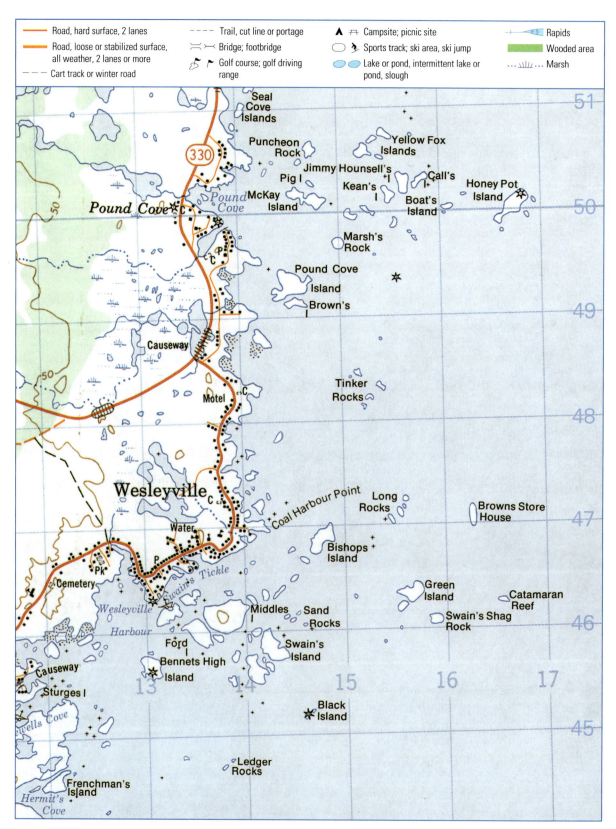

Figure 2.12 Topographic map of coastal area, Wesleyville, Newfoundland. Which water forms can you identify?

As ocean waves pound the coast, they act as powerful agents of erosion. Where coastal rock is weak, particles and even boulders are broken off. Wave action causes these materials to grind away at remaining rock until both are reduced to rounded rocks, pebbles, and gravel. This material is then deposited to form new features such as sand bars, bay beaches, and sea caves.

Figure 2.13 Sea stacks at Hopewell Cape, New Brunswick. Waves and the action of the large tides of the Bay of Fundy erode pieces of rock along fault lines in the headlands, to form arches. With continued erosion, the roof of an arch will collapse into the sea, leaving a pillar of rock known as a stack.

EXPLORATIONS

REVIEWING THE IDEAS

1. a) Identify the following terms in the text.
   i) pond; lake
   ii) bay; gulf
   iii) fen; bog

   b) Make Venn diagrams to show the similarities and differences for each of the pairs of terms.

APPLYING YOUR SKILLS

2. a) In Figure 2.12, identify a wetland area.
   b) Give its absolute and relative location.

3. a) Which term is used in Figure 2.12 to refer to an enclosed body of water?
   b) If you were living in Wesleyville, what directions would you give someone to help them get to this inland water feature?

4. a) Refer to Figures 2.12 and 2.17. What evidence is there that this area is a submerged coast?
   b) Identify some of the positive effects of a submerged coastline on tourism, industry, and leisure activities in Atlantic Canada.

5. Refer to the definition of "bay" on page 27.
   a) In Figure 2.12, which two terms are used instead of "bay" to refer to a partially enclosed body of water?
   b) How would the body of water referred to by these terms compare in size with that of a bay?

6. Refer to Figure 2.12.
   a) Identify a strait.
   b) Write a definition for this term.

CONNECTING AND EXTENDING

7. a) Choose three tourist destinations in the Atlantic provinces. Investigate the land and water forms in each one. Explain how land and water forms have contributed to the popularity of this destination.
   b) Compare your findings with those of other students who have studied other locations. What can you conclude about the diversity of landforms in the Atlantic provinces?
   c) If you were planning a vacation in the Atlantic provinces, which destination would you choose? Why?

People in Their Environment

Often the character of a region grows from the ways in which people interact with their natural environment. Just by examining a map, for example, you would expect that the lives of many Atlantic Canadians are influenced by the ocean. The items that follow give some examples of the close relationship between the natural environment and the people of Atlantic Canada.

In Legend and Spiritual Beliefs

THE GLOOSCAP LEGENDS

In the legends of the Mi'kmaq and Maliseet First Nations of Atlantic Canada, Glooscap is a powerful figure, sent by the Great Spirit to teach, protect, and guide their people.

One of Glooscap's enemies was Beaver (the ancestor of all beavers in the world today). While hunting on Cape Breton Island, Glooscap picked up Beaver's trail and followed it all the way to the Minas Basin. Glooscap found that Beaver had constructed a dam from Cape Split to Parrsboro which flooded Glooscap's herb garden at Advocate Harbour. Glooscap used his paddle to destroy the dam and expose Beaver. Then he threw stones and lumps of mud at his enemy. These landed in the water and formed what is known today as Five Islands.

At the end of his days, Glooscap gathered his people at Cape Blomidon for a feast. He told them how to live a good life. Then he, with his grandmother and his dogs, got into his stone canoe and paddled into the darkness. At the mouth of the Bay of Fundy, he turned his dogs into stone. They formed the rocky islands, The Wolves, to guard the Bay of Fundy until Glooscap would return to his people.

Source: Adapted from Stanley T. Spicer, Glooscap Legends (Hantsport, NS: Lancelot Press), 1989.

In Earning a Living

Figure 2.14 The St. John River Valley supports many human activities, including farming, salmon hatcheries, and the pulp and paper mill at Nackawic, shown here.

Figure 2.15 Cycling at Rocky Point, Prince Edward Island. How does the landscape of the Island contribute to its economy?

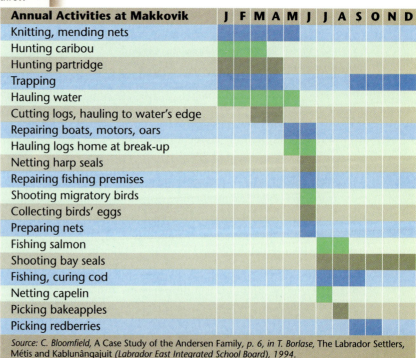

Annual Activities at Makkovik	J	F	M	A	M	J	J	A	S	O	N	D
Knitting, mending nets												
Hunting caribou												
Hunting partridge												
Trapping												
Hauling water												
Cutting logs, hauling to water's edge												
Repairing boats, motors, oars												
Hauling logs home at break-up												
Netting harp seals												
Repairing fishing premises												
Shooting migratory birds												
Collecting birds' eggs												
Preparing nets												
Fishing salmon												
Shooting bay seals												
Fishing, curing cod												
Netting capelin												
Picking bakeapples												
Picking redberries												

Source: C. Bloomfield, A Case Study of the Andersen Family, p. 6, in T. Borlase, The Labrador Settlers, Métis and Kablunângajuit (Labrador East Integrated School Board), 1994.

Figure 2.16 The annual round of traditional activities at Makkovik, Labrador. What patterns of activity can you find in this diagram?

In Making Global Connections

Charting a new course to prosperity

A MAJOR INTERNATIONAL initiative to develop stronger trading links among Atlantic Rim countries is under way. ...

Trading links with the United States and Europe are certainly nothing new, but there are always new and better ways to do business. Halifax's location as a port at the edge of the Great Circle Route — and one of the closest ports to Europe — makes involvement in a formal Atlantic Rim Network simply a matter of common sense.

Halifax has one of the world's best natural deep-water ports and is free of ice year-round. As the worldwide trend toward construction of superships with deeper keels continues, Halifax's advantage becomes even clearer over ports such as New York, where expensive dredging is required to keep shipping lanes open.

Source: The Chronicle Herald, *November 22, 1993, p. C1.*

The St. John River Society

Although the St. John River runs primarily through New Brunswick, its source is in Maine, USA, and part of its watershed lies in the province of Quebec. In 1992, The St. John River Society was formed to celebrate life along the St. John and its tributaries. The society promotes activities that express appreciation of the natural and cultural heritage of the river.

The St. John River Society has regularly proclaimed the fact that the river forms a cultural, economic, and physical link among thousands of people living in Maine, Quebec and New Brunswick. It should be seen as a great unifying symbol, and life along the St. John should be considered an uncommon but shared experience.

Source: The St. John River Society, The River, *Winter 1995–96, p.1.*

In Art

Figure 2.17 "Wesleyville: Night Passage Bennet's High Island" by Newfoundland artist David Blackwood. Find this island in the topographic map in Figure 2.12. What impression of the physical environment does this painting give?

EXPLORATIONS

REVIEWING THE IDEAS

1. **a)** What do you think is meant by the "Atlantic Rim"?

   b) Use an atlas and an outline map of the world to identify other ports that are part of the Atlantic Rim. What do you think is meant by the "Great Circle Route"?

APPLYING YOUR SKILLS

2. Look at Figures 2.12 and 2.17. List evidence that the physical environment has influenced where people live in the Wesleyville area.

3. David Blackwood said of the Wesleyville area, "The region is very flat and barren, the dominating features are the sea and sky. In winter you feel this even more, all shades of grey and white…."

   Source: William Gough, *The Art of David Blackwood* (Toronto: McGraw-Hill Ryerson), 1988.

   Examine Figure 2.17. How does Blackwood present the influence of the physical environment?

4. Work in a small group.

   a) Make a web diagram to show ways in which Atlantic Canadians are influenced by the natural environment. Find examples to add to those given in the text.

   b) Provide some examples to show how relationships between people and the natural environment are sometimes difficult.

CONNECTING AND EXTENDING

5. **a)** Make a chart of your family's yearly round of activities, as shown in Figure 2.16.

   b) How do your family's activities today differ from traditional activities of a Makkovik family?

   c) What does your chart indicate about your family's relationship with the natural environment?

SEEING THE BIG PICTURE

Assume that the exchange student from New Zealand has chosen to study at your school. She is scheduled to leave Auckland, New Zealand, on July 15 at 9:00 p.m. She will fly via Los Angeles and Toronto. Here are the details of her journey.

Journey	Flying time	Wait for next connection
Auckland to Los Angeles	13.5 hours	4 hours
Los Angeles to Toronto	5 hours	2 hours

Flying time from Toronto to local airport (research required)

1. Referring to atlas information, draw up the schedule of her journey. Include:

   a) the physical distance of her journey

   b) the time of arrival **in local time** at each of her destinations, including the major airport nearest to your community. You will need to consult a world time zone map to calculate local times. Note the effect of the international date line.

2. Use a relief map of New Zealand to compare the area around Auckland with the natural environment around your community. What similarities and differences can you find?

3. **a)** Make the postcard the student will send to her family to give an impression of the natural environment in your area. Use clippings from tourist brochures, take a photograph of a representative location, or make a painting or drawing. If you use a clipping, paste it on to a piece of card. Write a caption for the picture in one corner on the back.

   b) As the New Zealand student, write the postcard, giving your impressions. You may wish to mention similarities to or differences from New Zealand.

CHAPTER 3
The Changing Weather

Figure 3.1 Estimate the height of the snowbanks in this picture. Based on your estimate, if 10 cm of snow melts to approximately 1 cm of water, what depth of water would this snow represent?

Storm closes schools

Monday night's storm closed many schools in northern Newfoundland yesterday. Was this good news for students? For most of them it was not. Students have missed upwards of 15 school days this winter because road conditions and bad weather have prevented buses from transporting them to school. Many high school students have been kept busy in recent weeks, copying borrowed notes, getting extra help from teachers and "cramming" at night.

Raymond Hancock has been driving a school bus in Goose Cove for nine years and he says conditions this year are the worst he's seen. "The road has been treacherous," he notes. "Crews are working as hard as they can on the road, but there is just too much snow. They can't keep up with it. It's been storm after storm. The only way to keep the road clear is to have someone working on it for 24 hours a day."

Except for the headline "School's out for the summer," the newspaper headline at right probably gets the most smiles from students. Don't give all the credit to your school principal though. He or she may make the decision to close your school if you live in a remote rural area, but it's more likely that a number of different people are involved. School district officials, road and transportation crews, and provincial weather offices will have a role to play.
- How do we examine the weather so that school district officials, and many others, can plan for its impact?
- What are the factors that affect our climate, causing a variety of weather conditions?

What Is a Snowstorm?

Two factors are essential in the creation of a snowstorm: snow and wind.

Snow

Snow forms when water vapour condenses at a temperature below the freezing point. As it condenses, it forms ice crystals that join together to make snowflakes. **Condensation** occurs when moist air rises and cools, forming clouds. Air may rise for several reasons: it may be blown over high ground, it may be warmed from below, or it may encounter a colder and denser air mass (Figure 3.2).

You might think that schools would close most often in areas with the greatest annual snowfall. On its own, however, average snowfall cannot reliably predict your days off school. Figure 3.4 was created using averages — that is, figures based on measuring snowfall over as many as 30 years.

> ### Canadian January Night
>
> *Ice storm: the hill*
> *a pyramid of black crystal*
> *down which the cars*
> *slide like phosphorescent beetles*
> *while I, walking backwards in obedience*
> *to the wind, am possessed*
> *of the fearful knowledge*
> *my compatriots share*
> *but almost never utter:*
> *this is a country*
> *where a man can die*
> *   simply from being*
> *caught outside.*
>
> — Alden Nowlan

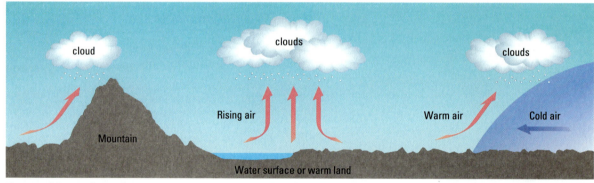

Orographic condensation: Air cools as it rises over high ground.

Convectional condensation: Air rises when warmed from below.

Frontal condensation: Warm, moist air rises over cold air.

Figure 3.2 Some conditions leading to condensation

Figure 3.3 What conditions are necessary for snow to fall?

CALVIN AND HOBBES ©Watterson. Dist. by UNIVERSAL PRESS SYNDICATE. Reprinted with permission. All rights reserved.

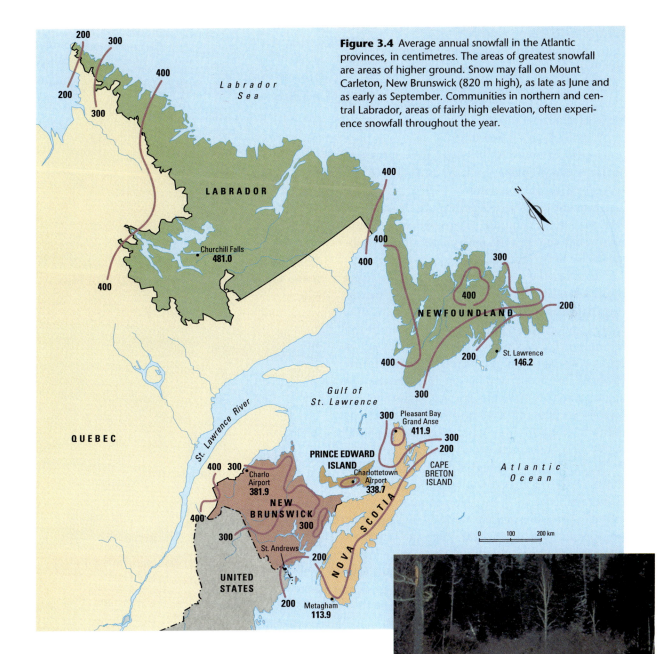

Figure 3.4 Average annual snowfall in the Atlantic provinces, in centimetres. The areas of greatest snowfall are areas of higher ground. Snow may fall on Mount Carleton, New Brunswick (820 m high), as late as June and as early as September. Communities in northern and central Labrador, areas of fairly high elevation, often experience snowfall throughout the year.

Exceptional snowstorms can skew the figures. For instance, an area might get all the year's snow in one stormy week, or it might have an exceptionally snowy year. In the winter of 1977–78, when Woody Point, Newfoundland, received a total of 893 cm of snow, schools were closed for more days than anywhere else in Atlantic Canada.

Snow is not the only necessary ingredient in a snowstorm. You also need wind — lots of it.

Figure 3.5 While students might suffer from the effects of the snowstorm, many people benefit. List the people and businesses for whom a snowstorm might be good news.

THE CHANGING WEATHER

Wind

Snow drifting down in soft white flakes generally does not present a danger to traffic. The same snow propelled by fast-moving air, however, becomes a biting, blistering blizzard that is hazardous to most forms of transportation.

Wind is air that is moving from an area of **high pressure** to an area of **low pressure**. Remember that hot air rises and cold air sinks. A warm surface will heat the air above it, making the air rise (see Figure 3.6). This creates an area of comparatively low pressure beneath the rising air. An area of high pressure forms when cool air sinks towards the surface, pushing the air underneath away (see Figure 3.7).

Air over the North and South Poles sinks because it is cold, producing an area of high pressure. Air over the equator rises because it is hot, producing an area of low pressure. Without the rotation of the earth, air would travel ceaselessly up and down from the poles to the equator. However, the earth does rotate on its axis once every day, so that a point on the equator travels approximately 40 000 km in 24 hours — a velocity of nearly 1700 km/h. Even a point on latitude 46°N (close to Moncton, New Brunswick; Charlottetown, Prince Edward Island; and Sydney, Nova Scotia) travels at over 1150 km/h. As a consequence, winds in the northern hemisphere blow counterclockwise into a low pressure area and clockwise out of a high pressure area. An area between high and low pressure feels the effects of both circulations (see Figure 3.8). High winds can develop when areas of very high and very low pressure come close together.

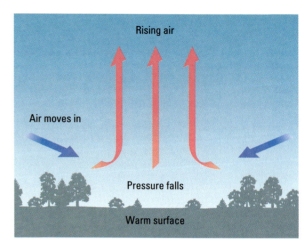

Figure 3.6 Air rising over a warm surface; a low pressure area

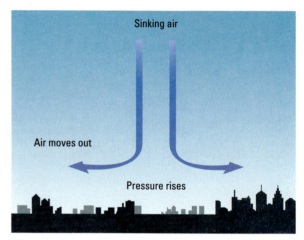

Figure 3.7 Cool air sinking; a high pressure area

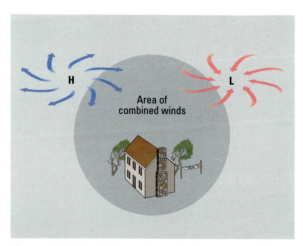

Figure 3.8 High winds can develop between areas of high and low pressure.

DID YOU KNOW...?

Wind can be used as a source of energy. The Atlantic Wind Test Site at North Cape, Prince Edward Island, develops and tests wind energy equipment. Windmills are used to drive turbines and generate electricity. Some of the electricity can be stored in batteries for times when there is little wind.

PHYSICAL SETTING

EXPLORATIONS

REVIEWING THE IDEAS

1. Compare the relief map of Atlantic Canada in Figure 2.2 (page 19) with Figure 3.4. What patterns do you see when you compare elevation and annual snowfall?

APPLYING YOUR SKILLS

2. **a)** Draw a diagram of a globe to show what the general flow of winds would be if the earth did not rotate.

   b) Use an atlas to find a map of world winds. Draw a diagram of a globe showing the actual general flows of the winds of the earth.

ANALYZING AND REFLECTING

3. Discuss the possible positive and negative impact of snow on an area.

CONNECTING AND EXTENDING

4. **a)** Work with a partner. Practise reading the poem "Canadian January Night" aloud.

   b) Which sounds are repeated often in the poem? How do these sounds relate to the topic of the poem? What effect do they create?

   c) Do you agree with Alden Nowlan's view of winter? Describe your own response to winter. You may wish to present your ideas in the form of a poem, painting, or collage.

FACTORS AFFECTING THE CLIMATE OF ATLANTIC CANADA

Of course there is more to the climate of Canada than just snow. **Climate** refers to the average conditions of temperature, **precipitation** (rain, snow, and any other forms of water particles that fall from the atmosphere), humidity, pressure, and wind. The climate of the Atlantic provinces is usually humid and relatively cool. At times, however, there are floods, droughts, cold snaps, or heat waves. These extreme conditions are averaged with other recorded figures to determine the climate, but they are also part of the region's ever-changing **weather** — that is the conditions of the atmosphere over a short period.

A number of factors influence the climate of Atlantic Canada. These include latitude, air masses, ocean currents, and proximity to water.

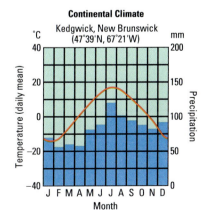
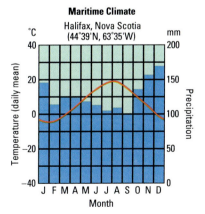
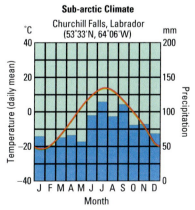

Figure 3.9 Three main climate types in Atlantic Canada. The numbers on the left of each graph and the red lines show temperature. The numbers on the right and the blue bars show precipitation. Write a description of each of the climate types shown, drawing generalizations from the information in the graphs. What is the climate type where you live?

Latitude

All parts of the world receive the same total number of hours of daylight in the course of a year. Because the earth's surface is curved, however, sunshine is more intense in lower latitudes (see Figure 3.10). Thus Cape Sable, Nova Scotia, at latitude 43°N, receives more intense sunshine than Belle Isle, Newfoundland, at 52°N, or Killinek Island, Labrador, at 60°N.

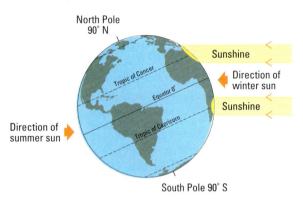

Figure 3.10 Intensity of sunshine varies with latitude. Because the earth is tilted on its axis, sunshine also varies with the seasons. Use a piece of curved black cardboard and a flashlight to show how the intensity of sunshine varies with latitude. How does intensity vary in northern regions in winter and summer?

Air Masses

Large volumes of air with similar temperature and moisture conditions throughout are called **air masses**. Wind is the movement of the air within these masses. Air masses affect the climate because they take on the temperature and humidity characteristics of the areas in which they originate (see Figure 3.13). When **Continental Arctic** air rolls in from northern Canada in winter, for example, it feels cold and dry. When **Maritime Tropical** air wafts in from the Caribbean, it feels warm and moist. When **Maritime Polar** air blows in from the Atlantic east of Newfoundland, it feels cool and moist.

Air masses, like wind, move as a result of changing pressure conditions. The leading edge of an air mass is known as a **front**. Fronts bring the characteristics of the air masses that drive them, and often bring sudden changes in weather. Most precipitation in the Atlantic provinces comes about when the cold and dry air masses from the north meet the warm and moist air masses from the south.

Figure 3.11 These teenagers at Covehead Beach, Prince Edward Island, are enjoying the summer sunshine. What should they do to protect themselves from the harmful ultraviolet rays, which are more intense at this time of year?

Ocean Currents

Just as air masses coming from distant places affect our climate, so do **ocean currents**. The waters of the world's oceans are constantly in motion. Tides move the water up and down while currents move water from place to place. The major ocean currents have considerable influence on climate. The **Gulf Stream**, an ocean current from the south, brings warmth to the southeastern waters of the Atlantic provinces. **The Labrador Current**, flowing from the north, brings cold waters to much of the Atlantic coast. The Gulf Stream warms and moistens the air masses above it, while the Labrador Current cools and moistens.

Fog is a common phenomenon along the Atlantic coast. It often forms when the warm moist air over the Gulf Stream waters moves over the waters of the Labrador Current and is cooled (see Figure 3.12). The water vapour in the moisture-laden air condenses into very small water droplets. Not big enough to fall as rain, these water droplets remain suspended in the slowly moving air.

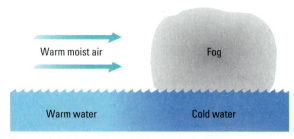

Figure 3.12 Formation of fog

Figure 3.13 Ocean currents and air masses affecting the weather of the Atlantic provinces. Although winds in the Atlantic provinces blow from all directions, the prevailing winds (the winds from the most usual direction) blow from the northwest in winter and southwest in summer. The places named all hold weather records. Suggest which records each one might hold.

Proximity to Water

Sunshine heats land and water at different rates. Water, and the air over it, heats up and cools down more slowly than land (see Figure 3.14). As a result, areas very close to large bodies of water stay cooler in summer and warmer in winter than do areas inland. This moderating effect greatly influences the climate of many Atlantic Canadian communities close to the ocean.

Elevation

Temperatures throughout the Atlantic provinces are also influenced by elevation. Generally, as height increases, temperatures decrease, largely because air is so much thinner at high altitudes.

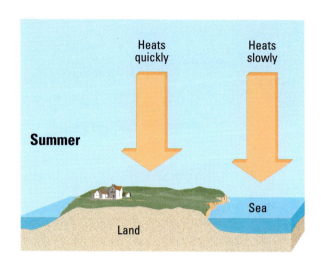

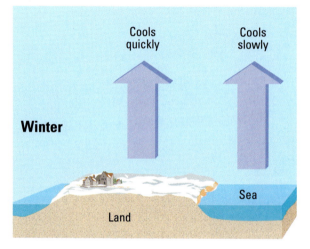

Figure 3.14 Variation in heating and cooling on land and sea

DID YOU KNOW...?

Our climate has sparked some remarkable inventions: the snowblower, snowplough, frozen fish, insulation, underground shopping malls, winter fuels and lubricants, the kerosene foghorn and all-weather asphalt.

Source: Environment Canada, The Climate: What a Difference a Degree Makes.

Table 3.1 Find these three locations on the map in Figure 3.13. What causes the differences in temperature? Speculate on why the warmest month of the year is July in Woodstock but August on Sable Island. Why is February much warmer on Sable Island than in Woodstock?

Place	Woodstock, NB	Charlottetown, PEI	Sable Island, NS
Location	(46°09′N)	(46°15′N)	(43°56′N)
Mean Daily Temperature (Coldest month)	−11.5° (Jan.)	−7.5° (Feb.)	−1.3° (Feb.)
Mean Daily Temperature (Warmest month)	19.3° (July)	18.8° (July)	17.6° (Aug.)

40 Physical Setting

FOCUS ON AN ISSUE

World Climate Change

In recent years, scientists have warned that the earth's atmosphere is being altered by gases produced through various human activities. These gases, many say, are producing a "greenhouse effect." The earth absorbs much of the sun's radiation, but some is reflected back into the atmosphere. The "greenhouse gases" in the atmosphere absorb or trap some of this radiation, rather than allowing it to escape to the upper atmosphere. The result is a change in temperature that threatens to alter the climate around the world. In some parts of the world, temperatures have increased over the last 50 years. In others, including the Atlantic provinces, the average temperature decreased over the same period. The gases primarily responsible for this climate change are carbon dioxide, nitrous oxide, and methane.

Climate Change: A Canadian Concern

Carbon dioxide (CO_2) accounts for 80% of Canada's total greenhouse gas emissions. The majority of CO_2 results from burning fossil fuels for energy. This means that when we use energy — whether driving our car, using the clothes dryer, watching television or leaving the lights on — we are usually burning fossil fuels and contributing to the problem of climate change. It also means that when we choose to ride our bike, hang our clothes to air dry, read a book or turn off the lights when we leave the room, we are directly contributing to a solution to climate change.

Methane and nitrous oxides make up the remainder of Canada's greenhouse gas emissions. Sources include landfills, agricultural practices, chemical processes and fertilizer production and consumption. We can reduce the emissions of methane and nitrous oxides to the environment by reducing the amount of waste we generate by composting, recycling and, most importantly, reducing our consumption of disposable items.

Source: Pollution Probe, ProbeAbilities: A Report to Pollution Probe Members, Fall 1996.

Figure 3.15 Mean annual temperature change from 1930–59 to 1960–89, as calculated in 1995. Note that temperatures need to be collected over long periods of time to establish changing patterns.

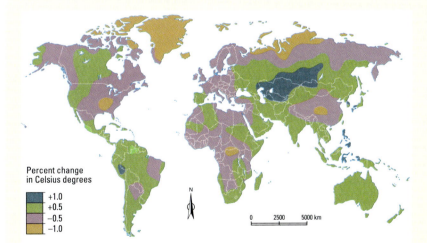

Table 3.2 Top producers of greenhouse gases

Country	Percent of global emissions
United States	18.4
Former U.S.S.R.	13.5
China	8.4
Japan	5.6
Brazil	3.6
Germany	3.6
India	3.5
United Kingdom	2.4
Mexico	2.0
Italy	1.8
France	1.7
Canada	1.7

ANALYZING THE ISSUE

1. Work in a small group to discuss these questions.

   a) How do you, personally, contribute to climate change?

   b) Environmentalists encourage us to "think globally, act locally." How is this view reflected in the article?

   c) Many environmentalists also believe that the problem of climate change can be controlled only through international cooperation. Why is this so?

2. Write a "letter to the editor" or make a poster to encourage one way of addressing the problem of climate change.

EXPLORATIONS

REVIEWING THE IDEAS

1. **a)** In what way are ocean currents and air masses similar?

   b) Which one has an effect that is less immediate but longer lasting? Explain.

APPLYING YOUR SKILLS

2. Give reasons why the locations identified in Figure 3.13 are the warmest or coldest areas of each region in January and July.

3. In terms of location, explain why these Atlantic records do not surprise you.

   a) The record highest temperature occurred at Woodstock, New Brunswick.

   b) The record lowest temperature occurred at Esker, Labrador.

   c) The record number of frost-free days occurred at Sable Island, Nova Scotia.

   d) The record number of foggy days occurred at Argentia, Newfoundland.

CONNECTING AND EXTENDING

4. Look at a world map that shows the world's major ocean currents. Identify the currents that affect the climate of Atlantic Canada.

5. Obtain information of monthly mean temperatures and precipitation for the weather station nearest your school. Plot this information to produce a climate graph for your area. Use Figure 3.9 as a model.

6. Work in small groups to gather weather information for your local area for a period of three weeks.

   a) Use your own observations or local weather reports. Each member of the group should focus on one of the items below and record information for:
   - **i)** temperature (maximum and minimum)
   - **ii)** wind (direction and strength)
   - **iii)** amount of cloud cover
   - **iv)** precipitation (type and duration)

   b) Combine your information to make a chart of the weather over the three-week period.

   c) What connections can you see among temperature, wind, cloud, and precipitation?

7. Work in a small group.

   a) Each student should choose one of the groups below. Do some research to find out the way in which climate affects how these people make a living, which seasons they work, and where in the province they tend to live. Also consider how they adapt their work to the climate.
   - potato farmers in Prince Edward Island
   - loggers in New Brunswick
   - crab fishers in Newfoundland
   - fur trappers in Labrador
   - fruit growers in Nova Scotia

   b) Organize your findings in a chart entitled "Effects of Climate on the Atlantic Way of Life."

8. Imagine you are a real-estate developer about to build a vacation resort somewhere in Atlantic Canada.

   a) Choose your location, basing your decision on the climate of the area, which should suit the recreational activities that you think will attract visitors.

   b) Produce a brochure to inform and attract visitors. Be sure to mention the relevant features of the climate of the area, including data such as rain or snow fall, number of frost-free days, average temperatures, and ocean currents.

9. Many people remember exceptional storms, extremely warm summers, or other weather events. Interview someone in your community about an outstanding weather event that he or she remembers. Write an account of this event. You might wish to use journalistic style or a short story format.

Examining Weather

From Land and Sea

Scattered throughout Atlantic Canada, weather observers note and transmit information about the state of the atmosphere at their particular locations. They use a variety of instruments to measure pressure, temperature, humidity, wind speed and direction, precipitation, and clouds.

Figure 3.16 Surface weather instruments, including a sunshine recorder (left), wind-speed and direction recorders (the poles with revolving cups), and Stevenson screens (the white boxes), which hold maximum and minimum thermometers

From the Air

Weather radar stations are located at Halifax, Nova Scotia; Holyrood, near St. John's, Newfoundland; and Mechanic Settlement, near Sussex, New Brunswick. Radar is especially useful in detecting, locating, and measuring the amount of precipitation in clouds.

From Space

Weather satellites travel far above the earth, in the outer atmosphere. At regular intervals these satellites take pictures of the earth's surface and transmit them to weather stations on the ground. **Meteorologists**, or weather experts, use these images to make long-term weather forecasts.

Figure 3.18 (on page 44) shows an image taken by a weather satellite at 2:45 p.m. Atlantic Standard Time on March 2, 1996. It shows a winter storm approaching the Atlantic provinces. Later that day, this storm dumped more than 30 cm of snow over much of the western areas of the Atlantic provinces, while the eastern shore of Nova Scotia experienced snow followed by rain. On the following day, Newfoundland experienced considerable snowfall. A meteorologist used a series of satellite images together with information from other sources to produce the weather map shown in Figure 3.19. This map shows the weather of the same area shown in the satellite image for exactly 2:00 p.m. on the same day. By using several sources of information, the meteorologist could make a dependable long-term forecast about where this storm was going. This information would have been used to prepare weather reports, warning you to prepare for snow if you were venturing out for the afternoon.

Figure 3.17 A weather radar station

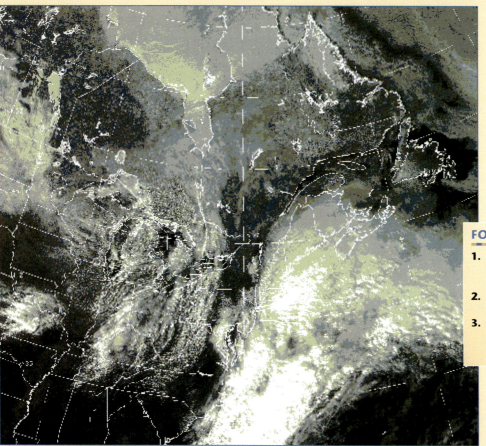

Figure 3.18 Satellite image of winter storm at 2:45 p.m. on March 2, 1996.

FOCUS ON FIGURE 3.18

1. Describe the shape of the cloud shown in the southeastern portion of the image.
2. Describe the relative position of the storm.
3. Using Figure 3.19, state the absolute location of the centre of low pressure.

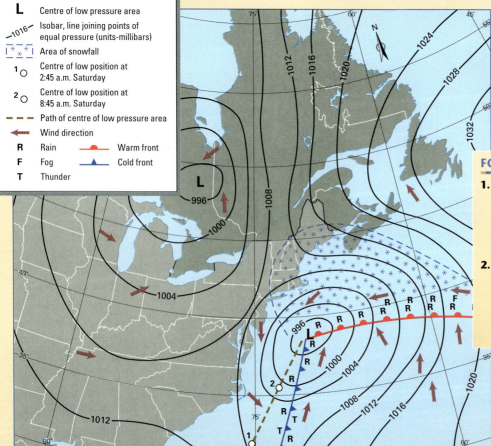

Figure 3.19 Simplified weather map of the area of the satellite image above, showing the weather at 2:00 p.m. on the same day

L	Centre of low pressure area
—1016—	Isobar, line joining points of equal pressure (units-millibars)
[* * *]	Area of snowfall
1 ○	Centre of low position at 2:45 a.m. Saturday
2 ○	Centre of low position at 8:45 a.m. Saturday
- - -	Path of centre of low pressure area
←	Wind direction
R	Rain
F	Fog
T	Thunder
•—•—	Warm front
▲—▲—	Cold front

FOCUS ON FIGURE 3.19

1. Assuming the storm continues on the path shown, how long will it take for the centre of low pressure to reach
   - Prince Edward Island?
   - Labrador?
2. At what time can snow be expected to start falling at
   - Charlottetown, Prince Edward Island?
   - St. John's, Newfoundland?
   - your school?

Career Focus: Meet a Meteorological Technician

Charlie Kennedy is an armed forces meteorological technician who works at the weather office at Canadian Forces Base Gagetown, New Brunswick. He studied mathematics, science, and computers as part of his training.

Figure 3.20 Charlie Kennedy, meteorological technician

Q: What do meteorological technicians do?

A: Generally speaking, we study the atmosphere. We examine changes in air pressure and temperature, movement of air masses, and vertical differences in the atmosphere. Most people think of meteorologists as weather forecasters. In fact there are many opportunities for meteorological technicians — in areas such as forestry, aviation services, mining companies, oil rigs, and the armed forces.

Q: What are your main duties here at Base Gagetown?

A: The meteorological unit provides information to the artillery for two purposes. First, atmospheric conditions affect the movement of shells. A shell fired a distance of 10 km may miss the intended target by as much as 1000 m if atmospheric conditions such as wind, humidity, and air pressure are not taken into account. Secondly, we provide a Fire Weather Index, which is based on air temperature, humidity, wind speed and direction, atmospheric pressure, precipitation, and underground temperatures (from sensors buried beneath the surface at 10 and 90 cm). This information helps to determine the danger of fires starting as a result of exploding shells.

Q: What major changes have taken place in your work during the last 15 years?

A: We used to collect and plot weather information. These were dull and tedious tasks; now they are handled by technology. Sensor information is fed directly into computers that in turn produce maps of current weather conditions and even maps of likely future conditions. It's a challenge now to keep up with the changes in the techniques used to gather information and to produce accurate forecasts.

Q: Which work experiences stand out in your mind?

A: While I was serving as a weather officer on the destroyer *HMCS Nipigon* in March 1993, we were hit by the "Storm of the Century." This storm dropped 3 m of snow on much of the New England coast and 1.5 m of snow on the Atlantic provinces. Winds of nearly 200 km/h produced a wave more than 25 m high, which caused the mast to move 54 degrees from the vertical. Several people had broken bones and there was havoc in the kitchen.

Another time we were sailing south of Newfoundland when freezing spray built up ice on the boat's superstructure — its surface above the main deck — to a thickness of 45 cm. Too much ice will make a ship top heavy and very unstable, so we spent 18 hours cutting at the ice with axes. The captain asked where he would find warm air, and I was able to advise St. Mary's Bay or the Gulf Stream waters. We sailed to St. Mary's Bay and the ice melted.

Q: Why do meteorologists and other weather forecasters sometimes "get it wrong"?

A: It is true that the weather we forecast does not always happen! There are so many factors to be taken into account when trying to predict upcoming weather. We have pictures of past and present weather based on information from weather stations across the land and sea, and we use computer models that show what is likely to happen, but we have to account for another dimension: time.

Making predictions is somewhat like trying to play a game of chess in which all the pieces are moving while you are planning your next move. As technology improves, our forecasts will become more reliable. We will also be able to provide a greater variety of weather information, such as information for travellers and tourists, a UV radiation index, beach forecasts in summer, and ski conditions in winter.

Explorations

APPLYING YOUR SKILLS

1. Locate the warm front in Figure 3.18. Suggest why areas immediately ahead of the warm front experience rain and fog while areas farther ahead receive snow.

2. What change in wind direction may be expected
   a) after the warm front has passed?
   b) after the cold front has passed?

CONNECTING AND EXTENDING

3. Work with a partner.
   a) Check your local newspaper for a weather map and a short- and long-range weather forecast.
   b) Use this information to write tomorrow's weather forecast for broadcast on television. Refer to the weather map. If possible, present the forecast to the class, using a projection of the weather map. You may even wish to make a video tape of your presentation.

4. Speculate why each of the following operations would require the services of a meteorologist.
   - the armed services
   - ministry of the environment
   - forestry company
   - airline
   - mining company in northern Canada
   - company with oil rigs off the Atlantic Coast
   - shipping company
   - ministry of tourism

CASE STUDY

THE FLIGHT OF A RADIOSONDE

Some weather stations, especially those at airports, use radiosondes to gather information about weather conditions. A **radiosonde** is a specialized piece of equipment that is carried into the atmosphere by a small balloon. In a highly coordinated effort, meteorologists all over the world send up radiosondes twice each day at exactly the same time.

The radiosonde is invaluable to weather experts because it transmits hard-to-get information about the upper atmosphere. It collects data such as temperature, relative humidity, pressure, elevation, wind direction, and wind speed that can be used to produce upper-air weather charts. The radiosonde transmits data continuously for about one hour. Later, the balloon bursts in the upper atmosphere, a parachute opens automatically, and the radiosonde falls gently to the ground.

Figure 3.21 Launching a helium-filled balloon ready to lift a radiosonde, at CFB Gagetown

1	2	3	4	5	6	7	8	9	10
Time	AscRate	Ht/MSL	Pressure	Temp	RH	Dewp	Dir	Speed	WndStat
min s	m/s	m	hPa	degC	%	degC	deg	m/s	
0 0	0.0	51	1001.3	11.2	95	10.4	350	2.5	———
0 30	4.4	184	985.4	10.5	89	8.8	13	7.9	ABCD–F
1 0	4.3	312	970.4	9.5	89	7.8	9	11.0	ABCD–F
1 30	4.3	441	955.3	8.7	91	7.3	4	12.4	ABCD–F
2 0	4.4	572	940.3	8.0	92	6.8	1	12.8	ABCD–F
2 30	4.3	701	925.7	7.4	94	6.5	356	13.0	ABCD–F
3 0	4.8	844	909.8	7.0	98	6.7	350	13.6	ABCD–F
3 30	4.6	981	894.8	6.5	99	6.4	340	14.9	ABCD–FG
4 0	4.6	1119	879.9	5.7	98	5.4	335	17.0	ABCD–FG
4 30	5.0	1269	863.9	4.9	98	4.6	333	18.7	ABCD–FG
5 0	5.4	1432	846.8	4.0	98	3.7	333	20.1	ABCD–FG
5 30	5.7	1603	829.2	3.0	98	2.7	337	21.6	ABCD–FG
6 0	5.8	1777	811.6	1.8	97	1.4	341	22.5	ABCD–F
6 30	6.0	1956	793.7	0.7	97	0.3	344	23.1	ABCD–F
7 0	5.9	2134	776.3	–0.3	97	–0.7	344	23.6	ABCD–F
7 30	5.0	2285	761.8	–1.1	98	–1.4	344	24.3	ABCD–FG
8 0	5.5	2450	746.2	–1.9	98	–2.2	346	25.3	ABCD–F

Column 1: Time from release of radiosonde in minutes and seconds.
Column 2: Rate of ascent in metres per second
Column 3: Height above mean sea level in metres (Note: Gagetown is 51 m above mean sea level).
Column 4: Atmospheric pressure in hectopascals (hPa). 1001.3 hPa is equivalent to 100.13 kilopascals (kPa).
Column 5: Temperature in degrees Celsius.
Column 6: Relative humidity as a percentage; the ratio of the amount of water present in the air to the amount of water vapour the air can hold at that temperature, multiplied by 100.
Column 7: Dew point; the temperature to which air has to be cooled to become saturated (incapable of holding more water).
Column 8: Wind direction in degrees based on a circle (360°). Thus a north wind would be blowing from 360 or 0, a southerly wind from 180, an easterly wind from 90.
Column 9: Wind speed in m/sec.
Column 10: The number of satellites being used to determine the position of the radiosonde. ABCD = 4, ABCD–FG = 6, A–CD–FG = 5. (A system of satellites similar to the GPS, as described in Chapter 1, is used.)

Table 3.3 Selected data collected during a radiosonde flight from CFB Gagetown, New Brunswick

EXPLORATIONS

APPLYING YOUR SKILLS

1. Refer to Table 3.3.

   a) Does atmospheric pressure rise or fall as the balloon rises?

   b) Does temperature rise or fall as the balloon rises?

2. a) At what height is the temperature 3°C?

   b) How long did it take for the balloon, after it was released, to reach this height?

3. What might occur if the air temperature and the dew point temperature were the same?

4. What direction is the wind coming from at the height of 572 m/MSL?

5. What happens to the speed of the wind as the radiosonde travels from the surface up to 2450 m/MSL?

6. Imagine you were flying a kite at Base Gagetown when the radiosonde was released. In which compass direction would you look to see your kite if it were 521 m above the surface of the ground? Remember that the wind direction in the chart indicates where the wind comes from.

7. What causes the helium balloon to burst?

CONNECTING AND EXTENDING

8. List all the kinds of information a radiosonde communicates. What course in school would help you interpret the information provided by a radiosonde?

SEEING THE BIG PICTURE

Work in groups to speculate on the possible effects of climate change.

1. Prepare an illustrated report or display showing the possible benefits or harmful effects of climate change in the Atlantic provinces. Take into account the impact of increasing and decreasing temperatures. How might sea levels, rainfall, and storm activity be affected? Each group member should choose a different topic from the following list, and then contribute his or her findings to the group project.

   a) agriculture
   b) fishing
   c) forestry
   d) tourism and recreation
   e) transportation
   f) home construction
   g) clothing

2. On an outline map of the world, and with reference to an atlas, show some fundamental changes that might occur in other areas as a result of climate change. Assume that temperatures will continue to change as shown in Figure 3.15. Each student should choose one of the following climate zones and speculate on changes that should be shown on the map.

   a) tropical climates
   b) arid climates
   c) warm humid climates
   d) polar climates
   e) mountain climates

PHYSICAL SETTING

CHAPTER 4

A Place to Live

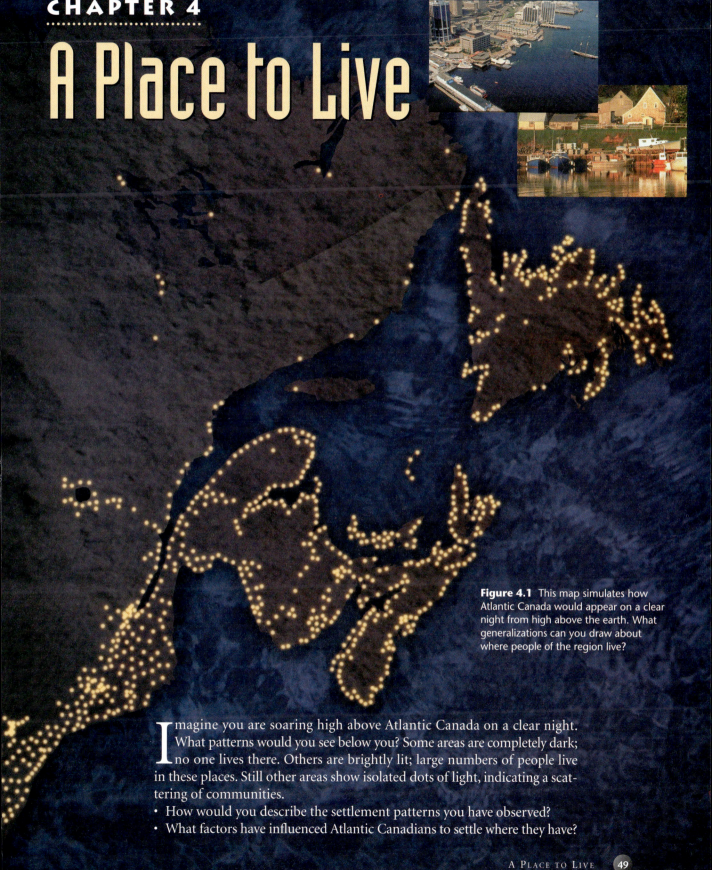

Figure 4.1 This map simulates how Atlantic Canada would appear on a clear night from high above the earth. What generalizations can you draw about where people of the region live?

Imagine you are soaring high above Atlantic Canada on a clear night. What patterns would you see below you? Some areas are completely dark; no one lives there. Others are brightly lit; large numbers of people live in these places. Still other areas show isolated dots of light, indicating a scattering of communities.

- How would you describe the settlement patterns you have observed?
- What factors have influenced Atlantic Canadians to settle where they have?

POPULATION PATTERNS

The people of Atlantic Canada are unevenly distributed across the four provinces. Where people live close together in a given area, the population is dense or crowded; where there are only a few people in an area of a similar size, the population is sparse. The term **population density** identifies how many people live on a given area of land. Population density is found by dividing the population of a given region by the area of that region (see Table 4.1).

Communities vary by population density and by settlement pattern or **population distribution** (see Figure 4.2). Even when areas have the same population density, they might have different population distribution patterns. When describing the population pattern of an area, both the density and the distribution of its population should be considered.

Table 4.1 Population density of the Atlantic provinces

Province	Population	Population density (Persons per km^2)
Newfoundland and Labrador	571 192	1.4
Nova Scotia	941 235	16.9
New Brunswick	761 973	10.3
Prince Edward Island	137 316	23.6
Atlantic Canada	2 411 716	4.5

Source: Statistics Canada, April 1996, Cat. 91-002-XPB, Vol. 10, no. 1.

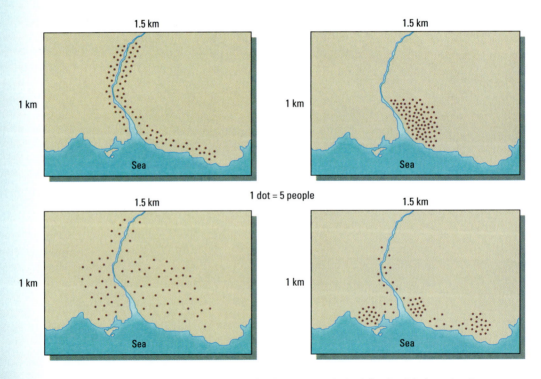

Figure 4.2 Common patterns of population distribution. Match the following labels to the diagrams: Clustered; Compact; Loose-knit; Linear.

PHYSICAL SETTING

The Rural-Urban Mix

Figure 4.1 indicates that people in Atlantic Canada live mostly in relatively small settlements scattered across the region. In some areas, however, there is a cluster with higher population density. These concentrations of people form **urban centres**. An urban centre has at least 1000 people and a population density of 400 or more persons per square kilometre.

In many parts of Canada, as in other countries, cities are growing in number and size. This trend is usually at the expense of populations in **rural areas**. People tend to migrate from the countryside to the city to look for work, especially when unemployment rates are high. The conditions that force people to leave the countryside are known as **rural push**. The conditions that attract them to move to cities are known as **urban pull**.

By the early 1900s, Atlantic Canada had a rail system that tied areas of the region together. People in rural areas produced food and raw materials for people living in larger centres. Workers in towns and cities produced finished goods and provided services for people in rural communities. As new technology was introduced in fishery, forestry, and farming industries, fewer workers were needed in rural areas. Many moved to cities and towns to look for work in manufacturing and services. Ports, such as St. John's, Halifax, and Saint John, grew in importance since exports and imports were routed through these centres.

Figure 4.3 Steam engine leaving the rail yard at St. John's, Newfoundland, c. 1900

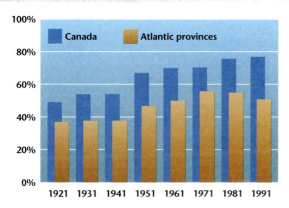

Figure 4.4 Urban population growth in Canada and the Atlantic region, 1921–1991. Describe the general trend shown here. How do the Atlantic provinces compare with the rest of Canada?

Province	Urban %	Rural %
Newfoundland/Labrador	53.6	46.4
Prince Edward Island	39.9	60.1
Nova Scotia	53.5	46.5
New Brunswick	47.7	52.3
Canada	76.6	23.4

Source: Calculations based on data in Statistics Canada, 1991, Cat. 93-305.

Table 4.2 Urban-rural population in Atlantic Canada, by percentage, 1991. Rank the provinces according to percentage of urban population. Using Table 4.1, rank the provinces according to population density. How do the rankings compare? Are you surprised at the differences? Why or why not? How can you account for the differences in rank?

Outmigration

People move from one area to another for a variety of reasons. While many stay within the same province or region, some move to other parts of Canada or even other parts of the world. Movement away from an area is known as **outmigration.** Much of the outmigration from the Atlantic provinces is to other parts of Canada, but some people also move to other parts of the world. Boston, Massachusetts; South-East Asia; and Japan have all attracted Atlantic Canadians in recent years.

	Total Outmigrants	NF	PEI	NS	NB	PQ	ON	MB	SK	AB	BC	YT	NWT
NF	18 867	—	208	2 710	815	382	9 140	314	116	2 447	2 204	61	470
PEI	2 623	157	—	674	435	65	757	43	33	207	298	4	—
NS	22 700	1 804	955	—	3 441	1 105	8 208	555	396	2 295	3 688	56	197
NB	16 130	545	719	3 191	—	2 618	5 580	396	157	1 546	1 306	—	72
PQ	43 042	351	92	1 098	3 035	—	28 143	719	346	1 954	7 101	28	175
ON	85 609	5 379	986	7 404	4 891	18 107	—	7 204	2 490	12 113	26 425	194	506
MB	25 448	197	45	510	429	699	7 180	—	4 020	5 112	6 871	46	339
SK	27 689	87	64	270	215	279	3 219	4 249	—	12 971	5 923	86	326
AB	66 727	1 027	153	1 910	1 065	1 655	11 412	5 025	10 793	—	31 649	633	395
BC	55 130	750	262	1 973	861	2 745	15 846	4 368	4 874	21 828	—	1 124	499
YT	2 289	—	4	9	16	39	133	17	41	560	1 308	—	162
NWT	4 373	160	—	184	94	154	593	396	256	1 616	769	151	—
Total immigrants	370 627	10 457	3 498	19 883	15 297	27 758	90 211	23 286	23 522	62 649	87 542	2 383	4 141
Net interprovincial migration	—	−8 410	875	−2 817	−833	−15 284	4 602	−2 162	−4 167	−4 078	32 412	94	−232

Province of origin (rows) / Province of destination (columns)

Source: Statistics Canada, CANSIM, matrix 6365, 1994–95.

Table 4.3 Migration between Canadian provinces, 1994–1995. What trends can you see for workers from the Atlantic provinces? What trends can you see for the country as a whole? Using data from Table 4.1 calculate the percentage of outmigrants for your province.

EXPLORATIONS

REVIEWING THE IDEAS

1. Atlantic Canada has a relatively low population density. Does this mean there are no crowded spaces in the region? Explain.

APPLYING YOUR SKILLS

2. Refer to Figure 4.1.

   a) Briefly describe the population distribution of each province.

   b) Choose one area that is sparsely populated and one area where population is evenly distributed. With reference to Figure 2.2 (page 19), explain how the physical features of these two areas influence the population distribution.

3. **a)** Look at Table 4.4 below. Which province has the highest percentage of its people employed?

   b) How does this province's urban-rural mix compare with that of other provinces, as shown in Table 4.2? What conclusions can you draw?

Table 4.4 Percentage of population employed, 15 years and older

Province	% employed
Newfoundland/Labrador	44.2
Prince Edward Island	59.8
Nova Scotia	55.3
New Brunswick	53.2

Source: Statistics Canada, 1991, Cat. 93–324.

ANALYZING AND REFLECTING

4. **a)** Work in a group to make a "pro and con" chart of rural vs. urban living.

   b) Where would you rather live, in a rural area or an urban centre? Why? Present your ideas in a short essay, speech, collage, or skit.

CASE STUDY

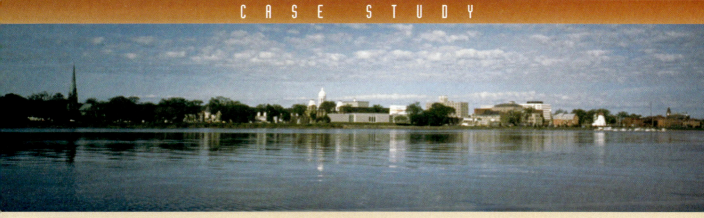

Figure 4.5 Fredericton was designed as a centre for government, culture, and education.

THE GROWTH OF FREDERICTON

The location, or **site**, of any settlement is influenced by geographic, political, and economic factors. This case study examines why Fredericton is located where it is, and why it became a provincial capital.

After the American War of Independence, the British were concerned that the newly formed United States of America might attack British colonies to the north. The less populated areas of upper New Brunswick were considered to be particularly vulnerable. As a result, in 1783, the British sent troops and their families into the St. John River Valley. Some settled at St. Anne's Point. In 1784, a group of Loyalists arrived. These were settlers from the United States who had remained loyal to Britain during the American War of Independence (see page 59). The area was surveyed into a grid pattern of streets with lots consisting of one-quarter of an acre each.

In the same year, New Brunswick was established as a province. Governor Thomas Carleton announced that St. Anne's Point, renamed Fredericton, would be its capital.

Letter to King George III, 1784

I have the honour to inform Your Lordship that having in the course of last winter visited the principal settlements forming on St. John River, I have fixed upon St. Anne's Point, about seventy five miles [120 km] from the mouth of the River, as a station well situated for the future seat of the provincial government. It has the advantage of being nearly in the centre of the Province and within a few miles of that part beyond which the River ceases to be navigable for vessels of any considerable size. Here the foundations are preparing for the Metropolis of New Brunswick to which, as a mark of respect to His Highness the Duke of York, I have given the name of Frederic'stown, which I hope may meet with His Majesty's approbation.

Thomas Carleton

Source: Collections of the New Brunswick Historical Society, 6 (1905), 405n.

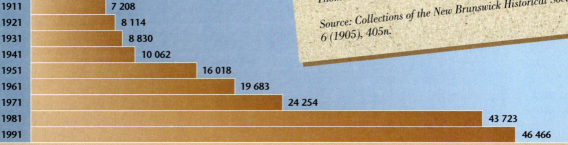

Year	Population
1832	1 200
1840	4 002
1851	4 458
1871	6 006
1881	6 218
1891	6 502
1901	7 117
1911	7 208
1921	8 114
1931	8 830
1941	10 062
1951	16 018
1961	19 683
1971	24 254
1981	43 723
1991	46 466

Figure 4.6 Population growth of Fredericton

A PLACE TO LIVE

Why Did Fredericton Grow?

- As provincial capital, it became an important government and military centre. Buildings were constructed to house the provincial legislature, municipal council, court, the Lieutenant-Governor's offices and residence, and military quarters.

- Transportation improved rapidly to meet the demand of new residents, especially the military. Fredericton's wheelwrights and wagon makers were in high demand. These skilled workers also produced iron products such as stoves, wood-working equipment, and farm tools.

- There were abundant resources in the area. Nearby forests were harvested to supply masts for ships and sawn into lumber at local mills. The rich soil supported a variety of crops that were marketed in Fredericton. Grist mills were built to process locally grown grains into meal and flour. Carding mills soon appeared to spin and weave local wool into homespun cloth. Tanning operations used the hides of local animals to produce leather to supply the demand for footwear and harnesses.

- The location of the city increased economic activity. Before roads and rail lines, the St. John River provided a major transportation corridor and a source of energy for manufacturing. Small river boats plied between Saint John and Fredericton carrying passengers and freight. Resources were transported by river and exported through the port of Saint John. In the mid-1800s, steam-powered river boats revolutionized river traffic. Fredericton's economy grew as river boats could easily connect with Woodstock and Grand Falls. In the last half of the nineteenth century, new rail lines connected Fredericton with Maine, Quebec, Saint John, and other points in Atlantic Canada.

DID YOU KNOW...?

Many Canadian cities belong to a "twin cities" program that promotes economic and cultural links between urban centres in different countries. Fredericton is "twinned" with Augusta, the capital city of the state of Maine.

EXPLORATIONS

REVIEWING THE IDEAS

1. Make a chart to show the geographic, political, and economic factors that determined Fredericton's site.

APPLYING YOUR SKILLS

2. A major urban centre needs an effective transportation system to connect it with the area it serves. Contrast the traditional transportation methods of water, rail, and road with current systems.

3. Refer to Figure 4.6.

   a) After World War II, Canada and the United States experienced a "baby boom." What evidence is there of the baby boom in Fredericton?

   b) How might you account for the population surge in Fredericton from 1961 to 1981?

CONNECTING AND EXTENDING

4. What factors determined the site of your community? Work in a group to research your community and prepare a diagram or model to illustrate the factors that affect its site.

5. Urbanization — the growth of urban centres — poses one of the greatest global problems. Find a list of the world's largest cities. Choose one and find out why it is growing. What problems is it experiencing? What are its prospects for the future? Present a report of your findings.

6. Today, urban developments are carefully planned, to ensure that they meet the needs of the community and have adequate services. Some computer programs allow you to design a community of your own. If possible, work with a program such as SIM TOWN® or SIM CITY® to locate and design your ideal community.

PHYSICAL SETTING

Roots of Our Population

The population of Atlantic Canada is made up of many cultures. This section will survey some of the population patterns created by the people who have made Atlantic Canada their home.

Aboriginal Peoples

There are differing views about the origins of Aboriginal peoples in the Atlantic region. Many Aboriginal experts believe that some nations have lived here since the beginning of time. Some archaeologists believe that Palaeoindian groups migrated here about 10 000 to 12 000 years ago, following game such as caribou and bison from as far west as British Columbia, as the glaciers of the Ice Age retreated. While these Aboriginal peoples all lived in harmony with their environment, different groups developed distinct spiritual traditions, languages, and cultures.

Figure 4.7 Distribution of Aboriginal peoples, AD 500, 1630, 1740, and present. What generalizations about changing population numbers and distribution can you draw from this map?

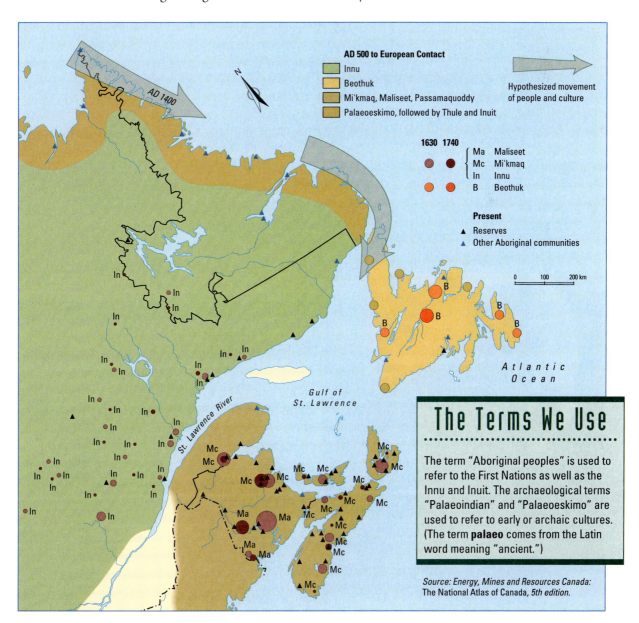

The Terms We Use

The term "Aboriginal peoples" is used to refer to the First Nations as well as the Innu and Inuit. The archaeological terms "Palaeoindian" and "Palaeoeskimo" are used to refer to early or archaic cultures. (The term **palaeo** comes from the Latin word meaning "ancient.")

Source: Energy, Mines and Resources Canada: The National Atlas of Canada, 5th edition.

A Place to Live

The Innu

Newfoundland and Labrador was home to the Maritime Archaic peoples between about 9000 and 3000 years ago. These peoples used resources from the land and sea. Some experts believe that the Innu are descendants of the Maritime Archaic cultures in the barren lands and sub-arctic climate of the Quebec/Labrador peninsula. The Innu were classified into two groups — the Montagnais and Naskapi — by early French explorers. Today, the Innu call their land Nitassinan and do not recognize the political boundaries of Quebec and Labrador.

Algonquian Nations

Three Algonquian nations lived in what is now called Atlantic Canada, hunting, fishing, trapping, and trading. These nations included the Mi'kmaq now living in Nova Scotia, parts of Newfoundland, Prince Edward Island, and New Brunswick; and the Passamaquoddy and Maliseet in parts of New Brunswick.

The Inuit

The north of the Atlantic region was home to Palaeoeskimo groups. Some archaeologists believe these groups crossed via the Bering Strait from Siberia, reaching Labrador about 3800 years ago. The Dorset, one of these Palaeoeskimo groups, disappeared about 1000 years ago. Legends about these early groups still exist among the Thule, who are thought to have arrived in about 1300, and are ancestors of today's Labrador Inuit. The Thule migrated south along Labrador's coast, so that the Inuit came into direct contact with Europeans.

The Beothuk

The Beothuk lived in Newfoundland, hunting and fishing both along the coast and in the interior. They suffered a fate now recognized as one of the tragedies of Canadian history. Susceptible to European diseases and further decimated by conflict with European settlers, the Beothuk became extinct. Their last known member, Shawnandithit, died of tuberculosis in 1829.

Effects of Contact

The first Europeans who came to the region learned from the Aboriginal peoples how to cope with the harsh environment. Nevertheless, the **ethnocentrism** (belief that their culture and beliefs were better than those of others) of the Europeans often kept them from appreciating and understanding the Aboriginal peoples. As a result, problems developed. In some parts of the region, there were conflicts. In parts of Nova Scotia, Prince Edward Island, and New Brunswick, Aboriginal peoples became regulated by Canadian law, and some were forced by treaties and other regulations off traditional lands and onto reserves. Today, in many parts of the region, Aboriginal peoples are beginning to claim back lands and the right to self-government. Aboriginal leaders and federal and provincial governments continue to negotiate settlements to such claims.

Figure 4.8 The only known portrait of a Beothuk is this one of Demasduit, also known as Mary March, painted in 1819.

> "Some people say that the treaties are treaties of peace and friendship, and not land treaties. These people haven't done their homework on the colonization of this area. There is no doubt that they can be called treaties of peace and friendship; they were treaties to end hostilities. But they do also have land and rights implications. They have been so recognized by the courts in many cases."
>
> Stewart Paul, former Chief of Tobique Nation, New Brunswick

Early European Settlement

In the early 1600s, immigrants from England and France began to settle in the Atlantic region to tap its resources, particularly fish and fur. Through the seventeenth and much of the eighteenth century, fierce competition arose between the British and French for control of the region. After decades of war, the Treaty of Paris (1763) gave England control of the Atlantic region.

Figure 4.9 *Top:* European territorial claims 1600–1690. *Bottom:* European territorial claims 1690–1713. In 1763, at the end of the Seven Years' War, France gave up its claims to the eastern part of North America to Britain.

> **FOCUS ON FIGURE 4.9**
> 1. How did European territorial claims change between 1690 and 1713?
> 2. How was the Atlantic region affected?
> 3. Compare the territorial claims in the period 1690–1713 with the distribution of Aboriginal peoples in 1630, as shown in Figure 4.7. What conclusions can you draw?

A PLACE TO LIVE

The Acadians

Although there was little immigration from France after 1650, Acadian settlements in the Annapolis Basin, established by farmers from the west coast of France, flourished. In 1671, the Acadians numbered approximately 440; by 1750, this figure had grown to 10 500. As the population grew, Acadian settlements spread over a wider area.

By the early 1700s, the Acadians found themselves in an uneasy situation. The British gained control of Acadia, Newfoundland, and Hudson Bay in 1713, and pressured the Acadians to swear allegiance to the crown. Some Acadians agreed, on the condition they could remain neutral in the event of a war between the British and French. Nevertheless, their relations with the British remained strained, mainly because Acadians continued to settle on marshland that was being held for new British settlers.

Figure 4.11 An artist's depiction of the expulsion of Acadians at Fort Amherst

In 1749, the British required the Acadians to swear an unconditional oath of allegiance or be deported. The Acadians refused. After failed negotiations, it was decreed in 1755 that the Acadians be deported and all their animals and land become British property. Some Acadians were sent to British colonies in the south; some were sent to France and England. Some fled before troops arrived to seek shelter among the Mi'kmaq in the interior. Others moved to Prince Edward Island and Cape Breton which were still under French control.

Many Acadians were unhappy in their new destinations and decided to return to Acadia. The Nova Scotia government agreed to give them land provided they would swear an oath of allegiance. Some returnees were settled in remote areas, such as the northern region of present-day New Brunswick.

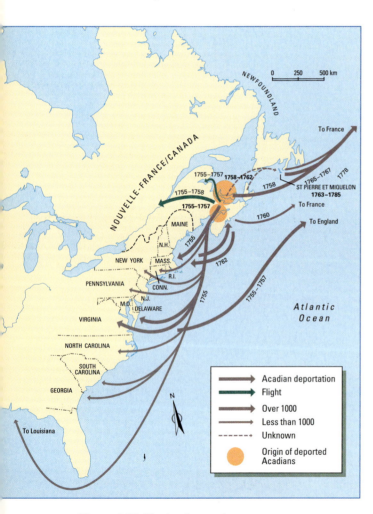

Figure 4.10 The Acadian exodus

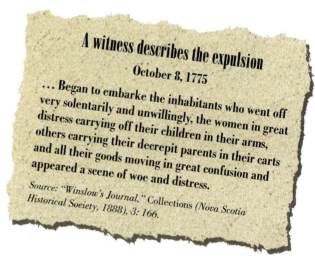

A witness describes the expulsion
October 8, 1775

... Began to embarke the inhabitants who went off very solentarily and unwillingly, the women in great distress carrying off their children in their arms, others carrying their decrepit parents in their carts and all their goods moving in great confusion and appeared a scene of woe and distress.

Source: "Winslow's Journal," Collections (Nova Scotia Historical Society, 1888), 3: 166.

Settlers of British Origin

Most European settlers from the 1600s onwards were English, Welsh, Irish, or Scottish immigrants.

- In Newfoundland, most early European settlers came to participate in the migratory fishery. Each spring English ships filled the harbours from Cape Race to Cape Bonavista. They fished all summer and returned home before the stormy fall weather arrived. As the English fished this area, the French fished along the south and west coasts of the island. Over time, a few fishers in each harbour began to stay through the winter to protect and repair fishing property. Gradually permanent settlements began, and then expanded along the northeast and south coasts of the island. When the territorial disputes between England and France were settled, and when large numbers of Irish immigrants arrived in the early 1700s, the population grew more rapidly.

  Some British fishers migrated directly to the coast of Labrador and, over time, some fishers migrated there from Newfoundland. In this way, permanent settlements were gradually established in Labrador as well.

- During the 1750s and 1760s, the British encouraged English-speaking settlers from the Thirteen Colonies to come to the Maritimes to counterbalance the number of people of French origin. Some of these newcomers were settled on land originally farmed by the Acadians.

- The Loyalists were colonists who supported the British against the rebellious American colonies in the American War of Independence (1776–1783). These colonists were regarded as traitors to the American cause. They were harassed and many of their homes were destroyed. In 1783 alone, close to 20 000 Loyalists colonists and ex-soldiers boarded ships to re-settle in Nova Scotia. In all, some 35 000 Loyalists left the United States. Many were attracted to the area to the north and west of the Tantramar marshlands and the St. John River Valley by government grants of 40 ha of land for the head of the household and 20 ha for each family member.

> Lester-Garland House traces some of the history of settlement in this part of the region. The house was built by Benjamin Lester who came to Newfoundland from Poole, in England, in the early 1700s, when he was 13. Lester came to work as an apprentice to his uncle who was a ship owner and merchant. By the 1760s, Lester, in partnership with his brother in Poole, was an established merchant in the Newfoundland cod trade. He had also built a home for his family, based on the plan of a country house built by his brother in England. The property was inherited by Lester's son-in-law George Garland, but over generations it fell into disrepair and was demolished in the 1960s. It was reconstructed in 1996 and is now open as a museum.

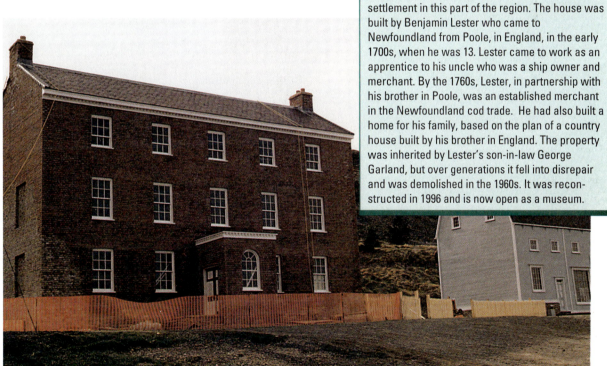

Figure 4.12 Lester-Garland House in Trinity, Newfoundland

- During the 1770s, many settlers came from Yorkshire, England, to the Chignecto, and from Highland Scotland to points along the north shore of Prince Edward Island and Nova Scotia. In the late 1700s, some 40 000 people left Scotland for North America. Of these, 8000 to 10 000 settled in Nova Scotia, many of them in Cape Breton. Many of the settlers were tenant farmers who came as a result of the Enclosure Movement. The open-field farming system of the time was being replaced by enclosed fields. This new system allowed landlords to operate more efficiently, but it forced many tenant farmers off the land.

- Between 1820 and 1850, a large number of English immigrants came to Canada. Of those who came to the Atlantic region, many settled in Prince Edward Island.

- In 1846, blight destroyed the potato crop in Ireland. Almost a million people starved to death and up to another two million emigrated. Many of these emigrants were tenant farmers, sent abroad by their landlords. Hundreds of thousands of immigrants came to the Atlantic provinces. Once here, many faced a hostile reception because they were destitute, and some moved on to the United States. Those who remained made important contributions, as did many other immigrant groups, to the culture, economy, and political life of the Atlantic provinces.

Figure 4.13 This announcement was published in the *New Brunswick Courier* in June 1847. What can you tell about conditions of the journey from this card? Why were these immigrants prepared to undergo such a dangerous and uncomfortable journey?

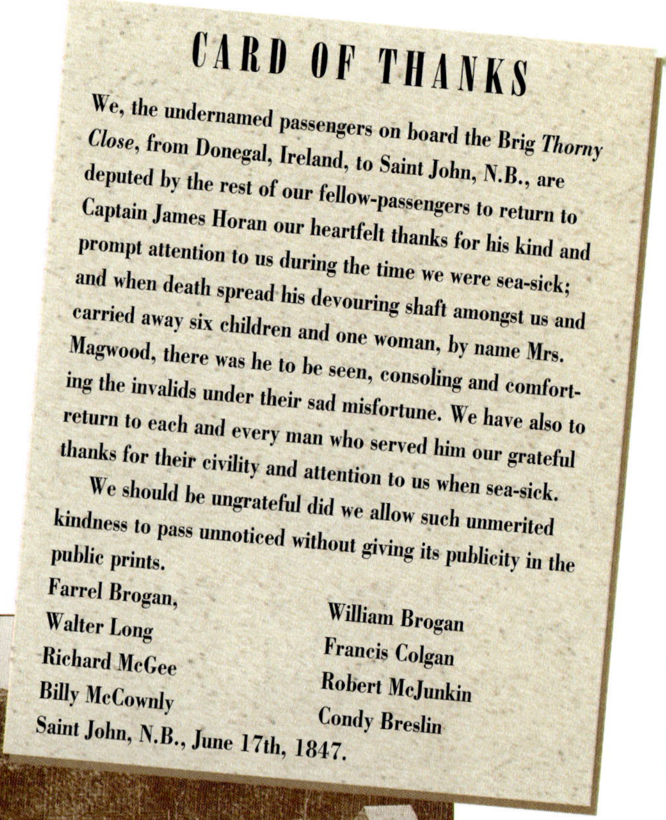

CARD OF THANKS

We, the undernamed passengers on board the Brig *Thorny Close*, from Donegal, Ireland, to Saint John, N.B., are deputed by the rest of our fellow-passengers to return to Captain James Horan our heartfelt thanks for his kind and prompt attention to us during the time we were sea-sick; and when death spread his devouring shaft amongst us and carried away six children and one woman, by name Mrs. Magwood, there was he to be seen, consoling and comforting the invalids under their sad misfortune. We have also to return to each and every man who served him our grateful thanks for their civility and attention to us when sea-sick.

We should be ungrateful did we allow such unmerited kindness to pass unnoticed without giving its publicity in the public prints.

Farrel Brogan,
Walter Long
Richard McGee
Billy McCownly
William Brogan
Francis Colgan
Robert McJunkin
Condy Breslin

Saint John, N.B., June 17th, 1847.

Figure 4.14 Artist's depiction of a Loyalist family establishing a homestead in the St. John River Valley

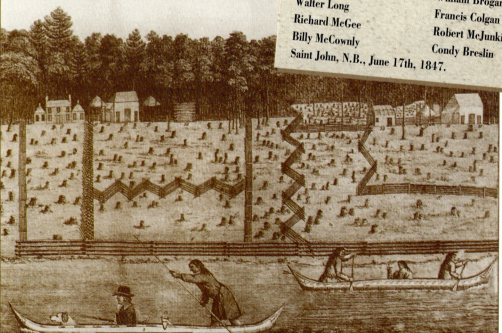

African-Canadian Communities

The first person of African descent in Canada is believed to have been Mathieu da Costa, who worked at Port Royal in 1608 interpreting Mi'kmaq for the French. Through the 1600s and 1700s, British traders captured people in West Africa and brought them to North America, to be sold as slaves. Although Halifax was not a major centre, it was part of the slave trade. While many early African-Canadians in this period were slaves, some were seaman, fishers, and landowners. Most people of African descent who came to the region arrived in later waves, as shown in Figure 4.16.

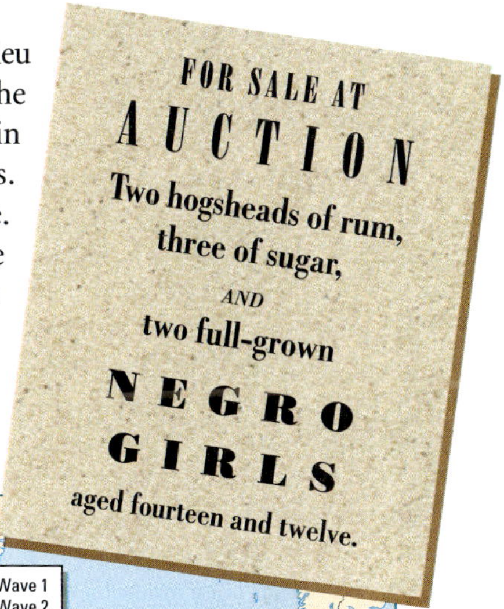

Figure 4.15 Auction notice, Halifax, 1769. What is your reaction to this poster? Discuss your response with a partner.

> **FOR SALE AT AUCTION**
> Two hogsheads of rum, three of sugar, AND two full-grown **NEGRO GIRLS** aged fourteen and twelve.

LEGEND

Wave 1
1782–1784 Over 3000 Black Loyalists arrive in the Atlantic provinces.
1792 1190 Black Loyalists decide their best hope for survival is to resettle in Sierra Leone, West Africa.

Wave 2
1796 About 550 Maroons are transported from Jamaica to Nova Scotia, after their attempts to resist British colonial rule and maintain their independence.
1800 Almost all Maroons sail for Sierra Leone, fearing the loss of their independence and culture in Nova Scotia.

Wave 3
1813–1816 About 2000 Black refugees arrive in Nova Scotia from the United States, following the British-American War of 1812.
1821 After much pressure by British officials for new African-Canadians to relocate, 95 Black settlers sail for new homes in Trinidad.

Wave 4
Late 1800s, early 1900s Sailors and other workers from the West Indies settle at ports in Nova Scotia such as Yarmouth, Weymouth, and Parrsboro. Some come to work in steel mills in Sydney, Cape Breton.

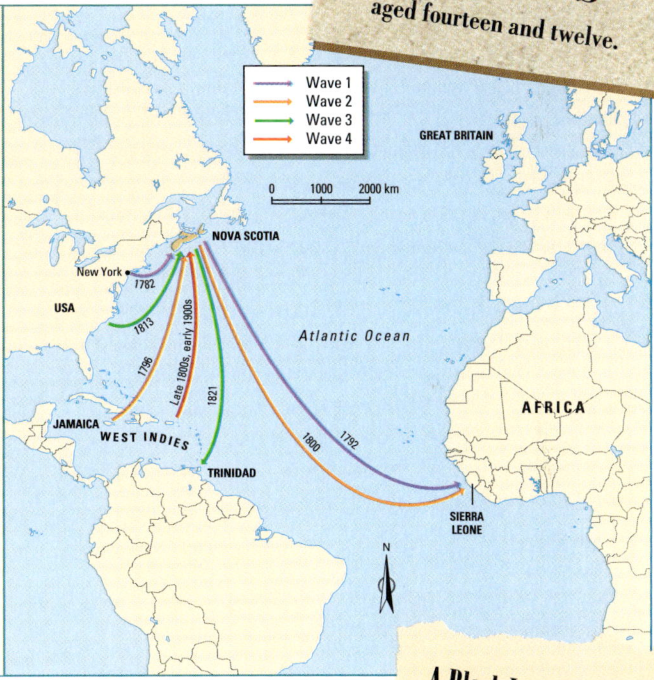

The British had offered freedom to any slave who would fight on their side during the American War of Independence. The response of the Black Loyalists is now considered the greatest slave revolt in the history of the Americas. Many of these Loyalists migrated to the Birchtown, Digby, and Guysborough areas, where they had been promised land and provisions. Once they arrived, however, they found that they were not to receive the same benefits as White Loyalists.

Figure 4.16 Waves of immigration and emigration by people of African descent

Figure 4.17 By 1851, African-Canadian communities were established in various parts of Nova Scotia.

A Black Loyalist's Account of Conditions in Nova Scotia

Instead of receiving our promised and proper allotments...the greatest part of us have received small allotments in a soil so over run with rocks and swamps that vegetation with our utmost care is barely enough to keep us in existence; nay some of us have actually perished from hunger and the severity of the climate.... It is therefore too late for the greatest part of us to reap any benefit in this country.

Source: Sylvia D. Hamilton, "On the Way to Africa" in Horizon Canada, 5: 1293.

A PLACE TO LIVE

Focus on an Issue

Africville

In 1848, the small community of Africville was established north of Halifax on Bedford Basin. As the city of Halifax grew, it started using the land around Africville for sewage and garbage disposal, industry, and railroads. City services improved rapidly in Halifax, but Africville was excluded, even though it was within Halifax city boundaries. While physical conditions in the settlement were far from ideal, the people of Africville felt a strong sense of community and culture. Over the years, and after much petitioning of government, community members succeeded in getting services such as schools, street lights, and a post office. Basic amenities such as water and sewers, however, were not provided.

Through the 1950s, residents of Africville pushed for improved services. Government officials, however, favoured demolishing the community altogether and relocating its residents in other parts of Halifax. It was calculated that providing adequate services to Africville would cost $800 000, but that relocation would cost approximately $76 000. In 1964, the first home was demolished; by 1970 Africville had gone. It was announced that the total cost of removing the community had actually come to $765 000. The extract from the poem to the right records the sense of loss experienced by the Africville community.

Figure 4.18 Africville, 1965. The church (centre left) played a large role in the community.

Africville My Home

Another time, another place
But the memories are vivid and strong.
From Big Town to Round the Turn,
We had a place to belong.

Remember the closeness of neighbours and friends,
Our elders so greatly respected,
And in our own small world, of that freedom and love,
Our unity kept us protected.

City living was fine for others,
But our haven out home reigned above,
Very true it is that we had our faults,
But our foundation was built on love.
In days gone by, our village stood strong,
City politics led us astray,
Let others learn from our misjudgments,
Trust never what they say.

Let the young ones learn what once was,
With pictures and tales of the land,
Each of us must teach them this,
Don't let go of what's yours, take a stand.

      Terry Dixon

Source: The Spirit of Africville *(Halifax: Maritext/Formac, 1992), p. 92.*

ANALYZING THE ISSUE

Work in a group.

1. **a)** Find the phrases or lines in "Africville My Home" that describe the community spirit.

   b) Terry Dixon says, "Our unity kept us protected." Why do you think community members felt they needed protection?

2. **a)** Make a diagram to show causes and effects leading up to the demolition of Africville.

   b) Identify as many places as possible on your diagram at which alternative steps could have been taken that might have resulted in a different effect. On your diagram, mark these steps and their possible effects.

3. **a)** What do you think Terry Dixon means by "Don't let go of what's yours, take a stand"?

   b) Is this view reflected in your diagram in any way? If so, highlight these steps. If not, adjust your diagram by adding steps that do reflect this view.

Immigration in the Twentieth Century

Although many immigrants came to Canada in the late 1800s and early 1900s, most of them were encouraged by the government to settle in the Western provinces. Similarly, in waves of immigration that followed, Atlantic Canada was not a major destination. In two important periods, however, some groups did make their homes here, contributing richly to the political, economic, and cultural diversity of the region. After World War II (1939–1945), a large wave of immigrants started coming from war-torn Europe. In the 1970s, many more immigrants started coming from the countries of Africa, Asia, and Central and South America. You will learn more about the contributions of different cultural communities in Unit 2. Through the 1980s and 1990s, Canada continued to accept immigrants from a wide variety of countries.

Figure 4.19 After the war, Canada and Newfoundland (which did not join Confederation until 1949) became home to thousands of "war brides" — women who married Canadians and Newfoundlanders serving in Europe during the war. These English war brides arrived with their children in Halifax in 1946.

Table 4.5 Some immigrants to Canada in the post-war years have been **refugees**, people forced to flee their homes. This table shows the main sources of refugees in the post-war period.

1956	Hungary
1968–72	Czechoslovakia
1972–78	Asians from Uganda
1973–79	Chile
1975–78	Vietnam/Cambodia
1976–present	Lebanon
1982–85	Poland
1982–present	Iran
1982–present	El Salvador
1983–present	Sri Lanka
1984–present	Guatemala
1992–present	Former Yugoslavia
1993–present	Zaire, Somalia, Ethiopia

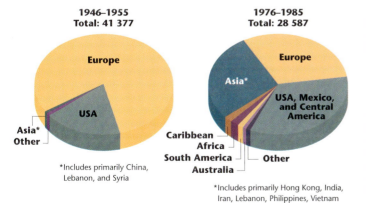

Figure 4.20 These two graphs show that the sources of immigration to the Atlantic provinces changed significantly between 1956 and 1976. Summarize the changes that you see.

Figure 4.21 As in other parts of Canada, many immigrants to the Atlantic provinces have settled in cities, contributing to the growth of our urban areas.

A Place to Live 63

EXPLORATIONS

APPLYING YOUR SKILLS

1. Work in a group. Make a display entitled "Settlement of the Atlantic provinces." Include the following:

   a) a time line of settlement by major groups

   b) "push" and "pull" factors for major groups

   c) an outline map of the world showing the origin of major groups

2. In the case study of Fredericton, you examined site factors that influenced the location of settlement. Identify, from this section, one other example of settlement influenced by site factors, and describe those factors.

CONNECTING AND EXTENDING

3. a) Research the topic of Aboriginal land claims. What is a land claim? If possible, view some of the specifics of a land claim by visiting some web sites of Aboriginal groups. Make a list of the issues usually included in land claim negotiations.

   b) Which of the issues in your list would, in your opinion, be the most difficult to negotiate? Why?

   c) Select one of the issues on your list, and with a partner, role play a discussion between an Aboriginal leader and a government spokesperson about this issue.

   d) Combine your arguments with those of classmates who have focused on different issues. Form a land claims strategy on behalf of:

   i) the Aboriginal group

   ii) the governments involved

4. a) Assume you can interview one of the passengers on the *Thorny Close* in 1847. Prepare a list of questions you would ask about conditions in Ireland, conditions on board the ship, and the passengers' hopes for a new life in Atlantic Canada.

   b) Either write a newspaper report based on these questions or role play your interview.

5. Since World War II, Canada has accepted many thousands of immigrants who fled persecution, famine, and war. Invite someone who immigrated to Canada to your class to describe his or her experiences. Alternatively, with the help of your teacher, find the story of one immigrant to Canada. Prepare a short report to describe his or her experiences.

SEEING THE BIG PICTURE

How does your own community fit into the population patterns discussed in this chapter? Do a survey for your community, and then create a profile of the community based on your findings. Base your survey on the following categories. Develop additional questions, as appropriate, for each category.

1. History
   • When was your community established?

2. Location
   • What site factors influenced its location?

3. Economy
   • What were the main occupations of early settlers?

4. Population density
   • What is the approximate population of the community?

5. Ethnic background
   • What is your own family background? Where did your family originate?

6. Facilities: What sorts of places does the community have for:
   • recreation?
   • health?
   • legal services?

7. Transportation
   • What forms of public transportation are there?

UNIT 2

Culture

CHAPTER 5 *What Is Culture?*

What forces shape culture and how is culture transmitted?

CHAPTER 6 *Our Cultural Mosaic*

How do different cultural groups in our society interact?

CHAPTER 7 *Expressions of Atlantic Culture*

How have expressions of culture in the past served as a foundation for contemporary arts and entertainment in the Atlantic provinces?

CHAPTER 8 *Occupation and Lifestyle*

How have occupations in Atlantic Canada influenced the lifestyles of the people who live here?

CHAPTER 9 *Culture and Politics*

How does our culture allow us to be active members of our society, with the power to make our voices heard on issues that affect us?

CHAPTER 5
What Is Culture?

Figure 5.1 At lunch, after school, on the weekend — just like young people everywhere — Atlantic Canadian teens love to hang out, enjoying each others' company.

You are meeting your friends outside the corner store. Maybe you will just hang out. Maybe you'll take your blades. You like the wall by the corner store. It is a good place to sit, to watch. There is a Chinese restaurant two doors down, where you and your friends can order eggrolls and stay as long as you like.

You talk. Your friend Dan tells about the new videos he saw, and Mu Ching tells about the fashion models in a new teen magazine. You discuss how unfair it is that Janet is not on the school volleyball team. Audrey tells her grandfather's story about the one-eyed sea captain who used to live on this corner, years ago.

The street corner where you and your friends meet, the wall where you sit, the restaurant where you hang out — these are some of your centres of culture. Much of your conversation — whether it's about videos, volleyball, or fashion models — deals with matters of culture.

- But what is culture? What different forms does it take?
- Where does our culture come from? How is it transmitted from one person to another, and from one generation to the next?

DEFINING CULTURE

Culture is a reflection of who and what we are. It refers to everything connected with the way humans live in groups. It includes all the ways people respond to their physical environment, their history, their economic life, their social life, and their political life. Culture includes arts and entertainment such as video-making, as well as beliefs such as what is or is not fair. It includes organizations such as city governments and schools, as well as behaviour patterns like hanging out after school.

Physical environment
How do people interact with their physical environment?

History
What are the origins of the culture, and how have events brought changes over time?

Social life
How do individuals and groups within the society interact?
What are their religions, values, and traditions?

Economic life
How do people make a living? How do their occupations influence their lifestyle?

Political life
How do people in the society organize themselves so that they can live together in peace and security?

Source: Adapted from R. Neering, S. Usukawa, and R. Kubicek, *Exploring World Cultures* (Vancouver: Douglas & McIntyre, 1988).

Figure 5.2 Aspects of culture. You have already learned about the physical environment of Atlantic Canada. In this unit, you will focus on the cultural impact of social, historical, economic, and political life.

Culture consists of all products of human work and thought. It includes the clothes you wear, the food you eat, the places where you live and shop, your beliefs and the things you value, the way you spend your leisure time, and the technology you use.

Culture is what earlier generations transmit to later ones; through a story of a one-eyed sea captain, for example, or through instructions such as "Keep your elbows off the table!"

Although culture is transmitted from one generation to the next, it is separate from genetic transmission of traits, or characteristics. For instance, you may have inherited your grandfather's broad shoulders. You may have inherited your mother's ability to play musical instruments by ear. These characteristics are not cultural. The clothes you wear over those shoulders, however, and the songs you play on the piano **are** based on your culture.

Figure 5.3 The ability to roll your tongue into a U, as shown here, is an inherited trait. About 70 percent of people can do it. The other 30 percent cannot. They could not do it even if their culture strongly encouraged the practice!

Culture: A Global Perspective

Scientists who study human cultural characteristics are known as **anthropologists**. Anthropologists have pointed out that there are important differences among cultures; for example, among the cultures of Saudi Arabia, Indonesia, and Atlantic Canada. In other words, there is **cultural diversity**. They also emphasize, however, that there is a lot of cultural similarity. One American anthropologist, George P. Murdock, made a long list of characteristics he found in every culture, all over the world. Some of these are shown in Table 5.1.

Table 5.1 Some common cultural characteristics from Murdock's list. Which five are most important to you? Why do you think these characteristics are common across cultures?

Art	Hairstyles	Music
Beliefs about good and evil	Hospitality	Numbers
Calendars	Housing	Personal names
Community organization	Jokes	Religion
Cooking	Kinship groups	Sports
Co-operative work	Language	Toolmaking
Education	Law	Trade
Folklore	Marriage	Visiting
Government	Mealtimes	

Figure 5.4 Although cultures are diverse, they share many characteristics. In addition, their characteristics may change over time.

EXPLORATIONS

REVIEWING THE IDEAS

1. Which of the following have to do with culture?
   a) Eye colour
   b) Eating with chopsticks
   c) Values and traditions
   d) Long fingers
   e) Fingernail polish
   f) School rules
   g) A keen sense of hearing

2. Choose two cultural characteristics from Table 5.1. Use drawings, diagrams, photographs, or clippings from magazines to explain how these characteristics are expressed in your culture. For example, you might show your culture's hairstyles. Make a class display of your work.

APPLYING YOUR SKILLS

3. What do you do in your spare time? Explain how the way you spend your spare time is a reflection of your culture. Be sure to include some of your centres of culture and some cultural topics that you and your friends might discuss.

CONNECTING AND EXTENDING

4. Assume you are an anthropologist. Choose any culture other than your own. From Table 5.1, choose three cultural characteristics to investigate in the culture you have chosen. Share the results of your investigations with the class in an oral or written report.

MEETING OUR NEEDS

All people, no matter what their background, have needs. We all have **physical needs**, such as the need for food, water, clothing, shelter, and safety. We also have **emotional needs**, such as the need for friendship, a sense of belonging, love, self-esteem, knowledge, excitement, and self-expression.

While all people share these needs, their ways of meeting them vary greatly. To a large extent, the culture of a group develops as people find ways to meet their needs. In the process of meeting their needs, they often adjust their physical environment, social environment, or both.

As you read the following examples, discuss which needs the people are meeting in each case. In addition, discuss how they are interacting with their environments.

- Every autumn the people of Twillingate Island, Newfoundland, hunt sea birds known as turrs, or thick-billed murres. These meaty birds were once an important part of the winter food supply.

- In the 1800s, many large, stately houses were built in Fredericton, New Brunswick. They are now regarded as some of the most beautiful homes in North America.

Figure 5.5 In many northern communities you may be teased or congratulated by your friends, depending on what kind of snowmobile you have.

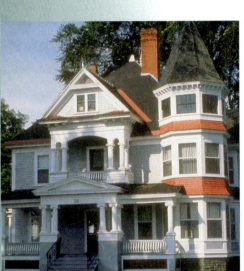

Figure 5.6 One of Fredericton's beautiful old houses

- In the 1780s, some of the Loyalist settlers in Atlantic Canada were starving. They were saved by members of the First Nations who brought them moose meat to eat.

- Prince Edward Island has powerful winds, and researchers at the Atlantic Wind Test Site at North Cape experiment with ways to harness this wind power to produce electricity.

- The Newfoundland economy has a growing high-tech sector. Companies in the province sell such products as telephone equipment, navigational programs, and computer files.

- There is a large community of Celtic background in Cape Breton, Nova Scotia. By celebrating their music, sports, and crafts, members of the community seek to preserve their Celtic heritage.

- Early New Brunswick settlers built covered bridges across the province's many rivers. The roofs of these bridges kept snow and rain from rotting the planks.

- Many young members of the Baptist Church in Atlantic Canada belong to a nation-wide organization called Canadian Baptist Youth (CBY).

- In 1982, Buddhist leader Chogyam Trungpa urged his followers in Colorado to join him in establishing a new Buddhist community in Halifax. He chose Nova Scotia because he believed traditional family values were important here. Today Halifax boasts the world's largest non-Asian Buddhist community.

MATERIAL AND NON-MATERIAL CULTURE

To understand cultures better, anthropologists examine their material and non-material aspects. When you look through your pocket, knapsack, purse, or school locker, what objects do you find? There might be a comb, a wallet, money, a photograph, a library card, a sandwich, a notebook, a pen, or a calculator. All these are part of your **material culture** — the physical objects produced and/or used by the society to which you belong.

Non-material culture, on the other hand, refers to the elements of culture that are not physical. It includes spoken language, ideas, stories, myths, legends, religious beliefs, and ways of behaving.

Among the most important aspects of non-material culture are our **values** — the ideas, beliefs, and ways of behaving that are valuable or important to people of a particular culture. One culture, for example, may value being exactly on time for appointments and social events. Another culture may value the wisdom of older people.

Figure 5.7 The teacher's wristwatch is one element of material culture in this photograph. What others do you notice?

Celtic culture in Cape Breton

Frances MacEachen is a tall woman in her twenties, sitting in a cluttered office in Mabou. She is editor and publisher of *Am Briaghe*, a newspaper of Celtic language and culture written in English and some Gaelic. Its 2000 subscribers span the world. It has a proper home in Mabou, where the sign on the post office says *Tigh Litrichean*: House of Letters. The Mull Restaurant serves Scottish oatcakes — bannock — and *marag*, a spicy white Scottish sausage....

The Celtic ideal has to do with honor and courage, with music and poetry, with hospitality, with loyal pride in family and ancestry....

Source: "Re-Gaeling Cape Breton" by Silver Donald Cameron in *Canadian Geographic*, January/February 1996, pp. 62–71.

Figure 5.8 Frances MacEachen. List five examples of material culture given in the article. List five examples of non-material culture. How many of the examples of non-material culture are also values?

DID YOU KNOW...?

Many cultures enjoy bannock. Members of First Nations and African Canadians share the pleasure of this biscuit-like bread with people of Scottish descent.

WHAT IS CULTURE? **71**

Explorations

APPLYING YOUR SKILLS

1. **a)** Keep a detailed diary of your activities over the course of a day to record your needs. Classify your needs as physical or emotional.

   b) Make a web diagram showing how your culture has drawn on or adapted the environment to meet those needs. For example, what resources have been harvested to meet your needs? Are your needs affected by the climate of your area?

2. Look back at Table 5.1. Divide the cultural characteristics listed in the table into material and non-material.

Traditional Culture, Popular Culture, and the Global Connection

You have seen that culture is often transmitted from one generation to the next. The customs, beliefs, opinions, and stories passed down from one generation to another are known as **traditions**. The older the traditions, the more powerful they often become.

For many years, people in your community may have harvested seaweed, or made sauerkraut from cabbages they grow themselves. For many years, they may have worn British woollens, made pewter jewellery, told Glooscap stories, or held annual rowing races on a local lake. All of these are examples of traditions. The **traditional culture** of a group is made up of practices established over many generations.

If your family belongs to a Christian Church, you may recently have had your *confirmation*. If your family is Jewish, you may recently have had your *bar mitzvah* or *bat mitzvah*. These are further examples of traditions. Such ceremonies, or **rites**, are part of the traditional culture of a family and the religious group to which it belongs.

The world has many traditional cultures that vary from group to group. There is, however, another, more widespread kind of culture, **popular culture**. This is the culture shared by many groups in Western society, both in the city and in the country. It is also shared, increasingly, all over the globe. Do you listen to popular music? Do you watch situation comedies on television?

Figure 5.9 Rowing race at the Royal Newfoundland Regatta on Quidi Vidi Lake, St. John's, Newfoundland. The Regatta, North America's oldest continuing sporting event, is part of the city's traditional culture. The Regatta has been held here since at least 1826.

Do you buy brand-name clothes, drink brand-name soft drinks, eat at fast-food restaurants, or admire internationally known sports stars? If so, you are participating in popular culture.

Suppose that you had a penpal in any one of the following places: Manitoba, the United States, Britain, Portugal, Jamaica, or Russia. You would probably find your penpal liked similar music, TV shows, brands of clothes, and sports stars.

The spread of these elements of popular culture in the modern world has much to do with technology. For example, popular culture spreads through the mass media — including television, radio, compact disks, newspapers, books, and movies. It spreads through communication and information technologies such as computers, fax machines, and telephones. It also spreads through transportation links such as expressways, ferries, causeways, bridges, undersea tunnels, and air travel routes.

DID YOU KNOW...?

Most of the popular culture shared by the people of the world comes from the United States.

- In Canada and in many other countries, most of the television programs people watch and most of the music they listen to are American. In Canada, most of the magazines we read also come from the United States.
- There are McDonald's restaurants in over 100 countries of the world.
- The American news service CNN World News is available on suitably connected televisions in all English-speaking countries of the world.

Figure 5.10 How does popular culture depend on each of the factors shown here?

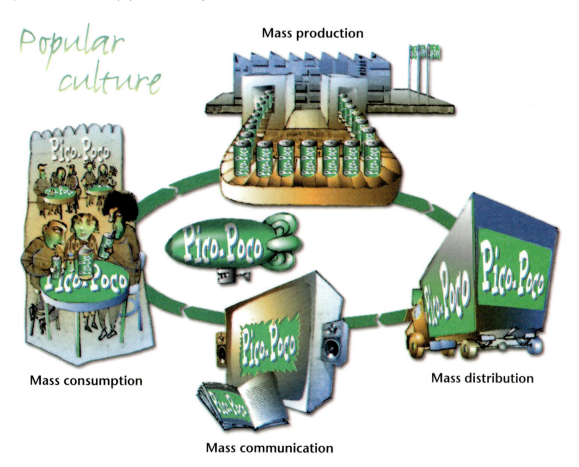

Source: Adapted from W. Sproule, People In Perspective (Scarborough: Prentice Hall Canada, 1994), p. 203.

Explorations

APPLYING YOUR SKILLS

1. Last Friday, Sharilyn helped her parents make the dinner her family always eats on Fridays. Then she tried out the cologne she had ordered from an ad on the Internet. After watching a TV show featuring her favourite popular singer, she read her younger brother a book about the Egyptian pyramids.

   In what ways was Sharilyn taking part in traditional culture on that evening? In what ways was she taking part in popular culture?

ANALYZING AND REFLECTING

2. **a)** Analyze one television drama or situation comedy, focusing on how that program transmits elements of culture. For example, what values are evident with regard to the following?
   - the way people look
   - their general lifestyle
   - the way they interact with each other
   - the way they solve conflicts or other problems

   b) How do commercials transmit elements of culture?

   c) Present your findings in a short written or oral report. Be sure to cite specific examples from the show and commercials you have watched.

3. Analyze one television show that you consider to be educational. How does this show transmit elements of culture?

4. **a)** Make brief notes on what you might do during an evening at home. Which of your activities relate to traditional culture? Which relate to popular culture? How many of your activities might be influenced in some way by American popular culture?

   b) How do you think popular culture affects traditional culture? For example, do fast-food restaurants decrease the tendency for people to cook and eat traditional meals at home? Are we losing valuable aspects of our local culture as we adopt the American values and lifestyles we see in the media? Or is popular culture a unifying force? Discuss these questions in a group. Make brief notes on your discussion.

   c) Debate: We need to protect our local and regional culture. Some limits should be placed on the amount of American programming and publications available in the Atlantic provinces.

5. With your classmates, brainstorm a list of cultural practices and products that have changed within your lifetime. You might start with family traditions, communication technologies, transportation links, or fashion trends.

The Many Agents of Socialization

Do you have a picture of yourself as a baby? What can you tell about yourself from that picture? Perhaps you can see some resemblance to other family members, but you probably can't tell much more. You were born with only your genetically inherited traits. In other words, you were born without culture. Yet today you may prefer to eat with a fork. You know how to put on your socks, tell time, greet your friends, read this page, obey traffic signals, and buy your favourite brand of soft drink. How did you learn all this? You did it through **socialization** — the process of learning behaviour that is considered suitable in your culture.

Many agents of socialization have operated in your life. They have included individuals, groups, and **institutions** (organizations with social, educational, and religious purposes). They have probably included the following:

- **Family**. For most people, socialization begins in the family. Your father, for example, may have taught you to wash your hands before meals. Your sister may have taught you to ride a bike. Most importantly, the values and attitudes you hold come most often from your family.

Figure 5.11 This baby could learn any language. Will it be French? Japanese? English? Gaelic? Inuktitut? That depends on the baby's family and other agents of socialization.

- **Schools**. They teach knowledge — what culture is or what history is, for example. They teach skills, such as reading and solving problems. They also teach attitudes and behaviours, such as cooperation and curiosity.

- **Peer groups**. Your peers are people of about the same age, who have similar interests to your own. Many of your friends, though perhaps not all, are your peers. From your peers, you may have learned such things as what clothes are in style, how to dance, and how to get a babysitting job.

- **Clubs, teams, and similar organizations**. Girl Guides may have taught you crafts and consideration for others. Playing on a hockey team may have taught you to be a good sport, whether you win or lose.

- **Community**. A summer job in a community business or other organization may have taught you skills such as running a cash register and dealing with the public. A community arena may have provided you with the opportunity to learn figure skating.

- **Government**, including government figures such as police and politicians. A warning from a police officer, for example, may have taught you not to walk alone in a certain park at night. A politician speaking on

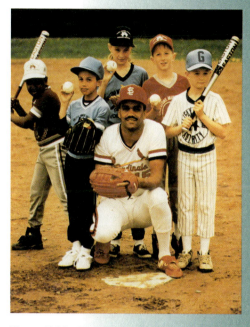

Figure 5.12 Cape Breton native and professional baseball player Curtis Coward takes time away from the St. Louis Cardinals to coach young students in Halifax. Why are sports figures powerful agents of socialization?

TV may have shown you how your community's recycling program works or how an offshore oil discovery might affect your province.

- **Religious groups**. From these you may have learned values such as honesty, kindness, and forgiveness. You may have learned the meaning behind special occasions such as Diwali, Christmas, Yom Kippur, Ramadan, or Kwanzaa.

- **Mass media**. As you have already seen, the mass media are an important means of spreading culture, especially popular culture. They are also becoming an important tool for education, as you will see in Unit 4.

The Role of Language

Christine Saulis is a Maliseet language teacher who regularly sees the power of language to socialize. She was hired to teach the language to Maliseet students who had been educated in English. "From day one the children ran to my room and did not want to leave. I still have to shoo them out of here every day. So obviously it's more than language that they are getting. It's — 'I can be myself!... I don't have to pretend to be anything or anybody else.'"

Source: R. M. Leavitt, Maliseet & Micmac: First Nations of the Maritimes *(Fredericton: New Ireland Press, 1995), p. 59.*

Focus on an Issue

School Culture: What Difference Can It Make?

In many ways, your school is a microcosm — a miniature model — of the society around you. It has a culture influenced by staff, students, and other members of the community. Various **formal**, or organized, groups contribute to that culture. These might include the chess club, a basketball team, or a student council. **Informal groups** also contribute to the culture of the school. They might include a group of students who meet after school to go skateboarding together, students who often eat lunch together, or students who volunteer to help out in the library during recess.

Most teenage students associate themselves with a group, either formal or informal, within the school culture. This is because most teens have a powerful need to "belong." While young people develop independence during teenage years, they still need to be part of a group — usually a group of their peers.

Many groups make a positive cultural contribution to your school. Think of a sports team, for example. How do the students, as a group, feel when the team wins a championship? How does the atmosphere of the school change? How does a student council help with the running of the school? On the other hand, some groups can have a negative effect. You may know, for example, of someone who has been excluded from a group — perhaps he or she was not included in arrangements to meet after school. How would this person feel? Why might he or she be excluded? What can happen when understanding and communication between groups break down? What can happen when understanding among members of the same group breaks down?

What role does the culture of the school play in these cases? In many cases, schools encourage interaction, cooperation, and communication among students. They value the ability to resolve conflicts. Usually they focus on three types of interaction: dialogue, problem solving, and mediation. Look at the lists in Figure 5.13 to learn more about these forms of interaction, and work through the activities below to analyze how the culture of the school can contribute to a positive environment.

ANALYZING THE ISSUE

1. Identify factors that contribute to the culture of your school.

2. **a)** Identify groups that are part of your school.
   b) Do you think any of these groups are misunderstood? If so, brainstorm ways in which they could improve understanding within the school.
   c) Show how various groups could work with each other to make a more positive contribution to school culture.

3. Role play a dispute between individuals or groups that might happen at your school. Are the guidelines on page 77 sufficient to resolve the conflict?

4. Discuss ways to improve communication and the quality of life for students at your school, at home, and in the community. Act on your ideas!

Figure 5.13 Resolving conflicts: Some basic guidelines

Dialogue

dialogue: interchange and discussion of ideas, usually between two parties

Basic rules
1. Listen to each other. Both parties have a chance to explain their position. Both parties must listen to each other.
2. No blaming. Parties must give their point of view about what happened without blaming the other.
3. Tell the truth. The object is not to blame one party or the other, but to find a solution. Therefore, there is nothing to be gained by not telling the truth.
4. Try to solve the problem in such a way that both parties feel better.

Problem Solving

1. When tempers flare, stop and think. Stay calm.
2. Identify the problem; collect as much information as possible.
3. Identify feelings. How do you feel? How does the other party feel?
4. Decide on a goal.
5. Identify as many possible solutions as you can.
6. Consider the consequences of each one.
7. Evaluate the options, and choose the best solution.
8. Think about possible obstacles, and make a plan for overcoming them.
9. Try your plan, and see what happens. Did it work?
10. If the first plan didn't work, try to find out why. Then try again.

Mediation

mediation: settling a dispute between two other parties in a diplomatic or friendly manner

DO	DON'T
Listen carefully.	Take sides.
Be fair.	Tell the parties what to do.
Ask how each party feels.	Ask who started the dispute.
Let each party explain what happened.	Try to blame anyone for the situation.
Treat each person with respect.	Ask, "Why did you do it?"
Keep what you are told confidential.	Give advice.
Mediate in private.	Look for witnesses to the dispute.

Source: Adapted from Earlscourt Child and Family Centre, *Peacemaking Skills* (Toronto, 1990).

EXPLORATIONS

REVIEWING THE IDEAS

1. Look back over the list of socialization agents on page 75. List all the agents in order of their influence on you. Beside each, give an example of something you learned from that particular socialization agent.

APPLYING YOUR SKILLS

2. Imagine yourself as a parent some time in the future. You are faced with the task of teaching your child appropriate behaviour, such as how to share toys with others or how to eat with others at the table.

   a) What types of behaviour would you model for your children?

   b) What you choose to convey to your child reflects your own culture. How does this culture reflect that of your parents? Your community? How does it reflect your personal convictions? Discuss these questions in a group.

ANALYZING AND REFLECTING

3. a) With a partner, investigate different ways in which you could respond to peer pressure. For each of the situations described, use the following problem-solving approach to reach a recommended course of action.

   i) What is the problem?
   ii) What are the possible solutions?
   iii) What are the pros and cons of each?
   iv) What is your plan of action?

   Situations
   - Your friend wants to copy your answers during a test.
   - You are out with a group of four or five friends one evening. Two or three of your friends have cans of spray paint and plan to spray some graffiti on a wall.
   - A group of three or four students have been "cornering" you each day and demanding your lunch money.
   - You have noticed a group of three or four students "cornering" another student each day and demanding his lunch money.
   - Your brother or sister is four years younger than you are. You have been given permission to go out with your friends as long as you take your sibling with you.
   - You are out with your friends when they suggest going to the video arcade. You are not allowed to go to the video arcade.

   b) For one of the situations above, prepare a flow diagram, cartoon, or skit to show the problem-solving process. Display the finished product in the classroom.

MAINSTREAM AND CONTRIBUTING CULTURES

Can a person have more than one culture at the same time? What if you are an Irish Catholic urban Newfoundland Canadian? You probably have at least five cultures: Irish, Catholic, urban, Newfoundland, and Canadian. What if you are a rural Dutch vegetarian New Brunswick Canadian? Or a francophone Prince Edward Island Canadian involved in theatre? Or a female Baptist African Canadian active in local politics? What would your various cultures be? How might they overlap? How might they conflict?

Mainstream culture is the general culture of the majority of people. Flowing into mainstream Canadian culture are many **contributing cultures** — cultures of smaller groups of people. A mainstream culture in a local area may be a contributing culture in a larger region. Like brooks running into a larger stream, Canada's contributing cultures add to and enrich the mainstream culture. You will learn more about contributing cultures and their relationship with the mainstream in the chapters that follow.

SEEING THE BIG PICTURE

1. Work in a group to predict changes that might occur in the culture of your area in the next decade. Organize your predictions into economic, social, and political changes. You might choose to complete this activity as a "jigsaw," by assigning the three different categories to different students, and then sharing and combining your findings afterwards. Consider the following topics:
   - clothing
   - food
   - shelter
   - family structures
   - transportation
   - communications
   - entertainment
   - medicine
   - music
   - sports

   Make broad, sweeping predictions. Will a rich natural resource be drained or discovered? Will people migrate away from your area or flock to it? Also make very specific, detailed predictions of changes likely to take place over the next ten years. Will the pen you write with, for instance, be disposable? Will it be recyclable? Will pens be obsolete?

2. Present your findings in the form of a chart, diagram, or other display.

3. Compare the predictions of different groups. Are there any common threads among all the predictions?

CHAPTER 6

Our Cultural Mosaic

Figure 6.1 Learning about other cultures is a good way to get to know your own culture better. Many travellers report understanding themselves better after a time abroad; perhaps that is because they have looked at themselves through someone else's eyes.

Imagine that you are part of a youth exchange to the Caribbean country of Haiti. You are visiting a school in a small coastal village. When you arrive, the head of the community quietly asks one of the boys to remove his earring. In hesitant English, he explains that he knows it's all right for boys to wear earrings in Canada; but in Haiti, only girls wear earrings.

At the end of your stay, your group visits many sites around Port-au-Prince, Haiti's capital. At the door to a museum, a guard stops your group. A girl who is wearing shorts has to wait outside.

- As an outsider to the mainstream Haitian culture, how would you feel?
- What do these incidents tell you about opportunities and problems that might arise when different cultures come into contact?
- How can cultural conflict be avoided so that cultural diversity can contribute to our society in a positive way?

Cultures Change

If you could visit your own community 100 years ago, you would find you had a lot to learn — that the culture of your community was different then. That is because cultures vary from place to place, and over time. Cultures grow and change. Cultures appear and disappear.

Some cultural changes are caused by internal forces. Cultures change because attitudes change. One hundred years ago, for example, it was unusual for most children to get more than two or three years of schooling. Today, most Canadians receive at least 13 years of schooling, and many receive much more. Why did attitudes towards schooling change over time?

Other cultural changes result from outside influences. As you have already seen, cultures around the world are changing rapidly as new technologies increase communication between cultures, bringing many outside influences. Travel and communication technology have created a popular culture that stretches around the globe.

For many years, Atlantic Canada developed with input from three main groups: Aboriginal peoples, the French and the British. Then, many other groups started to arrive, especially after the 1960s (see page 63). These groups have all contributed to cultural change, influencing the politics, economy, and social life of the region.

Figure 6.2 Fifty years ago, few homes had television. Today, Canadians from Iqaluit to Port Hardy depend on TVs for entertainment and information. Fifteen years ago, few people thought of owning a home computer. Today, many children learn how to run a computer before they learn how to read. How might such technological changes alter cultural beliefs?

DID YOU KNOW...?

Technology can provide powerful support for cultures. In Canada, for example, the main role of the CBC is to communicate Canadian culture from coast to coast.

OUR CULTURAL MOSAIC

Explorations

ANALYZING AND REFLECTING

1. Consider who or what has caused a recent change in your life. Think about the influence of your parents, peers, school, or any other socializing agent. Draw a cause and effect chart to show how this change might influence your life.

2. Choose a major invention such as the automobile, airplane, telephone, television, or computer. To appreciate how much this invention has changed mainstream culture, imagine life without it. Write a short story, essay or poem, or prepare a humorous skit, depicting life without the invention.

CONNECTING AND EXTENDING

3. Many cultures celebrate change by marking the "coming of age" in various ways. For example, getting your driver's licence, graduation, or ceremonies such as confirmation or a bar-mitzvah all mark coming of age. Explain the purpose of one coming of age celebration and the rites, or ceremonies, involved.

4. Use a library that keeps copies of old newspapers on microfilm or microfiche. Look at the newspaper for the day on which you were born. What was happening in the world? What kinds of products were advertised? What kinds of jobs were advertised? What kinds of fashions were popular? How much did products cost? Present a summary of your findings to the class. Then discuss how your culture has changed over the course of your lifetime.

Celebrating Cultural Diversity

Humans are social creatures. They develop by interacting with each other. Healthy humans belong to and interact with members of many groups.

◆ Most people belong to some kind of family or family grouping. During their school years, as we have seen, peer groups are very important. Later, they belong to a professional, employment, or volunteer group.

◆ Everyone belongs to an ethnic group and to a linguistic group. The members of an **ethnic group** share a common background, which can include country of origin. Note that there can be different ethnic groups within a racial group. Is your family Welsh, Icelandic, Filipino? There are more than 180 different countries from which you and your ancestors could have come.

◆ The members of a **linguistic group** share a common language. Do you speak Tamil, Swahili, German? There are more than 6000 different languages spoken world-wide.

◆ Many people also belong to a **religious group**: Lutheran, Brethren, Buddhist, Hindu. There are more than 122 000 different religious sects or groups.

◆ Everyone also belongs to at least one **cultural group**. As you have seen, in any society, there is one dominant culture, usually referred to as the mainstream culture. Members of other groups belong to contributing cultures. People of European ancestry who live in Canada are members of the mainstream culture. Europeans living in Japan, however, are members of a contributing culture.

In most countries, the members of all groups are encouraged to **assimilate** — that is, to become absorbed into the mainstream culture. Canadian society is also **multicultural**. This means that contributing cultures are expected to participate in Canada's economic, political, and social life but, at the same time, they are encouraged to maintain their own separate cultural identities. In this way, Canadian society is able to benefit from customs and attitudes of many cultures. By accepting many cultures, Canadians learn openness and flexibility and their lives are enriched.

In Atlantic Canada, as in other parts of the country, the differences that make each contributing culture unique are celebrated. For example, Miramichi, New Brunswick, is the home of an annual Irish Festival that offers music, food, and culture from Eire. This festival also provides a time to mourn the potato famine victims who died on their way to Canada in 1847. During the first Irish festival in 1984, a Celtic cross was erected in memory of these people.

In Dartmouth, Nova Scotia, people from a variety of cultures work together to plan an annual three-day celebration of the history, geography, customs, and peoples of many countries. During the festival each June, booths display food, drinks, arts, crafts, and entertainment from countries such as Nigeria, Lebanon, China, Scotland, the Philippines, Germany, India, Italy, Japan, Korea, Sri Lanka, Palestine, Greece, and Vietnam. As well as celebrating diversity, the festival features an *Anti-Racism Live Theatre* which makes people more aware of issues related to racism.

Figure 6.3 For many Canadians, Joe Ghiz (1945–1996) symbolized the success of Canada's policy of multiculturalism. A member of the Lebanese community, and a strong advocate for Canadian unity, Ghiz became premier of Prince Edward Island in 1986.

Figure 6.4 Events such as the Dartmouth Multicultural Festival celebrate cultural diversity. In the past, it was common for countries to expect immigrants to conform to the mainstream culture. Today, multiculturalism is a global trend.

OUR CULTURAL MOSAIC   83

Career Focus: Meet an ESL Teacher

Alice Foley-Keats is a teacher of English as a Second Language (ESL) with the English Language Program at the University of New Brunswick in Fredericton.

Figure 6.5 Alice Foley-Keats

Training for Teaching ESL

Entrance Requirements

Undergraduate degree from a recognized university, good command of spoken and written English, and a reference from a former teacher or employer.

Teacher Training

Training includes:
- field experience to observe teachers and students at work
- a period of internship to work with an experienced teacher and receive coaching
- various courses on educational psychology, how to teach, and how to evaluate what students are learning

Q: What does your work involve?

A: The program runs year-round and offers many different options. Some students study part-time, and some study in our total "Submarine©" immersion sessions. Depending on the course they choose, students live with a host family, in a residence, or in their own home. Students in the total immersion program sign a pledge promising to function only in English 24 hours a day, seven days a week. They attend English classes and experience English through cultural activities such as going to the theatre or enjoying a picnic and sing song.

Q: Who are your students?

A: Our students come from a wide range of ages, countries, and backgrounds. I have taught people as young as 14 and many well past retirement age. Our program deals with students from more than 50 different countries. We have some programs for people who know no English; and others for students with good English who need some help with improving their written communication. We have many local students, but also offer special programs to business people and professionals from national and international corporations, governments, and service groups. English programs are popular because English is the international language used both on the Internet and in international business. There are now more people in the world who speak English as a second language than people who have English as a first language.

Q: Some people say that language is one of the most important ways in which people learn culture. What cultural information do students learn from your class?

A: That depends on individual student needs. We encourage students to interact with people at farmers' markets, museums, handicraft studios, local historic sites, and Canadian celebrations such as Canada Day. We urge them to make observations that they bring back to class, then we discuss what they have seen and heard. We also expect students to interact with people from other cultures. We mix people from different backgrounds together; that way, they learn from each other. For example, I might have a student from Thailand work with others from Aruba, Japan, and Bangladesh.

Q: What have you learned about other cultures through your work?

A: I have learned so much — the way people in different cultures react, dress, interact, gesture. Teaching people from many cultures is like getting a chance to visit their cultures — to see through their eyes and memories. One Lithuanian student was keen on basketball. He explained that everyone in Lithuania is a basketball fan. From listening to him, I learned that basketball competitions between Lithuania and Moscow are more a political battle than a game. Now I understand better when I hear about riots after a sports match. In Saudi Arabia, it's offensive to shush someone, and you never hand anything to an Arabian with your left hand. The Japanese point to their nose when they use the word "me."

Q: How has teaching English as a Second Language contributed to your own life?

A: Although I'm a teacher, I'm also a learner. Teaching people from many cultures is like getting a chance to visit their cultures through their eyes and memories. Since I teach many different groups and clients, my job is always new and exciting, which I love. It keeps me in touch with world events.

EXPLORATIONS

APPLYING YOUR SKILLS

1. Imagine that you are the ESL teacher for a small group of immigrants. Choose one cultural event, either from mainstream culture (e.g., Canada Day or Remembrance Day) or from a contributing culture (e.g., Chinese New Year or Kwanzaa). Plan a series of activities that will help your students learn about this cultural event.

   a) Keeping in mind that some of your students may not speak much English, make a list of key terms that you would like them to learn.

   b) Plan ways of teaching the students about the institutions and traditions associated with the event.

ANALYZING AND REFLECTING

2. **a)** Complete a chart similar to the one below.

Aspect of Atlantic Canadian Life	Countries that Influence
Foods	
Music	
Clothing styles	
One other aspect	

   b) Write a paragraph discussing the benefits of living in a country that encourages multiculturalism.

3. Work in a group.

   a) Assume that you find yourself in a culture that is very different from your own. Perhaps you are working as an ESL teacher abroad; perhaps you are doing volunteer work in another community; perhaps your family has moved to another country. Consider the following:

   i) How might it feel to notice that there are few other people in the community whose skin is the same colour as yours?

   ii) In this situation, how might you feel and act toward other members of your own group?

   iii) What judgements might the people in the community make about your culture because of the behaviour of you and your group?

   Discuss these three points, and then develop a role play or skit to show what might happen.

   b) What have you learned from this activity about the way groups interact in Atlantic Canada? Discuss your observations.

4. Work in small groups.

   a) Many teenagers work very hard to assimilate — to "fit in." For example, many wear a "uniform" that consists of blue jeans and a T-shirt or sweatshirt with a specific brand name or logo. Brainstorm the ways in which people you know try to assimilate into the mainstream teen culture.

   b) Many teenagers work very hard to appear different from the mainstream culture. For example, some dye their hair green, others pierce their tongues. Brainstorm how people you know try to differentiate themselves from the mainstream Canadian culture.

   c) Discuss why it is often important for teens to feel both part of a group and different in some way.

5. **a)** List the skills and qualities that you think would be necessary to be a successful ESL teacher.

   b) How interested would you be in doing such a job? Explain.

   c) If you were interested in becoming an ESL teacher, which subjects should you focus on at school?

CONNECTING AND EXTENDING

6. Explore the Internet to find examples of how technology can support culture. You may wish to focus on one individual culture or on a range of different communities. Report or make a display of your findings.

7. Some cultures have disappeared. One such culture was that of the Beothuk of Newfoundland. Research and prepare an illustrated report on the culture of the Beothuk, including an explanation of why this culture became extinct.

What Is Racism?

While Canadians are encouraged to accept all members of contributing cultures, it is a reality that not everyone in our society is treated as equal.

You have already learned about the difference between inherited traits and cultural characteristics. Humans are born with similar physical and mental structures. Their cultures differ because they have developed in a variety of environments. Any of us, if born in another culture, would learn and follow the basic beliefs and values of that culture, and develop the necessary personality traits. For example, if our culture decided that all blue-eyed people were poor mathematicians, blue-eyed people would probably be treated as though they couldn't learn math. It is likely that many of them would come to believe this opinion, and many would never develop anything other than basic number skills. Their weakness in math would not be caused by their common inherited trait (blue eyes), but by the beliefs of their culture.

The view that all members of a group are the same — rather than individuals with differing abilities, personalities, and values — is known as a **stereotype**. Some people, for example, think that all teenagers are loud and thoughtless. This is a stereotype. There are some loud and thoughtless teenagers. Some teenagers — like many other people — are occasionally loud and thoughtless. This does not mean that all teenagers are like that. Some are never loud and thoughtless.

Figure 6.6 Racism has many negative effects on society as a whole, as shown here. Make your own diagram, based on this one, to show the benefits of eliminating racism.

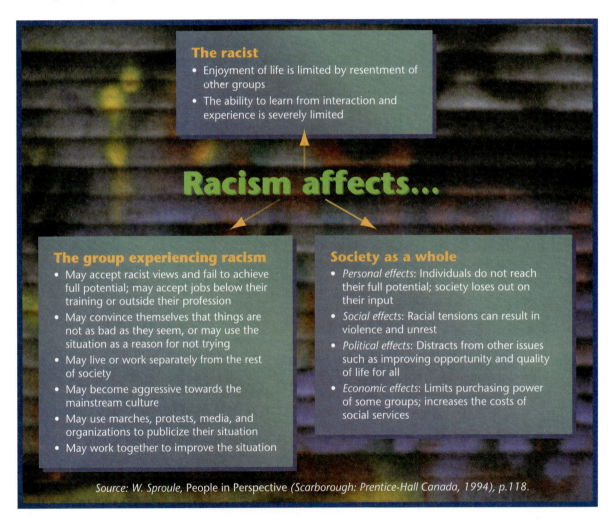

Racism affects...

The racist
- Enjoyment of life is limited by resentment of other groups
- The ability to learn from interaction and experience is severely limited

The group experiencing racism
- May accept racist views and fail to achieve full potential; may accept jobs below their training or outside their profession
- May convince themselves that things are not as bad as they seem, or may use the situation as a reason for not trying
- May live or work separately from the rest of society
- May become aggressive towards the mainstream culture
- May use marches, protests, media, and organizations to publicize their situation
- May work together to improve the situation

Society as a whole
- *Personal effects*: Individuals do not reach their full potential; society loses out on their input
- *Social effects*: Racial tensions can result in violence and unrest
- *Political effects*: Distracts from other issues such as improving opportunity and quality of life for all
- *Economic effects*: Limits purchasing power of some groups; increases the costs of social services

Source: W. Sproule, People in Perspective (Scarborough: Prentice-Hall Canada, 1994), p.118.

Someone who holds this stereotype of teenagers will expect that any young person he or she encounters will be loud and thoughtless. In other words, that person will hold a **prejudice** — a view based on previously held ideas, and not on knowledge or experience. That person might even **discriminate** against teenagers — that is, treat them unfairly, based simply on the fact that they are teenagers.

Racism is the belief that a person's abilities, personality, and values are influenced by race, colour, or ethnic origin. Racism is any action based on stereotypes that view all members of a racial, ethnic, or cultural group as being the same, rather than individuals. It is the mistaken belief that one group is superior to another, and is often the cause of discrimination by organizations, institutions, and individuals.

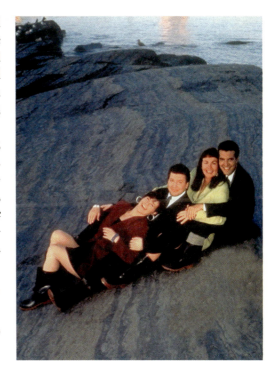

Figure 6.7 *This Hour Has 22 Minutes*, a series featuring Newfoundland comedians, satirizes Canadian culture. A **satire** uses sarcasm or wit to expose the silly or illogical things that people do or say. Watch an episode of the show. How does it poke fun at the tendency of people to stereotype? Why do you think this show has been so successful across the country?

FOCUS ON AN ISSUE

Canada's Immigration Policy: Who Gets In?

For many decades, Canada's immigration policy favoured applicants who were from northern and western Europe. In many ways it was a racist policy. For example, at one time immigrants from China had to pay a "head tax" and African-American immigrants were discouraged during settlement of the Canadian West. By the 1970s, however, attitudes were changing. Canadians now realized that immigrants from many countries had strong contributions to make.

In 1976, the federal government introduced new rules which state that immigration officers cannot discriminate against any applicants on the grounds of race, ethnic group, gender, or religion. The results of this policy can be seen in Figure 4.20 (page 63). Today, applicants are judged, regardless of country of origin, according to a number of criteria including age, languages spoken, education, job skills, occupational demand, job experience, and the presence of relatives living in Canada. Points are allotted for each of the criteria, and applicants who receive the required number of points are allowed to immigrate.

Figure 6.8 Refugees from war-torn Bosnia (formerly part of Yugoslavia) arrive in Newfoundland. In 1995, former Yugoslavians were one of the largest groups to immigrate to the Atlantic provinces. Why do you think this was so?

Different criteria are used to judge **refugees**, people who have fled their homelands because they are in danger as a result of their race, religion, political beliefs, or natural disaster. A certain number are accepted if immigration officers can find evidence that they face a genuine danger in their homelands.

In 1995, the federal government proposed a controversial change to immigration policy. It announced that each immigrant to Canada would have to pay a fee of $950. People who could not afford the fee would be admitted, but they would have to pay it in installments once they arrived in Canada. Critics claimed that this new fee was racist because it would prevent immigration by people from poor countries and by refugees — people in the greatest need. The government defended its decision by pointing to the expense of operating the immigration services and saying that all Canadians, even new immigrants, have to contribute their share.

ANALYZING THE ISSUE

1. Work with a partner or small group.

   a) Brainstorm the advantages and disadvantages of Canada's point system for immigrants.

   b) Brainstorm reasons why Canada uses different criteria for refugees.

2. Debate: The immigration fee of $950 per person conflicts with the intention of our immigration policy, and should be abolished.

EXPLORATIONS

APPLYING YOUR SKILLS

1. **a)** Review pages 55–62 in Chapter 4. List examples of discrimination and racism against groups or individuals. Research other examples.

   b) In the role of a member of one group that has suffered discrimination, explain how you feel about the treatment you have received. Explain also how you plan to respond. Present your ideas in the form of a monologue, journal entry, speech, or "letter to the editor."

ANALYZING AND REFLECTING

2. Most of us hold some stereotypical views, even if we would rather not. For example, do you believe that girls are bad at science? That Asian students are good at math? That people in wheelchairs can't play sports?

   a) Individually, or with a trusted partner, record three stereotypes that you hold.

   b) For each, identify at least one step you could take to change your way of thinking.

   c) Briefly list the benefits that might result from your changed way of thinking.

3. **a)** Over the course of a week, survey magazines, newspapers, and television to see how people of different ethnic and cultural groups, genders, and ages are portrayed. Are any under-represented? Are any portrayed in stereotyped ways? Can you find any conscious efforts to address problems of under-representation and stereotyping?

   b) In the style of a media critic either write a newspaper review or prepare a television or radio broadcast, summarizing your findings and giving your opinion of what you have seen.

4. **a)** Work with a partner or small group. Identify ways in which you believe teens are discriminated against.

   b) Choose one of these ways and discuss steps that you can take to deal with the discrimination. Identify the best course of action.

   c) Try to implement your suggested solution. Report on the degree of success you achieved to the class. How might you adapt your solution another time?

5. An African-Canadian female teenager faces the possibility of triple stereotyping. Write a paragraph or two suggesting the challenges that might be faced by such an individual.

Combatting Racism

As you have seen, racism harms individuals, groups, and society as a whole. But what can we do to combat it?

Institutional Responses

We have laws to protect us against racism. The Canadian Charter of Rights and Freedoms guarantees Canadians the right to live without discrimination on the grounds of race, national or ethnic origin, religion, sex, age, or mental or physical disability. Anyone who experiences discrimination on those grounds has the right to take legal action. In addition, many organizations today are "equal opportunity employers." This means they hire and promote workers regardless of race or gender.

> **DID YOU KNOW...?**
>
> On March 21, 1960, scores of people protesting peacefully against South Africa's racist apartheid policy were shot. Over 60 demonstrators were killed and many more wounded. In commemoration of this tragic event, the United Nations declared March 21 an International Day for the Elimination of Racial Discrimination. South Africa now has a government committed to racial equality, but this date remains a day of action against racism. In Canada, schools aim on this day to inform society about the nature of racism and to encourage everyone to do something, however small, to eradicate racism in all walks of life.

Personal Responses

Everyone in a multicultural society is responsible for recognizing individual prejudices and working to overcome them. What would you do, for example, if you heard someone you know make a prejudiced or racist statement? Clearly, your response would differ according to the circumstances, but educators have identified some effective steps to take.

Some people ignore racist comments or get angry, but these responses seldom help to change the other person's way of thinking. Effective alternatives include challenging the statement or trying to discuss your concerns. For example, a response such as the following might have some effect: "I am concerned about what you said about that group. My experience is not the same as yours. Can I tell you about my friends in that group?" In other words, education is an effective response.

Community Responses

As you saw in Figure 6.6, a community can respond to racism by working together to improve the situation. Community members sometimes organize protests and use different forms of education to publicize their situation and press for improvements.

Figure 6.9 Reacting to racist comments. Which of these responses is likely to be most effective? Why?

CASE STUDY

EDUCATING AGAINST RACISM

A Personal Response: The Example of Rita Joe

Rita Joe is a Mi'kmaq poet dedicated to reviving the traditional ways of her people. This task, as she sees it, is a process of education — both for members of the Mi'kmaq nation who have lost touch with their traditional roots, and for mainstream Canadian society which has seldom recognized the richness of her culture.

> ### I LOST MY TALK
>
> I lost my talk
> The talk you took away
> When I was a little girl
> At Shubenacadie school
>
> You snatched it away;
> I speak like you
> I think like you
> I create like you
> The scrambled ballad, about my word
>
> Two ways I talk
> Both ways I say,
> Your way is more powerful
>
> So gently I offer my hand and ask,
> Let me find my talk
> So I can teach you about me
>
> **Rita Joe**

Figure 6.10 Rita Joe's father, as a young man, together with his family

Rita Joe was born in 1932 in Whycocomagh, Cape Breton Island. She spent much of her early life in foster homes. To get away from one foster family, she put herself into the Shubenacadie Residential School. Until the 1960s, it was common for Aboriginal children to attend residential schools, where they were forced to abandon their traditional ways. At Shubenacadie, Rita Joe was not allowed to speak her native language or practise her spiritual traditions. In response, she took on the lifelong quest of encouraging other Mi'kmaq to educate themselves in traditional ways, and showing Canadian society how forced assimilation harmed members of her culture. This she did through her writing. In 1990, she was awarded the Order of Canada for her efforts.

Figure 6.11 Rita Joe receives the Order of Canada from Governor General Ray Hnatyshyn, 1990. Compare her clothes with those worn by her father and his family. What statement do you think she was making by dressing in this way?

CASE STUDY

A Community Response: The Black Cultural Centre for Nova Scotia

The Black Cultural Centre for Nova Scotia, situated in Dartmouth, was opened in 1983. Its aim is to educate people about the contributions of African-Canadians to our history and to celebrate African-Canadian heritage.

"Few people are aware of how African-Canadians have contributed to Nova Scotia's history. For example, Nova Scotia's Dalmore (Buddy) Daye was a Canadian light-weight boxing champion who was also the first African-Canadian ever appointed as sergeant-at-arms in a Canadian parliament. Because many African-Canadian children do not learn about people like Buddy Daye, they don't feel part of the mainstream Canadian culture. This is harmful to them, because it affects their self-esteem. Since Canada is a multicultural society, it's important for all children — African-Canadian and others — to learn about and celebrate the contributions of many communities, including the African-Canadian community."

Henry Bishop, Director of the Black Cultural Centre for Nova Scotia

Figure 6.12 The centre's museum displays cultural artifacts. It includes works by Edith Clayton, who adapted traditional African basket-making techniques to Canadian materials. Her unique maple-sapling baskets were so well-known that she was chosen to represent Nova Scotia's arts and crafts community at the 1986 Expo in Vancouver.

The centre consists of a museum, a library, and offices. It also provides space for people to attend lectures and seminars on subjects that concern the African-Canadian community. The centre focuses on educating teachers so that they can pass the information on to their students. It also produces a weekly program for the local cable television company. The overall aim is to help people understand cultural differences and to help African-Canadians maintain pride in their culture.

Figure 6.13 The military exhibit at the centre reminds visitors of the participation of African-Canadians in the country's armed forces.

OUR CULTURAL MOSAIC

EXPLORATIONS

APPLYING YOUR SKILLS

1. **a)** Explain the main message of Rita Joe's poem.

   b) What is the tone of the poem? How does Rita Joe convey this tone? Support your answer with examples of specific words and the types of language she uses.

   c) How effective is the poem in meeting Rita Joe's objectives? Explain.

2. Visit the web site of the Black Cultural Centre for Nova Scotia at www.nstn.ca/bccns/. How effectively does the web site meet the aims of the centre as outlined on page 91? What changes, if any, would you suggest?

CONNECTING AND EXTENDING

3. With the help of your teacher, find examples of people in your province who, like Rita Joe, are attempting to preserve a culture. Prepare a profile of one of these people.

4. **a)** As a class, investigate different steps young people can take to combat racism. Appoint students to take on the following roles and present their points of view on the topic in a classroom discussion:
   - representatives of student groups
   - teachers
   - representatives of community groups
   - politicians
   - police
   - social workers

   b) Take notes during the discussion.

   c) Make an anti-racism poster. You may choose to represent the many ideas resulting from your class investigation or simply one or two. Display your poster in the school.

SEEING THE BIG PICTURE

1. Make a chart or a collage to show the contribution of various cultural groups to your province.

2. As a class, plan and organize an event for your school to celebrate cultural diversity. Possibilities include bulletin board displays, a special assembly, or a multicultural meal.

CHAPTER 7

Expressions of Atlantic Culture

Figure 7.1 *Top*: Jeri Brown, Jazz Artist of the Year; *Bottom*: Great Big Sea, Entertainers of the Year, 1997 East Coast Music Awards

EAST COAST MUSIC AWARDS ROCK MONCTON

You are a newspaper reporter covering the East Coast Music Awards, hosted every winter in the Atlantic region. Each year sees growing anticipation of the event, the music, and the talent to be found there. Your task is to write a feature article on the awards as they showcase Atlantic Canadian music and culture.
- How will you decide if the awards represent and reflect Atlantic Canadian culture?
- How do the arts and entertainment of Atlantic Canada today draw on our historical background?

Traditional Music Meets Popular Culture

Different regions of Atlantic Canada have varied music traditions. From the Innu communities of Labrador to Newfoundland's Southern Shore, Cape Breton, Prince Edward Island, and Acadian New Brunswick, diverse music traditions span several hundred years. These traditions have evolved over time as people adapted to a new environment and interacted with other cultures.

Today, the East Coast Music Awards (ECMA) showcase musical talent throughout the Atlantic region. They feature almost every conceivable style of music. The ECMAs have done a great deal to enhance the profile of the region's performers on the world stage. They also show that music styles popular around the world are being embraced by Atlantic Canadians.

Figure 7.2 From tradition to today: Emile Benoit (right); Natalie MacMaster (below)

East Coast Music Awards Categories

Male Artist of the Year
Female Artist of the Year
Group of the Year
Atlantic Canadian Songwriter of the Year
Song of the Year
Video of the Year
Album of the Year
Country Artist of the Year
Pop/Rock Artist of the Year
Instrumental Artist of the Year
Alternative Artist of the Year
Jazz Artist of the Year
Children's Artist of the Year
Bluegrass Artist of the Year
Classical Recording of the Year
Roots/Traditional Artist of the Year
Francophone Recording of the Year
First Nations Artist of the Year
African-Canadian Artist of the Year
Dance/Hip Hop Artist of the Year
Entertainer of the Year
Dr. Helen Creighton Lifetime Achievement Award
Director's Special Achievement Award

DID YOU KNOW...?

One of Atlantic Canada's best known traditional musicians was Emile Benoit (1913–1992). In many ways, he represented the region's musical roots. Benoit was born in L'Anse-a-Canards on the west coast of Newfoundland and, as a youngster, taught himself to play the fiddle. His style was distinctively French, but also carried traces of the Irish, English, and Scottish traditions of the area where he grew up. Over his lifetime, he composed over a hundred jigs and reels and recorded many of them in his later years. Benoit was awarded the Order of Canada in recognition of his contribution to Canadian culture.

An Expert Speaks...
Interview with Rob Cohn

Rob Cohn is the organizer of the East Coast Music Awards (ECMA). He has been involved with the East Coast Music Awards since their inception in 1989.

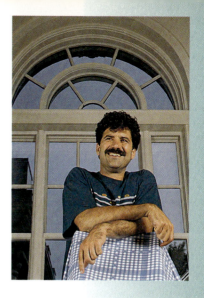

Figure 7.3 Nova Scotian Rob Cohn, a founding organizer of the East Coast Music Awards

Q: Where did the idea for the awards originate?

A: In the late 1980s, I was entertainment columnist for the *Halifax Daily News*, covering the local music scene. I was actively trying to encourage Atlantic acts to play their own music. I began talking with Ron Bryant, manager of a club in Dartmouth, about an awards show. In 1988, I approached the *Daily News* and the corporate world to raise some money and resources, and in April 1989 we had our first small awards ceremony. It was called the Maritime Music Awards because I didn't have the resources to figure out what was happening in Newfoundland. After I added a conference and "showcases" to promote particular acts in 1990, it was called the East Coast Music Awards because it was inevitable that we would have to include Newfoundland and Labrador.

Q: What impact has the ECMA had on the profile of music from Atlantic Canada, both nationally and internationally?

A: East coast music is now the "crown jewel" in the Canadian music industry. The ECMA can be said to be the catalyst for this for one simple reason: An awards show is all about promotion. The promotion we have given acts in the local, national, and international industry has focused attention on the region. It certainly helped that what we promoted was fresh talent that made its own brand of music.

The rise of East Coast music has changed the way the industry works in this country. In 1989, the industry was Toronto. Now the popular music in this country comes from the East Coast, the West Coast, Quebec, Alberta, Manitoba, and everywhere. The record labels travel around to events like the ECMA looking everywhere for talent, instead of waiting for it to come to them.

It's clear the industry on the East Coast would not be what it is today if we had remained a Nova Scotia organization and each province had its own event. The ECMA has managed to weave together all of the musical genres, contemporary and traditional, with five diverse regions (Cape Breton is a separate entity, along with the four provinces), and a diverse cultural mosaic (Aboriginal peoples, Celtic, Francophone, African-Canadian, European, and more).

Q: What would you say are the strongest national or international influences on the music of Atlantic Canada today?

A: The strongest influence is probably Celtic, which is a hybrid of Italian renaissance classical music. Some of the musical structures of Celtic are found in many "worldbeat" traditional musics such as South American and Japanese. Another strong influence is Los Angeles Pop, which is a hybrid of American rock and British pop. It is influenced by American roots, blues, soul, African spirituals, jazz, and classical.

Q: What advice would you give to young artists who want to succeed in this industry?

A: Don't expect anyone to do anything for you. No one owes you anything. If you have to tell someone how good you are, you're not. There's no one way to do any of this, so figure it out for yourself. Don't quit your day job. And remember, success in this business rarely means financial success.

EXPLORATIONS

APPLYING YOUR SKILLS

1. **a)** Research some of the winners of the last ECMA. For information, visit the web site at www.ecma.com or try e-mailing the organization at music@ecma.com

    b) Write the article suggested by the headline on the opening page of this chapter.

2. Review the ECMA award categories on page 94. What would these categories tell a person from another part of the world about Atlantic Canadian music and culture?

ANALYZING AND REFLECTING

3. Work in pairs or a small group. Choose one East Coast music act.

    a) Which musical traditions do you think have influenced this group or individual? Find recordings of musical styles that you think influenced this act.

    b) Present your findings to the class, using tapes or CDs to illustrate what you have found.

4. **a)** With the help of your teacher, obtain a recording of Emile Benoit. Does his music appeal to you? Explain.

    b) Do you think the popular music you listen to will appeal to young people of future generations? Why or why not?

CONNECTING AND EXTENDING

5. **a)** Which Atlantic music acts would you nominate for the ECMA? Visit the ECMA's web site at www.ecma.com to find out about eligibility and the nomination process. Would your favourite acts qualify?

    b) Make a presentation to a classroom panel of judges arguing for one act of your choice as winner in one of the ECMA categories. Use recordings, videos, and any other material in support of your nomination.

6. **a)** Country music from the southern United States became popular in the Atlantic provinces as radios became common in the 1940s and 1950s. The similarity between the narrative style of country songs and that of traditional music styles may have contributed to the popularity of this form of music. What reasons can you suggest for the continuing popularity of country music in Atlantic Canada?

    b) How do you think the Internet might influence the kind of music that is popular in Atlantic Canada today?

STORYTELLING AS ENTERTAINMENT

In Chapter 5, you were asked to describe some of your daily activities. The chances are that most of you included watching television for at least some part of the day. Television has become the central form of entertainment in our culture, and for many people, relaxing in front of the television means watching a story of some sort. While television is a relatively new medium, and an integral part of popular culture, storytelling has a long tradition.

In many cultures, storytelling was part of an **oral tradition**, in which the history of a group, the lessons it learned over time, and its morals were passed from one generation to the next. Often the stories took the form of fairy tales, myths, or legends. While storytelling was an important form of education, it was often the chief form of entertainment as well; stories would be told to while away long winter nights.

In the English-speaking traditions of Atlantic Canada, folk tales were rare. In the francophone tradition, however, folk and fairy tales thrived until recently. Some folk tales of the francophone areas were short, but many took hours to perform! Their very length suggests that they belonged to a society that moved at a leisurely pace, very different from that of modern-day North America.

In many parts of Newfoundland and the Maritimes, stories consisted of legends, anecdotes, and personal experiences. On the Port-au-Port Peninsula of western Newfoundland, however, the tradition was slightly different. In this and other francophone communities, fairy tales were typical. At one time, these fairy tales were considered strictly adult entertainment, because they contained gruesome details considered too horrific for children. Only as the tales declined in popularity among adults, did writers and storytellers adapt the stories for young audiences and give them a literary rather than an oral style.

Features of Traditional Stories

Generally speaking, traditional stories follow certain patterns. Here are some of the most common.

Single Plot: The plot is simple and focuses on one main idea or theme. All actions and scenes centre around this theme.

One Leading Character: The audience's interest lies with the actions and fate of one leading character.

Contrast: Contrasts between good and evil, rich and poor, beautiful and ugly, strong and weak, and foolishness and cleverness are common.

Two-to-a-Scene: Only two people appear at any one time in a scene.

Threes: The tales often feature three brothers, three princesses, three magical aids for the hero, or three great battles.

Repetition: Certain situations, words, sayings, or parts of speech are repeated through the story, sometimes many times.

Figure 7.4 Like folk stories, folk art is an expression of local culture. **Folk art** refers to works created by artists who receive no formal training. Usually it depicts everyday life and displays a simple, direct style. This painting is by Nova Scotia folk artist Maud Lewis. Lewis, who died in 1970, lived much of her life in poverty. Today her paintings are found in collections throughout North America, including the White House, home of the American president.

THE STRING OF TROUT

This folk tale was recorded from Mrs. Daniel Poirier of Egmont Bay, Prince Edward Island, in July 1957.
Which of the features of traditional stories can you identify?
In what ways does this tale reflect the culture of the region?

Once there was a man and he had a little boy. He lived near the church. There was a small river there and he loved to fish for trout, especially so he could give some to his parish priest. Every time he caught some lovely big trout, he would send his little boy to take a string of them to the priest.

One day he says to his little boy as usual, "Here, go and take these lovely trout to the priest."

"No, I'm not going," replied the little boy.

His father was surprised since the boy never ever answered him that way before. "What did you say? Go and take the trout to the priest."

"No. I'm not going."

"Why?" the father says.

"Just because I'm not going."

"Well," the man says, "If you go just this once, since they are so beautiful this time, I'll never ask you to go back again."

The boy doesn't answer. He takes the trout and sets out angrily for the priest's. He gets to the door, knocks and opens the door. The priest was seated on the far side of the room, farthest from the door. The boy takes the string of trout and throws them down on a chair, closes the door, and starts to go away.

The priest runs to the door. "Come here," says the priest. "Come here, my little boy. I'll show you that that is not the way to bring a string of trout to a priest."

The little boy was a bit ashamed.

"Come here. Come here, my boy."

Well, he had to go back. He goes back to the door and he's all ashamed.

"Come in," the priest says. "I'll show you how to bring a string of trout to a priest. Sit down in my big chair and you'll be the priest and I'll be the little boy."

The priest picks up the trout and goes outside. He knocks at the door.

"Come in," the little boy says.

He comes in and goes up to the little boy who is supposed to be the priest. He bows and says, "Here, Monsieur le Curé. My father sent you a string of trout."

The little boy isn't a bit slow. He puts his hand in his pocket and takes out 25 cents and gives it to the priest. Then, imitating the priest, he says, "Here, little boy. This is to pay you."

The priest was surprised and a little ashamed. "I can see now," he says, "why you did what you did. You want to be paid for your trouble. Very well, I will pay you."

There was a small table there. The priest takes 25 cents and puts it on one corner, puts 50 cents on another corner and a dollar on another corner.

"This is to pay you," he says to the little boy. "If you take the 25 cents, you will go to heaven when you die. If you take the 50 cents, you will go to purgatory, and if you take the dollar, you'll go to hell when you die. Now, choose."

The little boy doesn't waste time. He uses both hands. "Well," he says, "I'll take them all and then I'll be able to go where I want to."

The little boy goes out the door and on his way.

Source: Richard M. Dorson (ed.), Folktales Told Around the World *(Chicago: University of Chicago Press, 1975), pp. 448–50.*

How did such tales form a basis for modern forms of entertainment such as television drama? Interestingly, in Newfoundland's francophone community folk tales are referred to as "les contes," a name also used to describe the television soap operas that have become a large part of popular culture. Indeed, soap operas use formulas that are very similar to folk-tale patterns. The "soaps" tend to focus on romance, as do many folk tales. The story of Cinderella and her prince is an obvious example. Westerns, too, have similarities to folk tales. They are generally based on a hero formula, as are many traditional stories. Situation comedies, or "sit-coms," also draw partly on the format of folk tales, using traditional themes such as the consequences of cleverness, foolishness, deception, seduction, and laziness.

The oral tradition has not been entirely replaced by television and movies. While storytelling is not common, jokes are. In addition, we often hear **modern legends**. These are stories about ordinary people, often in urban settings, that describe events that could, in theory, happen. The setting of the legend often changes as the story circulates, so that its events occur in a familiar setting. You may have heard versions of legends such as "The Vanishing Hitchhiker" or "The Babysitter." Most of these stories are not true, but they often reflect common fears. Sometimes tabloid newspapers and television talk shows report these stories, which adds to their credibility.

EXPLORATIONS

APPLYING YOUR SKILLS

1. **a)** Explain the purpose of "The String of Trout." What messages, or lessons about life, does it give? Does it have any other purpose?

    b) With a partner, practise telling the story of "The String of Trout." Before you begin, plan which parts to emphasize and how to tell them to greatest effect. Remember that, in an oral tradition, stories are told rather than read, and they can change slightly with each telling.

    c) What do you think are the characteristics of a good storyteller?

2. Watch a western, sit-com, or other drama on television. Compare and contrast the structure of the show you watch with the structure of a traditional story.

CONNECTING AND EXTENDING

3. With the help of your teacher, if necessary, select one traditional story. It might be a regional folk tale or it might be a children's folk tale such as Cinderella. With a group, prepare to act out the story in the format of a soap, western, or sit com. Present your show to the class. Alternatively, make a comic strip of the story in modernized form.

4. Collect several modern legends from your area. They may be ones you have heard or ones that you have collected from tabloid newspapers. Analyze the stories, keeping in mind the following questions:

    a) Are they presented as truth?

    b) Is there any evidence to show they are factual?

    c) What makes the account believable?

    d) What makes you sceptical about them?

Literature and the Making of an Industry

Lucy Maud Montgomery is known worldwide, especially for her book *Anne of Green Gables*, first published in 1908. Montgomery wrote vividly about Prince Edward Island and its people, institutions, animals, plants, and weather, so that millions of readers have felt personally connected to her and, through her, to the Island. Montgomery's works were translated into many languages, and when she died in 1942, she had fans all over the world.

Through the decades, Montgomery's works have increased in popularity. Not one of her novels has ever gone out of print. What accounts for the continued success of her work? Partly, it can be attributed to a growing "L.M. Montgomery industry." Film, video, and television rights to the series *The Road to Avonlea*, based on several "Anne" novels, have been sold worldwide.

Figure 7.5 L.M. Montgomery, c. 1902

> Nothing I have ever written gave me so much pleasure to write. I…made my "Anne" a real human girl. Many of my own childhood experiences and dreams were worked up into its chapters. Cavendish scenery supplied the background….
>
> Source: M. Rubio and E. Waterston (eds.), *The Selected Journals of L.M. Montgomery, Volume I: 1889–1901* (Toronto: Oxford University Press, 1985), p. 331.

In 1997, *Emily of New Moon* — a television series based on Montgomery's *Emily* trilogy — followed on the success of *The Road to Avonlea*. Anne dolls, Anne china, Anne diaries, straw hats with attached red-yarn braids, and many other products based on Montgomery's characters are sold in gift shops across Prince Edward Island. And all of this merchandise is regulated by lawyers for Montgomery's heirs. All "spin-offs" from her work must have the approval of her heirs, and the producers pay a royalty on the money they make.

Figure 7.6 The musical *Anne of Green Gables* has played in Charlottetown every summer since 1965.

As a result, Anne has become a cultural **icon** — or symbol — not just of Prince Edward Island, but of Canada as a whole. In the last decade, tourism has replaced fishing as the second mainstay of Prince Edward Island's economy. It may soon replace farming as the main source of revenue. An important part of this tourist industry is based on the Anne phenomenon.

DID YOU KNOW...?

Anne of Green Gables was translated into Japanese in 1952. Since then, its central character has fascinated many thousands of Japanese readers. In the summer of 1996, more than 25 000 Japanese tourists visited Prince Edward Island, and most toured the Green Gables house in the Prince Edward Island National Park. Even though Montgomery's works describe the Island as it was 100 years ago, the tourists are not disappointed with its beautiful land- and sea-scapes today. Many express admiration of Anne, who exhibits a trait known by the Japanese as *oshin*, meaning *pluckiness or perseverance*. They also appreciate Anne's respect for tradition, especially the customs held dear by Marilla and Matthew.

Figure 7.7 Silver Bush Farm where L.M. Montgomery was married on July 5, 1911, is now a popular site for weddings. Some Japanese couples fly halfway around the world to have a wedding ceremony here, identical to that of Montgomery.

EXPLORATIONS

APPLYING YOUR SKILLS

1. Choose five pages from any novel by L.M. Montgomery or any other writer from the Atlantic provinces. Prepare a short written or oral report to:

    a) show how these pages reflect Atlantic culture.

    b) compare and contrast the culture illustrated in the pages with your own.

ANALYZING AND REFLECTING

2. Debate: Anne of Green Gables is a national cultural icon. The use of her character, even for commercial purposes, should be free and unlimited.

EXTENDING AND CONNECTING

3. **a)** What cultural icon would you choose to represent your area? Design a product to represent this icon. It should be a product that will appeal to a wide audience or market.

    b) Prepare an ad for your product: it could be a poster, magazine ad, or — if you have access to tape or video recorders — a radio or television commercial. Be sure to draw on the characteristics of the culture your icon represents.

A Focus on Fine Art

Artists of the Atlantic provinces have often painted the dramatic landscapes of the region. One such artist is Gerald Squires. Squires was born in Change Islands on Newfoundland's northeast coast in 1937, and spent much of his childhood on the island of Exploits. In 1950, his family moved to Toronto, where Squires finished school and planned a career in commercial art. He worked for a Toronto newspaper, but in 1969, he decided to return to Newfoundland to be an artist.

When Squires returned to Exploits, he found a community on the brink of death. While he had been away, the fishery — on which the economy and culture of the area were built — had been changing. As you will see in Unit 4, off-shore trawlers had replaced small-boat operators. Instead of being salted or sun-cured, fish were now fresh frozen in modern plants. As a result, the economy of the outports suffered. The government decided to resettle many people from such communities, offering them $2000 to settle in more urban centres.

Gail Squires, Gerry's wife, describes their reaction to the resettlement program that was underway in Exploits in 1970:

> There was a lot of anger towards the government. Word was that the school teacher and mailboat were to be taken away, forcing people to leave the island for these services.... [People were being forced] out of their centuries-long homes and livelihoods.... It was heart-wrenching to watch those proud people...being loaded aboard boats, pathetic and fearful, heading for an uncertain future amongst strangers. When we returned for a brief visit three years later, only three people remained as permanent residents....

Source: D. Walsh and S. Jamieson, Gerald Squires: Newfoundland Artist *(St. John's: Breakwater, 1995) p. 14.*

Figure 7.8 Gerald Squires working on his painting *Resettlement*. His daughter Esther is behind him. How did the painting change between this earlier version and the finished piece, shown on the next page? Which version do you think has more impact? Why?

In response to what they saw, Squires began a series of paintings called *The Boatman*. Since then, he has painted a number of series presenting Newfoundland images. Many draw on his cultural and spiritual roots on the island. Squires is now recognized as one of Newfoundland's finest artists. In 1992, he was awarded an honorary doctorate from Memorial University.

Figure 7.9 *Resettlement* was painted by Gerald Squires in 1975. What is the historical background to this painting? In what ways is the painting symbolic? In what ways does the painting reflect Squires' cultural roots?

EXPLORATIONS

REVIEWING THE IDEAS

1. Compare *Resettlement* with the painting by Maud Lewis on page 97. How would you describe the difference between folk painting and fine art?

APPLYING YOUR SKILLS

2. There are several paintings by Atlantic Canadian artists in this book. With a partner, analyze one of them, or any other painting by an Atlantic artist, by following these steps:

   a) Describe what you see in the foreground, middle ground, and background of the picture.

   b) What forms the focal point of the picture?

   c) What can you learn from the picture? Record three things.

   d) How does the picture make you feel? Explain.

   e) What is your opinion of the picture? Explain.

ANALYZING AND REFLECTING

3. Some artists are very successful, but most receive little financial benefit from their work. What do you think motivates them to paint? In pairs or small groups, role play an interview with any one of the artists whose work is included in this text. The interviewer should ask about the motivation and inspiration for the artist's work, and the artist should provide carefully considered answers. If possible, make a tape or video recording of your interview.

A Focus on Fashion

Clothing fashions often reflect the history, values, and lifestyle of a culture. Alan Syliboy, a Mi'kmaq artist from Millbrook, Nova Scotia, draws on his traditional culture to produce fashions for the modern market.

Ancient Inspirations

When Alan Syliboy discovered petroglyphs (rock drawings) done by his people in ancient times at Kejimkujik National Park, his career as an artist took a whole new direction. He decided to put his art, inspired by the petroglyphs, on T-shirts. Syliboy explains that, when he started, "There was no market for First Nations art, so I had to go door to door." Then he hit on another idea that would set his products apart from those of the typical T-shirt company. "Our shirts are made of recycled cotton saved from the manufacturing process," Syliboy says.

Syliboy's passion for resurrecting aboriginal traditions has become a thriving business. Red Crane Enterprises produces his fine-art designs on prints, cards, and plaques as well as T-shirts. His products are sold across Canada, in Germany and France, and also in Japan.

Figure 7.10 Alan Syliboy. Why do you think his designs appeal to modern consumers?

EXPLORATIONS

ANALYZING AND REFLECTING

1. **a)** Petroglyphs were a form of self-expression and communication in ancient times. In what way does fashion serve a similar purpose? Discuss, with reference to modern trends.

   b) Design your own T-shirt as a form of self-expression and communication.

CONNECTING AND EXTENDING

2. **a)** What sort of clothing was traditionally worn in your culture? Make sketches to show how you might adapt this traditional style to make a modern fashion statement.

   b) How might you be able to use recycled materials in the clothing you have designed? What might be the advantages of using recycled materials?

   c) Assume you believe there is a market for the clothes you have designed. Work with a group to draw up a plan of steps you would have to take to reach your market.

3. Describe the businesses in your area that are connected with fashion in some way. Write a short report on the importance of fashion to the economy.

CASE STUDY

THE ACADIAN RENAISSANCE

Acadian culture was once severely threatened. Today, however, the culture of Acadia is undergoing a dramatic renaissance, and various forms of the arts have played an important part in its revitalization.

As early as 1846, American poet Henry Wadsworth Longfellow drew attention to the Acadians' story with his poem *Evangeline*. A few decades later, in the 1880s, the Acadians in all four Atlantic provinces began actively seeking to preserve and promote their culture. They promoted French schooling and developed symbols of their unique form of French Roman Catholic culture.

Figure 7.11 New Brunswick-born novelist and playwright Antonine Maillet. In 1978 she won the coveted Prix Goncourt — France's award for the best novel in French. Her writing is inspired by the people, history, and geography of Acadia.

Some Acadian Symbols

 Flag The French tri-colour flag with a yellow star that stands for *Notre-Dame de l'Assomption* (Our Lady of the Assumption — The Virgin Mary).

 An Acadian holiday La Fête de l'Assomption, August 15.

 A slogan *L'union fait la force* (In unity there is strength).

Over the years that followed, the Acadians faithfully maintained their culture in their own communities. Through folk stories, traditions, and education, they transmitted it from one generation to the next. Then, beginning in the 1950s and 1960s, the outside world began to notice the Acadians. Anthropologists from Quebec, Ottawa, and France began publishing articles about this unique culture.

This interest encouraged the Acadians themselves to share their culture with the mainstream. They wrote books of poetry, legends, and recipes. They wrote novels and plays, with the works of Antonine Maillet being particularly notable. They shared their culture through music, painting, sculpture, and theatre. This lively expression of Acadian culture continues to the present time.

Figure 7.12 In 1994, Roméo LeBlanc became the first Acadian to hold the position of Governor General of Canada.

Global Connections

The Acadians have kept their connections with France, the country from which their ancestors came in the 1600s. For example, Acadian students are encouraged to read books written and published in France, and to attend universities in France. French ministers of culture and other government officials are often invited to important Acadian events.

One such event was the Acadian World Conference held in Moncton, New Brunswick, in August 1994. This conference, the first of its kind, was attended by about 300 000 people of Acadian descent from around the world. Among them were several thousand American Acadians. Some came from Louisiana (where they are known as *Cajuns*); some from Massachusetts; and some from other parts of the United States to which their ancestors were deported in the 1700s.

> "Acadia needs to say what it is: that it is part of Canada, that it is part of America, that it is part of the international fraternity of Francophone nations, and that it therefore has its own place in the world — a place that is unique, just as each of the world's peoples is unique."
>
> Source: Antonine Maillet, quoted in *New Brunswick Telegraph Journal*, August 11, 1994, p.5.

Figure 7.13 Numerous Acadian festivals celebrate their culture through music, song, storytelling, crafts, and traditional skills. Acadians from the United States often join those in Canada for festivals and other special events.

DID YOU KNOW...?

Although there are Acadians in all of the Atlantic provinces, the largest number are in New Brunswick. About one-third of New Brunswick's population is Acadian. Because of the large number of Acadians, the French language is officially protected in New Brunswick, Canada's only officially bilingual province.

Explorations

REVIEWING THE IDEAS

1. Make a cause and effect chart to show the role played by each of the following in the rebirth of Acadian culture.

   a) The poem *Evangeline*
   b) The Acadian flag
   c) Attention from the outside world
   d) Acadian writing and art
   e) French-language schools

ANALYZING AND REFLECTING

2. You have seen that the Acadians of Atlantic Canada are connected with both France and the United States. As a class, discuss how you think global connections can help a minority group maintain its culture.

CONNECTING AND EXTENDING

3. a) With the help of your teacher, choose a novel by Antonine Maillet. (Most of her work has been translated into English. However, if you read French well, you may wish to read it in the original.)

   b) Read part of the novel. Tell the class what you learned about Acadian culture from the novel, and what you particularly like about the selection you read.

4. a) Research any francophone community or region of your choice. Examples include Port-au-Port, Chéticamp, Evangeline, and Caraquet.

   b) Write a brief description of the community or region, perhaps in the style of an Internet site or tourist brochure. Be sure to include information on the area's forms of arts and entertainment. Include a map showing the location of the community or region and any other visuals you think are appropriate.

SEEING THE BIG PICTURE

1. Working individually or in a group, choose any one form of arts or entertainment from Atlantic Canada that you enjoy. Possible examples include:
   - dance
   - literature
   - music
   - comedy shows
   - comic books
   - fine art
   - music videos
   - drama
   - sports

   You can choose to focus on this form in general, or on one specific artist, entertainer, or other example.

2. Your task is to show how this form of art or entertainment reflects your culture. Study the outlines that follow and select the one you think most appropriate for your topic. Make a chart or collage based on the outline, to show the links between your chosen form of art or entertainment and your culture.

   Outline 1
   Physical Environment
   History
   Social Life
   Economics
   Politics

   Outline 2
   Popular culture
   Traditional culture
   Physical needs
   Emotional needs
   Material culture
   Non-material culture
   Socialization

3. Once your chart or collage is complete, think again about the outline you chose. Why did you choose it? Was it the most effective outline for your topic? Did you adapt the outline in any way? If so, how? If not, could you have benefited from doing so?

CHAPTER 8
Occupation and Lifestyle

Figure 8.1 What types of work are depicted in these images? How might the lifestyles of the workers shown here differ from each other?

It's the summer vacation. Most students over the age of 16 in your community have tried to get a summer job. Rashid is working as a counsellor at a summer day camp for six-year-old children, supervising sporting activities. He works from 8 until 4, Monday to Friday. Rita has started a craft business, making and selling jewellery. She works 10 hours a day, Monday to Saturday. Steven has a job in his aunt's restaurant, which is popular with tourists in the summer months. He helps out in the kitchen, stacking dishes, loading the dishwasher, and doing various other jobs. He works from Wednesday to Sunday. Monique works night shifts at the fish-processing plant, five nights a week. Susan has not managed to find a job this year. She hopes she'll be asked, at least, to do some babysitting.

- How might the different summer jobs of these students affect the way they live during their summer break? How might each one feel at the end of a working day? How might they spend their leisure time? How might their jobs affect their future occupations?
- In general, how do occupations influence our lifestyles?
- What can we learn about occupations and lifestyles from the examples of three groups in Atlantic Canada: The Labrador Inuit; the Lebanese community of Prince Edward Island; and the community of Lunenburg, Nova Scotia?

Why Do We Work?

Students like Rashid, Rita, Steven, and Monique often look for work during their vacations because they want to earn an income. Perhaps they are hoping to help out with expenses at home, saving for their future education, or simply looking forward to some extra pocket money. Most of them, however, work for other reasons too. Think of Susan who has not managed to find a job. She probably envies her friends who are working, not just because they are earning money, but because they are using their time constructively. Most of us look for ways to learn and achieve certain goals. Work gives us this opportunity. It meets a variety of important needs, as shown in the figure below.

Work is important because, in many cases, what we *do* gives us our sense of who we *are*. How often have you heard someone ask a new acquaintance, "What do you do?" The answer might be, "I am a miner," "I am a volunteer," or "I am a student." For this reason, people who find themselves out of work suffer from more than just a loss of income. The work we do for ourselves and others often gives meaning to our lives.

> **DID YOU KNOW...?**
>
> Even if a summer job bears no relation to a student's planned career, it can provide valuable experience. In almost all jobs, workers develop important skills and attitudes such as punctuality, cooperation, task commitment, and good communication.

FOCUS ON FIGURE 8.2

Choose one of the students described on page 108. Explain how his or her needs are being met by work. Rank these needs according to the levels shown in this illustration.

Level 4: A sense of identity:
We often define what we are by what we do.

Level 3: A sense of achievement:
Work allows us to set and reach goals, complete tasks, construct objects, and gain promotion. It gives us the opportunity to feel we are contributing to society in some way, or providing products or services that are valued by other people.

Level 2: Social interaction:
Work brings us into contact with other people, in both formal and informal ways.

Level 1: Economic reasons:
People work to earn wages so that they can pay for necessities such as food, shelter, and clothing, as well as "extras" such as entertainment and travel.

Figure 8.2 Why we work. A psychologist named Abraham Maslow (1908–1970) said that people have different levels of needs. When one need is met, people try to satisfy others, on a higher level. This illustration shows why people work, based on Maslow's theory.

OCCUPATION AND LIFESTYLE

Occupations and Lifestyle

So far, you have seen how occupations affect the way we feel about ourselves. How do occupations affect our **lifestyle** — the way we live within our culture?

Traditionally, occupations in the Atlantic provinces have been based on our rich resources: on fishing, forestry, farming and mining. Lifestyles often developed around these occupations. Many communities grew up close to the resources, with people working together in the industries. Life often revolved around families and the community. The church was often central to social activity, as were community gatherings for conversation, music, dance, and storytelling. People practised skills such as weaving and boat-making to produce goods they needed in their communities. Many traditional occupations were seasonal, as they still are today.

Today, however, occupations in our region are much more varied. There have been many changes in technology, in our use of natural resources, and in our global connections, as the following examples show.

Figure 8.3 Reconstruction of an Acadian kitchen. What can you tell about this woman's occupation and lifestyle?

Some elements of lifestyle

Types of relationships
Housing
Schooling
Types of work
Traditional skills
Entertainment
Leisure activities
Transportation
Clothing

NIGHT WORK

It was 3 a.m. and Milton Hay barely had a moment to chat. While the rest of the world slept peacefully and dreamed sweetly — or so it seemed — Hay was churning out photocopies. He does that all night long, Fridays through Mondays.

He was hardly the only one awake. Milton Hay is just one of 20 million night workers in North America — almost 20 percent of the full-time work force. They not only police our streets, tend our sick and keep our electricity humming, they also transport our goods, monitor our money, entertain us on TV, and will sell us a dozen eggs.

In Canada, approximately 3 million people work night shifts. About 1 million work on Saturdays, and half a million work on Sundays.

Source: Adapted from Sandy Bauers, "Night Work," Knight-Ridder/Tribune News Service.

FOCUS ON FIGURE 8.4

1. Make a line graph to show the rising percentage of women in the labour force.
2. Discuss why the number of women in the labour force has increased. Consider factors such as cost of living, numbers of single-parent families headed by women, increased education and technical skills, and enjoyment of work.

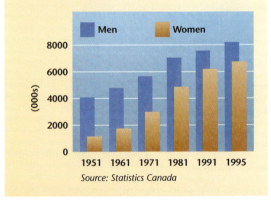

Figure 8.4 The number of women working outside the home has grown steadily since the 1950s, as this graph of Canada's labour force shows.

Why Do Occupations Change?

Occupations in a culture change for a variety of reasons. The most important are changes in the natural environment, historical events, and changes in technology. The case studies that follow will allow you to examine each of these types of change, together with the changes in lifestyle they have brought.

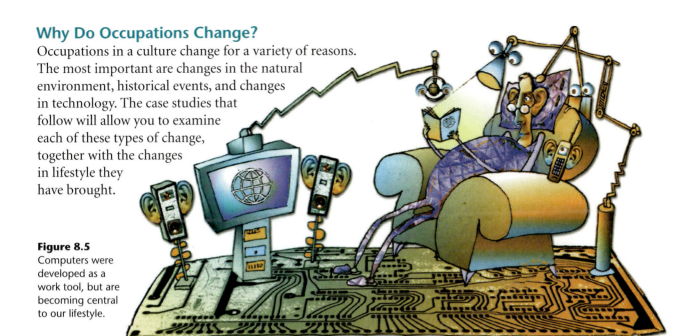

Figure 8.5
Computers were developed as a work tool, but are becoming central to our lifestyle.

EXPLORATIONS

APPLYING YOUR SKILLS

1. **a)** Make a list of your activities on an average day. Include activities such as school, work, entertainment, household chores, travel, eating. Estimate how much time you spend on each.

   b) Make a pie chart to show how you spend your time on an average day.

   c) Write a sentence or two to explain how your occupation influences your lifestyle.

2. **a)** Work with a partner or a small group. Brainstorm changes in lifestyle brought about by increasing numbers of women in the work force. Consider the following categories.

   Home life:
   Household chores (cooking, cleaning, etc.); child rearing; shopping; leisure time

   Working life:
   Women in management; pay equity

   "Spin-off" occupations:
   Child-care; housekeeping; preparing ready-made meals; selling women's work clothes; etc.

   b) Make an organizer of your conclusions.

3. **a)** Interview someone who works nights or weekends to find out the effect of shiftwork on this person's lifestyle.

   b) Present your findings in the form of a newspaper-style article or radio report.

4. Make a drawing, collage, or diagram to show the impact of computers on your lifestyle. Include the categories of home life, entertainment, education, and any others that seem appropriate.

ANALYZING AND REFLECTING

5. Many working women suffer from the stress of trying to be "superwomen." As one writer noted: "Women expect themselves not only to achieve at the office but also to sauté the vegetables, rotate the tires on the car, and raise at least one super-baby who is bilingual and can run a computer." What changes in society would help to solve the problems faced by working mothers? Discuss your ideas.

6. New Brunswick and Prince Edward Island allow seasonal "Sunday shopping": all malls, department stores, and supermarkets may be open for business. Debate the following topic: "Full Sunday shopping should be allowed in the Atlantic provinces." Be sure to refer to changes in lifestyle in your arguments.

CASE STUDY

THE LABRADOR INUIT

The Labrador Inuit are one of 15 groups of Inuit who inhabit the Canadian North. Over a very short time, and especially since Newfoundland entered Confederation in 1949, they have faced tremendous cultural change. As you will see, many found themselves living in a new environment. As a result, their occupations changed, as did their lifestyles.

The economy of the Labrador Inuit was traditionally based on a close relationship between themselves, the land, the sea, and wild animals. The Inuit had cultural rules that regulated wildlife harvesting. For example, they did not kill animals during their breeding season.

Figure 8.6 What can you tell about traditional occupations and lifestyles from this painting?

Table 8.1 Species traditionally hunted by Inuit, and their main uses. In addition to the food sources shown here, other small game, cod, capelin, and berries supplemented the diet of the Labrador Inuit.

Animal	Uses
Seal	Main source of food, boots, clothing, covering for shelter, oil
Walrus	Supplemental food, blubber for fuel, tusks for harpoon heads and other implements
Whales	Supplemental food, blubber for fuel, bones for implements
Caribou	Main source of food, clothing
Bears	Supplemental food, clothing
Common Eider	Supplemental food, feathers for lining clothes
Geese	Supplemental food
Bird eggs	Supplemental food
Salmon	Main source of food
Char	Main source of food
Arctic hare	Supplemental food, hats, mitts, boots

Such rules helped to reduce the chances of over-harvesting the animals on which they depended.

Traditionally, the Inuit lived in three different types of shelters. In winter, they lived in houses made of stone and sod, partially dug into the ground. The entrance was about 20 cm lower than the main part of the house. In this way it trapped the cold, and protected the house from the wind. On hunting trips, the Inuit built snow houses as temporary shelters. In summer, they lived in cone-shaped tents made of animal skins. All clothing was made from animal skins and was designed to provide excellent protection from extreme cold.

Figure 8.7 A traditional Inuit winter house at Hebron earlier in the twentieth century.

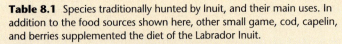

Sleeping platform

Entrance passage

112 CULTURE

Changing Times, Changing Lifestyles

The traditional Inuit way of life slowly began to change in the mid-1700s. Earlier contact with European fishers had caused some conflict between the two groups. The British government believed that the relationship between the Inuit and Europeans would be better if the Inuit were converted to Christianity. As a result, the government gave approval for the Moravian Church to establish missions in Labrador.

The first mission was established at Nain, with later missions at Hopedale, Makkovik, Okak, Killinek-Hebron, Zoar, and Ramah. The presence of full-time mission stations altered the traditional Inuit lifestyle. Rather than travelling inland in winter, some Inuit began to stay on the coast with the missionaries. Cut off from their traditional environment and source of food, they began to depend on government for support.

Figure 8.8 Wooden houses in Hopedale. These homes were sometimes referred to as "matchboxes." How does this house compare with the traditional home shown in Figure 8.7? Which home is better adapted to the environment? Explain.

Table 8.2 The Labrador Inuit now have a new range of economic activities. Which of these activities use traditional skills? Which use new skills? Which use both?

Natural resource	Economic activity
Wild meat	Meat from wild caribou is sold to domestic and international markets through the Labrador Inuit Development Corporation.
Fish	Like other Atlantic fishers, Labrador Inuit can no longer depend on traditional species such as cod, salmon, and char. They are experimenting with non-traditional species such as shrimp and turbot.
"Untouched" wilderness	Inuit hunters use their knowledge of the land and its animals to act as guides for tourists. Some visitors are interested in hunting, with a gun or a camera, and others are **ecotourists**, interested in learning about the sub-Arctic environment.
Natural products suitable for arts and crafts	Many Inuit communities produce arts and crafts from bone, ivory, soapstone, grass and skins. This artwork sells around the world.
Anorthosite	This stone is mined from Paul Island and exported to Europe for architectural use.
Labradorite	This semiprecious stone is mined from Tabor Island for craft use.

DID YOU KNOW...?

Seal, caribou, narwhal, fish, and walrus provide a much richer source of iron, magnesium, and calcium than beef. The harvest and use of these foods has an important economic value that is only now being recognized.

Figure 8.9 Ecotourists in Labrador. How does ecotourism illustrate one method of adapting traditional culture to new economic demands?

In the 1950s and 1960s, some Inuit communities in Labrador were relocated. Here, they are becoming self-sufficient. They have focused on recovering traditional skills, and developing them for use in a commercial economy.

Figure 8.10 Inuit art often reflects a cultural belief that all living things are interrelated and dependent on each other. How are these values evident in this sculpture? Why do you think Inuit art finds a market around the world?

EXPLORATIONS

APPLYING YOUR SKILLS

1. **a)** List the animals on which the Labrador Inuit depend. Which of these animals are available on the coast? Which are available inland? Which might be available in both areas?

   b) Make a chart or diagram or write a short paragraph showing how the natural environment influenced aspects of Inuit culture such as food, shelter, clothing, and transportation. Include information on how the search for food had an impact on Inuit lifestyle.

ANALYZING AND REFLECTING

2. Assume you could interview a member of an Inuit community about what he or she has retained of traditional language and lifestyle. With a partner, write at least three questions you would ask.

3. **a)** Define the term "ecotourism."

   b) Assume you are an ecotour operator. You are looking for a new tour guide. Write a job advertisement to be placed in the newspaper. Be sure to outline the skills and qualifications that you think are necessary.

   c) Prepare an ad to attract "ecotourists." Where will you place your ad to reach your target audience?

4. Referring to pages 62, 102, and 103 and this case study, compare and contrast the experiences of resettlement of the groups described.

CASE STUDY

THE LEBANESE COMMUNITY OF PRINCE EDWARD ISLAND

The first groups of Lebanese to come to Prince Edward Island arrived during the late 1800s and early 1900s. Some came to escape religious persecution: at that time, Christians in Lebanon and Syria were being oppressed by Turkish conquerors. Others came because opportunities were limited in their small, heavily populated homeland. Still others came to escape fighting in the war-torn Middle East. All of these immigrants attracted others, who came later, to join their extended families. Many of the Lebanese immigrants spoke some French, and settled on the western part of the Island, where the francophone population lived. Others decided to make a life for themselves in other parts of the island. The occupations they chose were influenced in various ways by history — by the past they shared and by the circumstances they found in Prince Edward Island in those years.

Lebanon is one of the great trading crossroads of the world. Most Lebanese immigrants had an understanding of buying, selling, and money-exchange. Many became pedlars, selling goods in isolated parts of the Island. Some pedlars had a horse and wagon, but many travelled to their sales territory by train, then carried their goods from house to house. They divided their wares between a large backpack and a small compartmentalized box carried on their front, often carrying a weight of almost 50 kg! Their stock included shirts, sweaters, underwear, pants, socks, braces, fabrics, needles, scissors, thimbles, salves, liniments, tonics, and toys.

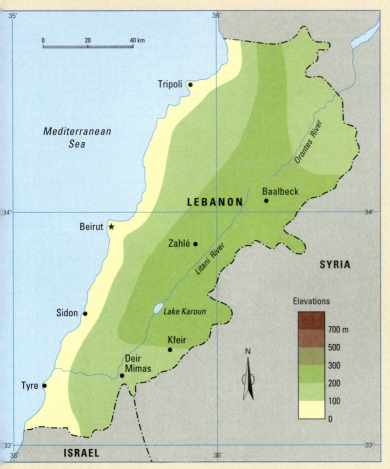

Figure 8.11 Locate Lebanon on a map of the world. Make a list of ways that Lebanon is geographically similar to Prince Edward Island. In what ways might the two cultures be similar?

Figure 8.12 Pedlars needed a government licence in order to do business. In 1905, it cost $20 for a horse and wagon licence, and $10 to peddle on foot.

OCCUPATION AND LIFESTYLE

In the early twentieth century, rural Prince Edward Islanders were isolated by winter storms and spring mud, which made travelling difficult. Television did not exist, and there were few radios and newspapers. News travelled by word of mouth. Imagine how welcome a Lebanese pack pedlar would be, bringing not only goods but also news.

Because of their occupation, many Lebanese immigrants got to know and be known by their Prince Edward Island neighbours. Although they maintained close family and community links, they soon adapted to the mainstream culture. Lebanon has long been a country where people from many cultures live together, and this experience with multiculturalism also helped the Lebanese immigrants feel at home in Canada.

> In the early years of the century, the Syrian and Lebanese pedlars who walked the muddy country roads beneath their heavy backpacks sometimes called themselves Angus or Alex so that they would sound more familiar to their potential customers. The pedlars…had very little English, so anything that aided communication was helpful. Sometimes they unfolded their bolts of cloth and displayed their shining needles before admirers who were unable to afford them, and sometimes — sensing the situation — they would leave the goods behind. Later, if money became available, the people would say, "Put aside what we owe Angus and Alex in the sugar bowl so that we can pay them when they come."
>
> Source: Alistair MacLeod, *As Birds Bring Forth the Sun* (Toronto: McClelland and Stewart, 1986), p. 157.

Figure 8.13 Most pedlars were men, but there were some women pedlars, too. They included Annie Kays, who came to Prince Edward Island early in the 1900s, and Mary Lubra, who worked as a pedlar while her husband stayed behind in Lebanon. Mary Fren started peddling in 1903 and was still licensed in 1911. Female pedlars carried their portable store divided between two stout suitcases.

Changing Times: Changing Occupations

By the early twentieth century, many pedlars had saved enough money to buy property in Charlottetown, where they opened corner stores. At first, married pedlars continued to travel in the countryside, while their wives stayed at home to look after the family and run the store. One reported that, while her husband was away, she made and sold enough ginger ale, root beer, doughnuts, and bread to buy a new house.

As Canada's culture changed, so did the way Lebanese immigrants made their living. Following World War II, automobiles became more common and transportation easier. Given these changes, the Lebanese immigrants directed their enterprising skills to a wide range of professions and businesses in Charlottetown.

Figure 8.14 Joe Ghiz with his aunt, June McKarris, in front of the McKarris store in Charlottetown, 1947. As you saw in Chapter 6, Ghiz later became premier of the province.

EXPLORATIONS

REVIEWING THE IDEAS

1. Make a web diagram to show how historical factors influenced occupations of Lebanese immigrants to Prince Edward Island.

ANALYZING AND REFLECTING

2. Review the extract from *As Birds Bring Forth the Sun*. With a partner, discuss your response to the extract. Did any of the information surprise you? What does the extract tell you about the culture of Prince Edward Island at the time?

3. Work in a group of four or five people. Assume you are a family of Lebanese immigrants in the early 1900s. Take roles of different family members, including grandparents, parents, teenage children, and any other family members you wish. The father is considering becoming a pedlar. In your roles, have a family discussion about the advantages and disadvantages of his doing so. How will his occupation affect your lifestyle?

4. Assume you are a pedlar or a corner-store owner in the early 1900s. Your business is doing well, and you would like an assistant. Write a job advertisement outlining the skills and qualifications you would like your assistant to have.

CONNECTING AND EXTENDING

5. **a)** How would you react to leaving a warm Mediterranean village for Atlantic Canada? What might surprise you? Consider weather, food, landscape, language, and any other aspects of life. In the role of a Lebanese immigrant, write a short letter to your family at home, giving your impressions.

   b) What would you try to find out first about your new home? Make a list of questions you would ask.

6. **a)** Brainstorm some "door-to-door" entrepreneurial activities in your community. Have some been replaced by telephone? Are some done by students? What do these activities suggest about lifestyles?

   b) Present your conclusions to the class.

CASE STUDY

Developing an Economy in Lunenburg

The area around Lunenburg, Nova Scotia, was traditionally inhabited by the Mi'kmaq. In the early 1700s, part of the area was cleared by Acadian farmers, but in 1753 Lunenburg was officially colonized by the British government in an effort to settle non-Acadians in the area. Most of the colonists were immigrants from German-speaking parts of Europe that now include Germany, Switzerland, and France. They came to Canada looking for economic security. Through generations, the people of Lunenburg have adapted their occupations and lifestyle in response to changes in environment, technology, and historical circumstances.

Figure 8.15 Lunenburg was designed as a model town. Streets were laid out in a formal grid of blocks, each with 14 house lots. Space was also set aside for public use and fortifications. What cultural attitude does the use of this grid pattern suggest?

Figure 8.16 Dories are still made in Lunenburg. Although they are no longer used for commercial fishing, they are in demand because they are so sea-worthy.

The colonists had been farmers in Europe, and they quickly set about clearing the land. Some settlers became craftsmen, using trees that had been felled to make items ranging from staves to ships. Many more made a living by farming. In the years around 1760, they grew hay, wheat, barley, rye, peas, potatoes, turnips, hemp, and flax. Lunenburg supplied Halifax with agricultural products and firewood.

Although Lunenburg harbour was full of all kinds of fish, the German settlers at first caught only enough for their own use. By the 1850s, however, Lunenburg crews were fishing on the Grand Banks. Most used the single-dory method, but in 1873, they experimented with new technology they had learned from American crews. This was the technology of "double-dory trawling." Fishing schooners were equipped with a number of two-person dories. At the beginning of each day, crews left the schooner in their dories, and set out hundreds of metres of trawl lines equipped with multiple hooks. After setting several lines, they went back, hauled up the line, and removed the fish that had been caught. When the dory was full of fish, the crew returned to the schooner, emptied their catch, then went back to their trawl lines. Using this technology, crews could catch far more fish, and fishing profits soared. Soon fishing became a new mainstay of the Lunenburg economy.

Figure 8.17 At the turn of the century, a fishing crew and apprentices gut mackerel and pickle them in barrels right on the wharf. How has new technology replaced the technology of the "Lunenburg cure"?

Figure 8.18 Sewing a canvas boat cover in Lunenburg. Make a list of jobs related to the fishing industry. Choose five of these jobs, and describe how skills used for them might be used in the tourist industry.

The processing of fish has also involved technology that has changed over the years. Originally, the fish were salted, then placed on flakes and dried in the sun. This process was called the "Lunenburg cure." The dried fish was used locally and exported to Europe and the West Indies. Lunenburg brigs and schooners carried dried fish south and returned with cargos of salt, liquor, sugar, molasses, and coffee.

The traditional method of air-drying codfish had its disadvantages. If the weather turned wet, hundreds of partially-cured cod spoiled. In 1939, a Lunenburg firm combined salt-drying techniques and air-conditioning technology to develop a process that allowed fish to be commercially dried in an indoor plant.

By the early 1900s, Lunenburg's economy was based very firmly on farming, fishing, and shipbuilding technology that had developed with the fishing industry. Through the years, however, the fishery declined. Many of the reasons for decline were related to new technology that allowed fishers to catch so many fish that stocks were depleted. With less demand for fish processing and fishing vessels, community members found themselves looking for new occupations. Today, Lunenburg still relies on fishing and related trades and technology such as sail-making, dory-building, and boat repairs, but the economy has **diversified** — that is, become more varied. Many community members are now occupied in three other sectors: tourism, manufacturing, and services.

TOURISM

In the 1970s, Lunenburg's local heritage society bought and restored historical buildings in the community that were then used as businesses. The society's efforts were so successful that Old Town Lunenburg, which has buildings dating from the late 1700s and early 1800s, was designated as a national historic district in 1991. In 1995 it was designated as an international UNESCO heritage site — recognized as being a unique record of past life. As a result, Lunenburg has become a popular tourist destination. In 1996, this town of fewer than 3000 full-time residents was host to between 250 000 and 300 000 visitors from around the world.

Figure 8.19 Visitors to Lunenburg appreciate the coastal surroundings and atmosphere. Ecotourists enjoy whale and seal watching and off-shore fishing. The area is so attractive that many people who have been for a holiday later buy a home in Lunenburg and retire there.

Table 8.3 Recreational facilities in Lunenburg. What do these facilities tell you about lifestyle in the town?

Lunenburg Arena
Community centre and gymnasium
Lunenburg Curling Club
Lunenburg Swimming Pool (outdoor)
Lunenburg Tennis Courts
Bluenose Golf Club
Lunenburg Yacht Club
Bluenose Bowlarama
Soccer and basketball fields
Various parks

DID YOU KNOW...?

Many houses in Lunenburg have a distinctive feature called the "Lunenburg Bump." Similar to the dormer found in many Nova Scotia homes, the Bump extends out from the roof to form an overhang above the front door. Some houses were also built with a large "coffin window" since it was considered bad luck to take a coffin through the front door.

Figure 8.20 This house was built in 1879. Known as "Wilson House," it is one of Lunenburg's best preserved examples of architecture from the late 1800s.

Manufacturing

The traditional occupations of shipbuilding and fish processing in Lunenburg allowed the people there to develop skills that have attracted other businesses. Plants now process vegetables as well as fish; manufacturers now make aerospace components as well as ship parts. Goods manufactured in Lunenburg sell in many other countries of the world. In addition, some international businesses have been attracted to Lunenburg because the town offers benefits such as good housing and a pleasant environment, as well as skilled workers. One Swiss firm located in Lunenburg partly because it was impressed with the education system.

> **DID YOU KNOW...?**
>
> National Sea Products, one of the world's largest fishing companies, is located in Lunenburg. Since the decline of the fishery it has refocused its activities, processing scallops and fish caught by Russian and Norwegian trawlers, and developing product lines such as fish sticks and chips.

Services

Service industries usually include banking, retail sales, communications, transportation, and other activities that meet the needs of the public. In Lunenburg many of the service industries are related to tourism. For example, the town needs a large number of inns, hotels, restaurants, craft shops, and art galleries. In addition, the town has become a popular location for movie making. This sort of activity boosts the economy further, by attracting additional visitors to the area.

There are also grocery stores, campgrounds, dive shops, bait companies, and dozens of other small businesses needed to serve local citizens and their visitors. Lunenburg has a high percentage of seniors who have come to retire there. As a result, the health-care and housing sectors of the local economy are growing.

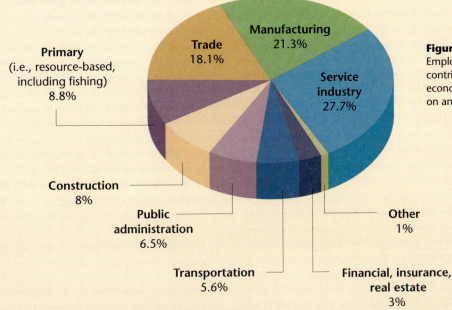

Figure 8.21 Lunenburg County: Employment by sector. Which sector contributes most to Lunenburg's economy? Does this sector depend on any others? Explain.

Occupation and Lifestyle 121

EXPLORATIONS

REVIEWING THE IDEAS

1. Make a web diagram to show the influence of the following on occupations in Lunenburg:

   a) environment

   b) technology (Brainstorm and include forms of technology that would feature in the new occupations of the community.)

   c) historical circumstances

APPLYING YOUR SKILLS

2. On an outline map of the world, show the following:
   - some historical economic links between Lunenburg and Caribbean countries
   - some historical economic links between Lunenburg and the United States
   - some current economic links between Lunenburg and the world

ANALYZING AND REFLECTING

3. As the economic development officer for Lunenburg, you know of a company that is looking for an ideal location for a new electronics plant. The plant will need a skilled work force. Develop a brochure that advertises Lunenburg as the best location for this plant. In planning your brochure, consider the following:
   - Lunenburg's history
   - Lunenburg's lifestyle
   - Atlantic Canadian culture
   - any other important information

   Design your brochure for maximum visual impact.

4. Lunenburg's unofficial motto is 'Proud past, promising future!' Develop a one-minute speech explaining how current development in Lunenburg exemplifies this motto.

CONNECTING AND EXTENDING

5. **a)** Research one other World Heritage Site in Atlantic Canada and one other anywhere else in the world. How does the United Nations program contribute to the preservation of these special sites?

   b) Prepare a short report or display of your findings.

SEEING THE BIG PICTURE

1. **a)** Make a list of occupations in your community. Include at least five different occupations.

   b) Prepare a display or collage to show how these occupations affect lifestyles in your community. Include the following:
   - Home life
   - Social/community life
   - Transportation
   - Forms of entertainment and leisure
   - Schooling and child-care services
   - Health care services
   - Any other appropriate categories

2. Compare your community with one of the groups described in this chapter. What do the similarities and differences in occupations and lifestyle tell you about your culture?

3. Think about the occupation you plan. How will it affect your lifestyle?

CHAPTER 9

Culture and Politics

Figure 9.1 Students getting involved in their communities. *Top*: Cleaning up for Earth Day. *Right*: Circulating a petition. How can you exercise your political power?

You enjoy canoeing on a local river that is a paradise for wildlife enthusiasts and nature lovers like yourself. A major industry has just announced that it is building a plant upriver. You and your friends believe the plant will spoil the environment you love. The industry promises many badly needed jobs, and few people seem to care whether steps are taken to protect the environment.
- As a teenage student, you feel powerless. What can you do to make your voice heard?
- How does our culture allow us to participate in the way our society is run — to exercise political power?

CULTURE AND POLITICS 123

WHAT IS POLITICS?

Politics is the way in which we organize ourselves so that the members of our society can live together in peace and security. As you have seen in the previous chapters, our society is made up of many groups with different values and concerns. Let's take the example of the previous page. You, as a nature lover, might oppose building the plant. If you were an unemployed worker who stood a good chance of getting a job at the new plant, however, you might feel strongly that it should be built. If you were a representative of the industry, you would have your own reasons for locating at that spot. Politics is the system we have for working out a balance among the interests of different groups in our society. Our political system gives each of these groups a variety of ways to make their concerns felt, as you will see throughout this chapter.

GOVERNMENT IN OUR LIVES

Canada is governed as a **democracy**. Democracy means government by the people. In our culture, one of the strongest values that we share is the right of people to participate in the way they are governed. Because people, together with their history, geography, and economy, differ widely across Canada — and even within a smaller area such as the Atlantic region — governments must respond in many different ways. They do so by operating on a variety of levels. We have a **federal government** based in Ottawa to deal with concerns of the nation as a whole. We have **provincial** and **territorial governments** that address more regional concerns. We also have **municipal governments**, or local councils, that look after local matters under the direction and authority of the provincial government.

Table 9.1 Government responsibilities: Some examples. Federal and provincial governments share some responsibilities, especially in the areas of health care, resources, social services, and job training. Where municipal governments don't exist, the provincial government looks after local matters.

Federal Government	Provincial Government	Municipal Government

Defence	Education	Fire protection services
International trade	Hospitals	Garbage collection
Banking	Health-care system	Street cleaning and maintenance
Natural resources	Natural resources	Building permits
Any area not included in the *BNA Act*, which established Canada's federal system in 1867 (e.g., radio, television, air travel)	Municipal government	Collecting property taxes and licence fees (e.g., for stores or pets) to pay for services

The politicians who work at all of these levels of government represent the people who elected them to their positions. You may have seen **representative democracy** in action in your school. Many schools have a student council or some other form of student government. Often, each grade will have a representative on the council to ensure that the concerns of students at different levels are considered. Our system of government works on a similar principle. Canada is divided into areas called **ridings** or **constituencies.** The voters in each riding elect one person to represent them at each of the various levels of government. **Representatives** elected to the federal level of government are called Members of Parliament (MPs). In the Maritimes, representatives to the provincial legislatures are called Members of the Legislative Assembly (MLAs); in Newfoundland and Labrador, they are called Members of the House of Assembly (MHAs). Representatives to municipal governments are usually called councillors. All of these representatives make decisions in government based on the wishes and needs of their **constituents** — the people who live in their riding.

DID YOU KNOW...?

The Aboriginal peoples of Atlantic Canada had political systems that developed over many centuries. The Mi'kmaq Nation, for example, consisted of seven districts each of which was governed by a district council and a chief. There were also annual Grand Councils, where each region was represented. These councils selected a Grand Chief to preside over the nation.

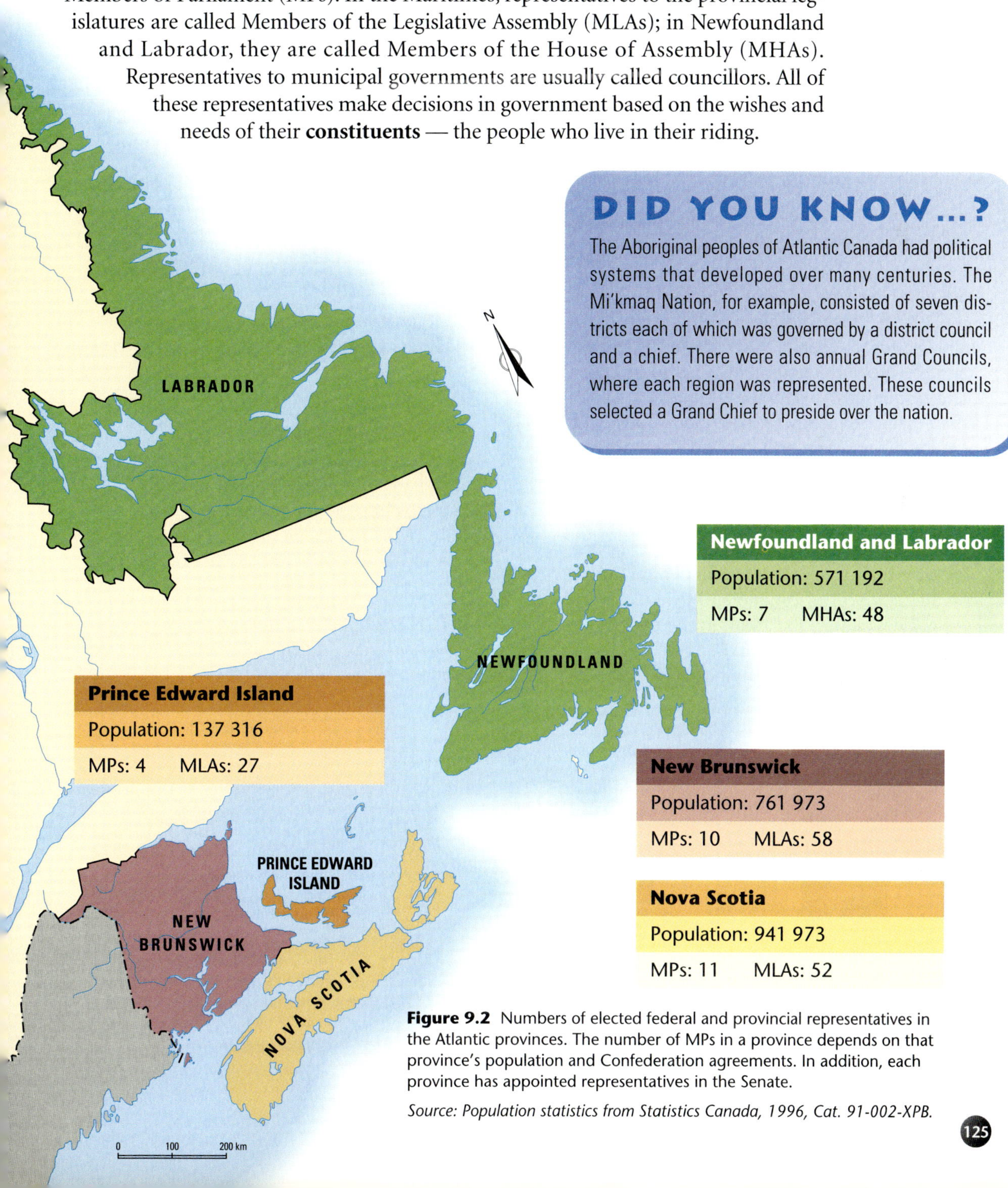
N
LABRADOR
NEWFOUNDLAND
PRINCE EDWARD ISLAND
NEW BRUNSWICK
NOVA SCOTIA
0 100 200 km
Newfoundland and Labrador
Population: 571 192
MPs: 7 MHAs: 48
Prince Edward Island
Population: 137 316
MPs: 4 MLAs: 27
New Brunswick
Population: 761 973
MPs: 10 MLAs: 58
Nova Scotia
Population: 941 973
MPs: 11 MLAs: 52

Figure 9.2 Numbers of elected federal and provincial representatives in the Atlantic provinces. The number of MPs in a province depends on that province's population and Confederation agreements. In addition, each province has appointed representatives in the Senate.

Source: Population statistics from Statistics Canada, 1996, Cat. 91-002-XPB.

Focus on an Issue

Does Our Federal System Work?

Our system of government was devised as a compromise. In the early nineteenth century, what we now call Canada was known as British North America. It was made up of several separate British colonies and territories, each with its own culture — each had a distinct government, a unique history, and its own economic needs. At the same time, there were forces drawing the peoples of British North America together. The building of the railway called for co-operation; growing economies promoted inter-colonial trade; and many colonists — particularly those of Loyalist stock — were fearful of an invasion from the United States.

The federal system of government, established by the *BNA Act* in 1867, was supposed to meet these conflicting needs. The system allowed for the federal government in Ottawa and the provincial governments to share power and responsibility. Over the decades, however, there have frequently been tensions between the federal government and the provinces. Since the 1970s, the separatist movement in Quebec has often been in the news, but other provinces, too, have been looking for ways to protect their interests. The federal government is often criticized for adopting policies that favour central Canada — the provinces of Ontario and Quebec, which have the highest populations in the country. In the early 1990s, the Reform Party gained much support by arguing that the needs of the Western provinces had been overlooked. In the East, the Atlantic provinces have been working for more co-operation among themselves, to benefit the culture and economy of the region. A number of organizations have been established to promote co-operation, including the Atlantic Provinces Economic Council (APEC), the Atlantic Provinces Transportation Commission, and the Atlantic Provinces Education Foundation (APEF), the organization responsible for producing this text book!

ANALYZING THE ISSUE

The federal compromise we call Canada has lasted for more than 130 years.

1. What forces are currently drawing Canadians together? Consider interests and concerns that Canadians across the country share. What forces are drawing us apart? Consider issues that separate provinces or regions.

2. What forces are currently drawing Atlantic Canadians together? Consider interests and concerns that people across the region share. What forces are drawing us apart? Consider issues that separate the provinces.

3. Debate: Canada's federal system of government is outdated; it should be replaced with a new system that gives more power to the regions.

SPEECH FROM THE THRONE   THROWN FROM THE SPEECH

FOCUS ON FIGURE 9.3

1. Identify all the people and objects portrayed.
2. How does the cartoonist want you to feel in response to the cartoon?
3. Summarize the message of the cartoon in one or two sentences.
4. Do you agree with the message of the cartoon? Explain.

Figure 9.3 The Speech from the Throne outlines the government's plans for a new session of Parliament. It is read by the Governor-General in Ottawa or by the Lieutenant-Governor in provincial legislatures.

EXPLORATIONS

APPLYING YOUR SKILLS

1. **a)** Use a telephone directory to list at least 15 services provided by federal government, provincial government, and municipalities. Try to choose services that you and your family might use in a typical month.

   b) In a group, make a concept map to show how government affects your daily life. Include categories and specific examples to demonstrate your ideas.

CONNECTING AND EXTENDING

2. Governments spend billions of dollars on delivering services. In recent years, they have tried to cut back on the expense.

   a) Conduct interviews with family or community members to find out the following:
   - Government services when your grandparents were your age
   - Government services when your parents were your age

   b) Compare these services with government services today.

   c) What do you think government services might be like by the time your children are teenagers?

   d) Make a chart or time line of your findings and conclusions.

3. Investigate one municipal service in your community, such as fire fighting or garbage collection. Prepare a short report including the following information:

   a) Who is responsible for the service?

   b) Who pays for the service?

   c) How is the service organized?

   d) Are there other ways to organize the service that might be more efficient? Explain.

THE POWER OF THE VOTE

How does our system ensure that politicians do, in fact, represent their constituents fairly? It does so through **elections** — asking all citizens 18 years of age or older to vote for their representatives. In each election, voters choose from a list of **candidates**. In the riding where our hypothetical industrial plant is to be located, an environmentalist might choose to vote for the candidate who promised to work to establish a provincial park in the area of your local river. An unemployed worker might be more likely to vote for a candidate who pledged to promote new industry in the area. The candidate who gets the most votes wins a seat in government, where he or she is expected to represent the interests of his or her constituents. If the politician fails to do so, he or she stands the chance of not being re-elected at the next election. In Canada, federal and provincial elections must be called no later than five years after the previous election. In this way, politicians answer to the public for their actions, and must be sensitive to the concerns of their constituents.

> ### DID YOU KNOW...?
> Canadians today vote by **secret ballot**, but this type of voting was not used in Canada until 1874. In the first Canadian election, in 1867, only men who owned property and who were 21 years of age or older could vote. Each voter had to declare his vote in public! Many were badgered to vote a certain way, even at the voting station.

Figure 9.4 The word "ballot" can refer to the paper on which you cast a vote or to the process of voting. In Ancient Athens the secret ballot was used by male citizens of the city voting on the banishment of individuals. Paper was a precious commodity in those days, so shards of broken pottery were used as ballots. This shard contains the name "Pericles."

The Party System

How do we know which candidates will best represent what we believe? Which ones will reflect the values that we hold as a result of our family life, religion, or education? Partly we know by watching and listening carefully to what they say. We can also get some idea of what they support by considering the party to which they belong.

A **political party** is a group formed by individuals who have similar views on public issues. The function of the party is to give a stronger, collective voice to people who hold those views. Over the years, there have been many political parties in Canada, each representing a different set of ideas. In the Atlantic region, the Liberals, the Progressive Conservatives, and the New Democrats have been the most influential parties. Legally, an individual does not need to be a member of a political party to be a politician. In practice, however, independent candidates are rarely elected because, without belonging to a political party, they will have little power.

After an election, the party with the most successful candidates forms the government. The other parties make up the **Opposition**. Members of the governing party decide which laws the government will propose, and the members of the Opposition act as critics of the Government. All members vote on new proposals, which are called **bills**. Once passed, bills are called **Acts** and become the law.

Figure 9.5 Each political party has a logo. Shown here are the logos of the three main parties that have been most influential in the Atlantic provinces. What message do you think each logo is intended to give?

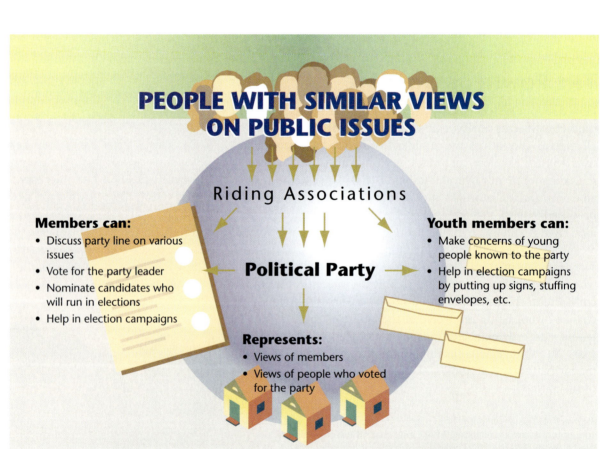

Figure 9.6 How political parties work. Anyone can join a political party by becoming a member of its riding association or youth wing.

The MPs of each party meet regularly as a group, known as a **caucus**. At these private meetings, MPs can explain the views of their constituents on various issues and argue for particular policies. Nevertheless, it is important for voters to choose a party that best represents their beliefs because, once elected, members of the same party tend to vote the same way. One MP, called the "whip," is assigned the job of making sure all party members are present for votes and "follow the party line." On many issues, MPs are expected to vote with the party, even if the majority of the people in their riding or their consciences tell them to vote otherwise.

Cabinet Government

When a government is elected, some of the elected representatives from the winning party are chosen by their leader to be in the **cabinet**. These are called **ministers**. The cabinet makes most of the major decisions of government, oversees the civil service, and prepares new laws. Cabinet ministers are the most powerful people in political life. They are, however, responsible, or accountable, to all the elected politicians. The cabinet meets privately and then takes its decisions to the entire legislature. The cabinet must have the support of a majority of the elected members in order to govern.

The leader of the party that forms the federal government becomes the **prime minister**, and the leader of the party that forms the provincial government becomes the **premier.**

Figure 9.7 Interior of the House of Commons, Ottawa. The Speaker — an MP chosen to act as "referee" in the House — sits at the end of the chamber. Members of the government sit to the Speaker's right. The opposition sits to the Speaker's left. The prime minister and cabinet members sit in the front rows. The remaining MPs on the government side are known, therefore, as "backbenchers."

DID YOU KNOW...?
Some linguists believe the word "caucus" is based on the Algonquian word *cau-cauasu*, which means "elder" or "councillor."

CULTURE AND POLITICS

CASE STUDY

WAYNE ADAMS: REPRESENTING THE PEOPLE

We have seen that the role of government is to represent the people. In the early 1990s, the government of Nova Scotia was concerned that the Mi'kmaq First Nation and African-Canadians were not adequately represented in the province's legislative assembly. The government asked the Provincial Electoral Boundaries Commission to examine ways of addressing this problem. No Mi'kmaq or African-Canadian had ever been elected to the province's legislative assembly.

The commission held hearings across the province. In particular, it sought advice on how to ensure representation of Nova Scotia's African-Canadian population, which lives in more than 30 small communities spread across the province. The commission rejected calls for a guaranteed African-Canadian seat in the legislature, one that would represent all African-Canadian voters from across the province. Instead, in 1992, it created a new riding called Preston, which would include three African-Canadian communities near Halifax (North Preston, East Preston, and Cherrybrook) and several non-African-Canadian communities. The Commission said this would "encourage but not guarantee" representation of African-Canadians in the legislature.

Early in 1993, a provincial election loomed, and there was great anticipation within the African-Canadian community. The Liberal party selected Wayne Adams, an African-Canadian municipal politician, as its candidate for the riding. The New Democratic Party endorsed Yvonne Atwell, head of the African Canadian Caucus. The Progressive Conservative party nominated Rev. Darryl Gray, a well-known Baptist minister. In February of 1993, with three high-profile African-Canadian candidates running for the major parties, it seemed assured that the people of the Preston riding were about to elect Nova Scotia's first African-Canadian MLA.

Then came an unexpected twist. David Hendsbee, a former ministerial aid in the ruling PC government, had wanted to become the PC candidate for the Preston riding, but Premier Donald Cameron had refused to support his nomination. A few weeks later Hendsbee decided to run as an independent candidate.

No longer was the Preston election a race between three African-Canadian candidates. Hendsbee, who was not African-Canadian, was well known in the riding. He was a potential winner.

Figure 9.8 Wayne Adams receives a hug from a supporter after winning the election in Preston.

130 CULTURE

Would the African-Canadian vote split three ways, assuring Hendsbee of victory? Did any African-Canadian candidate have enough support across the entire riding to muster a win? Did Hendsbee have enough support in African-Canadian neighbourhoods to combine with his expected popularity in other neighbourhoods? On election night, all eyes were on Preston. The result: Liberal Wayne Adams won with a margin of 491 votes.

The newly elected premier, John Savage, began to build his cabinet. His Liberal party had won 40 out of 52 seats, and many of the new MLAs, including Wayne Adams, had the qualifications to be effective cabinet ministers. Adams had the administrative experience and the personal skills necessary for the job. Leaders in the African-Canadian community and other supporters lobbied on his behalf.

No one was surprised when the premier made Adams Minister of Supply and Services and Minister Responsible for Communications and Information. The new cabinet was sworn in at a public ceremony in Halifax. Hundreds of onlookers erupted in a standing ovation when Wayne Adams took the oath of office to become Nova Scotia's first African-Canadian cabinet minister.

Wayne Adams's road to success

Since Wayne Adams was elected, he has had little time to reflect on what it all means. But people in the Black community know one thing is certain: his election and high-profile political appointment is a positive sign and a boost to morale for people of colour in Nova Scotia.

Adams agrees: "Black people in Nova Scotia have been invisible for too long." He laments the lack of Black role models, especially when he was growing up in Halifax's north end....

"There were times when I dreamed about being one of them," he recalled. "Yet at the same time, something in the back of my head told me I could never be like them. Only White people held those jobs."

Adams said he hopes his political success sends a strong message to young Black men and women to get involved in politics, business and other professional careers. "I always tell people, if you believe it and you focus on it, you can achieve it."

Success is something he knows well. He never lost an election in 14 years on Halifax County Council. And his resume reads like a catalogue of job listings.

Since graduating from high school in 1963, he has worked as an auto mechanic, owned and operated a service station, and was an affirmative action officer and later media information director with the province. He also worked part time as a newspaper reporter, produced and hosted a radio talk show that won a national award, and owned a small business in Halifax.

Adams is married and has one daughter. He has devoted his life to community activism, human rights, and economic development. At the time of his election he was executive director of the Black Cultural Centre for Nova Scotia and was a former president of the Nova Scotia Home for Coloured Children.

Source: Adapted from The Chronicle-Herald & Mail-Star, *September 24, 1993, p. B1.*

Figure 9.9 In 1996, Wayne Adams (centre) became Nova Scotia's Minister of the Environment. What would be his main responsibilities in this role?

EXPLORATIONS

REVIEWING THE IDEAS

1. Make a flow diagram to show the process of electing and forming a government. Include the following:
   - constituents
   - political parties
   - candidates
   - election
   - government
   - prime minister/premier
   - opposition
   - caucus
   - cabinet

ANALYZING AND REFLECTING

2. **a)** What values and beliefs would you look for in an elected representative? Make a list. Follow the example below.

   Values: honesty, family life, etc.

   Beliefs: Government should take an active role in managing services; Government should play less part in the economy, etc.

   b) Compare your list with those of other students. What values are most commonly shared? What types of beliefs tend to be different?

3. Work in a small group. Assume that the position of MLA or MHA could be advertised. Write a newspaper ad calling for suitable candidates. Outline required skills and experience.

4. **a)** Why do you think members of government are expected to follow the party line?

   b) Discuss ways in which elected members might be able to balance the wishes and needs of their constituents with the party line. (e.g., a free vote).

   c) In the past, some members of government who have chosen to vote against the party line but in accordance with their consciences or the wishes of their constituents have been expelled from the party, so that they have to sit as independent members. If you were a member and faced this choice, what would you do?

CONNECTING AND EXTENDING

5. **a)** As a class, discuss:

   i) What did Wayne Adams mean when he said that African-Canadian people "have been invisible for too long"?

   ii) What other Canadian groups are "invisible"? Have any people of Aboriginal ancestry been elected to the provincial legislature in any Atlantic province? Are various racial and ethnic groups represented in your provincial legislature? Are they represented in the cabinet?

   iii) Are women politically "invisible" in your province?

   iv) Do you think it is important to see others who are like us in positions of authority? Why?

   b) Prepare a profile of someone who serves as a political role model for you. Your profile can be in the form of a short essay, a display, a role play interview with the individual, or a special news report.

6. **a)** Who are your elected representatives? Give the names of your MP and your MLA or MHA. Are you represented locally on a municipal or town level? Explain.

   b) Find out if your representatives in government are members of the governing party or the Opposition. Determine their particular responsibilities (e.g., Member of the Opposition, Health critic).

   c) Examine one federal or provincial issue that made the news, and find out how your elected representative voted. Draw a political cartoon giving your view of the issue.

7. **a)** If young people can't vote until they are 18, why do parties have youth wings and why do elected representatives try to find out what young people think? Discuss as a class.

   b) Imagine that a federal politician has proposed lowering the voting age to 16. Prepare a short speech or write a "letter to the editor" supporting or opposing the proposal.

8. Identify and research one current issue and indicate how at least three political parties view the issue. Suitable topics include jobs, social programs, cutting government costs, and increasing corporate taxes.

Democracy in Action

While voting is an effective way to participate in government, there are other methods of exercising our political power — of making government listen to our concerns. Generally, these methods are most effective when they are used collectively — that is, by people working in groups.

- **Political activists** use direct action such as protest marches, distributing pamphlets, rallies, and public speeches to draw attention to a cause. Environmentalists in your riding, for example, might hold a protest rally outside the offices of the industry that is planning to build the new plant, or they might hold a large, public picnic on the banks of the river to draw attention to the area they are trying to save.

- The **media** are a powerful means of communication. The environmentalists might place advertisements in newspapers and on local radio or television stations, but — more importantly — they would probably try to ensure media coverage of their cause. The media reach a very wide audience, and can persuade large numbers of people to think one way or another. A report of a public picnic, together with striking images of a beautiful environment and an interview with parents of young children playing happily on the river bank, might persuade many people to support the creation of a park in an area zoned for industrial expansion. In contrast, a report of a hostile and disruptive protest outside business offices might persuade many people that the environmentalists who oppose the new plant are a group of troublemakers, not much interested in the greater good of society.

- **Lobbying** is another method of exercising political power. **Lobbyists** try to persuade politicians to support their cause, usually by supplying them with information. A lobbyist for the environmental group in your riding, for example, might give the Minister of the Environment a petition from nature lovers like yourself and documentation showing how the new industrial plant would destroy habitat for wildlife of the area. You have the freedom to lobby politicians on your own, but you are more likely to be effective if you form or join a **lobby group** of people who support the same cause. Today, there are an increasing number of professional lobbyists — people who are paid to represent the views of others to politicians.

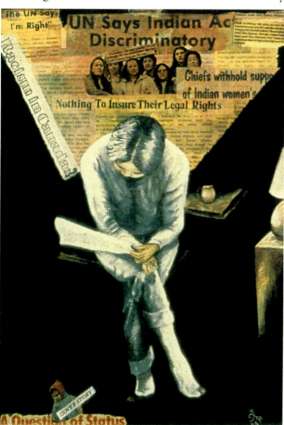

> ### DID YOU KNOW...?
> The term "to lobby" comes from the British Parliament buildings, where the House of Commons and the House of Lords are separated by a central public lobby. It was in this lobby that people traditionally met with politicians to seek their favour.

Figure 9.10 *A Question of Status* by renowned Maliseet artist Shirley Bear, a political activist who supports Aboriginal and women's rights. She believes that art and politics are connected with each other: "I use my art to express how I view and feel about the world." In what way can art be a political tool?

♦ **Labour unions, Non-Governmental Organizations (NGOs), and other groups** use various methods, including lobbying, to represent the concerns of their members. The environmentalists in your riding might gain support from an NGO such as Pollution Probe.

♦ The **court or judicial system** gives people the power to challenge actions that threaten their rights. You saw in Chapter 6 how we all have the legal right to be protected against discrimination. In the case of the dispute in your riding, if the environmentalists could prove that there was a good legal reason why the industrial plant should not be allowed, they could challenge the company and its plan to expand in court. If, for example, the law states that an environmental assessment must be done to predict the impact of any new industry, and the assessment has not been done, environmentalists would probably be able to get an injunction — a court order preventing the plant from being built until appropriate studies were complete. Similarly, if protesters were interfering with the operation of the company offices, the company could probably get an injunction to keep the protesters away.

Figure 9.11 Anti-poverty rally in Ottawa, organized by Canada's National Action Committee on the Status of Women. This NGO lobbies government on issues that affect women, such as pay equity, opportunities for promotion, and child care. What other actions do you think women could take to express their concerns on issues that affect them?

Table 9.2 Some Non-Governmental Organizations. NGOs often work to improve various aspects of the environment, health conditions, or the economy. Canada has a large number of NGOs that work to make a difference in other parts of the world. Do you recognize any of these names? Which organizations do you think are mainly political? Which are economic? Which are environmental?

Amnesty International	Canadian University Service Overseas
Canada World Youth	
Canadian Council for International Cooperation	Canadian Wildlife Federation
	CARE Canada
Canadian Organization for Development through Education	Oxfam-Canada
	Project Ploughshares
	Save the Children

DID YOU KNOW...?

In Sweden, anyone has the right to read the prime minister's mail, both incoming and outgoing. The letters are available in a government office. What do you think is the point of this law?

CASE STUDY

Janet Conners: Profile of a Political Activist

Nova Scotians Janet and Randy Conners turned personal tragedy into a political movement. Randy, a hemophiliac, required regular blood transfusions. He contracted the AIDS virus from a transfusion of tainted blood. Not knowing that he was infected, he passed the virus to his wife.

The couple decided that the public needed to be made aware of what had happened to them, in order to prevent such tragedies in the future. They made many public appearances to draw attention to the need to reform the way we collect and store blood. They also tried to heighten awareness about the AIDS epidemic and to combat the prejudice and fear surrounding it.

As a result of the Conners' quest for justice, in 1993 the government of Nova Scotia became the first province in Canada to compensate victims of tainted blood. Their efforts also helped to persuade the government to set up the Krever Inquiry, to examine how thousands of Canadians were infected with the AIDS virus and hepatitis C through blood transfusions in the 1980s. Randy died of an AIDS-related illness in 1994, but Janet continued to be an eloquent spokesperson for those who suffer from AIDS, and a vigorous campaigner for government funding of research.

She won't go quietly

Janet Conners — mother and activist, widow and educator — battles AIDS in her own very public way. Outspoken and determined, she fights ignorance and prejudice about the disease each day.

Conners has become adept at publicizing her message and pressuring government on AIDS-related issues. She sits on the board of the AIDS Coalition of Nova Scotia, and is busy with fundraisers and safe-sex talks in schools. She participates in candlelight processions in memory of those who have died of the disease. She argued forcefully against the federal government when it tried to prevent the Krever Inquiry from laying blame for the distribution of tainted blood in Canada.

Among her strategies:
- Asking Canadians to each send a nickel to contribute to Krever's defence;
- Crashing a government meeting that was discussing limits on the Krever Inquiry — ringing alarm clocks; banging pots; and dumping letters, BandAids, and money on the floor;
- Standing outside the House of Commons with duct tape and a Canadian flag across her mouth to demonstrate she's being gagged by the federal government, in an effort to get more funding that would allow her to prepare properly to fight the court challenge against the Krever Inquiry.

Source: Adapted from Halifax Chronicle-Herald and Canadian Press, various dates.

Figure 9.12 Janet Conners (right) and her mother, Irene Pritchard, hand out protest postcards in Halifax. They asked members of the public to send the postcards to their MPs protesting plans to limit the Krever Inquiry.

CASE STUDY

Labour Unions: The Politics of the Workplace

In 1997, approximately 30 percent of paid workers in Canada belonged to a labour union. A union can be formed when the majority of the workers in an industry or business vote to join. The government and the employer then recognize the union as the representative of all of its members. The union negotiates with the employer on behalf of its members on issues such as wages, job security, working conditions, vacation pay, pensions, medical or dental insurance, and other benefits. Because workers do not bargain with employers on their own, but collectively through the union, this process of negotiation is known as **collective bargaining** (see Figure 9.13).

Unions do more than bargain with employers on behalf of employees. They act as lobby groups at both the federal and provincial levels. Labour leaders often try to get governments to pass laws that will favour the members of their union. Often their lobbying is directed at economic issues such as job creation, minimum wage rates, or job-training programs. In addition, unions have been active on broader social issues. They have worked for the equality of women in the workplace, lobbied in support of social security benefits such as old-age pensions and medicare, and supported legislation prohibiting discrimination on grounds of race or ethnic origin.

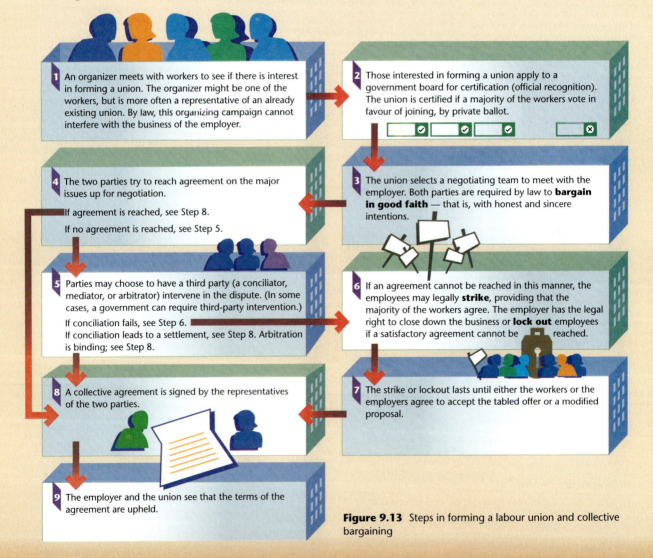

1. An organizer meets with workers to see if there is interest in forming a union. The organizer might be one of the workers, but is more often a representative of an already existing union. By law, this organizing campaign cannot interfere with the business of the employer.

2. Those interested in forming a union apply to a government board for certification (official recognition). The union is certified if a majority of the workers vote in favour of joining, by private ballot.

4. The two parties try to reach agreement on the major issues up for negotiation.
   If agreement is reached, see Step 8.
   If no agreement is reached, see Step 5.

3. The union selects a negotiating team to meet with the employer. Both parties are required by law to **bargain in good faith** — that is, with honest and sincere intentions.

5. Parties may choose to have a third party (a conciliator, mediator, or arbitrator) intervene in the dispute. (In some cases, a government can require third-party intervention.)
   If conciliation fails, see Step 6.
   If conciliation leads to a settlement, see Step 8. Arbitration is binding; see Step 8.

6. If an agreement cannot be reached in this manner, the employees may legally **strike**, providing that the majority of the workers agree. The employer has the legal right to close down the business or **lock out** employees if a satisfactory agreement cannot be reached.

8. A collective agreement is signed by the representatives of the two parties.

7. The strike or lockout lasts until either the workers or the employers agree to accept the tabled offer or a modified proposal.

9. The employer and the union see that the terms of the agreement are upheld.

Figure 9.13 Steps in forming a labour union and collective bargaining

Career Focus: Meet a Journalist

Ian Hanomansing grew up in Sackville, New Brunswick. He graduated from Mount Allison University in Sackville with a BA in Political Science and Sociology, and from Dalhousie University in Halifax with a law degree. Now based in British Columbia, he is national reporter for CBC Newsworld and host of Pacific Rim Report.

Figure 9.14 Ian Hanomansing

Q: How did you become a journalist?
A: Right after I finished high school, I got a summer job as a fill-in at night at a radio station in Amherst, and I really liked it. All through my university years, I worked in radio. I knew I wanted a job in broadcasting eventually, but I thought it would be a good idea to make myself more marketable as an employee by going to law school. In fact, a law degree can be useful for a reporter because you often deal with the courts or other legal issues.

After I graduated, I sent my resume to local stations. CBC called me for an interview for a job in television, and they liked my work. It was just one of those lucky breaks.

Q: Are television journalists trained in presentation?
A: Some people take training in presentation, but most don't. I learned from a combination of things. When I was 14 or 15 years old, I would take a newspaper and read the first page, pretending I was on radio, and listen to myself. I was also very involved in debating in high school. Debating helps you analyze an issue, think on your feet, argue a view, and be insightful. I also did play-by-plays with a friend for school hockey and basketball games. Then, when I was 17, and I first started working, I would tape myself on the radio and listen afterwards. I still make tapes of my broadcasts and review them a few weeks later. It's not vanity; it's a case of seeing how I can improve. You have to be self-critical.

Q: What work goes into the preparation of a news story?
A: A lot depends on the type of story. There are "spot" stories, where something happens at 2 p.m., and you have to have it ready to air at 6 p.m. Your job is to find out as much as you can as fast as you can, go into the edit room to put something together quickly, and get it on the air. In that case, there is virtually no preparation. It's just a matter of getting it on the air and getting it right.

On the other hand, there are stories you find on your own. You might see something that interests you. You do the research, interview people, and write a script. In television, a story is usually no more than two and a half minutes. This means the script is very short, but there is always so much information you have to cover, and you have to make sure to cover all sides of the story. It's a challenge.

Q: The news media are often seen as one of the key institutions in a democracy. Do you agree?
A: Yes, I think it's true. All you have to do is talk to people in other countries where the media aren't free to report what they like. They often don't get the whole story. News is fundamental information. We often tend to take it for granted, but it keeps us all aware of what is going on.

Q: What advice would you give a teenager interested in becoming a journalist?
A: First, find out as much as you can about the job. Talk to people to understand what it means to have to work with deadlines and tremendous pressure.

Second, be prepared to teach yourself. Even though you can go to journalism school, things change so rapidly — technology, for example — that you have to teach yourself a lot. You can start right away: watch television reports; see what the major networks are doing; think about aspects of a broadcast you like and don't like.

Third, seize any opportunity to practise. Get involved in debating activities, volunteer at a local station if you can, provide commentary for sports events.

Finally, remember that it's a competitive field out there. Luck can be the most important factor. That shouldn't be discouraging, but sobering. There are still a lot of things you can do to help yourself. With practice and hard work, you will be in a position to seize a lucky opportunity when it arises.

Culture and Politics

EXPLORATIONS

REVIEWING THE IDEAS

1. From the text or from your own general knowledge, give examples of the following:
   a) political activism
   b) lobbying
   c) a labour union
   d) an NGO

ANALYZING AND REFLECTING

2. a) What are the advantages of a union to its members?
   b) What are the advantages of a union for an employer? Why might an employer oppose workers' plans to form a union?

3. What is your response to the actions used by Janet Conners? Give your reaction in a short speech or "letter to the editor."

4. "It is both the right and the responsibility of individuals to participate in the political process." In a group discussion or short paragraph, give your response to this statement. Support your view with examples drawn from the chapter or from your own experience.

5. Review news stories in the newspaper and on radio and television for one day. Choose one story that is in the news, and compare its treatment in different media. How do the various treatments influence your view of the story? Explain.

CONNECTING AND EXTENDING

6. a) Identify an issue of concern to the students in your school. Which level of government would be responsible for this issue?
   b) How could you lobby your elected representative at the right level of government to make your concerns felt? Draw up an appropriate strategy.

7. a) Research one recent political issue. Suitable examples include the seal hunt, logging, pay equity, and child poverty. What evidence can you find of involvement by labour unions, NGOs, media influence, lobbying, or any other form of political action?
   b) Prepare a report or display of your findings.

SEEING THE BIG PICTURE

1. Work individually or in a group.
   a) Identify some political issues in your community. Review newspapers and magazines to find more information about groups or individuals involved in these issues.
   b) Identify the groups or individuals involved and make notes to record the ways in which they put their message across.
   c) Which methods appear to be the most common? Which methods appear to be the most effective?
   d) Make a collage or other display of your findings.

2. a) Do a review of newspapers and magazines to find out how people in other parts of the world get involved in the political process.
   b) Compare your findings with the information you gathered for question 1. Draw three generalizations based on your comparison. Present them to the class.

UNIT 3

Economics

CHAPTER 10

Economics: Close to Home
How do basic economic principles affect our daily lives?

CHAPTER 11

The Atlantic Economy
What types of activity form the basis of the economy of the Atlantic region?

CHAPTER 12

Our Economic Outlook
How does the economy of the Atlantic region compare with economies in the rest of Canada and the world?

How important will global links be in the future economy of the region?

How is the economy of the region changing?

CHAPTER 10

Economics: Close to Home

> If I had a $1 000 000
>   Well I'd buy you a green dress...
> If I had a $1 000 000
>   Well I'd buy you some art...
> If I had a $1 000 000
>   Well I'd buy you a monkey...
> If I had a $1 000 000 I'd buy your love
>
> — Barenaked Ladies

Figure 10.1 You might think of economics as the concern of governments and corporations, but individuals, too, need an understanding of economics in their everyday lives.

The song "If I Had A Million Dollars," by the Canadian rock group Barenaked Ladies, expresses an age-old human fantasy. From earliest times humans have daydreamed about having plenty and wanting for nothing. The ancient Hebrews dreamed of a promised land that flowed with milk and honey. In medieval England, Dick Whittington was lured to London by the promise that the streets were paved with gold. The Spanish explorers searched the Americas for the legendary gilded city, El Dorado.

In the twentieth century we continued our wishful thinking. The novelist James Hilton, writing at the height of the Great Depression of the 1930s, described a city called Shangri-La, where all human wants were satisfied and no one grew old. At the same time, as millions of North Americans went hungry, a popular song described "The Big Rock Candy Mountains" where lemonade gushed from springs, soda poured from crystal fountains, and lakes were filled with stew!

- If you had a million dollars, what would you choose to do with your money? Would you be able to afford everything you wanted? Would everything you wanted be available? Could you use your money productively — to produce more wealth?
- How do these questions relate to us, even if we don't have a million dollars?

What Is Economics?

Most of us do not have a million dollars. No matter how rich or poor we are, however, all of us continue to want something; we continue to dream. It appears that humans are unable to create a world where we have enough to satisfy all our wants. Candy will never grow on trees. In other words, our wants are boundless but **resources** are limited. The study of our efforts to satisfy our unlimited wants through the use of limited resources is known as **economics**.

Scarcity

If we could find that fantasy world where nothing was scarce, there would be no need to produce anything. No one would need to work or to buy anything. In short, there would be no economy. This is where economics begins — with **scarcity**.

To an economist, something is scarce only if someone will buy it for a price. If you want to know whether something is scarce or not, try to sell it or exchange it for something else of value. If you can get something in return for it, you know it is scarce. Economists divide scarce things into two groups: **goods** (meaning commodities or products such as sugar, lumber, or computer chips) and **services** (such as those of a barber, a musician, or an architect).

> **DID YOU KNOW...?**
>
> The word "economy" comes from a Greek term meaning "running a household." The economic system of a country determines the way it is run, taking into account three main questions: What should we produce in order to satisfy our wants? How should we use our scarce resources to produce it? Who should get the goods and services that are produced?

Figure 10.2 This painting by Richard Flynn depicts the City Market in Saint John, New Brunswick. People have visited marketplaces throughout history. They have been coming to this one since 1876. What attracts us to marketplaces? Do we go there for reasons other than to buy and sell? Can you think of modern markets where buyers and sellers do business without actually meeting?

Examine the following cases to understand the scarcity principle.

Case 1: Suppose that in the fictional land of Atlantis grow thousands of orange trees and only a few apple trees. Which fruit would be scarce? An economist would need more information to decide. If the people of Atlantis never eat apples but love oranges, then, in the *economic way of thinking*, it is oranges that are scarce.

Case 2: Suppose that you set up a booth in the schoolyard to sell fresh air. Your business would likely fail. An economist would say that this happened because you were trying to sell something that was not scarce. Yet there are circumstances where fresh air, pressurized air, or pure oxygen are quite scarce. In those situations it has a price. Oxygen vending machines were common in Tokyo, Japan, when smog smothered that city in the 1970s. If you felt short of breath you could put a mask on your face, insert a coin, and inhale.

Opportunity Cost

When something is scarce, it has to be **rationed**, or limited, in some manner. In our economy, the usual way of determining who gets scarce things is price rationing. If you have a million dollars, you can afford a scarce item like a luxury car, but most of us use cheaper forms of transportation.

The real cost of an item is not completely explained by its price in dollars. In determining the real cost of buying any good or service, you must take into account the things you sacrifice whenever you choose to spend money in a certain way. In other words, you need to ask, "What else can I do with the money?"

If you had a million dollars, there may not be much that you would have to sacrifice, but let's look at an example that is a lot closer to everyday life. Assume that you have decided to make some money by selling pizza at school during lunch hour. You are selling the pizza for $1 a slice. One student, Leila, has $200 in her wallet. She loves pizza and is rather

Figure 10.3 Customers at an oxygen stand in Toronto. Customers visit the outlet to inhale oxygen from special dispensers containing flavour enhancers. Would this kind of venture likely stay in business in your community? Explain. Think of three other situations where air would be scarce enough to have a price.

hungry. A second hungry pizza lover, Joe, has only $1 in his wallet. Who can best afford a piece of pizza?

The economist answers that question by looking at **opportunity cost**. The opportunity cost is what each student gives up in order to buy the pizza. What if Leila is a ski enthusiast who has been promised a trip to Marble Mountain if she raises enough money to buy new ski boots? She has saved for months and plans to buy the boots after school. If they cost exactly $200, then pizza will cost her the opportunity of going skiing. She probably will not buy the pizza, especially if she has a peanut butter sandwich in her locker. The opportunity cost is too high. If Joe, on the other hand, has no particular plans for his $1, his opportunity costs are low and he will probably become one of your customers.

Let's look at one other possibility. Suppose that your classmate Fred has $1 in his pocket when he smells your delicious pizza. Hunger speaks, he gives you the loonie, and wolfs down the pizza. As he swallows the last bite he thinks about other ways in which he could have spent the money: bus fare home, a box of juice, or a deposit in his savings account. He realizes he has bought on impulse. **Impulse buying** is what we do when we make a purchase without weighing the opportunity costs. Unfortunately for Fred, it began raining that afternoon and so his opportunity cost was high!

Figure 10.4 The opportunity cost can be seen as the opportunity lost.

EXPLORATIONS

APPLYING YOUR SKILLS

1. Most of us will never have a million dollars, but assume you have inherited the sum of $5000.

   a) Identify the goods or services that are scarce in your life. What do you want or need?

   b) Identify your options now that you have $5000. Which scarce goods or services are you able to buy?

   c) Make an economic decision: What will you do with the $5000? Identify your opportunity cost.

ANALYZING AND REFLECTING

2. The following comments suggest that our needs and wants are unlimited. With which do you agree? Why?

   a) "It's not so much that our wants and needs are unlimited. Advertising and the consumer society that encourages us to buy, buy, buy make us think they are."

   b) "I can satisfy my needs and wants for a short time. It's harder to satisfy them over a longer period."

   c) "Even if we had an ideal educational system, there would still be a shortage of workers."

   d) "Regardless of whether you are rich or poor, you should know the difference between needs and wants."

   (Adapted from C. Smith et al., *Canada Today*, Scarborough: Prentice Hall, 1996, p. 156.)

CONNECTING AND EXTENDING

3. In 1997, newspapers reported the story of a man in England who won a large sum of money in a lottery. He promptly quit his job and spent his days watching videos and eating junk food. The result? He died of a heart attack within several months. If you could have given this man some advice on his economic choices, what would it have been?

The Laws of Supply and Demand

Demand: The Consumer's Side of the Market

We sometimes talk about the difference between needing something and wanting something. Think again of the pizza example. It's lunch hour and you have a fully loaded, piping hot pizza. Ask your classmates if they *want* a slice of pizza. Most likely everyone will say yes. In fact those who did not eat breakfast might even convince you that they *need* a piece. But then ask who would and could *buy* a piece. Only some of your classmates will say yes. Those who are *willing* and *able to pay* create **demand** for your pizza.

We create a demand for an item when we are willing and able to give something of value — usually money — for it. Economists don't differentiate between needs and wants; both are classified as demand. Anything that is scarce enough to demand a price is classified as an **economic good or service**.

The demand for an item will vary with its price, as shown in Table 10.1. *As the price of something rises, people will buy less of it. As the price of something falls, people will buy more of it.*

Supply: The Producer's Side of the Market

Demand is only one side of your classroom market. Someone must **supply** the pizza. Supply is the mirror image of demand, the other side of the market. On the demand side of the market are **consumers**, or buyers, and on the supply side of the market are **producers**, or sellers.

Figure 10.5 At an auction, what happens to the number of bidders as the price rises?

The Law of Supply and Demand

The sentences in italics on this page and the next make up the "law of supply and demand." They can be summarized as follows:
high quantity demanded = high prices
low quantity demanded = low prices
high quantity supplied = low prices
low quantity supplied = high prices

Price	Demand: Number of slices that would sell	Supply: Number of slices offered for sale
$0.25	80	0
$0.50	60	0
$0.75	40	0
$1.00	20	24
$1.25	16	36
$1.50	12	40
$1.75	8	60
$2.00	4	96

Table 10.1 A demand and supply schedule. This fictitious survey shows what the demand and supply might be for pizza in your class. On a line graph, plot a demand curve and a supply curve from the data shown here. What can you tell about your market from the point at which the two lines intersect?

Figure 10.6 New Brunswickers Harvey McLeod and Christopher Freeman demonstrate a juggling toy called Devil Sticks that they adapted, manufactured, and made a commercial success. Many of us have seen buskers use these juggling props, but few of us saw them as an economic opportunity. Thinking of the supply side of the market led these young entrepreneurs to develop a highly successful business. Do you think we tend to see ourselves only as consumers and not as producers?

Imagine we survey your class to see who would be willing to supply pizza. Let's assume that you live next door to the school, so bringing pizza is easier for you than it is for anyone else. Because you only have a small oven, you could never bring more than two 12-slice pizzas. When you consider the costs involved, you determine that you must charge at least $1 per slice in order to make it worth your effort. At $1, no one else is willing to go to the trouble of bringing pizza. If the price were to rise, however, other classmates would probably become involved as sellers or producers, perhaps because they could afford to pay for a taxi to bring the pizzas to school. If the price rose again, more students would be trying to sell pizza, as shown in Table 10.1. *As the price of something rises, suppliers produce more of it. As the price of something falls, suppliers produce less of it.*

EXPLORATIONS

APPLYING YOUR SKILLS

1. You are on a fund-raising committee for a special school activity. Think of a product that you might be able to sell at school and in your neighbourhood to make money.

   a) Make up supply and demand schedules for your product, as shown in Table 10.1.

   b) Whether or not something is scarce, or in demand, is often a function of taste. How might you be able to change public taste in order to create more demand for your product? Make a list or sample of what you could do.

ANALYZING AND REFLECTING

2. Consignment stores that sell used designer clothing have become popular in recent years. Explain why you think this is so, with reference to supply and demand.

3. **a)** In countries impoverished by famine or war, many people want Canadian products yet these products do not sell there (i.e., there is no economic demand). Explain.

   b) Prepare a cause and effect diagram to show how sending foreign aid to such countries might create a demand for Canadian products.

ECONOMICS: CLOSE TO HOME

THE HIDDEN MARKET

When you look at Table 10.1, you notice that, if you sold your pizza at 50 cents per slice, there would be a demand for 60 slices. Remember, though, that you are selling the pizza at $1 per slice. This means that every day unspent coins jangle in the pockets of hungry consumers who have only 50 cents to spend. These consumers are known as the **hidden market**.

An astute business person would think of a way to reach this part of the market, with its potential customers. Could you add a 50-cent hot dog to your menu? Could you sell pizza by the half-slice? Could you produce a cheaper pizza? Some students would probably buy cheaper alternatives to your pizza if they were available. The **substitution effect** tells us that for any economic good or service there is a substitute. If the price of one product is too high, people will tend to buy a substitute — a hot dog or half-slice of pizza, for example. Wise consumers and astute business people use the substitution effect to their advantage.

Figure 10.7 Most of any market is hidden from view. The astute business person thinks of ways to reach the hidden market.

EXPLORATIONS

REVIEWING THE IDEAS

1. **a)** List some key economic terms that you have learned so far in this chapter.

   b) Choose five of these terms and describe how they apply to your life.

APPLYING YOUR SKILLS

2. Insert an economic good or service into the blank, and debate "There is no substitute for _____."

ANALYZING AND REFLECTING

3. Explain how advertisers put pressure on low-, middle-, and high-income families.

4. **a)** Work with a partner. Role play the following situation. One of you is selling pizza to your class at $1 a slice. The other enjoys East Indian cooking and wants to offer hot samosas for sale in the classroom at two for $1. In your roles, discuss what will happen to pizza sales if samosas are also available. Might the competition be good for business? Can you develop a strategy that might be good for both of you?

   b) Share your strategy with another pair.

CONNECTING AND EXTENDING

5. Visit some local stores or review newspaper ads to find examples of strategies that retailers use to increase their sales. Organize your information in the form of a chart or table.

ECONOMIC THINKING AND YOUR PERSONAL FINANCES

If you weigh opportunity costs, if you understand how supply and demand drive our market economy, and if you use the substitution effect to your advantage, you will have much more to spend on the things that you want.

We've all heard of get-rich-quick schemes. The most common of these is the lottery. Many others exist, ranging from speculating on high-risk stocks to panning for gold. In pursuit of these bonanzas, however, there are many more losers than winners. Here are five essential and safe steps to maximize your economic resources:

1. Set short-, medium-, and long-term goals for yourself, for example:
   - Short term: buy stereo equipment
   - Medium term: attend community college to become a chef
   - Long term: own your own restaurant

2. Make a financial plan to meet those goals, for example:
   - Save $20 per month so that, within 10 months, you can purchase stereo equipment that costs $200.
   - Together with your parents, save $100 per month towards the cost of attending college in three years ($8,000 required: $3600 cash, the remainder to be borrowed).
   - Work as a chef while repaying your student loan and accumulating $10,000 for restaurant start-up costs.

3. Examine your current financial position. How much employment income do you have? Do you have other sources of income? How much of it do you spend? How do you spend it? Do you have debts?

4. Prepare a monthly budget and relate it to your overall plans.

5. Stick to your budget by applying economic principles such as the substitution effect.

> "Young people who are learning how to manage their finances can follow some general guidelines. First, prepare your budget and make sure you don't overspend in any of the areas (see pages 148 and 149). Second, don't set any unrealistic goals for yourself, as you may not be able to achieve them. Then you might lose confidence in your ability to meet any financial goals. If you set realistic goals, you should be able to reach them. Third, if you are planning to borrow money, make sure that you will have a way to make the payments before applying for the loan."
>
> *Louis Gallant, Credit Union Manager, North Rustico, Prince Edward Island*

Figure 10.8 Your credit union or bank has experts who can advise you about your personal finances.

ECONOMICS: CLOSE TO HOME

Financial Statement for the month of _____

	Budget	Actual

INCOME

Employment Income (take-home pay)
Investment Income
Commissions and Tips
Other Income

                Total Monthly Income _____ _____

EXPENSES

Compulsory Savings
Emergency Account
Investments
                Total _____ _____

Home Costs
- Mortgage
- Electricity
- Heating
- Maintenance and Repairs
- Telephone
- Cable TV
- Home Insurance
- Taxes
- Other

                Total _____ _____

Food
- Groceries
- Restaurants
- Other

                Total _____ _____

Personal Expenses
- Life Insurance
- Restaurants
- Medical and Dental
- Hair styling
- Clothing
- Pocket Money
- Other

                Total _____ _____

Leisure Time
- Holiday
- Sports
- Movies, dances, etc.
- Magazines, newspapers
- Other

                Total _____ _____

Other
- School costs
- Child care
- Miscellaneous

                Total _____ _____

Total Monthly Expenses _____ _____
(includes savings)

Total Monthly Income _____ _____

Discretionary Income _____ _____
(total income less total expenses)

Figure 10.9 Budget forms such as this one are designed for adults. They are available free from many banks and credit unions and for a small cost from most stationers.

All budgets, whether for teenagers or adults, should have the following features.

- Income and expenses are separated and itemized.

- Two entries are made for each item. The budgeted amount is what you predict you will earn or spend over the course of the month. This amount is entered at the beginning of the month. The "actual" column records what happened and is completed at the end of the month. To complete this column, you need to note down how much you spend in each area each day.

- Fixed expenses, such as repaying a loan, rent, or life insurance, will be the same each month. Other expenses are flexible and have to be estimated.

- Under expenses, savings are listed first and described as compulsory. This is an important part of the budget process. Many people set aside some money for emergency use. This enables them to stick to their budget during months when they have unexpected expenses. It is a good idea to save some of your income, regardless of how little, on a regular basis.

- Any budget should be flexible, to ensure that bookkeeping is not too complicated. Some people enjoy keeping track of every cent, but most of us do not. Notice that there is a category for pocket money as well as a category for "other."

- The budget form should provide space for calculating discretionary income. This is the amount of money left over after you pay all your expenses and deposit the compulsory savings. If you end the month with a positive balance, you can then decide, at your discretion, how to spend or save it. There are several ways to increase discretionary income. You can reduce your spending; earn more by working; earn more through investments; or practise legal tax avoidance through such methods as registered education savings plans (RESPs).

EXPLORATIONS

APPLYING YOUR SKILLS

1. Obtain a budget form similar to the one shown in Figure 10.9. If you cannot obtain one for free, practise the substitution effect by making your own, by hand or on computer.

    a) Interview a parent to fill out a sample budget. This budget should remain **private**.

    b) Summarize which costs are the greatest. (There is no need to report on actual sums of money.)

    c) Write a private journal entry to explain how the family budget affects you. In what ways might you be able to make a difference to the family budget?

ANALYZING AND REFLECTING

2. "Take care of the pennies and the pounds will take care of themselves."

    "Don't be penny wise and pound foolish."

    Debate the relative merits of these two British proverbs. Are the two ideas compatible? Why or why not? Does the budget process described accommodate both of these ideas? Explain.

CONNECTING AND EXTENDING

3. **a)** Go to a bank or credit union and get information on plans such as registered education savings plans (RESPs) and registered retirement savings plans (RRSPs).

    b) Assume you or a parent is considering starting a RESP. Write down a list of questions you would like answered before investing your money.

    c) Do some research to find the answers to your questions.

ECONOMICS: CLOSE TO HOME

It's a Matter of Interest

It's a sunny Canada Day, and you're wandering along the beach. You discover Aladdin's lamp: out pops the Genie to make you an offer. She gives you the following choice, saying that if you choose the most lucrative option you will be able to keep the money. Make the wrong choice and you get nothing. Which option would you choose?

Option 1: You will be given a quarter of a million dollars now, and the same amount each and every day for the rest of the month.

Option 2: You will be given one cent today and then double the previous day's amount every day for a whole month. In other words, you would receive two cents on the second day, four cents on the third day, eight cents on the fourth day, and so on.

This example shows us that getting the most out of your money requires an understanding of interest and its compounding effects. When we borrow money from a bank to meet our needs and wants, we agree to pay back a larger amount after a period of time. Similarly, when we invest or save money, we earn back more than the original sum. The difference between the **principal** (the original sum) and the larger amount is known as **interest**. The amount paid per hundred dollars per year is known as the **rate of interest**. It is expressed not as dollars, but as a percent (%). Because interest costs can be very high, it is important to understand some basic facts about borrowing money or buying on credit.

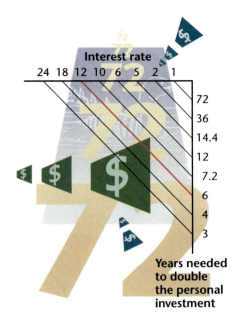

Figure 10.10 The "Rule of 72": You can calculate how long it will take a saved or invested sum of money to double at various interest rates by dividing the number 72 by the interest rate. If you saved or invested $1000 and the **compound interest** at the rate of 12%, your original sum would double in 6 years. The rule applies as well to borrowed amounts of money.

Know the difference between **consumer credit** and **investment credit**. If you borrow to attend university, finance a small business, or buy a home, you are investing. If you borrow to take a vacation or buy new stereo equipment, you are consuming.

Ask financial institutions for advice. Any credit union or bank has experts who are paid to advise you about borrowing money. It is in their interests for you to make wise financial decisions. It is in your interests to compare different options offered by different institutions.

Know the total cost of credit. The rate of interest advertised at an appliance dealer, a car dealer, or a bank may not tell the whole story. There can be extra, hidden costs. Further, payment schedules can make a dramatic difference to the cost of borrowing money (see Table 10.2).

Borrowing Money

Some Questions to Ask

- What is the rate of interest?
- What is the total amount of interest to be paid over the course of the loan?
- If interest rates drop can you renegotiate the loan? If they rise is your rate guaranteed?
- Can you make extra payments directly on the principal of the loan?
- Is there a penalty for paying off the loan early?
- Can payments be made weekly or biweekly as well as monthly? If so, what are the savings over the term of the loan?
- What will it cost to have life insurance on the loan?

Loan amount of $20 000 at 10% interest calculated on the declining balance	Monthly payments	Weekly payments
Payment per period	$424.94	$106.24
Total annual payments	$5099.28	$5524.48
Total interest	$5496.40	$4833.12
Amortization period	5 years	4.5 years

Table 10.2 The effect of weekly payments on the cost of a car loan of $20 000, compared with a more conventional schedule of monthly payments. Calculate the total amount paid for each plan. How much would a weekly schedule save you on this loan?

Figure 10.11 Credit cards sometimes give the illusion of unlimited wealth. In what way can this illusion be dangerous?

EXPLORATIONS

APPLYING YOUR SKILLS

1. Look through newspaper advertisements or store catalogues or visit some appropriate stores to find an expensive item that you might like to have. Suitable examples include a mountain bicycle, stereo equipment, a musical instrument, or a computer. Find out how much this item costs.

   a) Find out how much interest you would have to pay if you bought the item in each of the following ways:

   i) by credit card such as VISA or MASTERCARD

   ii) by borrowing from a bank or credit union (compare at least two institutions)

   iii) by using credit plans offered by the store (if any)

   b) Which option would be the best, if you were to buy the item?

   c) Apply the substitution effect. What other options could you choose to lower the cost of buying the item?

ECONOMICS: CLOSE TO HOME

CASE STUDY

A Financial Fable

Marie Newton felt embarrassed and discouraged the day the class discussed budgeting. How could she record her weekly income? She had none. She could not tell the class about her family's budget. There was none. Her classmates talked of savings accounts for college and weekly allowances and, when the teacher asked, some of them even knew about mortgages. To Marie these were just words.

> How could she record her weekly income? She had none. She could not tell the class about her family's budget. There was none.

What she knew about money was that there never seemed to be enough now that her father was gone. Her mother and younger brother and sister lived with her in the small apartment. Her mother worked hard, but her salary never stretched far enough. At home, discussions about money always started with apologies and ended in disappointment. "Rent" was an angry word.

"Record all your income and expenses for the next two weeks," Mr. Russell had said.

"Mine will be a blank sheet," Marie thought.

But Mr. Russell saw that she looked troubled, and stopped her as the class left.

"Marie, you look worried about the assignment."

After a few moments she raised her eyes and mumbled, "I don't get an allowance."

Mr. Russell said that the assignment would be private, and that she did not need an allowance in order to do the task. "You probably handle money even if it isn't yours. Keep track of it. If your mother sends you to the store, jot down the amounts. The point of the assignment is to get you into the habit of keeping track of money. You'll do just fine."

For the next two weeks Marie kept track of all of the money that passed through her hands. She was surprised at how much it was. Several times she ran errands for her mother. Once she went to the store for the woman who lived in the apartment across the hall. On the final Saturday, she was asked to baby-sit for her mother's friend. By the time the assignment was due, Marie had recorded more than $50 in expenses. She got an A on the assignment.

The experience set her to thinking about money, and she decided to apply some of the lessons she had learned in class. Looking over the records, she saw that her mother was already practising the substitution effect. Last week, when she went to the store, her mother asked her to buy "no name" brands if they were cheaper. "A penny saved is a penny earned," Mr. Russell had told the class. Now Marie understood what he meant.

152 ECONOMICS

It was spring, and Marie and her brother and sister needed new clothing. It was Marie who suggested that blue jeans from the second-hand shop would be just as good as new ones. That is where they went. After an hour of digging through the bins, each of them had a new outfit. To show her gratitude, Marie's mother said she would treat them to a movie. "If we wait and go on Monday it's half price."

Marie had learned to keep an eye on expenses. She could see how economizing had the effect of increasing the family income. Now she wanted to apply some of the other lessons she had learned. She also wanted an income of her own. What could she do aside from occasional baby-sitting?

At first nothing seemed possible. Marie, at 14, was not old enough to work for most employers, and working for her mother for pay was simply putting money into one family pocket by taking it out of another. It was at the flea market that Sunday that an idea came to her. Used toys, games, and children's books seemed to sell well. Often her mother would buy some little thing for her brother and sister. They had toys at home that were no longer in use. If they had some in their apartment, Marie reasoned, other people probably had similar caches. Would people sell their used toys to her? She could use her baby-sitting money to start her own business.

Marie made some flyers and delivered them door to door, introducing herself as a young entrepreneur. For every adult who was gruff, several were nice. She explained her flea market business, and asked if she could buy small items for children. Marie was pleasantly surprised to find that about one in five houses had something for her. She was careful not to pay more than half what she thought the item would bring. Some people didn't even want money, and were just glad the toys were going to be used again!

Marie cleaned and mended the toys and put price tags on them. Within two weeks she felt she had enough items to break even at the flea market. She had just enough money left to rent an $8.00 table for the Sunday morning market. Marie was anxious as the weekend approached, but when Sunday came it was all worthwhile. She took in $19.25 and had several items left over.

By going door to door after school two days a week, Marie had enough items on hand to sell at the flea market every second week. Some weeks sales were slow, but on one occasion she made more than $40. She found that the last week of the month was best because it followed pay day.

> Marie had learned to keep an eye on expenses. She could see how economizing had the effect of increasing the family income.

ECONOMICS: CLOSE TO HOME

Marie enjoyed earning an income and always kept an eye open for opportunities. On the way home from school she would pick up discarded cans or bottles. Hardly a week went by when she didn't make a dollar by recycling. In spring, she put a note on her flea-market table saying she was available for mowing lawns. This brought several offers. One day she overheard Mr. Russell say to another teacher, "That Newton kid is a real go-getter."

One day in June, after an exam, Marie stopped at the credit union on the way home. She was nervous at the thought of being in a bank, but she took a deep breath, and told the teller that she wanted to open an account. She was surprised when the teller dealt with her as though she were an adult. Soon she was going into the credit union on a regular basis with small amounts of money.

> "Get interest working for you instead of working against you and you'll prosper."

Late that fall Marie walked home clutching her credit union pass book. She stopped to open it and glance at the balance. She had broken the $200 barrier: $203.17! And better yet, the quarterly interest had been added: $2.42. "Get interest working for you instead of working against you," Mr. Russell had said, "and you'll prosper." Marie was proud.

When December came the sounds of Christmas filled the malls. The stores were bursting with tempting merchandise. Her younger brother and sister had asked for a video-game attachment for the television. Marie was shopping with her mother when they saw it. It was advertised for $189 cash or 24 monthly payments of $12 each. Marie's mother said she was going to buy it.

"If we scrimp we can afford the monthly payment. Your brother and sister will love it. They want it so badly!"

Marie did the multiplication and realized that the cost of the credit was nearly $100. She thought of the long time it had taken her to earn the $2.42 interest on her bank account. And she thought of how difficult it was for her mother to make ends meet already. For a moment she felt angry. She must convince her mother not to buy.

> "Be thrifty, not miserly, Marie. There's an old saying, 'It's well to be thrifty, but don't amass a horde of regrets.'"

Then Marie thought of her younger brother and sister. She thought of their faces Christmas morning. Something her grandfather had said when he came to visit came back to her. When she confided in him about her bank account he had said how proud he was of her. But then he had said,

"Be thrifty, not miserly, Marie. There's an old saying, 'It's well to be thrifty, but don't amass a horde of regrets.'"

It only took a moment for Marie to realize what she wanted to do.

"Mom," she said, "I've got a great Christmas idea!"

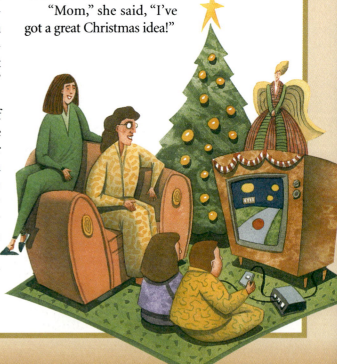

EXPLORATIONS

APPLYING YOUR SKILLS

1. In a role play, in a cartoon strip, or in writing, continue this story. Be sure to consider the following.

   a) What is Marie's "great idea"?

   b) How do you think her mother might react? What will be the opportunity cost for Marie's mother in dollars if she chooses to arrange credit from the store?

   c) If Marie's mother agrees to her idea, what will be the opportunity cost to Marie in dollars? Assume that she is getting 5% interest on the money in her bank account.

2. The gap or **disparity** in wealth within our own society can often be enormous. How is this illustrated by the fable?

SEEING THE BIG PICTURE

1. **a)** Make a list of one short-, one medium-, and one long-term economic goal. These goals can be real or imaginary.

   b) What do you need to do in order to achieve your goals? Determine the opportunity costs for each goal.

2. Prepare a personal budget that will allow you to meet your goals.

3. Complete your budget sheet for one month.

4. What does your budget reveal? Could you save more? If so, how? Could you increase your discretionary income? If so, how? What would you do with the additional money?

CHAPTER 11
The Atlantic Economy

Figure 11.1 What goods can you identify in these photographs? All of them are produced and/or distributed as part of our economy.

If you were to list all the goods and services you use on any day, the number and variety would probably surprise you. Goods would include items of clothing, classroom materials, reading materials, sports equipment, and more. Services would include schools, transportation, restaurants, and more. These goods and services meet your needs and wants. They also form the basis of our economy.

- What sorts of goods are produced, processed, and distributed in Atlantic Canada? What sorts of services are provided?
- How do these goods and services contribute to our economy?
- How is the economy of the Atlantic region changing?

Sectors of Our Economy

All the goods and services that you use in a day — be they your sneakers or your cafeteria lunch — are related to different types of activity in our economy. These types of activities can be broken into four sectors.

Table 11.1 Percentage of labour force employed by economic sector, 1993

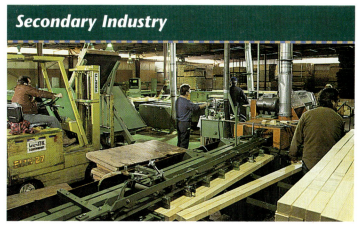

Province	Primary	Secondary	Tertiary and Quaternary
Newfoundland and Labrador	8.2	19.5	72.3
Prince Edward Island	13.1	16.4	70.5
Nova Scotia	6.2	17.3	76.5
New Brunswick	5.8	18.2	76.0

Primary Industry

Primary industry refers to activities in which people use, extract, or harvest natural resources such as water, soil, fish, animals, plants, and trees. The products of primary industry are only slightly altered before they are used. Fishing, mining, forestry, and agriculture are all primary industries.

Secondary Industry

Secondary industries process raw materials into finished goods. During this manufacturing process, raw materials are processed into products that are substantially different from the original materials. The materials are worth more in their manufactured form than they were as unprocessed materials. This increase in value is known as *value added*. Manufacturing and construction are part of the secondary sector.

Tertiary Industry

Tertiary industries enable consumers to obtain and use the finished goods. Workers in the tertiary sector of the economy provide services rather than goods. Sales, repair services, banking, and insurance are all part of the tertiary sector.

Quaternary Industry

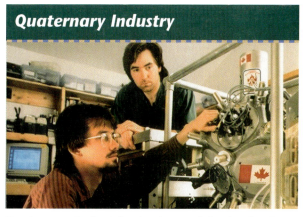

Quaternary industries involve specialized technology. Research scientists and computer software designers are examples of people who work in quaternary industries. Because quaternary activities usually provide services rather than goods, they are often grouped together with tertiary industries.

THE ATLANTIC ECONOMY

These sectors of the economy combine to produce the **Gross Domestic Product (GDP)** — the total value of goods and services produced within a given area in a given year. GDP can be given for a province, a region, or a country. Most economists pay close attention to GDP because the figures, taken over time, indicate whether an economy is growing, staying the same, or declining.

The following sections of this chapter will take a closer look at the contribution of each of the sectors to the economy of the Atlantic provinces.

Table 11.2 Gross Domestic Product of the Atlantic provinces, $ thousands, 1995. Sometimes the economy is measured in terms of **GDP per person** or **per capita**. This figure is the total GDP divided by the number of people who live in the area (see Table 12.2 on page 185).

Province	Total GDP
Newfoundland and Labrador	6 450 534
Prince Edward Island	1 833 755
Nova Scotia	13 127 655
New Brunswick	10 218 924

EXPLORATIONS

APPLYING YOUR SKILLS

1. Copy the following chart into your notebook and fill in the blanks with appropriate activities. Follow the example.

Primary activity	Secondary activity	Tertiary activity	Quaternary activity
wood harvesting	making books from paper	sales in book store	designing computerized inventory control system
gold mining			
	making bread		
		retailing fish fillets	
	making leather shoes		
	making potato chips		

2. **a)** Conduct a survey of the students in your school to determine the sectors in which people in their household work, or have worked. Present your results in a chart similar to the one below.

Economic sector	Number of people employed in that sector	% of surveyed people employed in that sector
Primary		
Secondary		
Tertiary		
Quaternary		

b) According to your findings, which sector is most significant in your area in terms of the percentage of workers employed in it? Which is the least significant?

ECONOMICS

Primary Industry

As you have seen, primary industries are based on natural resources; but what is a natural resource? **Natural resources** are the materials found in the natural environment that humans can use to satisfy their needs and wants. In the strictest sense, a natural material is considered to be a resource only if three conditions are met. First, society must feel it needs the material. Second, technology must be advanced enough to extract, or harvest, the material. Finally, it must be economical to extract the natural material and put it to use.

For centuries, primary industries have formed the basis of this region's economy. Some, such as fishing, have even influenced our culture. However, just as cultures change, so does the economy. Today, primary industries remain important, but they do not play as large a part as they did in the past. In some cases, primary industries are in decline because resources are depleted. This is the case in some areas of the fishery.

Figure 11.2 Primary industry in Atlantic Canada is based on the natural resources of the sea, forests, mineral deposits, and agricultural land.

DID YOU KNOW...?

Primary industries create many jobs in other industries. First, the raw materials must be processed. Wood produced by the primary sector, for example, might create jobs in a furniture factory. Further, when forestry workers spend their earnings, they help create jobs for even more workers — in banks, restaurants, and stores, for example. Although some primary industries may contribute only a low percentage of a province's GDP, if they close down, secondary and service sector industries also suffer.

Others are in decline because of changing consumer demand. This has been the case with coal mines, for example, as other sources of energy have become more widely available. Still others have suffered in the face of stiff **competition** from other countries. For example, producers in the southern United States can supply lumber to that region more cheaply than Canadian producers can. The primary industries that do continue are changing, as well. Traditionally, primary industries required large numbers of manual workers, with very specific skills. Today, many are using new technology that has changed these requirements to some degree. Primary industries may now require fewer workers with a broader range of skills and a higher level of education. You will learn more about these topics in Chapters 15 and 16.

Figure 11.3 Major primary industries of the Atlantic region, 1997

Harvesting the Sea

For centuries, the economic well-being of much of Atlantic Canada rested heavily on the fishery. For much of our region's history, the breeding stock was able to replace the numbers of fish caught. By the middle of the twentieth century, however, several factors combined to cause a decline of groundfishing, as you will see in Chapter 15. The federal government closed the cod fishery in July 1992, causing much hardship for many families. Some fishers took training and started new careers. Others began **aquaculture** — or "fish farming" operations — and still others fished for species whose survival was not threatened, such as crab and hake.

Province	Value of fishing	% of GDP contributed by the fishery
Newfoundland and Labrador	59 449	0.9
Prince Edward Island	37 021	2.0
Nova Scotia	237 414	1.8
New Brunswick	94 723	0.9

Table 11.3 Contribution of the fishery to the provincial GDP, $ thousands, 1995. Which province relies the most on fishing?

An Ideal Fish Habitat

The waters off Atlantic Canada are ideally suited as a fish habitat. In these waters, the warm Gulf Stream and the cold Labrador Current mix together, attracting an array of fish species. In addition, the continental shelf off the coast of Atlantic Canada creates conditions that aid the development of phytoplankton, or microscopic floating plants that form the foundation of a complex food chain that supports fish and the humans who harvest the sea.

Figure 11.4 The banks of the continental shelf off Atlantic Canada form large areas of shallow water, where light can penetrate to the ocean floor, creating conditions favourable for the development of microscopic plant life.

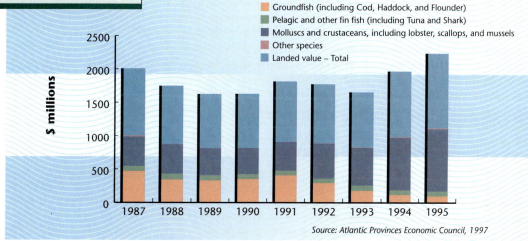

Source: Atlantic Provinces Economic Council, 1997

Figure 11.5 Value of the fishery in Atlantic Canada, showing changing trends

THE ATLANTIC ECONOMY

Using Our Forests

In Atlantic Canada, some trees are harvested for use in construction of various sorts. Much of the annual cut of timber, however, goes to the region's pulp and paper mills. Most of the forested areas are owned by provincial governments.

To protect the forest resource, some provinces set a limit on the amount of timber that can be cut each year. This amount is referred to as the **allowable annual cut** (AAC). To set the AAC, the government considers factors such as rate of tree growth; loss from fires, insects, and disease; impact of cutting on wildlife; and number of trees to be replanted. About 8 percent of the forest in Atlantic Canada is cut each year.

Table 11.4 The contribution of forestry to provincial GDP, $ thousands, 1995. Which province relies the most on forestry?

Province	Value of forestry	% of GDP contributed by the forestry sector
Newfoundland and Labrador	75 111	1.2
Prince Edward Island	9 883	0.5
Nova Scotia	94 465	0.7
New Brunswick	212 057	2.1

Figure 11.6 Forests are a treasured resource for many reasons. They provide materials we need and they create employment. They produce oxygen, protect the soil from erosion, and provide habitat for birds and other wildlife. They also provide many opportunities for people to enjoy their natural environment.

Mining: Treasures From the Earth

Mining refers to activities that take mineral substances from the earth. These substances may be metallic, non-metallic, or fossil fuels. We use minerals to produce a wide range of items: heavy equipment, construction materials, heating fuel, household appliances, and much more.

Different methods may be used to extract minerals. A mineral deposit consisting of horizontal layers close to the earth's surface, for example, would be mined in the open-pit method. A deposit deep beneath the earth's surface would be mined using the shaft method.

Table 11.5 Contribution of mining to the provincial GDP, $ thousands, 1995. Which province relies most on mining?

Province	Value of mineral production	Contribution of mining to GDP (%)
Newfoundland and Labrador	251 497	3.9
Prince Edward Island	403	<0.1
Nova Scotia	230 776	1.8
New Brunswick	183 101	1.8

Economics

Farming in Atlantic Canada

Farming can be defined as a set of activities devoted to producing food and other products from the land. Types of farms include vegetable, livestock, dairy, egg, fur, and mixed farms. Farming involves three main stages. The first, called "input," includes everything needed to grow a crop. In the second stage, "process," the farmer carries out all the activities needed to bring the crop to maturity. If the farmer carries out these steps correctly, and nature does not bring any unwanted surprises, the result will be the final stage, "output."

Table 11.6 Related elements of farming

Inputs	Processes	Outputs
• labour • tools • equipment • suitable soil • suitable climate • knowledge • energy • seed	• selecting crops • location of crops • planting • fertilizing • spraying • tilling • harvesting • removing wastes	• crops • waste products

Table 11.7 Contribution of farming to provincial GDP, $ thousands, 1995. Which province relies the most on farming?

Province	Value of farm production	Contribution of farming to GDP (%)
Newfoundland and Labrador	18 539	0.3
Prince Edward Island	143 898	7.9
Nova Scotia	146 674	1.1
New Brunswick	110 213	1.1

EXPLORATIONS

REVIEWING THE IDEAS

1. Work in groups of four. Each member of the group should select one of the resources described in this chapter.

   a) In point form, show how your resource meets the three conditions described in the first paragraph on page 159.

   b) Share your conclusions with your group.

2. Why are forests a treasured resource? Include your own opinion in your answer.

APPLYING YOUR SKILLS

3. **a)** Using data from Tables 11.3 to 11.7, make a pie graph to show the importance of forestry, fishing, mining, and farming in your province. If possible, use a computer program to make your graph. Keep this graph; you will add to it as you learn more about the other sectors of the economy.

   b) Discuss which secondary and service industries in your province benefit from the leading primary industry.

CONNECTING AND EXTENDING

4. Find a newspaper article related to any primary industry. What changes in the industry are evident from the article?

THE ATLANTIC ECONOMY

CASE STUDY

MINING AT VOISEY'S BAY

In the summer of 1993, Albert Chislett and Chris Verbiski were collecting rock samples from river beds in northern Labrador. The partners, owners of an exploration company known as Archean Resources, were looking for diamonds on behalf of the Diamond Fields Resources company. At the same time, they kept an eye out for "rusty zones" — areas where rocks are stained by minerals carried in groundwater and run-off.

During a helicopter flight to Nain one afternoon in late September, Chislett and Verbiski noticed a hill near Voisey's Bay.

Figure 11.8 Discovery Hill, Voisey's Bay

Part of this hill caught their eye: it was a deep red colour. They returned to the site two days later and collected 25 samples to be analyzed in a lab in Newfoundland. Geologists discovered that the samples contained 1.5 to 6 percent copper and significant amounts of cobalt. Chislett and Verbiski soon staked out areas around what became known as Discovery Hill.

It took Chislett and Verbiski almost a year to convince Diamond Fields Resources to explore the area further but, by a majority vote of one, the company finally agreed. Archean Resources, Chislett and Verbiski's company, managed the exploration program for Diamond Fields Resources. In November 1994, it was announced that samples taken from around Discovery Hill contained high concentrations of nickel, copper, cobalt, and precious metals. Immediately, exploration companies, armed with geological maps and reports, began beating a path to northern Labrador. By January 1996, over 170 Canadian companies had staked land for exploration.

> **FOCUS ON FIGURE 11.7**
> 1. What industries might locate here, based on the deposits? Consider all sectors of the economy.
> 2. How might materials from Voisey's Bay be transported to market?
> 3. This area is covered with ice for parts of the year. What problems might this cause?

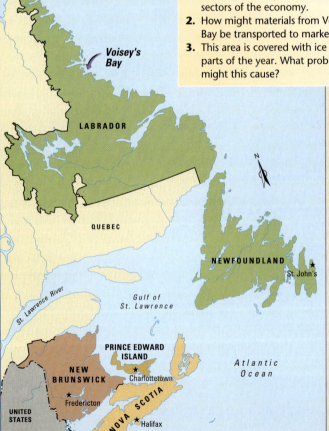

Figure 11.7 Location of Voisey's Bay

> **DID YOU KNOW...?**
> The ore from the deposit at Discovery Hill is so dense that a chunk the size of a small microwave oven weighs 1000 kg. At 1996 prices, a piece of rock this size, containing nickel, copper, and cobalt, was worth about $500.

By this time, Diamond Fields had estimated that the mineral deposits in the area were some of the richest in the world. Their high concentration meant that more metals could be extracted from less ore. In addition, the ore was very large grained, which meant it would not need to be crushed to the same extent as a fine-grained ore. Both of these factors would reduce the cost of separating the metals from the ore.

The deposits lay in a bowl-shaped area, with ore thicknesses of up to 100 m, located relatively close to the earth's surface. As a result, companies would be able to extract the ore relatively cheaply. The ore is also concentrated in a small area: you can walk from one end to the other in an hour. This factor would help contain possible damage to the environment.

Since the initial discovery, further deposits have been found. Before long, the International Nickel Company (INCO) became involved. INCO operates huge nickel mines in Ontario and Manitoba. In 1996, when INCO bought Diamond Fields Resources, it gained control of the deposits at Voisey's Bay.

SOME ISSUES AT VOISEY'S BAY

In the past, mining, milling, smelting, and refining activities have damaged the environment. INCO will have to use the most modern technology available to minimize the effects of mining and processing on the environment around Voisey's Bay. Federal and provincial laws set standards for care of the environment; nevertheless, critics remain concerned about air quality, dumping of refuse, disturbance of land-fast ice, and tailings.

Both the Innu and Inuit have land claims in the Voisey's Bay area. Some of these lands, where Innu and Inuit hunt, trap, and fish, are targeted for exploration and mining. The Innu and Inuit claim that they should be accepted by both governments and developers as equal partners in all decisions that affect the land and wildlife.

> The Innu used to call the place Kauipuskats Shipish (Burning Spot Brook) where the drill sites are at Voisey's Bay.... I see the beauty of the land. What I'm worried about is the animals and rivers, and I don't want to see a lot of land destroyed. I know there are some graveyards north of the drilling sites. It seems like the government has stolen our land. I begin to realize the change in our way of life in the midst of poverty.
>
> — *Tshenish Pasteen, Davis Inlet elder*

EXPLORATIONS

APPLYING YOUR SKILLS

1. Prepare a newspaper or video report announcing details of the discovery at Voisey's Bay. Try to convey the importance of the find in the tone of your report.

ANALYZING AND REFLECTING

2. Work in a group. Research the issues at Voisey's Bay, and complete a chart listing different viewpoints. Use the following headings across the top of the chart: Groups, Points of view, Possible conflict, Possible solution. Consider the views of the following groups: government, industry, Innu and Inuit, environmentalists, any others.

3. Suggest ways in which the Innu and Inuit could get involved in the development of the mining project.

4. a) Identify an issue related to industry and the environment in your province. Research the issue so that you understand the viewpoints of the groups involved.

   b) Role play a discussion among these groups, in which you try to find a solution.

THE ATLANTIC ECONOMY

CASE STUDY

Potato Farming in Prince Edward Island

Figure 11.9 Gordon Sobey, potato farmer

Gordon Sobey operates a farm 8 km from Borden-Carleton, Prince Edward Island. Sobey owns 80 hectares of land but rents an additional 56 hectares at approximately $120 per hectare. The farm grows mainly potatoes for seed and table use, but also produces grain, hay, and sows, as well as wood for private use.

Soil conditions are an important factor for potato farmers. The soil on the Sobey farm has a balance of clay and sand that is good for potato farming. Nevertheless, Sobey — like all farmers — has to manage the soil carefully. To maintain soil fertility, Sobey practises **crop rotation**, growing one crop on land where another crop was grown previously. This practice helps restore nutrients that have been depleted. He also applies up to 1350 kg of fertilizer on every hectare per year.

FOCUS ON FIGURE 11.10

1. Describe the location of the outbuildings, such as the barn and warehouse. Does their location provide an advantage? Explain.
2. What evidence do you see that Gordon Sobey has taken measures to protect the farm from wind?

1 House
2 Hedgerow
3 Potato warehouse
4 Machine storage
5 Feed room and office
6 Grain storage tanks
7 Manure storage
8 Dry sow barn
9 Farrowing barn
10 Food storage and area for equipment repair
11 Feeder barn

Figure 11.10 The Sobey farm

166 ECONOMICS

Table 11.8 Rotation system on the Sobey farm. What will be the pattern in the fourth year?

	Field 1	Field 2	Field 3
Year 1	potatoes	hay	grain
Year 2	grain	potatoes	hay
Year 3	hay	grain	potatoes

To help reduce soil loss, Sobey plows along slopes instead of up and down slopes. **Contour plowing**, as this practice is called, allows the deep plow furrows to prevent soil from running off during heavy rains.

Productivity of a farm can be greatly reduced by insects and disease. The Colorado Beetle, for example, strips the leaves off potato plants. On Prince Edward Island, farmers also battle fungi (or blight) in the soil during wet periods. Potatoes infected with fungi turn dark, and will not be bought by consumers. To fight insects and disease, Sobey applies pesticides to his fields during the planting and growing season.

The Business of Farming

To maintain his operation, Sobey relies on both equipment and farm labourers. His equipment includes tillage machinery (for preparing land for crops), grading and packaging equipment, three tractors, and three trucks. He employs one full-time worker besides himself. During peak periods, an additional 4 to 6 workers are hired from the local area. Sobey will hire only workers who demonstrate a willingness to work long hours and have a thorough knowledge of the equipment. An inexperienced worker might cause damage, resulting in costly repairs and a loss of profit because of down-time.

At one time, the federal government subsidized transportation for farm goods and funded research into new farming practices. With budget cuts, these programs have been reduced. Farmers like Gordon Sobey are now charged a fee every time they have their potato seed inspected and the soil on their farms tested for disease. These changes have driven up costs.

Figure 11.11 *Left*: Colorado Beetle. *Below*: Farming equipment is expensive to buy and has to be maintained.

Table 11.9 Work on Gordon Sobey's farm is organized into a sequence of major activities.

Time	Activities
Early May	• Plant barley
Middle to late May	• Plant Burbank potatoes
	• Clean up equipment
Early June	• Prepare spray equipment
Middle to late June	• Spray grain and potatoes to control weeds
Middle July	• Cultivate potatoes to ensure roots are covered
Late July	• Spray again to control blight and disease
Early to middle August	• Repair equipment
Late August	• Harvest grain
Early to middle September	• Continue harvesting grain
Late September	• Complete equipment repair
October	• Harvest potatoes
	• Clean, sort, grade, package, and store potatoes

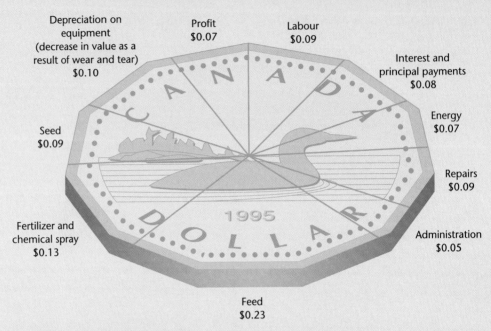

Figure 11.12
Where a dollar goes on the Sobey farm. Which three items account for the greatest expense?

- Depreciation on equipment (decrease in value as a result of wear and tear) $0.10
- Profit $0.07
- Labour $0.09
- Interest and principal payments $0.08
- Energy $0.07
- Seed $0.09
- Repairs $0.09
- Fertilizer and chemical spray $0.13
- Administration $0.05
- Feed $0.23

Like most business people, Sobey has to ensure that he will make a profit. He uses computer technology to organize his activities and purchase supplies and services. His computer also helps him keep an accurate record of expenses.

Gordon Sobey produces over 1 million kg of potatoes per year, over 7 tonnes of hay and grain per hectare, and 80 sows. The pork is marketed each week through a meat company in Charlottetown. The potatoes are sold to two or three local produce dealers who export them to provincial, regional, and international markets.

EXPLORATIONS

REVIEWING THE IDEAS

1. a) What is the relative location of Gordon Sobey's farm?

b) What are the advantages of this location?

APPLYING YOUR SKILLS

2. a) Using Table 11.6, identify which inputs Sobey can most easily control in order to keep his operation cost efficient. Explain.

b) Select an input and explain how it affects the kind of farming activities in which Sobey is engaged.

c) At what time of year would Sobey most likely hire the additional four to six workers? Explain.

3. If you were a farmer who practised good soil management, how would you convince other farmers to do likewise? Explain.

ANALYZING AND REFLECTING

4. a) Some consumers prefer to buy "organic" produce that is grown without chemical fertilizers or pesticides. In a group, brainstorm the advantages and disadvantages of organic farming for customers. As a farmer, where might your savings be? What additional costs might you incur?

b) Debate: We should buy only organically produced vegetables.

SECONDARY INDUSTRY

Secondary industries include manufacturing and construction. Transportation and utilities (such as hydro and gas) are often included in this sector, as well. As you have seen, many secondary industries in the Atlantic provinces are related to the primary sector. Shipbuilding and food-processing, for example, have grown out of fishing and agricultural industries.

Manufacturing can be broken into two types. **First-stage manufacturing** refers to processing raw materials. For instance, ore from Voisey's Bay must be processed in a smelter to produce nickel. **Second-stage manufacturing** uses processed materials to make finished products. Nickel is used, for example, to make stainless steel for pots, pans, knives, and forks.

Table 11.10 Contribution of secondary industries to provincial GDP, $ thousands, 1995. In which province is the secondary sector most important?

Province	Value	% of total
Newfoundland and Labrador	870 493	13.3
Prince Edward Island	328 747	17.9
Nova Scotia	2 493 868	19.0
New Brunswick	2 027 605	19.8

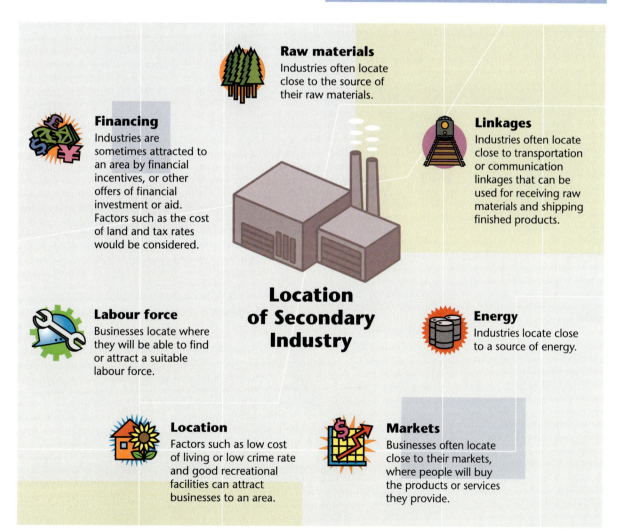

Figure 11.13 Why do industries locate where they do? The factors shown here usually play a part, although the importance of each one often varies, depending on the type of industry.

CASE STUDY

PROCESSING POTATOES: HAVE A FRENCH FRY!

It's possible that the French fries you recently had at a fast-food restaurant were produced by McCain Foods of Florenceville, New Brunswick. McCain Produce was established in 1914 to export seed potatoes. In 1956, brothers Harrison and Wallace McCain came up with the idea of frozen French fried potatoes. At that time, restaurants and other food service operators used the labour-intensive method of peeling and cutting potatoes into fries on site. The McCain brothers managed to convince many of these operators that frozen French fries would cut their costs, since peeling by hand would not be necessary. They also had to convince operators to buy freezers! In 1957, 30 workers at the plant in Florenceville produced about 700 kg of fries per hour. Today, workers produce a variety of frozen foods at McCain plants around the world.

Figure 11.14 Location of Florenceville, New Brunswick. What evidence can you find to show why McCain might have located here? Check the factors in Figure 11.13.

Figure 11.15 In what ways is this commercial designed to appeal to the market? Most corporations hire advertising agencies to prepare their commercials. In which sector of the economy does an advertising executive work?

What accounts for the success of McCain Foods? The company has a policy of using quality ingredients. It also employs the latest technology to reduce costs, and has an aggressive marketing strategy. Probably the most important reason for its success, however, is **diversification**. A successful company has to anticipate what consumers will buy, and then market the idea. McCain has not restricted itself to producing plain French fries. Other potato products include battered fries, nuggets, wedges, and hash browns. Based on its success with potato products, the company has been able to process a wide range of other foods, such as pizza pockets, frozen vegetables, frozen dinners, and juices.

McCain has also considered consumer concerns about healthy eating habits. Health Canada recommends that people should obtain only 30 percent of their calories from fat and 10 percent from saturated fat. As a result, McCain developed the "Superfry." Cooked in non-hydrogenated canola oil, this fry has only 28 percent of its calories from fat and less than 3 percent from saturated fat.

Table 11.11 McCain has plants in all of the countries shown here, employing more than 12 000 people world-wide.

Canada	France	Spain
Argentina	Germany	United Kingdom
Australia	Japan	United States
Belgium	Netherlands	
Colombia	New Zealand	

170 ECONOMICS

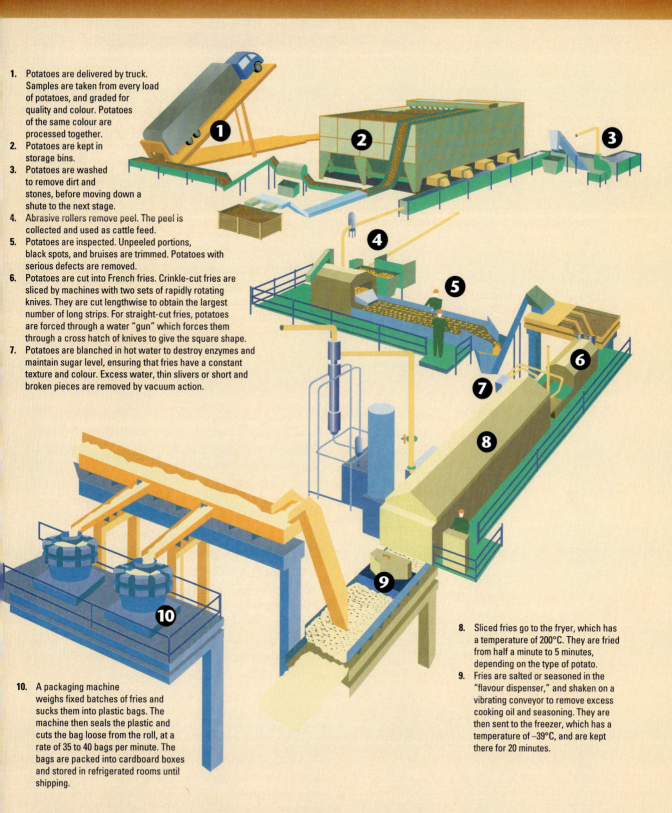

1. Potatoes are delivered by truck. Samples are taken from every load of potatoes, and graded for quality and colour. Potatoes of the same colour are processed together.
2. Potatoes are kept in storage bins.
3. Potatoes are washed to remove dirt and stones, before moving down a shute to the next stage.
4. Abrasive rollers remove peel. The peel is collected and used as cattle feed.
5. Potatoes are inspected. Unpeeled portions, black spots, and bruises are trimmed. Potatoes with serious defects are removed.
6. Potatoes are cut into French fries. Crinkle-cut fries are sliced by machines with two sets of rapidly rotating knives. They are cut lengthwise to obtain the largest number of long strips. For straight-cut fries, potatoes are forced through a water "gun" which forces them through a cross hatch of knives to give the square shape.
7. Potatoes are blanched in hot water to destroy enzymes and maintain sugar level, ensuring that fries have a constant texture and colour. Excess water, thin slivers or short and broken pieces are removed by vacuum action.
8. Sliced fries go to the fryer, which has a temperature of 200°C. They are fried from half a minute to 5 minutes, depending on the type of potato.
9. Fries are salted or seasoned in the "flavour dispenser," and shaken on a vibrating conveyor to remove excess cooking oil and seasoning. They are then sent to the freezer, which has a temperature of –39°C, and are kept there for 20 minutes.
10. A packaging machine weighs fixed batches of fries and sucks them into plastic bags. The machine then seals the plastic and cuts the bag loose from the roll, at a rate of 35 to 40 bags per minute. The bags are packed into cardboard boxes and stored in refrigerated rooms until shipping.

Figure 11.16 The making of a French fry. Systems vary from one plant to another, but the overall process is similar to the one shown here. At McCain Foods in Florenceville, the process of making French fries is almost completely automatic. Fries are untouched by human hands except in the trim and inspection areas.

EXPLORATIONS

REVIEWING THE IDEAS

1. **a)** Brainstorm a list of food service operators (e.g., hospitals, restaurants, etc.).

   b) How did the introduction of frozen French fries cut costs for these operators?

APPLYING YOUR SKILLS

2. In the role of a McCain's sales representative in 1956, convince a food service operator to buy your frozen French fries.

3. Return to the pie chart you made for activity 3 on page 163. Add a segment to show the contribution of secondary industries in your province.

4. Using examples from this case study, make a diagram to show the links between a secondary industry and primary and tertiary industries.

ANALYZING AND REFLECTING

5. Some economists believe that technology has reduced jobs; others believe that it has created more than it has replaced. What is your opinion? Support your views with examples from the case studies in this chapter, as well as any other relevant examples.

CONNECTING AND EXTENDING

6. **a)** Choose and research one secondary industry in Atlantic Canada. Make a poster of your findings.

   b) As a class, use your posters to create a display entitled "Secondary Industries in Atlantic Canada."

TERTIARY AND QUATERNARY INDUSTRIES

The tertiary sector of the economy provides services rather than goods. People who work in the service sector include workers in the tourism and hospitality industry, stockbrokers, business consultants, clerks, doctors, couriers, and many more. The quaternary sector includes specialized and "high-tech" activities.

Some tertiary and quaternary industries have a close link with the primary and secondary sectors. In the fishing industry, for example, fishers rely on weather forecasters to determine what ocean conditions will be like. They rely on mechanics and technicians to check and repair equipment. Plant owners often rely on marketing specialists to find new opportunities to sell their fish products. Other tertiary and quaternary industries develop wherever there are large groups of people who need services in their everyday lives.

In the Atlantic provinces, as in other parts of Canada, the tertiary and quaternary sectors have become extremely important to the economy. Since the 1950s, these industries have been growing steadily.

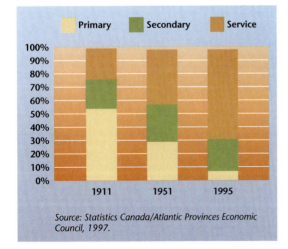

Source: Statistics Canada/Atlantic Provinces Economic Council, 1997.

Figure 11.17 Labour force in Atlantic Canada by occupation group. Describe the trend shown by this graph.

Table 11.12 The contribution of tertiary and quaternary industries to provincial GDP, $ thousands, 1995. Which province relies the most on these sectors?

Province	Value	% of total
Newfoundland and Labrador	5 175 445	80.2
Prince Edward Island	1 313 801	71.6
Nova Scotia	9 924 458	75.6
New Brunswick	7 591 225	74.3

CASE STUDY

The Prince Edward Island Food Technology Centre

Assume you are a potato farmer with an idea for a new type of potato snack. You would like to open a small processing plant on your farm, but you have some important questions that need to be answered. What types of potatoes would be most suitable for your snack? How can you make some test batches? How can you be sure that the method you use is completely safe for consumers? You will be required to provide nutrition labelling on your snack. How will you find out what the label should say?

In a case such as this, the Prince Edward Island Food Technology Centre (FTC) can provide direction. The FTC was established in 1987 on the campus of the University of Prince Edward Island in Charlottetown. It provides scientific and technical expertise to agricultural and fisheries industries. The centre operates from state-of-the-art laboratories, with advanced scientific instruments, on-line data, and statistical systems. The FTC employs about 30 food scientists, technicians, and support staff.

FTC Services

- **Analytical services:** FTC can test a product such as a snack food to determine attributes such as taste, texture, appearance, and colour.
- **Statistical services:** FTC employees record and interpret information from the tests they run on products.
- **Sensory analysis:** The FTC can advise producers on how to improve textures of new products. For example, laboratory tests have been done on the texture, moisture content, sugar content, starch content, and cell walls of different types of potatoes to find out which make the best frozen fries.
- **Food safety:** The Centre can ensure that the new product will remain safe to eat through all manufacturing processes.

Figure 11.18 *Above and below, left:* Testing facilities at the Food Technology Centre. What characteristics of tertiary and quaternary industries are evident in these photographs?

- **Nutritional labelling:** Scientists at the Centre analyze new products for protein, fat, carbohydrates, moisture, vitamins, and minerals. This information is needed for nutritional labels. They also conduct tests that allow manufacturers to make such claims as "low-fat", "low-cholesterol", "salt-free", and "good source of protein" on their packaging.
- **Partnership:** The FTC offers partnerships with any company who wishes to use their services. Producers who use the Centre's services can "pay" for these services by offering FTC part ownership of the new product.

The Atlantic Economy

EXPLORATIONS

REVIEWING THE IDEAS

1. a) What is nutritional labelling?

b) Look at the nutritional labelling on some products that you buy regularly. What does it tell you about the products?

APPLYING YOUR SKILLS

2. a) Return to your pie chart. Add a section showing the contribution of service sector industries in your province.

b) Mark the remaining segment of your chart as "Other." This segment would include resources other than the four described in this chapter and some industries not included in the classification by sector.

c) Write a paragraph describing the contribution of different sectors to the economy of your province.

ANALYZING AND REFLECTING

3. The cost of setting up and running a food technology centre such as the one in Charlottetown is very high. Some of the funds are provided by government. Assume the role of a provincial politician who is trying to explain to taxpayers why the investment in the FTC is worthwhile. Write or present a speech giving your view.

THE NEW ECONOMY

You have seen how the economy of Atlantic Canada is changing. Service industries are the biggest employers. The primary and secondary industries that remain are calling for new technical skills. These changes are not unique to the Atlantic region; they are part of a global shift. Since the 1980s, computers and information technology have revolutionized the world of work. Today, workers with "high-tech" skills and experience are in demand in all sectors of the economy, and the demand for this type of employee will increase in the future. These changes have been given several names, including the "new economy," "the knowledge-based economy," and the "technology economy." Table 11.13 shows many of the characteristics of this new economy. You will learn more about the skills required in the new economy in Chapter 16.

Atlantic Canada moving toward knowledge-based economy

Atlantic Canada clearly has the basic ingredients for success in developing a strong knowledge-based economy, concluded participants in an Atlantic Technology Forum in Halifax....

"Atlantic Canada is on the move," asserted Forum speaker Dr. Kelvin Ogilvie.... "Most importantly, success is occurring in knowledge-based industries."

He highlighted a number of the region's key advantages: "Atlantic Canada is one of the most beautiful and diverse regions of the world. Atlantic Canadians have been incredibly resourceful, have demonstrated a capacity for work and dedication, and are remarkably inventive. Atlantic Canada has produced some of the world's most successful entrepreneurs."

Source: St. John's *Weekly Extra, December 8, 1996, p. 3.*

Table 11.13 Comparison between the "old economy" and the "new economy"

	Old economy	New economy
Main industries	Resource-based	Knowledge-based
Labour force	Manual workers	Information processors
Education	Basic	Advanced
Literacy (ability to read and write)	Desirable	Essential
Reliance	Dependent	Self-reliant
Main organization	Large corporation	Small firms
Entrepreneurship	Undeveloped	Highly developed
Labour relations	Confrontational	Cooperative
Number of industries	Few	Many
Technology	Slow moving; distinct fields	Rapid change; merging fields
Competition	Little foreign competition	Strong foreign competition
Markets	Focus on domestic markets	Focus on global markets
Products	Mass-produced products for mass markets	Complex products for sophisticated consumers
Human resources	Low changing skill requirements for workers	Rapidly changing skill requirements for workers
Areas of growth	In large firms, mainly through attracting outside investment	In new and small firms, through new investment in new developments

Source: Economic Recovery Commission, At the Crossroads (1994), p. 7.

Figure 11.19 Manufacturing electronic circuit boards, Amherst, Nova Scotia. Computers and other communications technology form the basis of the "new economy."

Career Focus: Meet an Entrepreneur

Economists predict that the "new economy" will have a large number of **entrepreneurs** — people who turn ideas into businesses. Some entrepreneurs run small businesses that employ just a few people; others operate businesses that have grown and employ a large number of people. Together, they make a large contribution to our economy. Adeline Misener is an entrepreneur whose idea was to make a business out of the need for workers trained in high-technology skills. She started a business called JOT — Job Oriented Training — based in Fredericton, New Brunswick.

Figure 11.20 Adeline Misener, President, JOT Inc.

Characteristics of an Entrepreneur

- Applies creative ideas
- Takes informed risks
- Uses resources effectively
- Produces goods or services profitably

Q: Where did you get the idea for your business?

A: I was working with the John Howard Society, helping young offenders get back into the workforce. I saw a very strong need to develop programs that would train people to help them get a job.

Q: What kinds of services does JOT provide?

A: JOT Inc. focuses on technology and human resources development. We have four divisions: professional training in computers and information technology, corporate consulting, software and multimedia development, and biosystems engineering. The services we offer include basic computer training, building and applying data bases for customers, producing educational and entertainment software, and developing interactive training systems that can be distributed on the Internet and CD-ROM.

Q: Did you require a large investment to get started?

A: Not really. I was very fortunate at the very beginning in that I won a contract to provide training services that gave the company some financing up-front.

Q: Why did you select Fredericton as the location for JOT?

A: New Brunswick is an acknowledged leader on the "information highway." Here, we have access to a large network of technology specialists, strong business support, and a tradition of cooperation and collaboration that's hard to match. Fredericton is home to more than 70 percent of the province's knowledge industries and is rapidly becoming the advanced learning technologies and multi-media capital of Canada.

Q: How many employees do you have? How did you obtain them? What skills and attitudes did they need to have?

A: The people who work here are the most important resource the company has. Our success depends on our human resources. The number of employees fluctuates between 25 and 50, depending on current projects. We advertise positions that need highly qualified and specialized individuals, and we also match resumes that we get with openings, as they arise. Our employees need a good academic background, but more importantly, they need communication skills. We are a customer-service company, so our

176 ECONOMICS

employees need to be able to communicate effectively with our clients.

Q: What kinds of equipment do you use?

A: For our software development, we use the most advanced multimedia machines available. In addition, we have three computer labs in the building where we do training. We also have four other sites in other parts of the province for technology training.

Q: Do you experience much competition?

A: Yes; we have very heavy competition in all of our areas. We compete well, though, by maintaining high quality and standards. We know that we need to offer our customers service, we need to care about our customers, and we always have to be thinking of innovative ways to make ourselves just a little bit different.

Q: How do you develop your markets?

A: We inform potential clients of our services by going to trade shows, by showing our wares, by using e-mail, by developing a home page on the World Wide Web, by talking to people, and just by letting people know who we are and offering good service so they come back again. We also rely on word of mouth: satisfied clients will recommend us to others. Most importantly, we ensure that the products and services offered by JOT Inc. are of international standard.

To hold on to our markets, we must always be looking ahead, watching developments, talking to people. We need to know what the big software and hardware producers are developing, so we can design training programs. We need to watch the marketplace to see what consumers are buying to get a sense of what sorts of software programs are in demand. We have to determine where the big markets are, and then gear ourselves towards that.

EXPLORATIONS

REVIEWING THE IDEAS

1. According to the article on page 174, what does Atlantic Canada have to offer knowledge-based industries?

2. **a)** Briefly describe some important differences between the "old economy" and the "new economy."

    b) Explain how these changes might affect you.

APPLYING YOUR SKILLS

3. Make a chart to show how JOT matches the characteristics of the new economy, as shown in Table 11.13.

CONNECTING AND EXTENDING

4. **a)** Work in a small group. First brainstorm the sorts of risks an entrepreneur takes. Then brainstorm the possible rewards of entrepreneurship.

    b) Review this chapter to find as many examples of entrepreneurs as you can. What characteristics do all of these people seem to share?

    c) Interview an entrepreneur from your community to find out about his or her experience.

    d) If you were interested in becoming an entrepreneur, what skills do you think you would need? Make a list of skills. Pick three of the skills that you think are most important and indicate how and where you might be able to develop them (e.g., through college, specific work experience, etc.).

5. Kelvin Ogilvie notes that Atlantic Canada has produced some world-renowned inventors and entrepreneurs. Investigate one famous Atlantic Canadian inventor or entrepreneur and present a report of your findings.

SEEING THE BIG PICTURE

1. Use the chart below to match your interests and strengths to a type of occupation.

2. Find out about some of the jobs in the type of occupation you have chosen. Your school's counselling centre should be able to provide information.

3. Identify a few jobs that might interest you, and then focus on just one. In what sector does this job fall? Do you think job prospects in this sector are good? Explain.

4. Make a list of educational qualifications you will need to do that job.

Working with Ideas and Information

I enjoy:
- Expressing myself through writing, music, or art
- Doing experiments or researching a topic
- Solving puzzles or problems
- Studying or reading

Types of occupation:
Arts and entertainment
Business and finance
Scientific research
Law

Working with People

I enjoy:
- Caring for, helping, or serving people
- Persuading people or negotiating
- Working as a member of a team
- Leading or supervising others

Types of occupation:
Health care
Education
Tourism
Religion
Sales

Working with Things

I enjoy:
- Using tools, machines, or equipment
- Making things with my hands
- Maintaining or fixing things
- Finding out how things work

Types of occupation:
Equipment repair
Manufacturing
Transportation
Construction
Trades

Source: Adapted from D. DesRivieres et al., In Business: Work and the Canadian Economy (Scarborough: Prentice Hall Canada, 1997), p. 47.

CHAPTER 12

Our Economic Outlook

Figure 12.1 Chad Smith, of the rock group Red Hot Chili Peppers, and many other first-rate drummers around the world use Sabian cymbals made in the small town of Meductic, New Brunswick, shown above.

The main street of Meductic, New Brunswick, population 254, is as busy as an abandoned western movie town on a hot afternoon, with tumbleweed rolling past the saloon. But beyond this single-street settlement of white clapboard houses stand two buildings that are extremely important to the world of music. On one side of the road is a small factory built in 1969. On the other is a much larger facility, opened in 1996. These buildings are the production facilities of Sabian Ltd., the second largest manufacturer of cymbals in the world.

- What does the Sabian Cymbal company tell us about our economic links with other provinces and other countries?
- How does the economy of the Atlantic region compare with economies in the rest of Canada and the world?
- How important will global links be in the future economy of the region?

Sabian Cymbals: An International Success Story

Not everyone plays cymbals. Some young people are even discouraged from playing them! Fortunately for Sabian Cymbals, these instruments are in demand by music makers around the world, making Sabian a highly successful company. Among the outstanding performers who use Sabian cymbals are Phil Collins (Genesis), Alan White (Oasis), Chad Smith (Red Hot Chili Peppers), Steve Ferrone (Tom Petty and the Heartbreakers), and Mike Portnoy (Dream Theater). In addition, many of the world's leading orchestras use Sabian cymbals, including the Berlin Philharmonic, the Montreal Symphony, and the New York Philharmonic. Drum corps and marching bands throughout the world also choose Sabian cymbals.

Locating at Meductic

Sabian was formerly owned by the Zildjian company, based in Massachusetts, USA. Through the 1960s, the use of cymbals increased with the growing popularity of rock 'n' roll. Demand for Zildjian cymbals grew, especially when Ringo Starr of the Beatles started using them. In 1969, Zildjian opened a **branch plant** in New Brunswick, in order to avoid paying import taxes on cymbals they produced for Canada and Europe.

There were several other reasons for locating in New Brunswick. Wages were lower than in the United States, and New Brunswickers had a reputation for producing goods of the best quality. In addition, many were farmers and forestry workers, so they were familiar with tools and machinery. The factory could be built near the Trans-Canada Highway, which would allow for easy transportation of raw materials and finished products. Lastly, Robert Zildjian, son of the owner, enjoyed the fishing and scenery of the St. John River in the Meductic area. He notes today, when asked about the advantages of manufacturing in Meductic, "It lacks all urban problems."

Sabian was established as a separate company in 1982, following the death of Zildjian's founder and a split between his sons. Starting over was not easy for the new company, and sales fell in each of the first three years. The situation improved when Sabian developed a new series of cymbals that gave drummers greater control over the sound they produced. The company also adopted aggressive marketing strategies, sending employees around the world to meet with salespeople and customers.

Figure 12.2 Sabian Cymbal sales 1983–96

Figure 12.3 A good drum kit. Percussionists may use 20 or more pieces, with hi-hats counting as two cymbals, together with half a dozen drums or so, to produce the desired effect.

Making Cymbals

Figure 12.4 To produce bronze, raw materials (mainly copper and tin) are smelted in exact proportions in an electric furnace. The molten bronze is then poured into moulds to make castings.

Figure 12.5 The castings are shaped in a hot-rolling mill that makes it possible to work the metal, which would otherwise be very brittle.

Figure 12.6 Workers then shape the cymbals by pressing and hammering them.

Figure 12.7 Some cymbals are hand finished while others are finished by machine.

Figure 12.8 The cymbals are then shaped on a lathe to the required thickness, smoothed, rounded, polished, and labelled.

Figure 12.9 The finished product, each with its own musical qualities, is then tested prior to packing and shipping. What skills would a good cymbal tester require?

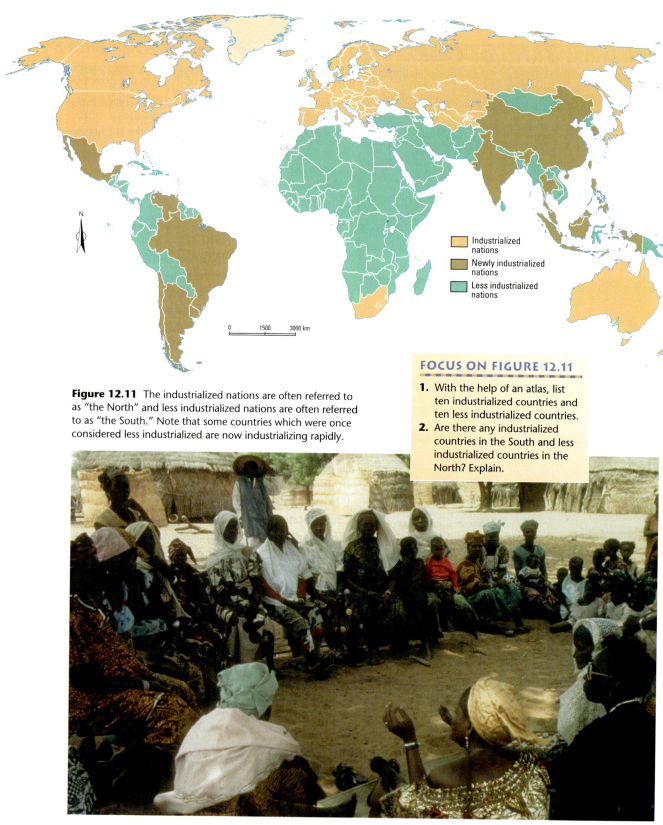

Figure 12.11 The industrialized nations are often referred to as "the North" and less industrialized nations are often referred to as "the South." Note that some countries which were once considered less industrialized are now industrializing rapidly.

FOCUS ON FIGURE 12.11

1. With the help of an atlas, list ten industrialized countries and ten less industrialized countries.
2. Are there any industrialized countries in the South and less industrialized countries in the North? Explain.

Figure 12.12 The Canadian International Development Agency (CIDA) was set up by the Canadian government to coordinate aid to less industrialized countries such as Niger. This photograph shows a health class for women and their children. The main aim is to help people in these countries develop their own solutions to their economic problems in harmony with their natural environment. Why is interaction between the countries of the North and the South important?

The Atlantic Provinces

Just as some countries of the world are wealthier than others, so some provinces in Canada are richer than others. The wealth gap among provinces is known as **regional disparity**. As Table 12.2 shows, the **GDP per capita** in the Atlantic provinces is lower than the Canadian average.

Many people argue that a lower GDP does not necessarily mean a lower quality of life. Other factors contribute to a very good quality of life in the region, as shown in Figure 12.13. In addition, GDP does not account for self-sufficiency. For example, produce from the garden may supplement income and better people's lives, but it is not included in the GDP.

There are several reasons why the average GDP is lower in Atlantic Canada. First, incomes are lower. In 1994 the average salary was $31 737 in the Atlantic provinces, while the national average was $35 861. Second, the unemployment rate has been higher in Atlantic Canada for much of the twentieth century. Much of the employment available in the Atlantic provinces is **seasonal**, which means a large number of workers are employed for only part of the year. Major resource industries such as agriculture, fishing, and forestry operate on a seasonal basis, as do many of the manufacturing industries that process the resources. Tourism, too, has a limited season, from late May until October. In addition, as you have seen, many primary industries have been changing.

Table 12.2 GDP per capita, Canada and the Atlantic provinces, 1995.

Canada	$ 26 324
Newfoundland and Labrador	17 306
Prince Edward Island	19 037
Nova Scotia	20 004
New Brunswick	20 830

Source: Statistics Canada, Cansim Matrices 2623–2631, 4997, 4998 and 6950.

FOCUS ON FIGURE 12.13

1. Which factors contribute most to a high quality of life in your province?
2. Considering the GDP (Table 12.2) and the quality of life indicators, why might people choose to live in Atlantic Canada? What other factors might influence their decision?

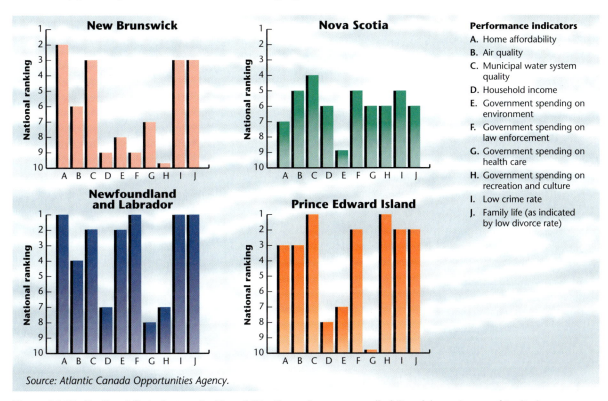

Source: Atlantic Canada Opportunities Agency.

Performance indicators
A. Home affordability
B. Air quality
C. Municipal water system quality
D. Household income
E. Government spending on environment
F. Government spending on law enforcement
G. Government spending on health care
H. Government spending on recreation and culture
I. Low crime rate
J. Family life (as indicated by low divorce rate)

Figure 12.13 Quality of life indicators: Ranking of Atlantic provinces among all of Canada's provinces and territories.

OUR ECONOMIC OUTLOOK

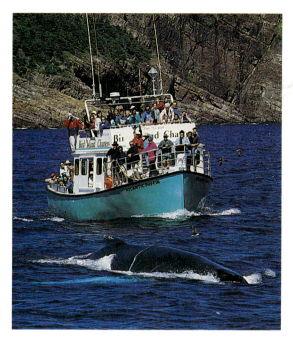

Figure 12.14 Many industries in the Atlantic provinces create seasonal employment, although **diversification** of the economy is creating a wider range of jobs.

Another reason for disparity may be the **brain drain** from Atlantic Canada. Almost 250 000 people have migrated from the region in the last 30 years. These migrants tend to be the younger, better-educated members of the labour force. (See Table 4.3 on page 52 for a chart of **outmigration** from the Atlantic provinces.) People with a higher level of education tend to earn the most money. As a result, Atlantic Canada has not had as many high-wage earners as other parts of the country. At the same time, few immigrants to Canada settle in Atlantic Canada; most head for Vancouver, Toronto, and Montreal.

> "All the research I have examined indicates immigration is good, especially when it brings human capital [experience, education, knowledge] to Canada, or if it brings investment capital money. We should be trying to attract more immigrants to Atlantic Canada, to get a share of that knowledge and capital."
>
> Source: Professor W.J. Milne, University of New Brunswick, quoted in Atlantic Review, July/August, 1994.

DID YOU KNOW...?

Across Canada, the population is aging. On average, Canadians are living longer than they did in the past. In addition, Canada experienced a **baby boom** from the mid-1940s to the early 1960s. As "baby-boomers" age, the number of seniors in our society will increase dramatically.

The baby boom has had an important impact on the economy. For example, many new schools were built in the 1960s to educate the baby-boomers and companies began to target teenagers as a large new market for their products. Baby-boomers are going to have an even greater effect on society when they reach retirement. It is likely that costs for social and medical services for our aging population will increase. On the other hand, many seniors remain active and healthy, and enjoy retirement as a time of increased leisure and travel. There will probably be many more job opportunities in servicing the needs of seniors.

Figure 12.15
Changing age structure in the Atlantic provinces

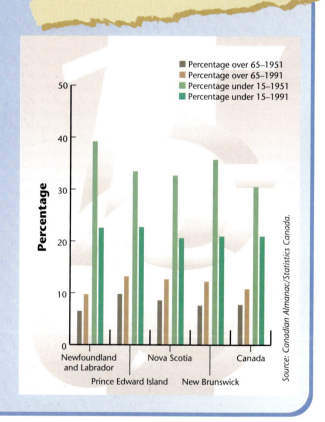

EXPLORATIONS

APPLYING YOUR SKILLS

1. Assume you have a penpal in Niger. Write a letter describing conditions in Atlantic Canada. In your letter, include at least three questions to your penpal about life in Niger.

ANALYZING AND REFLECTING

2. Work with a partner or in a small group.

   a) Discuss the following topics:

   i) Why do so many young people leave the Atlantic provinces for other parts of Canada and for foreign countries?

   ii) What is the effect of this outmigration on Atlantic Canada?

   iii) What can be done to encourage young people to stay in the region?

   b) Present your ideas to the class.

CONNECTING AND EXTENDING

3. a) Make a chart showing industries in your community that offer seasonal employment and those that offer year-round employment. Categorize the industries according to economic sector.

   b) At the bottom of the chart, write a few sentences comparing the importance of both kinds of employment to your community.

4. a) Make a list of the types of jobs that you think are likely to become available as a result of the increasing number of seniors.

   b) Find out more about one of the jobs you have listed. Write a short description of that job, including skills and qualifications required and main duties. Alternatively, think like an entrepreneur, and describe a business that would cater to the needs of seniors.

   c) Brainstorm other emerging opportunities in the new economy. Choose one that interests you, and discuss.

5. Would you prefer to stay in Atlantic Canada or to leave? Provide reasons for your answer, including push and pull factors and quality of life indicators.

ATLANTIC CANADA: LOOKING FOR SOLUTIONS

Despite regional disparity, the economy of Atlantic Canada has been maintained and is now showing signs of growth. To ensure that important services such as health care and education are similar throughout the country, the Canadian government introduced a system of **transfer payments**. Since 1957, it has transferred some of the taxes collected in provinces with the highest GDPs to provinces with lower GDPs. All provinces except Ontario, Alberta, and British Columbia have received transfer payments.

At the same time, the federal government has tried to encourage economic development. For example, in 1987, it established the Atlantic Canada Opportunities Agency (ACOA). This agency encourages new businesses by providing business loans and expertise, and helping companies to make **strategic alliances** — partnerships that will help them develop. The aim is to help the Atlantic economy **diversify**, by producing a wider range of goods and services. A more diverse economy means we will rely less on traditional industries that may be in decline or that offer mainly seasonal employment.

Since 1990, the federal government has been tightening its overall budget. Transfer payments and funding for agencies such as ACOA have shrunk. At the same time, the economy of the Atlantic region has started to grow. Many analysts believe that the stronger economy is the result of a large number of new small businesses and a growing spirit of entrepreneurship. In early 1997, the Atlantic Provinces Economic Council reported that the percentage of entrepreneurs in Atlantic Canada had risen from 7 percent to 14 percent.

The Importance of Trade

In the search for activities to boost the Atlantic economy, trade plays a central role. The economy of the Atlantic provinces developed through trade with Europe, the West Indies, and New England. After Confederation, more emphasis was placed on trade with the rest of Canada. Today, the Atlantic provinces trade with the world. International and interprovincial trade provided employment for about 222 000 people in Atlantic Canada in 1990. This number has risen as exports increased dramatically from 6 billion dollars in 1992 to more than 10 billion dollars in 1995.

Table 12.3 Atlantic exports, $ thousands, 1995

Paper and paperboard	2 065 257
Mineral fuel products	1 873 565
Fish and crustaceans	1 672 441
Wood pulp	1 218 498
Rubber and products	688 112
Ores	677 014
Processed fish and crustaceans	162 705
Processed vegetables and fruit	153 286
Machinery and boilers	127 096
Steel products	89 880
Plastics and products	88 454
Iron and steel concentrates	60 095
Lead and products	50 137
Special class products	47 406
Furniture	41 298
Animal fodder	29 579
Inorganic chemicals	29 284
Art of stone and plaster	27 264
Optical, photo, lenses	24 423
Chemical products	13 457
Others	1 329 649
Total	**10 468 900**

Source: Statistics Canada, Catalogue # 65-003.

FOCUS ON TABLE 12.3

1. Construct a bar graph to show the comparative importance of products exported from the Atlantic provinces.
2. What percentage of the total value of exports is made up from the four leading products?

Figure 12.16 A multi-billion dollar Gravity Base Structure (GBS) went into operation in 1997, drilling wells and extracting oil at the Hibernia oil field off Newfoundland's east coast. How will the Hibernia project contribute to the economy of the region? Consider its effect on all sectors of the economy.

Focus on an Issue

Free Trade

Since the late 1950s, world trade patterns have been changing. Many countries now belong to **trading blocs**. These organizations encourage trade among member nations, especially by **free trade** — that is, eliminating **tariffs**, or taxes on goods imported from other member countries. In 1989, Canada joined a trading partnership when the government signed a free-trade agreement with the United States. In 1992, this agreement was extended to include Mexico, with the signing of the **North American Free Trade Agreement** (**NAFTA**). In 1996, Chile was drawn into the agreement. There are plans to include, eventually, all of South America in a consolidated Americas trading bloc.

There has been much disagreement about the benefits of free-trade agreements. On the one hand, some producers benefit because new markets open up for their products. As a result of NAFTA, for example, trade with Mexico — a market three times that of Canada — is expected to expand. Some goods that will likely flow to Mexico in greater volumes include forestry products, iron ore (from Labrador), non-ferrous metals (especially from New Brunswick), cattle, meat, fish, and shell fish. In return, Mexico will supply Canada with larger amounts of coffee and vegetables that do not grow in our climate.

Table 12.4 Major trade blocs and date of formation

1957	EU:	European Union
1967	ASEAN:	Association of South East Asian Nations
1970	WAEC:	West African Economic Community
1973	CARICOM:	Caribbean Community
1979	SADCC:	Southern Africa Development Coordination Community
1980	LAIA:	Latin American Integration Association
1994	NAFTA:	North American Free Trade Agreement

On the other hand, some local producers find that their goods cannot compete with the cheaper imports that have begun to enter the Canadian market. Some goods can be produced more cheaply in other countries for a variety of reasons. For example, the growing season is longer in the United States and Mexico. In addition, wages and benefits may be lower, the cost of borrowing money for automation may be lower, and health and environmental standards may be lower. These producers believe that NAFTA could force them out of business.

ANALYZING THE ISSUE

1. List three Mexican goods available in your community and three goods produced in your community that are exported to Mexico.

2. a) Do a survey of business people in your area, asking for their opinion on free trade with the countries of North and South America.

   b) Make an organizer to list arguments they give both in favour of and against free trade.

3. Find three articles in your newspaper that describe businesses in the area. Describe how these businesses may have benefited or suffered as a result of trade agreements.

4. Write a letter or make a speech giving your opinion of free trade.

Figure 12.17 Prime Minister Jean Chrétien and the provincial premiers have led several trade missions to countries in Asia, including China, India, and Korea. Here they are shown in Korea in 1997. Why do you think they have focused on Asian countries?

OUR ECONOMIC OUTLOOK

CASE STUDY

The new economy, government policies, and private efforts have all contributed to an Atlantic economy that is steadily growing and diversifying. A number of new industries have joined the region's exporters. This group of case studies will examine four: one connected with the land, one with the sea, one with the air, and one with space.

ON THE LAND: ATLANTIC-ALLSTAR GENETICS

In 1991, Larry Jewett started Atlantic-Allstar Genetics (AAG) in Keswick, New Brunswick, with financial help from ACOA. His company started by shipping frozen cow embryos to milk-producing countries throughout the world. After several years, the company began shipping pregnant cows overseas from the port of Saint John. As can be seen in Figure 12.18, his business has grown rapidly.

Figure 12.18 Atlantic-Allstar Genetics pregnant-cow exports

The United Kingdom and Eire have bought pedigree (purebred) stock to upgrade and replace existing herds, especially after the required slaughter of many British cattle following an outbreak of *Bovine Spongiform Encephalopathy* (mad cow disease) in 1996. Most of AAG's customers, however, want cows that will increase their milk production, so they import pregnant *non*-pedigree cows, which are less expensive.

AAG draws on cattle from all parts of Canada for its shipments. The cattle are transported in locally designed and built containers, which are lifted from the dockside onto the ships. Each shipment calls for careful organization. As Debbie Graye, AAG's office manager, explains: "There's lots of red tape, inspectors, insurance brokers, customs officials, shipping contracts, and port authorities!"

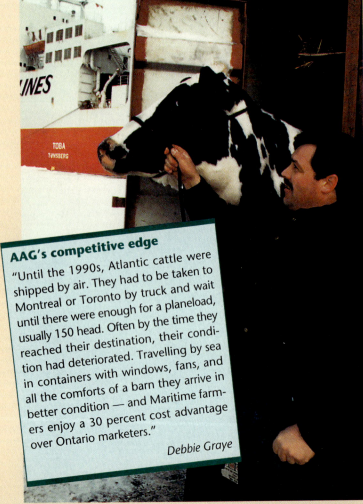

AAG's competitive edge

"Until the 1990s, Atlantic cattle were shipped by air. They had to be taken to Montreal or Toronto by truck and wait until there were enough for a planeload, usually 150 head. Often by the time they reached their destination, their condition had deteriorated. Travelling by sea in containers with windows, fans, and all the comforts of a barn they arrive in better condition — and Maritime farmers enjoy a 30 percent cost advantage over Ontario marketers."

Debbie Graye

Figure 12.19 Larry Jewett bids bon voyage to a Holstein cow. Jewett says aggressive marketing accounts for the company's success: "We've been prepared to take risks, marketing for the most part in unknown territory."

From the Sea: Blue Mussels, Prince Edward Island

In 1995, the mussel harvest in Prince Edward Island was as large, by weight, as the lobster catch. Why have mussels become so popular? Phyllis Duffy, of Enterprise PEI, a government-sponsored marketing agency, notes, "weight for weight they have the protein content of beef but far fewer calories and a very low fat content. They are also a good source of calcium, iron, thiamin, and riboflavin — all at a surprisingly low cost. Mussels may be used as an appetizer or as a main course; they are big, clean, sweet, and tender, and because they're grown on long lines suspended in the clear waters surrounding the island, Island Blue mussels grow quickly and are free of sand and grit."

Mussel Cultivation

Some 100 aquaculturists around Malpeque Bay are benefiting from this industry. They grow mussels on long lines (often 200 metres) anchored at each end and supported by floats. Water draining into the bays and estuaries in the area are rich in fertilizer that pours off fields where farmers grow potatoes and other crops. In the sea this fertilizer encourages the growth of phytoplankton, a major part of the mussel diet.

While suspended, mussels may fall victim to such predators as eider ducks, crabs, and starfish. Aquaculturists frighten off eider ducks and other birds with an electronic device that emits a high-pitched sound when the birds come near. Hydrate of lime is used to control starfish.

Sometimes shellfish toxins, from certain plankton, cause health problems, so mussels are rigorously tested before marketing to make sure they are safe to be eaten. Water temperature can also present problems. If the water temperature rises much above 20°C, which is not unusual during July and August, the mussels may drop to the sea floor and die. To combat this problem some farmers increase the depth of the longline so that the mussels are in deeper, cooler water. Similarly, mussels may be lowered in winter to warmer, ice-free waters.

Farmers harvest the mussels when they are 18 to 24 months old. They can be harvested throughout the year except during summer. The summer months follow the spawning period, after which mussels need time to reach their peak condition. Winter harvesting may involve the use of a chain saw, to cut holes in the ice, and divers to retrieve the ends of the longlines.

After harvesting, mussels are graded, washed, and cooled — mainly by machines. They then go to market. PEI Blue mussels are served in restaurants throughout North America. Ambitious aquaculturists can sometimes sell their mussels in western Europe during April and May, when European supplies are not normally available.

Table 12.5 Production of mussels in Prince Edward Island (kg)

Year	Production
1978	11 800
1990	2 500 000
1991	3 350 000
1992	4 100 000
1993	4 500 000
1994	5 900 000
1995	7 250 000

Source: Enterprise Prince Edward Island, Charlottetown.

Figure 12.20 Mussel aquaculture

IN THE AIR: INSTRUMAR LIMITED

The Instrumar company of St. John's, Newfoundland, has devised technology that makes flying safer. In winter, ice that builds up on the outer surfaces of an aircraft can present a serious hazard. The ice affects the aircraft's aerodynamics, making it extremely difficult to control during takeoff and landing. Aircraft must be sprayed with de-icing fluid to avoid the danger.

In the past, pilots have had to make a visual inspection of the aircraft before takeoff, to decide whether or not to de-ice the wings. Visual inspections are not always easy or effective, especially at night or in stormy weather. Dr. Stuart Inkpen, president of Instrumar, worked with a number of engineers in St. John's to develop a sensor that detects the presence of ice, snow, de-icing fluids, and water. The sensor determines whether or not de-icing is necessary. In this way, it reduces delays in takeoff, reduces the use of environmentally unfriendly sprays, reduces the cost of flying, and increases flying safety.

After the sensor was first designed, Instrumar executives realized that they needed help in refining and manufacturing the device. With help from ACOA, Instrumar made a **strategic alliance** with a company that could help it put its plans into action. It joined with a partner, Allied Signal Canada, an Ontario aerospace company. Together the companies will be able to develop the device further. In alliances with other companies, Instrumar is developing sensors to measure and monitor a variety of other situations.

Figure 12.21 Instrumar uses high-technology to analyze when de-icing is required.

Figure 12.22 De-icing, or removing built-up ice, prevents accidents during takeoff and landing.

Into Space: The Aerospace Industry Association and IMP Aerospace

Nova Scotia gave the British Empire its first aircraft, the *Silver Dart*, in 1909. The province is now helping develop an International Space Station, *Alpha R*. This space station will be the largest combined international technology effort ever undertaken. The United States, Europe, Japan, and Canada will all co-operate in the project. The first space-shuttle mission to carry hardware to space for the assembly of the station was scheduled for late 1997, with operation of the station planned to begin by 2000.

In 1995, the Aerospace Industry Association (AIANS) was established to represent the aerospace industries of Nova Scotia, some of which are involved with the Canadian Space Agency. One such company is IMP Aerospace of Halifax. Together with a number of companies from across Canada, IMP is building the Mobile Serving System (MSS). Following initial work by the Canadarm operating from the shuttle, the MSS will be used to help assemble and maintain space station *Alpha R* while it orbits earth. It will move equipment, recover satellites, assist astronauts, and berth shuttle orbiters.

Meanwhile, down on earth, AIANS will be helping member aerospace companies pursue further aerospace contracts around the world for the benefit of Nova Scotia. The primary aim of AIANS is to create strategic alliances among members, bringing them together so that Nova Scotia aerospace companies will complement and help one another.

Figure 12.24 Model of international space station *Alpha R*

▲ **Figure 12.23** Engineers from IMP. Projects such as *Alpha R* employ many people, and reduce the brain drain from Atlantic Canada. If you were planning on becoming an engineer, how could the work of these engineers benefit your future career?

EXPLORATIONS

REVIEWING THE IDEAS

1. Look back at the characteristics of the new economy listed in Table 11.13 (page 175). Make an organizer showing evidence of the new economy in the four case studies presented here.

2. Give examples from the four case studies of co-operation at the following levels:
   a) provincial   **b)** national   **c)** international

APPLYING YOUR SKILLS

3. Choose one of the companies described in the case studies. Prepare a brochure or advertisement for the product or service provided by the company. Be sure to focus carefully on an appropriate audience.

CONNECTING AND EXTENDING

4. The use of natural resources by industry sometimes causes difficulties. For example, boating off Prince Edward Island was disrupted by mussel lines. A solution was reached when mussel growers agreed to anchor the mesh tubing socks below the water.

   a) Describe instances in your community in which the use of resources by industry is compatible or incompatible with resource use by the public.

   b) Choose one case in which resource use is incompatible. Suggest solutions to the problem. You will find the problem-solving approach on page 78 (activity 3a) useful.

5. Work in a group to suggest a new manufacturing industry for your area.

   a) Brainstorm ideas for a suitable product.

   b) Consider the impact of the new industry on your community. Include demand for the product, location of the manufacturing plant, plans for financing, availability of labour, skill requirements for labour, sources of raw materials, transport of raw materials and finished product, location of markets, and environmental impact.

   c) Consider whether or not your company will need to make any strategic alliances. What specific benefits would you seek from a partnership?

   d) List any problems that might result from your new manufacturing industry.

SEEING THE BIG PICTURE

1. Look around your home at various products, such as food, clothing, footwear, appliances, books, electronic games, and sports equipment. Note the country of origin of these items, and plot the information on an outline map of the world. Be sure to include a legend and give your map a creative title.

2. **a)** Develop a definition of the term "global economy."
   b) In what ways do the industries mentioned in this chapter show that the Atlantic provinces are part of a global economy?

3. Explain, with reference to the examples contained in this chapter, why so many goods and services are developed and exchanged throughout the world instead of being produced and consumed locally.

4. Prepare a chart to suggest trading possibilities of the Atlantic provinces with each of the following countries: Niger, Chile, Mexico, Israel, Japan, and the United States. Use the following headings for the columns of your chart:
   - Country
   - Relative location
   - Population
   - GDP per person
   - Locally produced goods and services that might be exported to the Atlantic provinces
   - Goods and services that might be imported from the Atlantic provinces
   - Trading difficulties (e.g., a shortage of money to pay for imported goods or services, imports would displace workers, excessive distance between the two countries)

UNIT 4

Technology

CHAPTER 13 *Technology: Past to Present*
What is technology?
How have we used technology over the centuries?

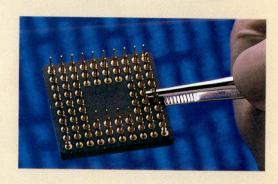

CHAPTER 14 *Technological Links*
How has technology affected transportation and communications in Atlantic Canada?

CHAPTER 15 *Technology and Resources*
What has been the effect of technology on our resource industries?

CHAPTER 16 *Technology at Work*
How has technology affected the way Atlantic Canadians work?
What is the social impact of new technology in the region?

CHAPTER 13
Technology: Past to Present

Figure 13.1 *Top*: Alexander Graham Bell experiments with the technology of flight. *Centre*: Technology today. *Bottom*: Bell and his wife Mabel, whose hearing impairment helped to inspire his invention of the telephone.

If you could travel back in time to the Bras d'Or Lakes of Cape Breton at the turn of this century, you might be surprised at some of the things you would see. The town of Baddeck was the second home of Alexander Graham Bell. We know Bell as the inventor of the telephone, but he also conducted pioneering experiments with human flight, built hydrofoil craft for travelling on water, and engaged in experimental farming. *Beinn Bhreagh*, the Bell estate, was more than a tranquil retreat for the family of one of the world's great inventors. It was a centre that attracted great minds and placed the village at the cutting edge of invention.

- If Bell were alive today, what would inspire his great curiosity: Space travel? Telecommunications? Genetic engineering?
- How have we used our inventions — our technology — to change our physical world over the centuries?

WHAT IS TECHNOLOGY?

For a moment, look around you. Divide all of the things that you see into two categories: naturally occurring and human-made. All those things made, or manufactured, are products of our technology. **Technology** is the application of knowledge and skills to make goods or to provide services. It includes the tools and machines that people use to convert natural resources into the items they need. It also includes the methods they use to convert their resources. Technology is, therefore, both **product** and **process**.

Technology is any product or process that allows humans to extend their natural abilities. Let's return to the example of Alexander Graham Bell. Look at some of his inventions listed below. How did each of these forms of technology extend human abilities?

Table 13.1 Some of Alexander Graham Bell's inventions

- The telephone, developed after experiments in voice communication with people who were hearing impaired. Bell's mother and his wife Mabel were both hearing impaired. Bell and his father both worked as teachers of the deaf.

- The hydrofoil, a craft that could skim across the top of water at great speed.

- A sheep that would birth twins, triplets, or even litters of lambs. Unfortunately neither the wool nor meat of these sheep was of good quality.

- A metal detector to locate bullets inside a wounded person, developed when President Garfield of the United States was lying near death after being shot by an assassin. The invention did not save the president but remained in use until the development of the X-ray a generation later.

- A "vacuum jacket," a precursor of the iron lung. This invention was motivated by the death of two of Bell's children in infancy.

Figure 13.2 Bell developed a "photophone," which could transmit voice using light waves. It could only work with an unobstructed view, so was dismissed as a novelty. Its importance was not recognized until a century later, when fibre-optic cable was introduced to carry information rapidly over long distances.

TECHNOLOGY AND CHANGE

Technology is one of the most powerful agents of change in any society. New inventions bring new ways of doing things. Change has been part of all societies in the past. Today, however, there are some important differences. In particular, the pace of change is far more rapid than ever before, and the scope is far greater, with the impact of new technology stretching around the globe. Exciting developments in areas such as medicine, communications, home technology, workplace technology, and many other aspects of life are changing the way people live in all parts of the world.

> **FOCUS ON FIGURE 13.3**
> 1. Identify important forms of technology in each of these images.
> 2. Speculate on the impact of each form on the lifestyle of people in each period.

Figure 13.3 New technology sometimes has such an important impact that it is thought of as a "revolution."

Revolution in Agriculture

Early humans moved from one place to another in search of food. When they learned to plant seeds, use tools, domesticate animals, and practise irrigation, their lifestyle changed dramatically. As civilizations developed, people learned how to produce more food, they became healthier, and lived longer.

Revolution in Industry

As civilization developed, so did the focus on scientific thinking, new ideas, and innovative ways of doing things. Dramatic changes in the area of manufacturing, transportation, and communication further transformed everyday life.

The "High-Tech" Revolution

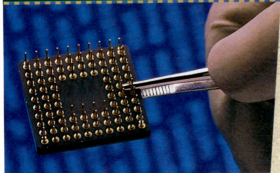

Today's "high-tech" revolution is based on the application of scientific knowledge that is increasing at an astonishing rate. The key to many new developments is the tiny but immensely powerful microchip.

> The computer chip — that small piece of sand, glass, and metal containing the capability to process information — has reshaped and changed our world. You will find computer chips everywhere — not just inside computers, but inside your car, your telephone, in some cases even your microwave and toaster ovens.
>
> And so far, for the most part, all these little computer chips have lived in splendid isolation. They've existed mostly by themselves, doing what they are supposed to do, and usually doing that quite well. That is about to change. The Internet is making all of these little computer chips aware of each other and providing them with the ability to link together.
>
> Digitize the information of the world, add the Internet, and you have a global computer of massive proportions.
>
> Source: J. Carroll and R. Broadhead, 1997 Canadian Internet Handbook (Scarborough: Prentice Hall Canada), p. 9.

A Global Technological Time Line

Agriculture

50 000 to 4 000 BC Humans learn to plant seeds and use simple farming tools.

3000 BC Egyptian farmers use cattle and horses as draft animals.

2500 BC Irrigation used for farming in Egypt, the Middle East, and India.

2000 BC Cotton cultivated by Aboriginal peoples of Peru.

1000 BC Chinese farmers use plant-based insecticides on crops.

1000 BC Agriculture develops in sub-Saharan Africa, north of the equator.

100 BC First wheeled plows used in southern Europe.

100 AD Agriculture spreads in southern Africa.

700 AD Water wheels used to turn grind stones in flour mills in Europe.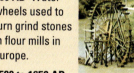

1500 to 1650 AD Crops grown by Aboriginal peoples in the Americas, such as potatoes, tobacco, and tomatoes, introduced into Europe.

1550 to 1800 New methods of crop rotation, seed selection, and mechanization bring Agricultural Revolution to Western Europe.

1785 Cast iron plow shares, drawn by horses, developed in England.

1829 First steam-powered tractor developed in United States.

1884 First chemical fungicide and fertilizers.

1889 First tractor with internal-combustion engine.

1980s First genetically engineered plants and animals developed for commercial use.

1990s Computerized management of livestock herds becomes common.

Manufacturing and Industry

50 000 to 4000 BC Fire used to melt copper, tin, gold, and silver to craft metal jewelry, tools, and utensils.

3500 BC In Egypt and Middle East, copper and tin mixed to make a stronger alloy, bronze.

2000 BC Bellows used to melt copper in western Africa.

1500 BC Furnaces capable of smelting iron developed in Egypt and Middle East.

100 AD Use of iron spreads in southern Africa.

285 AD Pappus of Alexandria describes five machines of the ancient world: the pulley, the screw, the lever, the wedge, and the cogwheel.

615 AD Petroleum, known as "burning water," used in Japan.

720 to 800 AD Arab scientists begin the study of chemistry.

1000 to 1500 AD Metals, cogwheels, and springs used in clock-work devices in Europe.

1400 AD Crank and connecting rod mechanical system developed in Germany, allowing inventors to turn lateral motion (e.g., a piston) into rotary motion (e.g., the wheels of a car).

1705 Development of steam engine starts the Industrial Revolution.

1800 Development of the battery ushers in age of electricity.

1860 First internal combustion engine, developed in France, brings new industrial growth and makes automobile possible.

1933 Electron microscope developed in Germany, allowing for developments in microbiology and nuclear medicine.

1951 First nuclear power station for civilian use opens in Russia.

1962 First industrial robots mass produced in United States.

1980s and 1990s Production becomes increasingly automated and computerized.

High Technology

2500 BC The abacus, developed in Babylon, spreads throughout ancient world.

600 AD Book printing in China.

1445 First printing press with movable type developed in Germany by Johann Gutenberg.

1609 Microscope developed in the Netherlands.

1645 Blaise Pascal develops the first calculating machine.

1833 Charles Babbage develops the Analytical Engine, the forerunner of the modern computer.

1837 Samuel Morse invents the telegraph.

1876 Alexander Graham Bell invents the telephone.

1895 X-ray developed.

1920s First commercial radio broadcasts.

1927 First long-distance television transmission.

1929 Discovery of penicillin revolutionizes human ability to control disease.

1951 First commercially manufactured computer.

1959 Integrated circuit allows for miniaturizing electronic equipment.

1962 First commercial telecommunications satellite.

1967 First heart transplant, in South Africa.

1978 Birth of first "test-tube baby."

1988 First transatlantic fibre-optic cable.

1990 The Internet links computers worldwide through telecommunications satellites.

1997 First cloning of a mammal announced.

Technology in Everyday Life: Then and Now

Education

Figure 13.4
Far left: Model school, attached to a teacher's training college, Fredericton, 1886.
Left: Modern classroom. How has technology changed?

Recreation

Figure 13.5
Far right: The Kananites, a Nova Scotia women's hockey club, c. 1900.
Right: How has equipment changed?

Transportation

Figure 13.6 Wooden bridges such as this one in Hartland, New Brunswick, were common. This was, and still is, the longest such bridge in the world. Laws required "horses and other beasts, and carriages of all description, to proceed no faster than a walk." A galloping horse could set up vibrations that would collapse a bridge.

DID YOU KNOW...?

The phenomenon of "resonant vibration" can cause even a solidly built bridge to collapse. All structures vibrate naturally, and elements such as wind, movement, or sound can cause the vibration to increase. If the additional vibration occurs at the same resonance or frequency as the natural vibration, the vibration can be greatly exaggerated, causing the bridge to sway, buckle, or even collapse. Today technology used to build bridges such as Confederation Bridge, linking New Brunswick and Prince Edward Island, takes account of this possibility to prevent such disasters from occurring.

Communication

Figure 13.7
Far right: All telephone calls had to be routed manually through a switchboard. *Right:* Cellular phones allow us to remain in touch wherever we are.

In the Office

Figure 13.8
Left: Typing machines first came into use in the 1870s, and electric typewriters did not become common until the 1960s. *Far left:* Today it is standard for offices to have computers, fax machines, and multifunction photocopiers.

EXPLORATIONS

APPLYING YOUR SKILLS

1. Make a series of small diagrams to show the purpose and impact of at least five different forms of technology. Follow the example.

   Problem to be solved → Technology ← Resources used
   How it changes our lives ↗ ↘ How it extends human abilities

ANALYZING AND REFLECTING

2. Even though his invention of the telephone made Alexander Graham Bell a wealthy man, he continued to experiment and invent. Why do you think human beings invent things? With a partner, brainstorm a list of reasons. Then rank these reasons. You might get some ideas by referring back to Figure 8.2 on page 109.

CONNECTING AND EXTENDING

3. Research any technological invention, and write a brief biography of its inventor. What motivated the inventor? How did he or she finance the experiments needed to make the invention? What resources and technology were available to the inventor? What was the impact of the invention?

4. Make two or three "Then and Now" scenarios of your own, similar to those above, showing the development of technology in everyday life in the Atlantic provinces. Combine your scenarios in a bulletin board display.

CASE STUDY

Technology of Water Transportation: A Comparative Study

One way to understand how technology changes is to focus on one form, and see how it has developed. Water transportation in Atlantic Canada provides a good example. Canada has thousands of kilometres of coastline, hundreds of rivers, and thousands of lakes. Not surprisingly, water travel has played a major role in our history. The water craft featured in this case study were all built in southern New Brunswick. As you follow their development, think about the knowledge, skills, and natural resources needed to make these technological changes happen.

The Canoe

No technology is more associated with Canada than the birch-bark canoe. The First Nations of the Eastern woodlands developed the craft as a precision-built vessel that was both functional and a work of art.

The skills required to build a canoe were numerous, and there were many problems to overcome. Canoe builders needed to know how to harvest bark; prepare pitch; fashion tools; fell trees; split cedar for gunwales, sheathing, and ribbing; bend wood with hot water, lace joints, caulk seams, and etch designs, among various other skills.

Caulking the Seams

Building a canoe was a complex procedure. The extract below describes just one stage: preparing to caulk the seams. The best artisans joined the seams so skillfully that, at first glance, the vessel would appear to have none. Careful engineering placed the seams only above the waterline, and following the contours of the canoe.

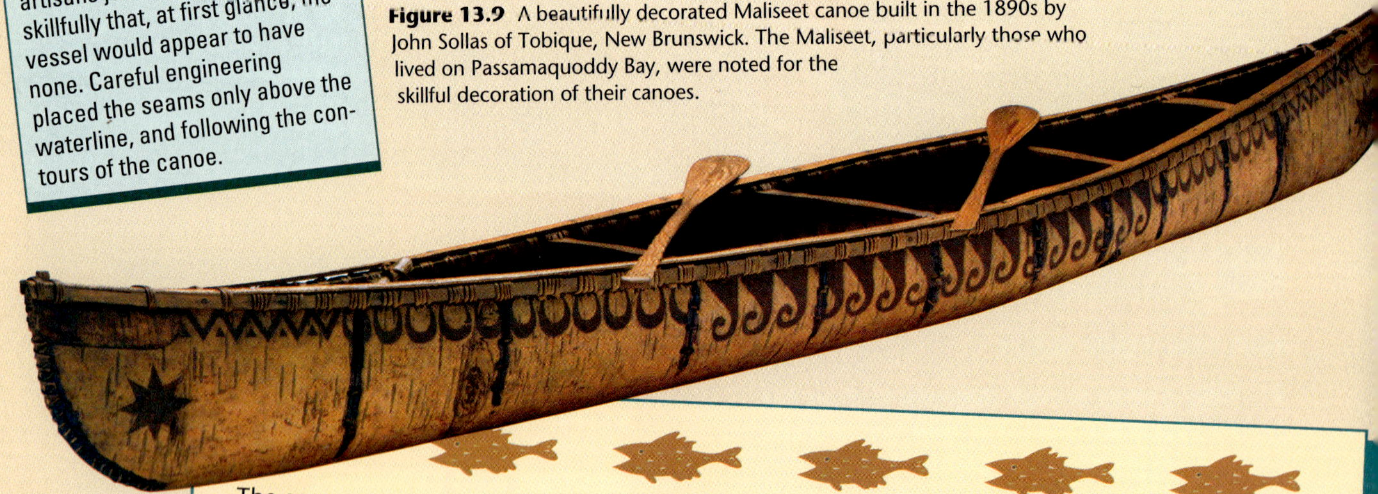

Figure 13.9 A beautifully decorated Maliseet canoe built in the 1890s by John Sollas of Tobique, New Brunswick. The Maliseet, particularly those who lived on Passamaquoddy Bay, were noted for the skillful decoration of their canoes.

The spruce gum was gathered and tempered.... It was heated in a number of ways. One method was to heat it in a wooden trough with hot stones.... Another method was to boil water in a bark container and drop in the spruce gum, which melted and floated on top of the water....

Tempering, done after the gum was melted, consisted of adding animal fat and a finely powdered charcoal. The mixture was then tested by dipping a strip of bark into it and then into cold water. The strip was bent to see if it cracked the spruce gum; if it did, too much tempering material had been added and more gum was required. If no cracking occurred, the gum on the strip was held in the hand for a few moments to see if it became tacky or could be rubbed off the strip; if either occurred more tempering was needed.... Red ochre or vermilion were sometimes added, often together with charcoal made from the willow.

Source: Edwin Tappin Adney, apprentice to Peter Joe, a Maliseet master canoe builder, c. 1887. Published in E.T. Adney and H.I. Chapelle, The Bark Canoes and Skin Boats of North America (Washington, DC: Smithsonian Institution Press, 1983), pp. 24–25.

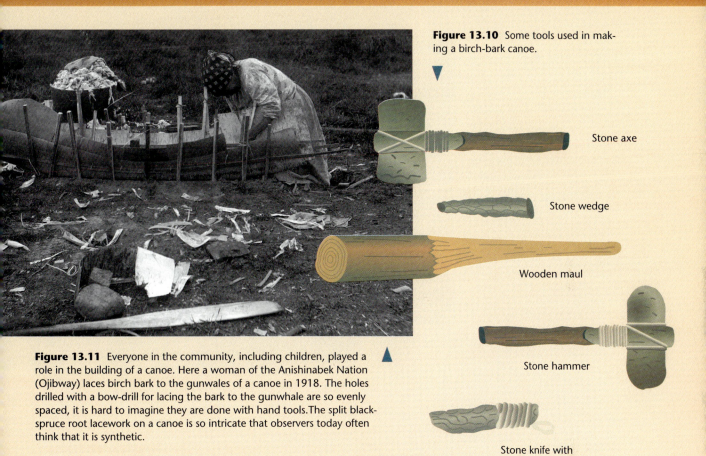

Figure 13.10 Some tools used in making a birch-bark canoe.

Stone axe

Stone wedge

Wooden maul

Stone hammer

Stone knife with rawhide thong handle

Figure 13.11 Everyone in the community, including children, played a role in the building of a canoe. Here a woman of the Anishinabek Nation (Ojibway) laces birch bark to the gunwales of a canoe in 1918. The holes drilled with a bow-drill for lacing the bark to the gunwhale are so evenly spaced, it is hard to imagine they are done with hand tools. The split black-spruce root lacework on a canoe is so intricate that observers today often think that it is synthetic.

Wooden gunwales ran along the top sides of the canoe, and on the inside thinly cut boards were held in place against the birch bark by cedar ribs. All of this intricate wood work was neatly finished using hand-made stone tools. The bending of the slender cedar ribs after they were soaked in hot water was one of the most delicate operations, requiring great skill and patience.

The skill of canoe building was passed from one generation to the next over centuries. European settlement, however, virtually destroyed this technology of thousands of years. Birch groves dwindled as settlers cleared the forests for farming. As the First Nations moved onto reserves, traditional lifestyles, including the use of canoes, were restricted. Furthermore, the settlers began mass producing canvas canoes. Canoe-building technology was kept alive by only a handful of Aboriginal artisans.

Figure 13.12 Cedar ribs for a canoe, bent and hung to dry.

The Snow

Thousands of ships were built in Atlantic Canada during the age of sail. Many of them were built on the Bay of Fundy. For example, the town of St. Martins on Quaco Bay had shipyards that built more than 500 ocean-going vessels. One type of vessel was the brig, a two-masted square-rigged ship. The Canadian brig was called a "snow."

Figure 13.13 The 204-ton snow *David* was launched from St. Martins, New Brunswick, on Quaco Bay, in 1825 and sold in Scotland a year later.

> August 22, 1825
>
> Gentlemen
> I am gitting on pretty well with the ship timber. I have the greater part of the fraim cut in the woods and considerable of it hawled to the river, and if I git a good freshet to git it down I shall git the ships fraim very cheap. I have got a fine lot of timbers and have imployed none but axemen. Havin some knoledge of ship timbers myself, I can manage without any carpenters in the woods which will be a great savin. I have engaged a master workman at ten shillins per day for the winter & twelve & six pence for the summer, and have ingaged several workmen at the customary wages. Likewise agreed for the boarding of the men at 10/6 per week….
> Mr Washburn who is to be the master workman is a smart man and has a fine vessel almost ready to launch which he has built for Mr. David Vaughan.
>
> Your obedient servant
> James McLean

The logs for ships' timbers were cut in the nearby forests and brought to the building site. They were squared with a broad axe and then hand sawn into planks. The lumber was steamed for bending, a blacksmith made the iron work on site, and horses or oxen pulled materials on wagons.

The *David* (Figure 13.13) was built at the small McLean shipyard near Quaco Head. The letter at left, from shipbuilder James McLean, was written to the merchant-bankers who financed the building of another vessel. It gives some insight into the technology of the day.

Figure 13.14 St. Martins, New Brunswick, now a popular tourist destination on the Fundy coast, played an important role in nineteenth century commerce. What geographical features made it an ideal shipbuilding centre in the age of sail?

The skills involved in building wooden ships created several trades. At the height of the great age of sail a shipyard would employ a sawyer, plankers, caulkers, joiners, carvers, blacksmiths, sail makers, mast makers, pump makers, rope makers, painters, and riggers as well as many labourers. Over all of these was the shipwright or ship's carpenter, the most prestigious of the trades. In smaller yards, the ship's carpenter often acted as overseer of all the other trades as the "master workman."

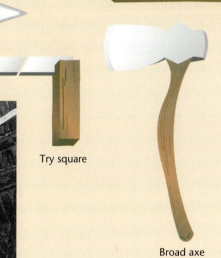

Figure 13.15 Some tools used in the building of a snow. How do they differ from the ones shown in Figure 13.10?

Figure 13.16 Ship-building crew with a schooner under construction on the Bay of Fundy coast. On March 22, 1826, McLean informed his Saint John partner that "the vessel is raised and the fraim's up." The vessel would have resembled the frame pictured here.

CAULKING THE SHIP'S SEAMS

To caulk the sides of a ship, the caulker first separated a few strands from a coil of oakum and twisted them into a single stranded rope. Then, using a mallet and a thin caulking iron to wedge the oakum, he sealed the planks, which had already been bevelled to fit together. The seams were then compressed by two men, one holding a hawsing iron and the other a "beetle" (see Figure 13.17). Following this, a mop was used to pay (waterproof) the seam with a heated mixture of pitch and turpentine.

Source: Adapted from Eileen Reid Marcil, The Charley-Man (Kingston: Quarry Press, 1995) pp. 266–267.

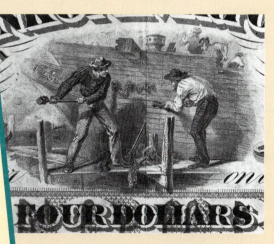

Figure 13.17 This detail of an 1871 $4 bank note of the Bank of Liverpool, Nova Scotia, shows caulkers using a hawsing iron.

TECHNOLOGY: PAST TO PRESENT

The Frigate HMCS Halifax

Figure 13.18 *HMCS Halifax.* A frigate is a high-speed warship, designed as an escort-vessel. It is a little longer than a football field. The *Halifax* carries a crew of 195 sailors as well as an air detachment of 30 people to operate its on-board helicopter.

Figure 13.19 This aerial view of the Saint John Shipbuilding yards shows three frigates in various stages of completion. Three are standing in the graving dock, a dry dock for working on ships below the water line.

The Royal Canadian Navy commissioned the *HMCS Halifax* in June, 1992. The *Halifax* was the first of 12 patrol frigates to be built by the Saint John Shipbuilding Company Ltd. (SJSL) between 1983 and 1995. The frigate project was the largest building contract undertaken in Canadian military history. The *Halifax*-class frigates are 134.1 metres long and sturdy enough to withstand the rigours of the North Atlantic, yet they can reach a speed of 27 knots (approximately 50 km/hour) in just over two minutes. Their computerized operational and weapons systems place them amongst the most sophisticated warships on earth.

The huge project had many critics. The awarding of the contract to a New Brunswick-based company drew criticism from competing companies in other provinces. In addition, critics believed that the cost of the project — more than $9 billion — could not be justified at a time when governments were cutting back on their spending in many areas. Furthermore, legal wrangling between SJSL and a Quebec sub-contractor filled the news. A hostile press constantly publicized glitches in the program. Nevertheless, the building of the frigates was one of the most remarkable technological feats in Canadian history.

> ### DID YOU KNOW...?
> Saint John Shipbuilding is an Irving-owned company. The Irving empire of companies is controlled by the family of New Brunswick industrialist K.C. Irving, who has played a major role in developing industry in the Atlantic provinces in areas such as transportation, pulp and paper, oil, and media, amongst others.

Throughout the huge task, project engineers faced the challenge of keeping up with computer technology, which was advancing at a breathtaking pace. When plans were first being laid for the frigate program, the "point and click" computer mouse had not been developed, IBM had not begun to make personal computers, and the CD-ROM did not yet exist! Hundreds of engineers and technicians found they had to upgrade their skills constantly, learning about new equipment and systems, so that the frigates would not be obsolete before they were finished. SJSL developed a "centre of excellence" that drew on expertise from around the world. The store of knowledge and skills required to build the vessels was immense. Just the operational equipment manuals for the frigate fill more than 175 000 pages of text!

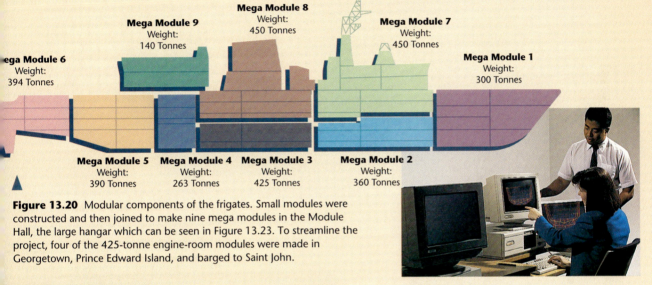

Figure 13.20 Modular components of the frigates. Small modules were constructed and then joined to make nine mega modules in the Module Hall, the large hangar which can be seen in Figure 13.23. To streamline the project, four of the 425-tonne engine-room modules were made in Georgetown, Prince Edward Island, and barged to Saint John.

Figure 13.21 Engineers using computer-aided design (CAD) to develop plans for the frigate. In 1990, SJSL purchased a new CAD system which transferred 22 000 sheets of engineers' drawings to computer graphics. Tens of thousands of design changes were made over the course of the project to keep pace with rapidly changing technology.

Figure 13.22 Welders using computer aided manufacturing (CAM) to make precision cuts in steel plates. The steel work — moulding 250 000 pieces of steel plate and bars to cover 33 000 m^2 — was done by a process known as numerically controlled (NC) plasma steel cutting.

Figure 13.23 A bow module leaves the Module Hall headed for the graving dock. At the height of the project the shipyard employed more than 3800 workers. The first ship off the assembly line, the *HMCS Halifax*, took 5 million person-hours to build. When the twelfth vessel was finished, increases in productivity had cut this time in half.

EXPLORATIONS

ANALYZING AND REFLECTING

1. Make an organizer similar to the one below for the three vessels described in this case study.

Vessel	Resources used	Knowledge and skills

   a) Consider the training and skill levels of the builders. What skills and training did they need for each of the three vessels?

   b) For each of the vessels, what general knowledge did the builders require?

   c) How did each project involve team effort and specialization?

   d) With a group, discuss how builders from one age would have had difficulty in learning the trades of another age. Choose the vessel you would like to have built. Give reasons for your view.

2. The Saint John Shipbuilding Company describes itself as "an equal opportunity employer."

   a) What does this phrase mean?

   b) Compare the role of women in the building of the three vessels. In which case was there the greatest division of labour along gender lines?

3. What satisfaction do you think the workers on each vessel experienced from their building job? Explain.

4. In a group, brainstorm to find a solution to the following problem. It was solved regularly by people in the First Nations, using technology available to them. All of the information you need is given.

   It is spring in the Wolastoq (St. John) River Valley 700 years ago. Your parents are gathering maple sap and boiling it down to make syrup. You have been asked to fell three large cedar trees which stand on a knoll above a winding clay-bottomed brook. The trees will be used to build canoes in the summer. You know which trees to fell because their bark was girdled a year ago so that they would season while standing. You have a stone axe and knife. Your younger brother and sister look at the tree trunks, which are too large for them to reach around with their arms. "You can never chop these down," they say. "They're too big." You laugh and tell them, "Don't you remember how grandfather showed us what to do last spring? There is an easy way to do this but you will have to help me." How would you fell these trees?

CONNECTING AND EXTENDING

5. In the past, shipbuilding was a thriving enterprise in all four Atlantic provinces. Research shipbuilding in the region in the following ways.

   a) Investigate the triangular trade that developed between Britain and its colonies in the Americas in the nineteenth century. How did the technology of wooden shipbuilding influence the economy of the British North American colonies?

   b) Develop a glossary, illustrated chart, or time line of various types of sailing ships produced in Atlantic Canada. You might also wish to make a model of one or more of these vessels.

   c) Research what is being done today to revitalize our shipbuilding enterprises.

Technology: A Double-Edged Sword?

As the engineers of the *HMCS Halifax* discovered, this is an exciting world to be living in, especially if you like rapid change. In many ways, we are living in a world that our great-grandparents could not even have imagined. We have the ability to explore the deepest oceans and outer space. Scientists are unfolding the mysteries of the atom and the gene. What changes do you imagine technology will bring in your lifetime? Think about the visions of the future portrayed by the movies and science fiction. What images of progress do they present? What problems do they predict arising from technology? Will the science fiction of today become the reality of tomorrow?

> **FOCUS ON FIGURE 13.24**
> 1. Think about images of technology you have seen in the movies or in science fiction. Which aspects of these images have become reality or near-reality?
> 2. What are some of the positive aspects of technology as shown in these sources or in the images on this page? What are some of the negative aspects?
> 3. What do you think the future holds with regard to technology?

Figure 13.24 Some images of technology

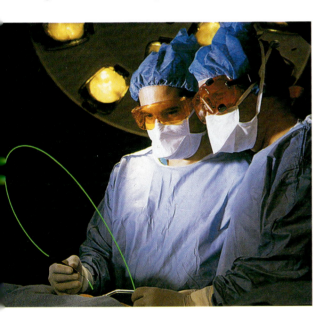
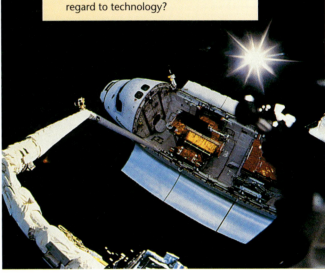

Internet connects northern communities

Anti-nausea drug Thalidomide now known to cause birth defects

WHO announces eradication of smallpox

Laser beams promise new uses in surgery

Traffic jams now a way of life

ozone layer continues to thin

Canadian-designed "V-chip" can help adults control what children view

Technology: Past to Present

FOCUS ON AN ISSUE

Genetic Engineering: An Ethical Dilemma

Some of the most important advances in technology have been made in the fields of science and medicine. **Genetic engineering** is a form of science in which basic characteristics of a plant or animal are changed by removing, splicing, and altering genes. The result is an organism that does not exist in nature. For some years, genetic engineering has been a topic of heated debate. Many people believe genetic research serves valuable purposes. Others think it is not ethical for humans to alter nature and that, by doing so, they might make problems more serious than any they solve. Examine the following information to see what you think.

Aqua Bounty Farms

The following extract comes from the promotional brochure of Aqua Bounty Farms, an aquaculture company based in Newfoundland, with operations in Prince Edward Island and New Brunswick.

Most experts believe that our planet is at a critical juncture in its ability to derive fish and seafood from our oceans. There are 16 major fishing areas in the world today. Edible fish are endangered in 14 of these areas. The United Nations has estimated that, to meet worldwide demand for fish and seafood by the year 2025, we will have to increase our present annual harvest sevenfold. We need to implement better ocean management and conservation efforts, but, at the same time, we must put our technology to work to improve the productivity of fish grown inland and along our coasts....

Aqua Bounty Farms has discovered a safe, practical method to increase the growth rate of salmon and other fish several times over. The technology, based on splicing growth and other genes, allows salmon to grow an average of 400% to 600% faster than traditional salmon during the first year following hatch.

Through AquAdvantage breeding, farmers will be able to sell their fish at a lower price, and more fish will be available to consumers seeking delicious, high-quality, low-fat protein food sources.

Aqua Bounty farms will license AquAdvantage salmon to be bred only in enclosed tank systems or net pens where the fish have been sterilized. This will prevent farm-raised fish from escaping into the oceans and interfering with the breeding of wild stocks.

Source: Adapted from Aqua Bounty Farms, Update, Vol 1. No.1, June 1996

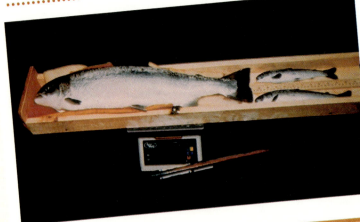

Figure 13.25 An AquAdvantage salmon next to two natural salmon of the same age. Will genetically engineered fish be a part of the solution to the problem of overfishing? Will they succeed in the market?

Are we flying too close to the sun?

Humans now have the power to manipulate the genetic building blocks of life, to invent new life forms. But doing so raises many ethical questions.

New life forms promise great benefits for humanity: cures for stubborn diseases, plants that resist insects, bacteria that will produce medicine. But how do we know where these new life forms will lead? What if they prove to be harmful to the environment, or cause damage in other ways? And who has the right to decide where they should stop? Doctors already have the ability to "screen" genes, identifying possible problems in unborn babies. Will they soon have the ability to go one step further and alter the genes in a foetus? Should humans be using technology to tamper with nature in this way?

It might be timely to recall an ancient Greek legend that warned of human arrogance. Icarus fashioned wax wings, but once he gained the power of flight, he grew proud and flew too high. As he got closer to the sun, his wax wings melted and he plunged to his death. Are we flying too close to the sun? Perhaps the wisest course of action is to proceed with great caution. As we fly, let us remember that our wings are made only of wax.

Figure 13.26 In 1997, scientists in Scotland announced a major step in genetic engineering. They had cloned a mammal for the first time, reproducing the lamb shown here from single cells of another sheep. Named Dolly, this lamb was an identical reproduction of the sheep from which the cell was taken. Dolly presented the possibility that, one day, humans could be cloned.

Mother Goose and Grimm

Figure 13.27 Why are many people concerned about cloning?

TECHNOLOGY: PAST TO PRESENT

ANALYZING THE ISSUE

1. **a)** The article on Aqua Bounty Farms points out that "we need to implement better ocean management and conservation efforts." What is meant by this statement? What role do you think technology has to play in these efforts?

    b) In what ways do the activities of Aqua Bounty Farms support ocean management and conservation efforts?

    c) Why would it be a concern if genetically engineered salmon escaped into the oceans?

    d) How might the story of Icarus apply in this case?

2. Brainstorm some possible consequences if further research into genetic engineering were banned.

3. Brainstorm some possible consequences if research into genetic engineering continues without limits.

4. What is your own view about the ethics of genetic engineering? Should humans have the right to make life forms that do not exist in nature? Should restrictions be placed on genetic engineering? If so, by whom? If not, why not? Share your views with your classmates.

SEEING THE BIG PICTURE

1. Work with a partner or a small group. Develop generalizations in response to the following questions:
    a) What is the purpose of technology?
    b) What sorts of benefits do humans derive from technology?
    c) What sorts of problems does technology present?

2. Keeping these generalizations in mind, develop some "Guidelines for Responsible Research" for scientists of the future. Be sure to cover the following points:
    a) What should the main goal of all research be?
    b) What should the responsibilities be with regard to society at large?
    c) Which areas of research (if any) should be limited in some way?

3. Based on these guidelines, design or make a plan for one of the following:
    a) a city of the future
    b) a farm of the future
    c) a school of the future
    d) transportation of the future
    e) one industry of the future

CHAPTER 14
Technological Links

Figure 14.1 The Westmoreland Street Bridge, Fredericton, New Brunswick, designed by ADI. The engineers at ADI drove over this bridge before it was built. What advantage did that experience give them?

Figure 14.2 ADI uses CAD software to simulate road conditions and predict possible hazards.

Imagine that you are designing a new highway. What factors do you need to consider to ensure that your new road will be as safe as possible? What will be the effect of different weather conditions? How good will visibility be on the curves? Is there a chance that rocks might fall on the road? How can you account for all of the different hazards that drivers on your road might encounter? ADI Limited, a company based in Fredericton, New Brunswick, and Charlottetown, Prince Edward Island, has some solutions. It uses computer systems to simulate driving conditions over a new route, even before construction begins. ADI has won engineering contracts all over the world. The company operates a control room in Fredericton, from where it can "troubleshoot" its customers' problems through telephone links.

- How is the technology of transportation and communication changing?
- How are these changes affecting Atlantic Canada?

Transportation in Atlantic Canada

It is not surprising that Canadian companies like ADI should be at the leading edge of transportation technology. Canada's varied geography and vast size have always challenged and inspired us to find new ways to link one part of the country with another. Transportation and communications have both had a special role to play in creating unity, by linking people across the land.

The Iron Horse

People across North America greeted the coming of the railways in the early 1800s with great excitement. Americans Mark Twain and Charles Dudley Warner wrote "Coaches that fly over the ground at twenty miles an hour—heaven and earth....It makes a man's brain whirl!" The railway was known as the "iron horse" but some called it the "iron civilizer" because it brought industry and awareness of the world at large to many small communities. Canadian writer T.C. Keefer described how, in excitement, "the young men and the maidens, the old men and the matrons, daily collect around the railway cars."

Until 1989, all four Atlantic provinces had rail lines. For the most part of a century, trains had been used as the main method of transporting passengers and freight. In 1997, only New Brunswick and Nova Scotia continued to have a rail service. Most Atlantic Canadians travel within the region by automobile, and most freight is carried by truck.

The transportation systems of today move people, goods, and services more rapidly than ever before — not just within Canada, but around the world. At one time, sailing ships or steam ships were the only means of travel across the Atlantic or Pacific oceans. A journey across the Atlantic Ocean in a ship like the *David* would take weeks. The *HMCS Halifax* could, of course, do the trip in far less time, but — more importantly — we now have aircraft that move passengers and goods rapidly all around the globe. The Concorde offers the ultimate in trans-Atlantic travel, flying at 2300 km/hr (faster than the speed of sound).

Figure 14.3
Technology has affected the transportation of both passengers and freight. *Above:* Although few of us will travel on Concorde, many Atlantic Canadians will fly at least once in their lives. The busiest route from the Atlantic provinces is between Halifax and Toronto. *Below:* Container technology allows goods to be transferred easily from one form of transportation to another — from a truck or rail car to a ship, for example.

Focus on an Issue

The Automobile: Benefit or Blight?

Ever since Henry Ford produced the first "horseless carriage" in the early 1900s, North Americans have become increasingly dependent on automobiles. In fact, the automobile now plays a central role in our popular culture. Cars have also had a major impact on lifestyle and economics around the world. Huge amounts of public money have been spent in building road systems for cars and trucks. Practically any aerial photograph taken today in the industrialized world will show road systems. The same could not have been said less than 100 years ago.

Figure 14.4 An electric car produced by Saturn Corporation, a Division of General Motors. How would this vehicle help to address environmental concerns?

DID YOU KNOW...?

Canada has one of the highest rates of car ownership in the world. While the automobile has brought many benefits, it has also introduced problems. The main areas of concern are fuel consumption, safety, and traffic congestion. In addition, emissions from auto exhausts cause smog and contribute to environmental problems. Furthermore, gasoline for cars is refined from oil, a non-renewable energy source. Researchers have been working for decades to address these concerns. Safety features such as air bags and stronger vehicle frames are constantly being refined. Electronic monitoring systems control engine performance, fuel economy, and other aspects of vehicle operation. Advances have been made, but we have a long way to go.

ANALYZING THE ISSUE

1. Brainstorm the benefits and disadvantages of automobiles. Use a table similar to the one below. Give examples for each category.

Benefits	Economy Working life Recreation Independence
Disadvantages	Energy problems Environmental problems Safety problems Traffic problems

2. Work in a group

   a) Make some suggestions for creative ways to address the problems you have identified, without giving up the benefits of the automobile.

   b) Discuss ways in which you, personally, could address some of the problems. For example, would a change in your lifestyle help in any way? Could you persuade any other individuals or groups to make changes? Give reasons for your answers.

3. Debate the impact of rail closures on the highway systems of Atlantic Canada.

CASE STUDY

TRANSPORTATION LINKS: CONFEDERATION BRIDGE

When Prince Edward Island joined Confederation in 1873, Canada pledged to provide an efficient steamship service that would link the Island to the mainland. Through the winter months, however, the Island was isolated. As early as 1885, engineers suggested building a tunnel under the Northumberland Strait, between Prince Edward Island and New Brunswick, to improve communication. While this suggestion was turned down, ice-breaking ferries did start a year-round service to and from the Island in 1917. Still, the dream of a more permanent connection did not go away. In 1956, the government of Prince Edward Island asked Ottawa to investigate a permanent crossing. After many years of negotiation and considering designs, a contract was signed for the building of a fixed link, or bridge, across the Northumberland Strait. Construction began in 1995. The fixed link was named Confederation Bridge.

> ### DID YOU KNOW...?
> Confederation Bridge reflects our region's growing global connections. The construction and operation of the bridge was awarded to a Canadian, French, and Dutch consortium (group of companies). The *Svanen* (see Figure 14.6) was built in the Netherlands and brought to Prince Edward Island from another project in Denmark.

The bridge is an exciting technological achievement. At 12.9 km, it is the world's longest continuous marine-span bridge. Never before has a cantilevered design been used with sections this heavy or with spans this long. On most bridges, the piers that support the bridge are embedded in the ocean floor. The piers of Confederation Bridge, however, rest on grooves carved into the rock of the ocean floor; the bridge is held in place by its own sheer weight and some concrete bonding.

Figure 14.5 Location of Confederation Bridge

Figure 14.6 The *Svanen*, a huge twin-hulled floating crane, prepares to place a double-girder section of Confederation Bridge, during construction in 1996. A bridge whose sections project from piers and are connected by girders in this way is known as a cantilevered bridge.

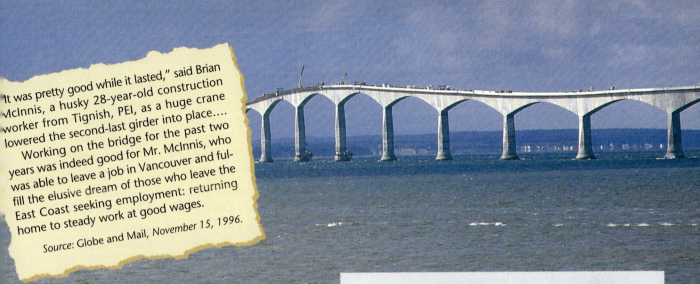

"It was pretty good while it lasted," said Brian McInnis, a husky 28-year-old construction worker from Tignish, PEI, as a huge crane lowered the second-last girder into place....
Working on the bridge for the past two years was indeed good for Mr. McInnis, who was able to leave a job in Vancouver and fulfill the elusive dream of those who leave the East Coast seeking employment: returning home to steady work at good wages.

Source: Globe and Mail, November 15, 1996.

Figure 14.7 Confederation Bridge is two highway lanes wide. It stands, on average, 40 m above sea level. One section, in the centre of the span, stands approximately 60 m high, to allow for the passage of ships.

A huge floating crane called the *Svanen* put the pier and span sections of the bridge in place. Construction workers placed about five huge sections each week. During each 12-hour shift, one section, built on shore, would be transported and accurately placed to within specified centimetres using the Global Positioning System (GPS).

The construction of Confederation Bridge brought up to 2400 jobs to the area. Many people believed that the fixed link would also bring more development and jobs to Prince Edward Island in the long term, because people could get to and from the Island more easily. They also believed that more tourists would come — because they wanted to see the new bridge and because it would now be easier to take their cars onto the Island.

Others, however, were not so sure of the effects of the bridge. Some were concerned that the Island would lose its unique character once it was joined to the mainland. They argued that new development and greater numbers of people would actually damage the tourist industry. Many pleasure travellers to Prince Edward Island, for example, looked forward to the ferry ride as part of their vacation.

Figure 14.8 Working on the supporting girders for the bridge. These girders were precast on an assembly line. Each one is 197 m long.

Opponents pointed out that jobs created in the construction would be short-lived and that 600 people who worked on the ferries would lose their jobs when the service was suspended with the opening of the bridge.

Environmentalists were also concerned that the bridge would harm the fishery in the Northumberland Strait. They claimed the structure would delay melting of the ice in the Strait, leaving the water too cool for lobster and scallop. Other opponents criticized the cost of the project, saying that it would have been more economical to update and maintain the ferry service.

Nevertheless, the majority of Prince Edward Islanders supported the building of the bridge, and welcomed its opening in June 1997.

Explorations

ANALYZING AND REFLECTING

1. Imagine that you are living on Prince Edward Island in the year 1885. Remember that the use of telephones is not yet widespread. What would be the advantages to you of a year-round link to the mainland? Give your views in one of the following forms:

    a) a letter to a friend or relative living on the mainland

    b) a public speech by an engineer suggesting a tunnel under the Northumberland Strait

    c) a skit

CONNECTING AND EXTENDING

2. Develop a set of "Did You Know…?" boxes about transportation in your province. This activity could be completed as a "jigsaw," by assigning different categories to individuals in a group, and combining your findings in one display.

3. a) With the help of your teacher, find some books, poems, and songs about the railway and its importance to Canadian culture. Share your findings with your classmates.

    b) Many environmentalists point out that trains are more fuel efficient and environmentally friendly than automobiles or airplanes, and that we should be using them more. Others argue that they are slow, inconvenient, and expensive to maintain. What do you think? Prepare your response in the form of a poem, song, cartoon, or opinion paper.

4. a) Find some pictures of automobiles built in the 1950s. Describe their general design.

    b) Compare these automobiles with cars of today. What are the significant differences?

    c) Write a few paragraphs or make an illustrated display to show how automobiles have reflected changing values and popular culture. If necessary, refer back to the definition of popular culture on page 72.

5. a) Develop a time line of changes and innovations for land, sea, or air transportation.

    b) What improvements in this form of transportation would you like to see?

    c) Design, draw, or tell about a vehicle from your chosen form of transportation for the year 2020.

Communications: Reshaping Our World

In spite of advances in transportation, getting from point A to point B can still be time consuming and expensive. Our planet is physically large. The remaining barriers are rapidly being overcome, however, by means of communications. Our homes and our workplaces are now "wired" with many types of technology. Computers, cable networks, and cellular or satellite telephone systems are all expanding our ability to communicate with other people. In school life, home life, recreation, entertainment, and business, communications technology is revolutionizing the way we live.

Figure 14.9 When Giovanni Caboto left Bristol, England, in 1497 he was not heard from again until his return from the "New Founde Lande." Five hundred years later, the recreated caravel *Matthew* had state-of-the-art communications, and its voyage could be tracked worldwide on the Internet.

Communications technology, even more than improved transportation, has really "shrunk" the globe. Through satellites, our news media are able to inform us almost instantly of events in distant parts of the world. Many of us send and receive information on the Internet as a routine part of our daily lives. Communications and computer-based information services are growth areas, filled with possibility for individuals and businesses. Together, they are virtually eliminating the problems of time and distance in sending and receiving information within the countries of the industrialized world.

Figure 14.10 Much of today's communications technology relies on fibre-optic cables, which are made of very thin strands of glass. Information can be transmitted very quickly through fibre-optic cables in the form of light waves. Fibre-optic cables can carry far more information, far more rapidly, than metal cables. Canada has one of the most sophisticated fibre-optic networks in the world.

Figure 14.11 Canada's women's rowing team wins the silver medal at the Olympic Games in Atlanta, 1996. At one time, seeing the Olympic Games was a rare privilege. Today, millions of people across the world watch from the comfort of their own homes.

THE INFORMATION AGE

Stop for a moment and brainstorm a list of the communications systems in your life. Consider everything from a doorbell to portable GPS. No matter how long your list, it is likely that it will grow rapidly within the next few years. All of these communications systems are part of the **Information Age**. In today's world, information is probably the fastest growing **commodity**, or product that can be bought or sold. No other product is increasing in sales to the same extent. One of the most versatile and fastest-growing transportation systems for information is the Internet.

The Internet was developed by the United States military in the 1960s, as a network linking a series of military computers. It started as a security measure: officials believed it would be harder for an enemy to destroy a computer network than a computer complex, which could be wiped out in a military attack. Through the 1980s, the network grew as it was joined by universities and other institutions. By the 1990s, millions of individuals had joined, subscribing to a network with links around the world.

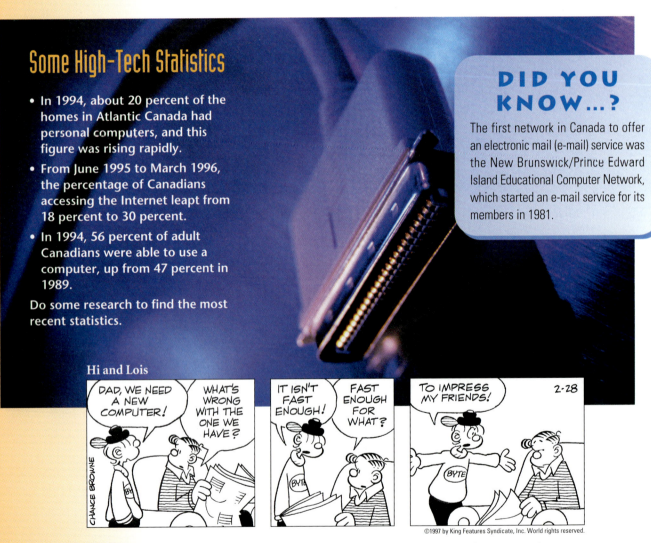

Some High-Tech Statistics

- In 1994, about 20 percent of the homes in Atlantic Canada had personal computers, and this figure was rising rapidly.
- From June 1995 to March 1996, the percentage of Canadians accessing the Internet leapt from 18 percent to 30 percent.
- In 1994, 56 percent of adult Canadians were able to use a computer, up from 47 percent in 1989.

Do some research to find the most recent statistics.

DID YOU KNOW...?

The first network in Canada to offer an electronic mail (e-mail) service was the New Brunswick/Prince Edward Island Educational Computer Network, which started an e-mail service for its members in 1981.

Figure 14.12 Communications technology has become part of popular culture, and our expectations for what it can do are constantly growing.

The Internet has given us the capacity to transmit large text files, pictures, sound clips, and video from computer to computer around the globe. It is widely used for gathering information and sending e-mail. People can now communicate and collaborate effectively in many creative ways. Team members in both small- and large-scale projects can work together, even though they may work at different locations. They can share documents, ideas, and designs as if they were sitting next to each other. The potential exists for communicating in thousands of ways never before thought possible.

1. Focus on the topic
Make a list of questions to ask about the topic you are researching.

2. Organize and plan
a) Organize your list of questions into a logical sequence that will form the plan for your research project.
b) Identify possible subtopics.

3. Locate information
a) Find a variety of sources. Consider:
 Print sources:
 • Books
 • Periodical index
 • Catalogue system
 CD-ROM sources:
 • Encyclopedias
 • Data bases such as ESTAT
 On-line services:
 • Internet
 • Infoglobe, etc.
b) Decide which material is related to your topic.
c) Decide which information is reliable to use.
 • Is the source likely to be accurate?
 • Is the information up to date?
 • Is the information based on facts rather than opinion?
 • Is the information supported by footnotes, references, and bibliography?

4. Record information
a) Find and record main ideas.
b) Summarize in your own words.

5. Evaluate your findings
a) Is your information relevant and logical?
b) Have you answered all of the questions raised in the "Focus on the topic" step?
c) Do the "Focus" or "Organize and plan" steps need to be adjusted?
d) Is more information needed?

6. Draw conclusions
a) What relationships can be seen in your information?
b) What conclusions can you draw from your information?
c) What opinions can you form?
d) What evidence supports your opinions?

7. Apply and communicate
Decide on the best way to communicate your findings. Remember your audience and time available. Consider using:
• a written report
• an oral report
• a visual presentation
• an essay
• a group discussion
• a skit
• a panel discussion
• a debate

Source: Adapted from A. Scully et al., *High Technology: Canada and the Information Age* (Scarborough: Prentice Hall Ginn Canada, 1997).

Figure 14.13 Research skills for the Information Age. In today's world we have access to vast amounts of information. As a result, it is important to develop research skills, learning how to find information efficiently and how to focus on the data we need.

CASE STUDY

ON-LINE SERVICES

Companies everywhere are developing new services that can be accessed "on-line" — through a computer system linked to a cable system. These services come directly to our homes. They include pay-per-view movies, shopping services of all types, or training courses, and the range is increasing constantly. Others are used in fields such as education and medicine.

On-line programs provide many advantages. People who live in rural areas may not have access to health care and education. They might have to travel away from home for these services, far from their families and at great cost. The examples that follow show how technology is helping to provide education and some health care services in some areas of the Atlantic provinces.

Telemedicine in Nova Scotia

Two Nova Scotia women are showing Canada — and the world — how to make telemedicine a reality

THE LATEST BUZZ in the medical field is **telemedicine** — the use of computer systems that help doctors to see, diagnose, and treat patients who may be hundreds of kilometres away. Telemedicine was pioneered in Newfoundland and Labrador by Dr. Maxwell House and Memorial University. Today, new methods are being used to make telemedicine a commercial venture. One company with a leading edge in the field is Nova Scotia's TecKnowledge Health Care Systems.

The concept of telemedicine is that if Buddy in Yarmouth drops a huge rock on his foot, it's faster to send his X-ray to Halifax by electronic means first, to ask a specialist if the patient really needs a three-hour ride in an ambulance to come up for surgery. If the diagnosis is particularly difficult, several sites can be linked together so that doctors can consult from several locations at once.

TecKnowledge is the brainchild of two engineers, Linda Weaver and Dorothy Spence. Weaver is the home-base half of the dynamic duo: she looks after product development and servicing while Spence travels the globe seeking markets....

Weaver attributes the success of the company to its emphasis on clients' needs. "We start by asking the question, 'What do you want to do?' and then design a system to answer the question. We customize off-the-shelf equipment, like computers and cameras, to the specific needs of clients, and follow with on-site training so that the equipment can be easily used."

Weaver sees the development of telemedicine as inevitable, given the huge size of Canada. "So it's better that we do it ourselves and sell it to others because, if we don't, other people will develop these systems and sell them to us."

Source: Adapted from Robert Martin, Innovations: Technology in Nova Scotia.

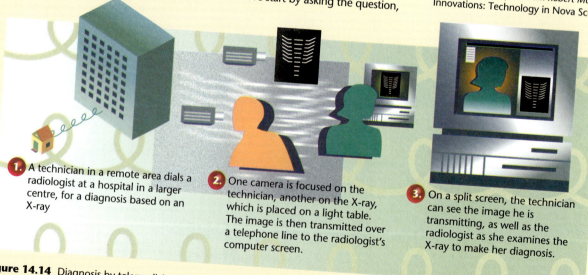

1. A technician in a remote area dials a radiologist at a hospital in a larger centre, for a diagnosis based on an X-ray.

2. One camera is focused on the technician, another on the X-ray, which is placed on a light table. The image is then transmitted over a telephone line to the radiologist's computer screen.

3. On a split screen, the technician can see the image he is transmitting, as well as the radiologist as she examines the X-ray to make her diagnosis.

Figure 14.14 Diagnosis by telemedicine. The system uses video cameras to transmit images over phone lines. This example shows diagnosis from an X-ray. The system can also transmit images of a live patient and other kinds of information.

Distance Learning in Newfoundland and Labrador

Each school day, high-school students Beverly Collier, Jennifer Freake, and Holly Stinson head off to attend classes at Lakewood Academy in Glenwood, Newfoundland. They spend some of their time in the regular classroom, but they take some of their classes with students in other schools that might be many kilometres away. Beverly, Jennifer, and Holly chose to take Chemistry and Advanced Mathematics. Their school, however, could not run these courses because the number of students who selected them was too small. Instead, the school enrolled the three students in **distance education** programs.

Every second day, the three students work from a specially equipped classroom, where they go on-line with other students in rural communities to take classes. An instructor at a different location teaches them through an audio-conference system and a "telewriter," which works as an electronic blackboard. The instructor is able to transmit graphics and free-hand writing or sketches during a session. The students are able to ask questions, observe problem-solving activities conducted by the instructor, and use the telewriter to demonstrate solutions they have developed. In addition, they can interact with other students at other locations. In this way, the classes are completely interactive. The students also fax work samples back and forth and complete assigned work and laboratories during off-line classes.

Each school has a staff member who acts as a distance education coordinator. The coordinator at Lakewood supervises chemistry labs with the students, oversees exams and tests, distributes assignments, and handles any problems that arise with equipment. The school has a fully equipped chemistry lab, so the students can fulfill all the requirements of the program.

Figure 14.15 Distance Education students Beverly Collier, Jennifer Freake, and Holly Stinson in the chemistry laboratory at Lakewood Academy.

"We feel that distance education has allowed us to develop the ability to work independently and efficiently. Through the program, we have learned good work and study habits, both in and out of school. We have also enjoyed the distance education classes and feel they have prepared us well for post-secondary education."

Holly Stinson, Jennifer Freake, Beverly Collier

Figure 14.16 TETRA operates a studio control room to monitor the technical requirements of on-line sessions.

Providing a Network

The network used to link Jennifer, Beverly, Holly, and other students with their on-line instructors is provided by Newfoundland's Telemedicine and Educational Resources Agency (TETRA), an organization established in 1988 by several departments of the provincial government and the Telemedicine Centre at Memorial University. The first TETRA pilot course was offered to 13 remote schools. In 1996–97, about 1100 students in 78 different locations received part of their high-school program through the service. TETRA services are also used by hospitals and other health services, colleges, and universities. The programs produced by TETRA are recognized as being among the most innovative in the world.

In the future, distance programs will provide "open learning," with opportunities for learners to study at the time, pace, and place of their choosing. Students will be able to use distance programs to accumulate all the credits they need for high-school graduation. As the system develops, Beverly, Jennifer, and Holly will likely look back on themselves as pioneers in their field — as, indeed, they are.

EXPLORATIONS

APPLYING YOUR SKILLS

1. **a)** Make an organizer to compare distance learning with learning in the more common classroom setting.

   b) What do you think the role of each kind of learning will be in the future? Make some predictions, giving reasons for the trends you foresee.

2. **a)** Identify services in your community that are already delivered through communications networks.

   b) Propose other services that you think could be delivered in this way.

   c) Create an advertising strategy to market your new service, including methods such as personal presentation, an information brochure, a home page on the World Wide Web, etc.

ANALYZING AND REFLECTING

3. **a)** Consider a world in which most of the services and goods people need can be ordered and received at home through electronic means or delivery services.

- Would you interact or communicate with your friends in the way you do now?
- What do you think would happen to the "art of conversation"?
- Would you go to the mall to pass the time or to shop? Would there be any need for malls?
- Would our needs for transportation increase or decrease?
- Where would we work and what kinds of jobs would we do?

b) Prepare a cartoon, collage, or skit to show the potential impact of home services.

4. **a)** Summarize the attitudes that you think have made Linda Weaver and Dorothy Spence successful entrepreneurs.

   b) Prepare an advertisement for TecKnowledge. Before you begin, think about the following question: Who will you try to sell your product or service to? What sort of advertisement might appeal to this audience? What aspects of the product or service will you emphasize?

CONNECTING AND EXTENDING

5. How do you communicate and for what purposes? How much of your communication is social or recreational and how much is related to work, school, and personal development?

   a) Make a Personal Communications Log. Log your interaction through communications systems and methods for a one-week period. Track each system used, noting frequency, total time, and purpose.

   b) Form pairs and compare charts.

   c) As a class, create a master chart indicating the methods of communication used, the general purposes for communication, and the frequency.

   d) Speculate on how your communication patterns might change as technology continues to evolve.

6. Innovative technological advances are happening across Atlantic Canada. Investigate advances being made in your province.

SEEING THE BIG PICTURE

1. In a small group, brainstorm a list of "high-tech" careers that are available as a result of the types of changes you have read about in this chapter. Be as wide-ranging as you can, including examples from road engineer to astronaut, and from web-page designer to help-line service agent for computer users.

2. Each group should identify one person whose work is related to the careers you have listed, and do one of the following:

   a) Invite the people identified to your class to participate in a panel discussion on opportunities and future trends in their line of work. Be sure to prepare questions for discussion, focusing on the kinds of skills and qualifications needed in their jobs, the best ways to gain those skills and qualifications, and emerging trends.

   b) In your groups, interview the people you have identified. Use the guidelines given in (a) above. Prepare a report of your findings to share with other groups in the class.

TECHNOLOGICAL LINKS

CHAPTER 15

Technology and Resources

From this...

...to this

Figure 15.1 The collapse of the North Atlantic cod fishery cast doubt over the economic future of thousands of Atlantic Canadians.

It is July 1992. You are 15 years old. For five generations your family has made its living from the Atlantic fishery. Their "bread and butter" has always been the northern cod. You have fished a fair bit yourself and you think that your future, too, will be in the fishery. On Friday July 3, 1992, you are listening to the radio and hear government officials declare that the cod fishery has been stopped dead, because fish stocks have been drastically reduced. A complete moratorium is in place. Your parents, along with almost 19 000 others who make their living in the fishery, are out of work for at least two years, perhaps more.

- How did you get to this point? Who or what is to blame?
- How has technology affected the fishery and other natural resources in the Atlantic region?

Technology and the Northern Cod

In 1497, John Cabot returned to England from North America, proclaiming that cod were so plentiful off the Atlantic coast that the fish sometimes stopped the progress of his ships. Cabot may have been exaggerating, but it doesn't stretch the truth to say that, since that time, the cod fishery has shaped the lives of generations of Atlantic Canadians. It has been part of where we live, our economy, our culture, our diet, and even our songs.

Until the closure of the cod fishery in July 1992, cod had been the cultural and economic cornerstone of hundreds of communities in Atlantic Canada for over 400 years. Many factors may have contributed to the collapse of the northern cod fishery, but overfishing is seen as a major problem. Most people agree that it was technological change that allowed the overfishing.

Figure 15.2 The Newfoundland outport community of Trinity. How would a community like Trinity be affected by changes in the fishery?

Some of the most significant changes were the advances in navigational aids, including radar, echo sounders, and Loran C. With these new tools, vessel operators could determine the exact location of fishing grounds and their own vessels. They could return to good fishing sites time and time again, and could go farther from shore to find new fish stocks.

Before the wide use of this kind of equipment, fishers navigated and found the best fish stocks by using skills they had built up through years of fishing. New technology meant fishers did not need the knowledge and skills gained by experience. They could use technology instead. This opened the door for new fishers, many of whom had less experience but could — with the right equipment — catch more fish.

Technology and the Cod Fishery

1954: Stern factory trawler introduced by Britain.

1957: Sailing ships replaced by motorized vessels.

1960s: Fish finders (echo sounders) first used to locate fish electronically.

1962: Cotton nets replaced by longer-lasting nylon nets.

1973: Dories used to catch fish with handlines in off-shore fisheries for the last time.

1970s: Stern trawlers become an important part of the Canadian fishing fleet.

1970s: Machines used to haul nets, bait hooks, and set trawls.

1970s and 1980s: The mesh size of nets decreases so that smaller fish can be caught.

1980s: Electronic navigation devices such as Loran C used to determine position and locate fishing gear.

1990s: Satellites allow the use of global positioning devices.

Figure 15.3 Even small in-shore fishing vessels were equipped with sophisticated equipment for locating schools of fish.

TECHNOLOGY AND RESOURCES 227

This song extract tells of changes to the fishery. Find an older song about fishing and compare it with this one. How do the content and tone differ?

Empty Nets

by Jim Payne

…It's empty nets, that's what he gets,
When you're out on the water no time for regrets,
Those empty nets, that's what he gets.
How's a poor fisherman to pay off his debts
When he goes out each morning to haul empty nets.
You can blame it on foreigners, blame it on feds,
Cast all the blame on each other instead.
But when all's said and done, it's still something I dread—
To see Newfoundland give up the fishery.
What of our communities? Will they just die?
"Pack up your duds, give the mainland a try."
But I'm staying here, 'til someone tells me
why I should put up with this misery.

Even more influential than the new navigational equipment was the **factory-freezer trawler**. Most of these vessels could hold from 2000 to 4000 tonnes of fish, though one Russian ship was known to carry as much as 8000 tonnes! These trawlers became the vacuum cleaners of the sea. Between the mid-1950s and mid-1960s, the total catch of Northern cod almost tripled. The trawlers were so good at catching fish that, even though fish stocks were going down, operators were able to find and catch even more fish. Of course, this bounty was not to last. By 1978, the catch had dropped dramatically. It fluctuated somewhat after that year but remained low until the government closed the fishery in 1992.

Why was action not taken sooner? For most of this period, there were no accurate ways to estimate how many fish were in the ocean and to analyze all the factors influencing them. The technology of resource management was lagging far behind fish-catching technology. Fish stocks were overestimated for many years, so that a disaster became inevitable. By the early 1990s, the numbers of cod were falling sharply. By the time the political decision was taken to stop the fishing, cod stocks were so low that many wondered if the species would survive. What is the status of the fishery today?

Figure 15.4 Cod landings, 1959–1991

FOCUS ON FIGURE 15.4

1. How much and when was the highest annual catch?
2. How much and when was the lowest annual catch, and what was the trend after this point?
3. Describe the balance between the inshore and offshore catch. Why do you think the inshore fishery fell in the late 1960s and early 1970s?

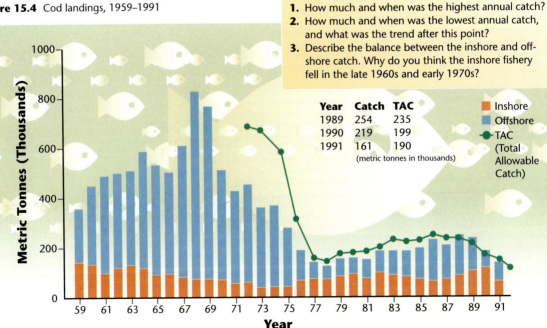

Figure 15.5 Factory-freezer trawlers are equipped to catch, process, package, and freeze fish on board. Notice how large the nets in the foreground are, in comparison with the size of the vessel, as indicated by the bird's-eye view diagram.

Fisheries Around the World

Atlantic Canada has not been alone in overfishing. All over the world, fish stocks are declining to the extent that they may not recover. Among the many other populations in crisis are Peruvian anchovy, North Sea cod, Californian sardines, Alaskan king crab, Alaskan pollock, and South African pilchard. The reasons for these problems are not always well understood but, in many cases, modern technology seems to play a part. We are just too good at catching fish! In addition, 60 percent of the ocean is outside the control of individual countries, so there are relatively few restrictions on how much fish can be caught. Global fish harvesting in the mid-1990s was five times what it was in 1950.

Aquaculture shows much promise for continuing to supply the world with fish, but we still have much to learn about its impact on humans and on the environment. Many environmentalists hope that the technology of resource management improves, so that the world's people can learn to manage their use of wild fish stocks.

DID YOU KNOW...?

- The open end of a large, cone-like trawler net can be 100 metres across — big enough to engulf a soccer field if it were floating in the sea.
- The factory freezer trawlers of the 1960s could catch in two 32-minute tows the same amount of fish that were caught in one whole year by the entire French fishing fleet of the 1500s.
- In spite of their incredible ability to catch fish, factory freezer trawlers operated through the 1960s and 1970s with no government-set limits (quotas) on how much they could catch.

Figure 15.6 Off-loading tuna in the Seychelles

Technology and Resource Use

What does the case of the fishery tell us about the way we use our natural resources? Some resources, like fish, are renewable. **Renewable natural resources** are living resources that have the ability to replace themselves. Trees and wildlife are other examples of renewable natural resources. As the example of the fishery shows, however, renewable resources may not last forever. If we use a renewable resource faster than it can regenerate, then the resource will disappear.

Non-renewable natural resources are non-living things. Minerals and fossil fuels such as oil and gas are examples of this type of resource. Once we use up a non-renewable resource, it is gone. Some non-renewable resources, such as fossil fuels, *can* be replenished by natural processes, but it would take as long as a million years. Some, like most metals, can be reused many times, which is why we have recycling programs.

Figure 15.7 Explain why each of the resources shown here is classified as it is. What resources can you add to each group?

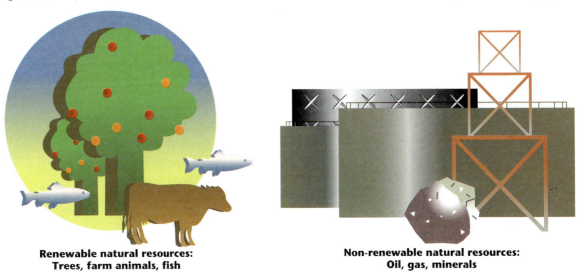

Renewable natural resources: Trees, farm animals, fish

Non-renewable natural resources: Oil, gas, minerals

Figure 15.8 Sustainable development must reconcile the competing needs of the economy, the environment, and the health of society.

Sustainable Development

To avoid losing resources forever, we have to use them wisely, by practising **sustainable development**. Sustainable development generally means the use of resources to meet our present needs without reducing the ability of future generations to meet theirs. Sustainable development requires us to live within our means. If we place limits on how much we take from the environment, we can ensure that we do not hurt it beyond its ability to heal.

Sustainable projects are those that serve our needs while keeping the earth healthy. Developments that harm the earth, such as the production of chemicals that damage the atmosphere, are not sustainable.

Sustainable development is a relatively new idea. It is not yet widely practised, but many people believe that it should be a goal for industries and individuals alike. If individuals live by the principles of sustainable development, their choices and actions — multiplied thousands of times — will allow sustainable development to become a reality. It is up to the present and future generations to make it work.

EXPLORATIONS

APPLYING YOUR SKILLS

1. Examine the time line on page 227 showing technological changes in the cod fishery. Choose three of the changes and make flow diagrams to show their impact. Follow the example:

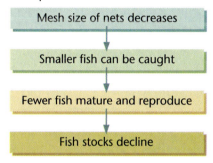

CONNECTING AND EXTENDING

2. Identify one of the hundreds of fishing communities in Atlantic Canada that relied heavily on Northern cod until 1992. If your community is one of these, identify another. With the help of your teacher, identify a school in that community that is also doing this course. Write a letter to that class to find out how the community, families, and individuals have been affected by the cod-fishery collapse. If possible, use the Internet to make contact.

3. Research several other locations where fishing is an important industry. Look for at least one place where the industry is sustainable and one other where resources are depleted. Use the research model on page 221 as a guide.

4. To learn more about using renewable resources in a sustainable way, conduct the following experiment. You will need a package of beans and a jar or similar container.

   Step 1: Place 50 beans in the container. The beans represent a renewable resource.

   Step 2: Case 1. Assume that five beans are added to the resource each year and eight beans are harvested each year. Record your data for five years. Use a table showing the year, the amount added, or regeneration, of the resource for each year (5), the harvest each year (8), and the total resource at the end of each year.

   Step 3: Case 2. Assume that five beans are added to the resource each year and five beans are harvested each year. Again, record your data for five years.

   Step 4: Case 3. Assume that five beans are added to the resource each year and three beans are harvested each year. Once again, record your data for five years.

   Step 5: On a single sheet of graph paper, plot size of resource vs. time for each case.

   Step 6: Answer these questions:

   a) Which case represents good management of a resource, so that it will be preserved for future generations?

   b) Which case might represent the management of the cod population from 1960 to 1992?

   c) In this activity, we have assumed that harvest is the only factor influencing the size of a resource. In a natural setting, other factors might also influence it. Suggest three.

   d) In this activity, it was easy to determine the size of the resource by counting the beans in the container. Determining the size of a population in the wild can be very difficult. Why do you think this is so? How do you think this uncertainty should influence management of the resource?

   Source: Adapted from D. Murphy et al., Finding the Balance, *Teacher's Resource (St. John's: Breakwater Books, 1993).*

5. a) Name two natural resources in your area to which you think the principles of sustainable development should be applied. Justify your opinion.

   b) Write a "letter to the editor" or make a poster showing actions that could be taken by businesses, community organizations, governments, individuals, or unions to manage the resource in a sustainable way.

Technology Below Ground

From the time you awake with the alarm clock until the time you turn off the faucet before going to bed, mineral products are close at hand. Minerals surround us, even in the ground below our feet. Only in a few places, however, are they so concentrated that we can extract them from the earth's crust. As you saw in Chapter 11, the processes involved in extracting and processing minerals are all part of the mineral development industry. Changing technology has influenced all the steps of this industry, from finding mineral concentrations, to extracting them, separating important minerals from waste, concentrating minerals into a usable form, and providing them to the producers of finished goods.

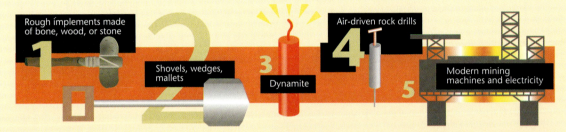

Figure 15.9 The development of mining technology

Mining is often thought of as a difficult and dangerous occupation. There have been some terrible mining disasters in the Atlantic region, including those at the Springhill and Westray coal mines in Nova Scotia. Even miners who do not encounter disaster in the mines often suffer ill health from working long hours in unhealthy conditions. And to make matters worse, mining towns often experience a cycle of "boom and bust." They thrive while the minerals are plentiful and easily accessible, but become "ghost towns" once the resources run low or demand declines. Unless alternative activities boost the economy, families have to leave or face long-term unemployment.

Figure 15.10 *Glace Bay* by Lawren Harris. What does this image of a Cape Breton coal mining community, painted in the 1920s, say about conditions there? The United Mine Workers of America gathered much support from the miners of Cape Breton in the 1920s. Why do you think this was so?

Figure 15.11 Reporting progress of search for victims at Springhill, the deepest mine in North America. Seventy-four men died here in 1958.

Figure 15.12 Underground salt mine and processing facilities of the Canadian Salt Company in Pugwash, Nova Scotia

DID YOU KNOW...?

Modern mining technology can extract materials from beneath the ocean bed. Off the coasts of Newfoundland and Nova Scotia, mining operations are extracting oil and gas from the Hibernia and Sable Gas deposits.

Today's technology promises to make mining safer and easier. Across the region, mines are introducing new machinery. One of the most exciting areas of change is **robotics** — the use of machines controlled by computer. Imagine sitting in a comfortable room in a building on the surface, controlling the movements of machines hundreds of metres below ground. The robotic machines drill holes in the rock and set explosive charges, all with direct instructions you give from the surface. The robots might also scoop up the ore blasted free from the parent rock and deposit it in automated vehicles for transport to the surface. Some of this technology is already a reality; some is being developed.

In order for robots to be effective in the ever-changing mine environment, they must be able to work in three dimensions. They must also be able to sense their surroundings and handle a variety of objects. This presents a major challenge. In order to give robots these abilities, designers are experimenting with sophisticated cameras mounted on the robots. These cameras transmit images back to an operator who can then control the robots. This form of remote-control may allow mines to go deeper into the earth's crust, where heat and rock pressure would present too great a danger for humans.

Some experts predict that as many as half of all mine workers might be replaced by machines by the early 2000s. One day we might even see "minerless mines." What does this mean for jobs and the economy? The miner of the future may never wear a hard hat. He or she will probably work with a computer instead of a drill. And it's likely that more people will be employed in designing, producing, and maintaining automated machinery than in more traditional mining jobs.

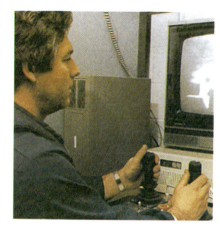

Figure 15.13 How does this miner's job differ from that of a traditional miner?

Technology and the Forest

The forests of Atlantic Canada are one of our most valued renewable resources. Managing our forests provokes controversy — probably more than the management of any other resource. Technology helps us to protect our forests — playing a role in the way we gather the information we need to make decisions and in the way we protect trees from pests and fires. On the other hand, it also allows us to harvest trees in ever more efficient ways.

Clear Cutting

The most common harvesting method in Canada is clear cutting, which means that virtually all the trees in a large area are harvested. Ninety percent of all trees cut in Canada are taken by clear cutting. Although this method is very common, it is also extremely controversial.

The Role of the Forest

In the early 1990s, a national public-opinion poll asked Canadians to rank the reasons why they value their forests. The results were surprisingly consistent across the country. Forests were ranked as being important for the following reasons, from most to least important:

1. Protecting water, air, and soil
2. Balancing the global ecosystem
3. Supplying wildlife habitat
4. Preserving wilderness
5. Producing economic wealth and jobs
6. Providing a place for recreation and relaxation

Do these results surprise you? Why or why not?

Source: Adapted from D. Minty et al., Resources for Tomorrow (St. John's: Breakwater Books, 1994).

Figure 15.14 Environmentalists in Temagami, Ontario, protest logging of old-growth forest, hundreds of years old. Many residents in the area supported logging because it meant more jobs. There have been protests against logging in other provinces, including New Brunswick. What would your opinion be in these circumstances?

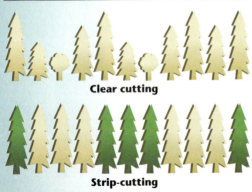

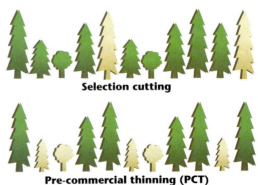

Figure 15.15 Various methods of harvesting the forest

Some lumber companies are modifying their methods to reduce the impact of large-scale clear cutting. They might clear cut in strips or in blocks. Both of these methods allow the bordering forest to shelter the cleared area and help the soil retain moisture and nutrients. Foresters can then replant trees in a more protected and controlled situation.

In favour

- Clear cutting is often the most economical method of harvesting trees.
- Foresters argue that it causes much less environmental damage than most people think. They compare clear cutting with a forest fire: removing all the old trees allows a new cycle of growth to begin.
- Fewer roads are needed for clear cutting than for other harvesting methods. Road construction can be one of the most damaging activities of a tree-harvesting operation. If soil is not eroded, and if adequate tree regeneration is ensured through good forest management, the forest will grow again.

Against

- Clear cutting leaves an appearance of devastation.
- While some tree species grow again in clear-cut sites, the practice can lead to soil erosion, loss of soil moisture, and damage to animal and fish habitats.
- In old forests, clear cutting destroys the complex relationships among soil, plants, and animals that have evolved over long periods. It can favour one group of plants and animals, but eliminate others.

Clear Cutting and the Rainforests

Tropical rainforests once stretched in a continuous belt around the earth's middle, covering about 20 percent of the world's area. Today, this environment is one of the most threatened on earth. Clear cutting has broken it into pockets, reduced now to about 7 percent of the earth's land area, and continuing to disappear at an alarming rate. Even though these forests are far from Atlantic Canada, their destruction has an impact on all of us. The rainforests function as the "lungs of the earth," cleansing the air. They are home to countless plant and animal species that are now being driven to extinction. Some of these plants and animals are vital in producing medicines used around the world.

There are many complex reasons for the destruction of the rainforest. Primarily, people of the tropics are trying to improve their standards of living. They are encouraged to clear the forest, often to farm beef cattle or to supply wood. The meat is frequently sold to industrialized countries, ending up in the fast-food industry or in pet food. Industrialized countries also make up the main market for tropical wood. Does the responsibility for the rainforest then rest with the people who live there, or do we also have a part to play?

Figure 15.16 The World Resources Institute has estimated that the tropical rainforests are being destroyed at the rate of about 7 million hectares per year, or 13 hectares per minute!

Mechanical Tree Harvesting

There are two types of mechanical tree harvesters. One is a full-tree harvester, which uses its mechanical arms to grasp a whole, standing tree and cut it off at the base with a rotary sawblade. The tree is then transported whole to a processing area where the limbs and tops are removed. The second type is a cut-to-length harvester, which fells the tree, removes the limbs and top, and cuts it into log lengths.

As with clear cutting, there are advantages and disadvantages with this type of technology. Mechanical harvesters require fewer workers and can cut and remove trees very quickly. Operators are safe in an enclosed cab and can work in poor weather. However, the machines are expensive and require maintenance.

There are also concerns that these machines harm the forest environment. In manual harvesting, tree branches are left in the forest, where they protect the soil from damage by large vehicles. These branches also retain the moisture in the soil and provide a protective cover for new seedlings. When whole-tree harvesters remove the branches from the forest, they leave the soil exposed. This can lead to degradation of the forest soil, so that the next forest to grow on this land will be less healthy than the one just cut down.

Figure 15.17 *Left*: Harvesting trees in the traditional manner. Why might someone today choose to use traditional technology to harvest trees? *Right*: Using a full-tree harvester. Why might someone choose this form of technology? The full-tree harvester is as efficient as farm machinery. How can a forest be compared to a crop of wheat? How do the two resources differ?

TECHNOLOGY ON THE FARM

Farms in the Atlantic region are rapidly becoming "high-tech." For example, most farmers depend on chemical technology for pesticides and fertilizers that protect food and improve crop production. Many now use farm machinery that is increasingly sophisticated — from harvesters, to potato graders and sorters, to computers that control conditions in milking sheds, greenhouses, and storage warehouses. New varieties of crops have been genetically engineered to grow more quickly or to resist pests. New techniques, such as embryo implants, are also available for breeding more productive livestock.

As part of the high-tech revolution in agriculture, cows in some places are wearing computerized collars. Wildlife managers commonly use radio collars to monitor the movements of wild animals, but why would anyone want to put a radio collar on a cow within the confines of a farm?

All over Atlantic Canada, dairy farmers like Calvin Samms of Howley, Newfoundland, are building new barns or modifying older ones to take advantage of **remote sensing technology**, which allows them to gather information from a distance. Each cow wears a special collar. Inside the barn, a computer system is linked to the milking machines and automatic feeders. Information on each cow — such as size, birth date, number of calves, and pregnancy status — is entered onto the computer.

> **DID YOU KNOW…?**
>
> Pesticide use in Canada is well tested and controlled, but elsewhere in the world — especially in less industrialized countries — dangerous chemicals banned in Canada are still used. In addition, higher crop yields resulting from fertilizers use up soil nutrients more rapidly, so that ever-increasing amounts of chemicals are needed. Researchers are now working on more environmentally friendly forms of technology. These include specialized forms of crop rotation and biological pest control, based on the introduction of natural predators.

Figure 15.18 The cows in this barn have their every move tracked by the radio collars they wear, but they don't seem to mind. In fact, the controlled environment lowers their stress level.

Other information, such as milk production and amount of grain eaten, is updated automatically as the cow feeds or is milked.

Typically a barn is divided into two parts: the main barn and the milking area. In Calvin Samms's main barn, cows roam freely and eat at feeding stations. When a cow enters a feeding station, a receiver picks up the radio signal from her collar and sends it to the computer. The computer determines which cow has entered the station, and instructs an automatic feeding machine to supply a fixed portion of grain. The amount given depends on the information already entered in the computer about that particular cow. Throughout the day the cow gets several small feed rations, because cows fed in this way produce more milk than those who eat a lot of feed at once. The computer has a record of how much feed each cow should receive in a 12-hour period, and simply does not give a particular cow more food after she has consumed her full ration. Cows can consume as much water and hay or silage as they want.

In the milking area, Calvin Samms and his son can milk over 90 cows in approximately 1.5 hours. If the need arises, however, Samms can easily handle all the milking himself. When a cow approaches a milking machine, the machine registers the signal from the animal's collar. As milking progresses, the computer records the volume of milk produced. It also measures the temperature of the milk to check if the cow has a fever. At any time, Samms can find out how much milk a cow has produced and compare it with how much she has eaten by examining the cow's file in the computer. The milking area is spotless, as wastes are automatically pumped away.

Does all this technology make a difference? Samms thinks it does. Because the barn environment is so well controlled, the cows experience little stress, and milk production is fairly constant throughout the year.

Source: Adapted from D. Minty et al., Resources for Tomorrow *(St. John's: Breakwater Books, 1994).*

EXPLORATIONS

APPLYING YOUR SKILLS

1. It has been said that "technology is a wonderful servant, and a terrible master."

   a) Make an organizer to show the advantages and disadvantages of some of the technologies described in this chapter.

   b) Write a short essay to show how the saying applies to natural resources in the Atlantic region.

ANALYZING AND REFLECTING

2. One trend in livestock farming has been to confine animals more closely. This practice allows farmers to maintain greater control over the factors influencing production. It is used most often for hens, which are confined in small row cages for egg production. Do you think such practices are ethical? Argue your views in a class debate.

CONNECTING AND EXTENDING

3. Pick an ordinary object you use every day that contains some mineral, either metallic or non-metallic. Research where the mineral came from. Develop a flow chart showing how it got from the earth's crust to you.

4. **a)** Conduct your own opinion poll in your community on the role of forests. Ask residents to rank the same six functions shown in the box on page 234.

   b) How do your results compare with the national ranking? How would you explain any differences?

   c) Consider submitting your results, along with a letter, to the provincial or federal government department responsible for forests.

5. Research any community in the Atlantic provinces that has, at any time, based its economy on mining. If mines in the area have

closed, find out why. If mines in the area are still open, find out how long they are expected to last. Look at the possible social effects on the community if the mine were either to close or to continue operating. Present a short report of your findings.

6. Research developments in drilling technology that have allowed for off-shore mining operations such as Hibernia or Sable Gas. Make a time line to show key innovations in drilling technology or prepare a short report on the types of technology used in off-shore mining.

7. **a)** As a group, develop a set of questions to ask about the use of new technology in farming. New technology might involve new equipment, new breeds of animals or plants, or new methods of pest control, to name a few.

   b) If possible, arrange a field trip to a farm and ask the farmer to help you answer the questions you have developed.

SEEING THE BIG PICTURE

1. Working either in a group or as an individual, find answers to the following questions. If you work in a group, you could do this activity as a jigsaw.
   a) Of the resource industries in your area, which one contributes most to the economy?
   b) Which one involves the largest number of people?
   c) Is the work force in each industry increasing, decreasing, or remaining stable? Why?
   d) Which ones cause the least, and most, environmental damage?

2. **a)** Choose one resource industry in your area, and identify a current technology that is used within it.
   b) Describe that technology and evaluate its impact on society and the environment.
   c) Do you think that the technology represents a good or bad example of sustainable development? Explain your answer.

3. For a resource industry of your choice, construct a web diagram to illustrate the influences that industry has on your society.

CHAPTER 16
Technology at Work

Figure 16.1 In what ways is your education preparing you to enter the work force?

Do you ever look forward to having your first full-time job? Imagine yourself at the age of 21, about to start work. You're excited as you dress for your first day. You want to look smart, but not too formal. You have invested many years in your education. You feel confident and skilled, but a little nervous. You arrive at work 15 minutes early, but the place is already bustling. One of the company's managers comes to meet you. She tells you a bit about your job and introduces you to some of your co-workers.

Then she says, "The first thing you will have to do is take a three-week training program to learn about the kinds of technology we use here and how we try to keep up with technological change."

"What's happening?" you wonder. "I have lots of technological training, and now I have to get more!"

- Does training in new technology ever end? Explain.
- How is technology changing the world of work for employers and workers?
- How can we prepare ourselves for a world of work that is constantly changing?

Businesses in the New Economy

At one time, most people completed their schooling and then launched into a single career for the rest of their lives. That era is over. In the new economy, conditions are changing rapidly for both businesses and workers. In this section we will look at some of the major issues affecting businesses today.

New Technology

Of all the changes in the Canadian workplace, the introduction of computers has probably been the most revolutionary. In 1985, about one in five employed Canadians used a computer at work. By 1989 the number was one in three. In 1994 almost half of the employed Canadians used computers on the job! Businesses today need to invest in new technology — not just computers, but other machines that can help them produce high-quality goods and services rapidly and efficiently. They also need to train their employees on an ongoing basis, as new technology is introduced. They need to keep up with changes in technology if they are to compete successfully with other companies.

Figure 16.2 Many companies aim to replace office technology about once every five years, to keep pace with new advances.

Customer Service

Companies today find that working hours are no longer restricted to the period between 9:00 and 5:00. Because of information technology, customers can place orders around the clock. They also expect to receive their goods and services quickly.

Figure 16.3 Why is it important for a business to deliver its goods or services without delay?

Downsizing

One of the ways some employers have responded to economic changes is by reducing staff and services. This is called **downsizing**. A company that downsizes might then **outsource** — that is, hire part-time, temporary, and contract workers or entrepreneurs who can supply services if and when they are needed. Many companies that downsize expect their remaining employees to maintain productivity, arguing that workers can be more productive with the help of new technology.

Figure 16.4 Machines can now handle many of the tedious or dangerous tasks that used to be done by hand.

The Global Economy

Computers allow information and money to move practically anywhere very quickly. This has allowed many to sell their goods or services abroad more easily than ever before. Some Atlantic businesses have developed **strategic alliances** with other companies abroad, to help them make or market their products. Others practise **offshore outsourcing**, which means they produce their goods in another country and then transport them back to Canada or another country to be sold. These goods are often produced in less developed countries where the cost of labour is low.

Figure 16.5 Why are Atlantic Canadian companies keen to trade abroad?

Restructuring

Many companies have found that, in the new economy, they need to change the organization of the company and the way in which employees work with one another. **Project teams** and **telework** are two changes in organization that are becoming more common.

- At one time, most companies expected their managers to tell others what to do and how to do it. Today, companies often assemble teams of workers with specialized skills and knowledge to work on specific projects. These **project teams** may not have a leader, or if they do, the leader's job is to serve as a coordinator who keeps the team working together. This role is important since members of the team don't have to be in the same place, or even in one country. In fact, Atlantic companies that trade outside of the region sometimes try to include team members from other provinces or other countries where they hope to do business.

Figure 16.6 Do you think team work would appeal to you? Why or why not?

- Working with a widespread team is made possible by telework. **Telework** refers to the activities of people who use computers to connect with other computers, perhaps at a head office or some other location. Usually telephone lines are used to link systems, but other kinds of connections are being developed that will allow for a faster flow of information. Teleworkers may operate from a home, a car, a hotel, or another office. They file reports, get new information, check the availability of products, place orders, leave messages, give and receive directions, and do any number of other things that are possible when two or more computers are linked.

Figure 16.7 Lap-top computers are just one of the innovations that have made telework a growing trend.

Focus on an Issue

Health in the Workplace

Since the 1940s, employers throughout Canada have had to follow government regulations that ensure the workplace is a healthy and safe environment. Most provide no-smoking environments and break periods, and some provide facilities such as gym space or day care centres. Today's technology, however, has brought some new health problems. For example, some workers in modern buildings complain of "sick-building syndrome." They become ill, often with headaches and nausea. The cause of sick-building syndrome is a mystery, but some engineers believe the problem is caused by air circulation. In most modern buildings, temperatures are controlled by heating and air-conditioning systems. Windows don't open, so there is no fresh air. The air that circulates through the building continually recycles pollutants such as tiny fabric particles from furniture or fumes from carpet glue, photocopiers, and other sources. These pollutants might be making some people sick. Improved ventilation sometimes helps, but researchers are working on other solutions, such as the one shown in Figure 16.8.

Other health problems are related to computers. Many people complain that long hours of using a mouse and keyboard have given them sore wrists and stiff hands. Others suffer eye-strain from staring at video monitors or back pain from sitting in one position too long. At least one company has developed software that interrupts the computer-user and coaches him or her through some physical exercises. Other companies are developing office furniture and accessories that relieve some of the physical stress that comes with extensive computer use.

ANALYZING THE ISSUE

1. Research some current health benefits and health problems related to the use of today's technology.

2. Work in groups to brainstorm some solutions to the problems you have identified. Then, as a class, decide on the top ten solutions.

3. Share your ideas with other schools by joining a newsgroup or developing your own home page for the World Wide Web. Try linking with Canada's SchoolNet at http://schoolnet2.carleton.ca/

Figure 16.8 The "Breathing Wall" consists of 800 species of plants, 50 water animals in an aquarium, and a large number of insects. This ecosystem draws in office air, together with its pollutants, and then purifies it. The air that then recirculates through the building is clean.

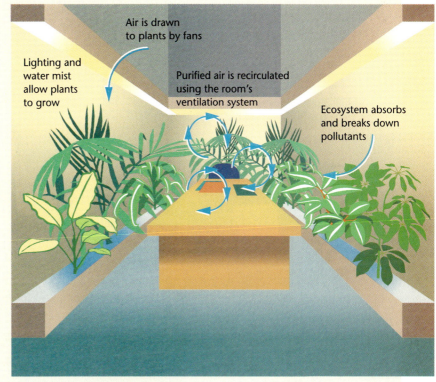

TECHNOLOGY AT WORK

Career Focus: Meet the Owner of a High-Tech Company

Mona El-Tahan is the president and chief executive officer of CORETEC Inc., a high-tech company in St. John's, Newfoundland.

Figure 16.9 Mona El-Tahan

Q: Can you briefly describe what you do?

A: My company specializes in developing technology to predict the movement of floating objects at sea through the use of computer models. The floating objects might be vessels, icebergs, oil, or sea ice. The user of our program feeds information into the computer about the wind and ocean currents, the original position of the object, and other details. Then the computer can display where that object will move over a certain period of time. We sell these programs to shipping companies and offshore oil companies.

Q: What is the purpose of the service you provide?

A: Objects like icebergs are major hazards when working at sea. Workers need to know if an iceberg or other object is likely to interfere with their operations, so that they can take appropriate action. They may need to move out of the way or divert the iceberg from its predicted path.

For example, I recently got a request for a model from Hibernia. The main structure is designed to withstand the impact of an iceberg, but the workers still have to protect all the off-loading facilities, the supply boats, and the shuttle tankers. They need to be able to predict what an iceberg is going to do. We also developed a model for Environment Canada to predict what an oil spill will do in the presence of sea ice. There are several other models for predicting the movement of an oil spill in open water, but ours is the only one that considers ice. This is very important in the North Atlantic. Now we are even serving as advisors to Norwegian and American companies.

Q: How did you get into this kind of work?

A: I did my graduate studies in ocean engineering at Memorial University in Newfoundland. The main topic of my thesis was modelling, or predicting, iceberg drift. My model was the first one developed in North America. It was purely theoretical: I didn't know I could use it in real life. I developed procedures for ice observers, including ways to protect their platforms from icebergs and to tow the icebergs away. I come from Egypt, so some people ask how

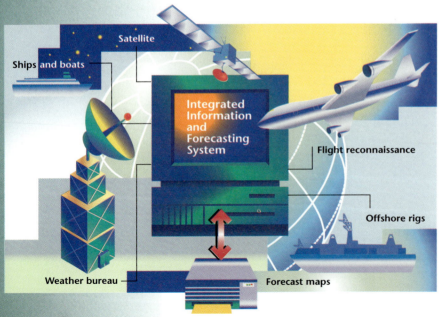

Figure 16.10 CORETEC's Integrated Information and Forecasting System tracks the movement of floating objects with information collected by the methods shown here.

I ended up working with icebergs. I laugh and tell them that they look much like the Pyramids.

Q: Dealing with icebergs is pretty unusual work. Can you describe any experiences that are especially memorable?

A: I received a call one stormy night around midnight. It was from Mobil, the drilling company working on the Grand Banks. They were in a panic because an iceberg had suddenly been spotted on the horizon. This was shortly after the *Ocean Ranger* disaster, when many people died, and I'm sure that was on their minds. There were over 80 people on board the rig. It was too stormy to send a helicopter to rescue them. I did a forecast in less than a half hour. Luckily it indicated that the iceberg would come close to the drill ship, within about a kilometre, but that it would pass by. Mobil officials asked me how confident I was about my forecast. I answered, "99 percent." When they saw the detailed model, with information on where the iceberg was and where it was going, they relaxed. They suspended their operations for the night and went to sleep. The next morning they sent a helicopter to see where the iceberg was. It was where I predicted it would be.

Q: Does computer technology play a significant role in your work?

A: Computer technology is really the key. Predicting the behaviour of a floating object that is being acted upon by many forces at the same time requires very sophisticated mathematics with numerous calculations. The computer is programmed to do all this calculating. That's what my models do and they do it fast. If it were not for the computer and the software, the problem could not be solved quickly enough to be of any use as a prediction. It is also essential to display the results in a format that is easy to understand—complete with tables, charts and maps. This helps people using the information to make the right decisions, even in an emergency.

Q: As well as being an engineer and software specialist, you are also an entrepreneur. Did any of your formal schooling prepare you for that?

A: No. We were not as fortunate as some young people now. I learned everything I know about business through real-life experience. I took some short training courses in project and personnel management, business development, and accounting that were very good. But I believe we never stop learning. You never graduate from life.

EXPLORATIONS

APPLYING YOUR SKILLS

1. How has technology had an impact on your place of work — that is, your school? Write a brief description of how you use technology during the course of the day, and of how this technology has changed school life.

ANALYZING AND REFLECTING

2. Labour unions have traditionally represented groups of workers in bargaining collectively with employers on issues related to wages and conditions of work.

a) How do you think the changes described in this section affect the way labour unions work?

b) If you were a union organizer in a workplace that was downsizing and restructuring, what goals would you set for the union?

c) If you were a manager in the workplace, what plan would you try to make for your relationship with the union?

CONNECTING AND EXTENDING

3. Work in groups.

a) Survey people in your community to find people who work at home, part-time or on contract for companies that outsource.

b) Call some companies in your area. Ask to speak to the Human Resources Office, and find out if any employees are teleworkers. Find out what jobs they do. Try to interview a teleworker to find out more about how this person does his or her job.

c) Prepare a short report of your findings.

4. Identify local companies or individuals using some kind of new technology in their work. Consider engineers, warehouse workers, office workers, sales people, farmers, artists, or any other occupation or workplace you can think of. Pick a few and find out more about how they are using innovative technologies. Write a short essay on your favourite success story.

Workers in the New Economy

What will changes in the workplace mean to people's lives? Consider some of the implications by reading about the experiences of some workers in the new economy.

"I'm an accountant. I work for a fairly large accounting firm, but I do most of my work at home. One of the benefits of working this way is that my children don't have to come home to an empty house after school, but there are also some disadvantages. I miss the camaraderie of working with other people, and sometimes I worry that I will be overlooked for promotion just because I'm not in the office very often."

Figure 16.11 Dianne Fuller, Prince Edward Island

"I own a garage that specializes in engine repairs. The last few years have been very interesting. Fixing an engine is not as straightforward as it used to be. I'm constantly looking for information that will help me keep up with technological changes in auto engines. Even in my own shop, I need to invest in new equipment to test and repair the vehicles that are brought here."

Figure 16.12 Gilbert Nochasak, Labrador

"I'm a freelance book editor. I work from home, which is good, because sometimes I have to work long hours to meet deadlines. But there are some disadvantages too. Because my work is based here, it's sometimes a challenge to separate my working and non-working life! Clients and authors know where to find me, so they often call me outside normal working hours. All the same, there are far fewer distractions at home than there would be in the office, so I can get more done in less time."

Figure 16.13 Patti Giovannini, Newfoundland

"I'm a carpenter. At the moment, I'm working in a plant that manufactures doors and window frames. This isn't steady work; usually I have a contract to help out on a special order for a new high-rise or housing development. The contract lasts for as long as it takes to complete the order. I like the flexibility of this sort of arrangement, and I use the time when I'm not working to upgrade my skills. I'm taking a distance learning course in marketing so that I'll soon have a wider range of job prospects. I have to make sure, though, that I plan my finances carefully. I don't have a pension plan, of course, as I would if I were a permanent employee, or a dental or health plan, so I need to make sure that I put money aside for emergencies. I take care to save so that I will have a financial cushion for times when I'm not at work."

Figure 16.14 George Phillips, New Brunswick

"I'm an aerobics instructor at a health club. People today are very health conscious, and they try to exercise regularly. A lot of them find that exercise really helps to relieve the stress of working life. Some of them really need to stretch out after a day spent huddled over a computer, and others who don't have much contact with other people in their work come here for social reasons."

Figure 16.15 Christine Hatsis, Nova Scotia

"I am a stockbroker. After 10 years in Toronto, I decided to come back to New Brunswick because I can now do all the transactions I need to do using my computer at home, hooked up to various networks through a modem. I can trade in stocks and keep contact with the main office. There are lots of advantages to working this way. I'm living where I want to be, and I don't have to face the traffic every morning. Think of the improvements in traffic congestion and air quality, if enough people worked this way!"

Figure 16.16 Anthony Saunders, New Brunswick

Focus on an Issue

How Can We Prepare for a Changing Workplace?

Even though we can't predict changes in technology, we need to prepare for the future. We can be certain that we will all need positive attitudes towards change. We will need to be ready for **life-long learning**, training and upgrading our skills constantly. We will need to be ready to change from one job to another and to adapt the way we work as new technology becomes available.

While education and training will be an asset in the new economy, we will also need some general or "generic" skills. These are skills that allow us to transfer more easily from one job to another, or from one contract to another. Employers will also continue to look, as they do at present, for attitudes that make their employees valuable to the company.

FOCUS ON FIGURE 16.17

1. How might a low education level impact on your lifestyle?
2. How do job prospects for people with low education levels differ in Atlantic Canada and Ontario?
3. If you want to maximize your chances of being employed, regardless of where you live, what level of education should you strive for?

Figure 16.17 Education and unemployment rates, 1981–1991

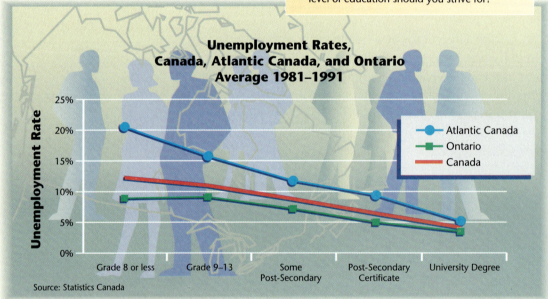

Table 16.1 Generic skills

Basic/academic skills	Technology skills	Thinking skills	Personal qualities
Literacy	Use of computers	Creative thinking	Responsibility
Numeracy	Use of other forms of technology	Decision making	Teamwork skills
Communications	Systems maintenance	Problem solving	Enterprising skills
Time management	Systems design	Knowing how to learn	Adaptability
		Critical thinking	

Table 16.2 Enterprising skills: Some characteristics valued by businesses and organizations

- Honesty
- Loyalty
- Respect for fellow workers
- Positive attitude towards work
- Striving for excellence
- Readiness to learn
- Ability to work with others and resolve conflicts when they occur
- Ability to focus on an end product and work towards it
- Self-confidence

ANALYZING THE ISSUE

1. Look at the list of generic skills in Table 16.1. Which of these skills have you refined as a result of this course? Which do you need to develop?

2. Make a plan that outlines the skills you need to develop and ways to do so.

3. You have thought about the role of employees; now consider the responsibilities of employers. Make a list of what you believe to be the main responsibilities of employers to their work force.

EXPLORATIONS

APPLYING YOUR SKILLS

1. Complete a chart similar to the one below, for at least three types of change in the way people work.

Change	Benefit to society	Cost to society, if any

2. **a)** Think of several summer jobs available to students in your community. Choose one, and imagine that you are applying for it. Write or update your résumé. Be sure to describe your experience and skills, especially where they are relevant to the job.

   b) Imagine that you are the employer. Would you hire yourself? Why or why not?

ANALYZING AND REFLECTING

3. Debate: The main aim of new technology should be to serve society as a whole, rather than individual corporations.

4. As more and more people use computers in their jobs or at home, they are interacting with other people less. What are the disadvantages of a world with less face-to-face interaction? Discuss as a class.

CONNECTING AND EXTENDING

5. **a)** Interview an adult about changes he or she has witnessed in the way people work. What caused some of the changes? How did he or she react to the changes? Were the changes stressful? What was the impact of the changes?

   b) In the style of a newspaper or magazine advice column, respond to the following question: "I am thinking of changing my career. How can I best prepare for change, and what steps can I take to reduce the stress that change brings?"

6. Research one of the following topics. Present your findings in a short essay, report, or display.

   a) Technology and health care

   b) Technology and education

   c) Technology and food production

   d) Technology and leisure time

   Your report should include brief descriptions of new types of equipment and what they can do, the benefits of new technology, and the manner in which technology is changing the way people work.

CHANGES IN MANUFACTURING AND MARKETING

Technology has had a major impact on the way products are manufactured, and in the way they are presented to you, the consumer. To develop a new product, be it a circuit board or a bar of soap, manufacturers follow certain steps, as shown in Figure 16.18. At each step, new technologies are being developed, most of which use computers in some way.

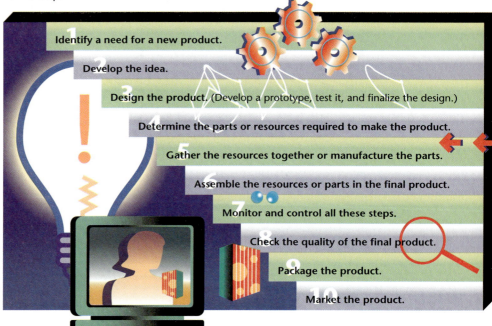

1. Identify a need for a new product.
2. Develop the idea.
3. Design the product. (Develop a prototype, test it, and finalize the design.)
4. Determine the parts or resources required to make the product.
5. Gather the resources together or manufacture the parts.
6. Assemble the resources or parts in the final product.
7. Monitor and control all these steps.
8. Check the quality of the final product.
9. Package the product.
10. Market the product.

Figure 16.18 Steps in developing a new product

Some New Manufacturing Technologies

With **computer-aided design** (CAD), engineers can develop three-dimensional objects on a computer screen and manipulate them in various ways. CAD saves time and money by allowing designers to streamline designs and test them without actually making the new product. Assume, for example, that a snowmobile manufacturer is producing a new vehicle. Engineers can check the aerodynamics of the design on computer. They can adapt the design as many times as they need to, and test the effect of wind on each variation, all on the screen.

With **rapid prototyping** (RP) engineers can easily make real models of the objects they have designed on the computer. For instance, the snowmobile designers and company owners would probably want to see a model of the new vehicle. An RP computer can instruct a special machine to cut accurate sections out of a plastic-like material that, when put together, will form a model of your snowmobile.

DID YOU KNOW...?

Many products are mass produced. They are made in large quantities, and every item coming off the production line is nearly identical. Computer systems, especially CIM, are now allowing in some cases for "custom production": customers can ask for special features in a product and have it assembled to meet their specific needs.

250 TECHNOLOGY

Once the design is finalized and the resources to produce it are collected, manufacturing can begin. Through the manufacturing process, machines squirt, pick up, drill, move, rivet, solder, or do any number of things. When these tasks are done automatically with computers controlling them, the process is called **computer automation**. Computer automation has existed for years, but only within single steps in the manufacturing process. For example, on a snowmobile production line, the instructions for mounting the engine onto the chassis (the base or frame of the vehicle) were not linked to the instructions for the machine that places the body on top. Today, **computer integrated manufacturing** (CIM) links various machines, so that each "knows" what the other is doing. In other words, if the machine that places the body on the engine has a problem, the machine that mounts the engine on the chassis will "know" immediately that it needs to slow or stop its output to prevent the system from backing up.

Figure 16.19 The Manufacturing Technology Centre, a joint project of Memorial University and the College of the North Atlantic in Newfoundland, has state-of-the-art equipment and technical experts for training engineers and manufacturers in the use of systems such as CAD, RP, and CIM.

Some New Marketing Methods

Marketing is the selling of an idea, product, or service. Technology is revolutionizing the way products are marketed, especially through the World Wide Web (WWW). Many companies are setting up web sites to "display" their products. With a computer and Internet link you can find out the very latest information about a whole range of goods, place an order, and then track the progress of that order. All while you sit at home!

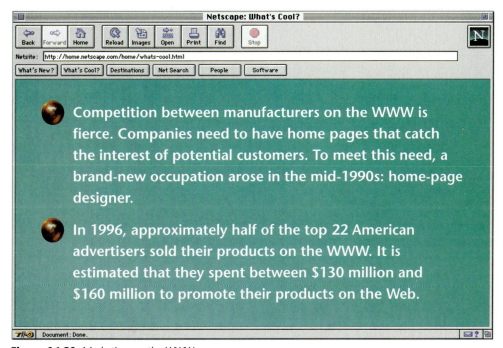

- Competition between manufacturers on the WWW is fierce. Companies need to have home pages that catch the interest of potential customers. To meet this need, a brand-new occupation arose in the mid-1990s: home-page designer.

- In 1996, approximately half of the top 22 American advertisers sold their products on the WWW. It is estimated that they spent between $130 million and $160 million to promote their products on the Web.

Figure 16.20 Marketing on the WWW

CASE STUDY

MAKING A CD

Atlantic Canada boasts an abundance of musical talent. You might have dreams of being a recording artist yourself. Let's look at the technology that brings the sound of Atlantic talent to the market.

Assume that you belong to a band that is about to make its first CD. Let's say your band has four main instruments: drums, lead guitar, bass guitar, and your voice. You have practised for days until you sound perfect. Now you are ready for the recording studio. You enter a sound-proof room that's wired with microphones and earphones. Outside the room, a sound engineer controls all the recording devices and a producer coaches you through the whole process. The producer gives you the cue and you start the opening chords of the first song. The process has begun.

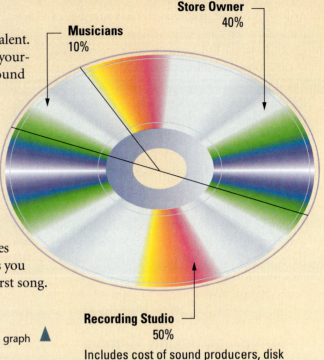

Musicians 10%
Store Owner 40%
Recording Studio 50%
Includes cost of sound producers, disk engineers, artwork for cover and disk, marketing and advertising, distribution

Figure 16.21 Who makes money when you buy a CD? This graph shows the *approximate* distribution of the money you spend. Figures shown are percentages of the final selling price. They do not include taxes.

1. A highly polished glass disk is coated with a light-sensitive chemical.

2. A laser shines pin-points of light onto the light-sensitive coating, creating tiny holes in it.

3. The disk becomes a mould. It is coated, by electroplating, with layers of nickel each only one molecule thick.

4. When the nickel is thick enough it is removed from the glass to become the master disk or "stamper" used to create other copies. The stamper is checked by laser for defects.

If you are very good and very lucky, you might get a song done in only a few "takes." It's much more likely that you will be interrupted many times and asked to make a small change or try something different until the producer and sound engineer are satisfied that they have the best possible recording of each instrument.

Although the band might be playing together, each instrument is recorded on tape separately. The sound engineer will later manipulate the sound of each one and add them all together to create the final mix. He or she will adjust the volume, pitch, and speed in tiny degrees to reach a satisfactory result. The sound engineer might even add special effects and new sounds. When everything is as good as it can be, a master tape is made and sent to the company that manufactures CDs.

Because of the huge demand for CDs, a manufacturer must be able to produce thousands per day in a high-speed assembly-line process. However, the assembly-line itself must be rapidly adaptable to produce different CDs for new recording artists. Follow the process in the diagrams below.

How a CD Works

Compact disks (CDs) are made of clear plastic and aluminum. The aluminum is encoded with tiny pits that reflect light and give the disk the rainbow colours you see as you move it in your hand. If you lined up all the pits from a single CD in a straight line it would be almost 5 km long! On the CD, they are organized in a spiral pattern from the centre to the edge. As the disk spins in a player, light from a tiny laser is reflected from the pit and converted into a digital signal that translates the information into sound.

Figure 16.22 Steps in the manufacture of a CD. A speck of dust could ruin a recording, so a dust-free environment is essential in the CD manufacturing plant. It might cost up to $1000 to make the master disk, but copies can be made for just $1 to $4 each.

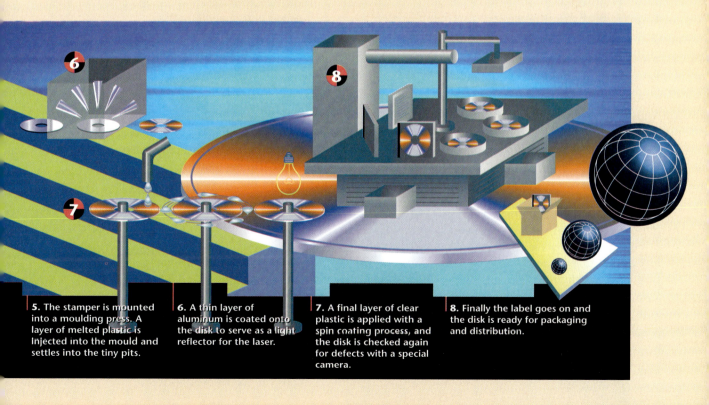

5. The stamper is mounted into a moulding press. A layer of melted plastic is injected into the mould and settles into the tiny pits.

6. A thin layer of aluminum is coated onto the disk to serve as a light reflector for the laser.

7. A final layer of clear plastic is applied with a spin coating process, and the disk is checked again for defects with a special camera.

8. Finally the label goes on and the disk is ready for packaging and distribution.

EXPLORATIONS

APPLYING YOUR SKILLS

1. **a)** Compare three examples of manufacturing that you have learned about in this book: making French fries (pages 170–171), making cymbals (pages 180–182), and making CDs. Which process is the most "high-tech"? Explain.

   b) Explain how CIM could be used to advantage in any one of these cases.

ANALYZING AND REFLECTING

2. How could technology be used to market a new CD?

   a) Brainstorm as many ways as possible.

   b) Make a marketing plan for a new CD, using all the technology available to you.

3. **a)** If you could order a custom-produced CD, what would you put on it?

   b) Do you think there would be a demand for custom-produced CDs? Why or why not?

CONNECTING AND EXTENDING

4. **a)** If you have access to the Internet, search the WWW to see how Atlantic Canadian companies are marketing their products. Start by identifying some large companies from telephone directories, newspapers, and magazines.

   b) You have probably heard the saying "Buyer beware!" This means that consumers should think carefully before spending their money. They should make sure, for example, that goods are of satisfactory quality or that the supplier will replace the goods or refund the cost if there is any problem. Why should people who buy goods over the Internet be particularly careful? Work in a small group to develop a list of guidelines for shopping on-line.

5. Visit a local electronics store. Ask one of the salespeople what technology is likely to replace CDs and CD players. Write a summary report on your findings. Use a word processor, if possible.

6. Develop a web site to "market" your part of Atlantic Canada. Include any information that would be interesting for visitors or newcomers to your area. Include links to other sites with information on Aboriginal peoples, cultural diversity, cultural activities, and any other interesting or useful information.

SEEING THE BIG PICTURE

1. Investigate manufacturing in Atlantic Canada.

   a) Choose a manufacturing company in your area. Work in small groups to investigate the points listed below. You could use the WWW, newspapers, magazines, or the telephone. You may be surprised to learn about what's going on "in your own backyard."

   i) What does the company make, and how does it make these products?

   ii) Does the company use any new technology such as CAD, RP, CIM, or robotics?

   iii) Do you or your family use products made by this company?

   b) If possible, try to arrange a visit to the manufacturing plant. Ask what changes, if any, the manufacturer is expecting in the technology used in the plant.

   c) Prepare a presentation of your findings for your class.

2. To get an idea of the bigger picture of manufacturing in Atlantic Canada, see if you can connect with other classes doing this course, perhaps through the Internet or your school computer network, and share your information.

3. Identify several careers in manufacturing. Decide on one or two that might appeal to you, and investigate what skills and qualifications you would need.

UNIT 5

Interdependence

CHAPTER 17 *Our Views of the World*

In what way are we all "global citizens"?

What factors influence the way we see the world?

How can we become contributing members of the global community?

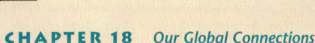

CHAPTER 18 *Our Global Connections*

How is Atlantic Canada part of the global community?

In what ways does our future well-being involve cooperation with the national and global community?

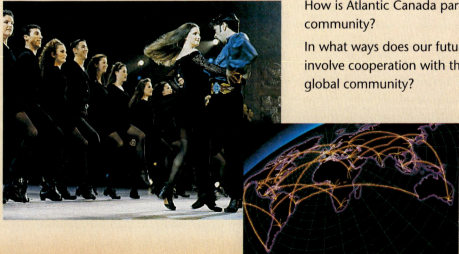

CHAPTER 17

Our Views of the World

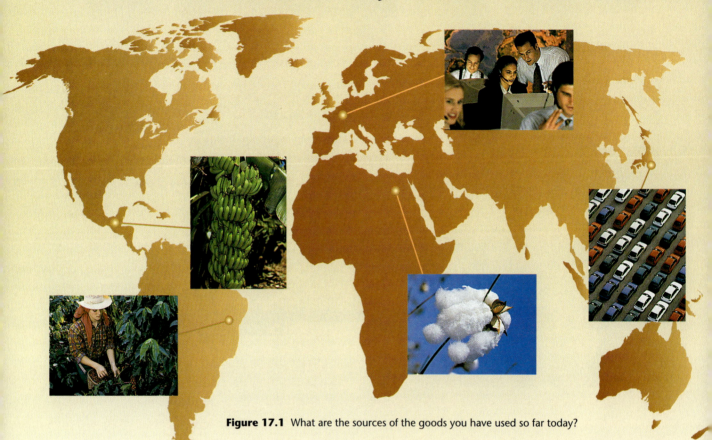

Figure 17.1 What are the sources of the goods you have used so far today?

Cecile pulls on a cotton T-shirt and jeans. She has breakfast — cocoa, toast with cheese, and a banana. Cecile's brother drives her to school in the family Toyota. On the car radio they hear a song by the new South American band everyone is talking about.

"My company might get a contract for a job in France," Cecile's brother tells her. "I might get to work there for awhile."

"Great!" says Cecile. "Oh, I almost forgot. I won't need a drive home after school. I'm playing basketball. There's a team coming up from Maine."

- Cecile lives in a small town in Atlantic Canada, but in what way is she linked to other countries?
- In what way are we all "global citizens"?
- How do our views of the world influence the way in which we participate in the global community?

GLOBAL CITIZENS

Cecile is from New Brunswick. Perhaps you are, too; or perhaps you live in Newfoundland and Labrador, Prince Edward Island, or Nova Scotia. You are most likely a Canadian citizen but, in a sense, you are also a citizen of the world. Like Cecile you are linked to many places all over the globe. Did an alarm clock wake you up this morning, for example? Perhaps it was made in China. Where were your shoes made? Perhaps they came from Portugal, Brazil, or Britain. Your T-shirt might be made from Egyptian cotton. Do you watch TV shows made in the United States? Do you write letters or send e-mail messages to friends or relatives in other countries?

In today's exciting times, we all benefit from many kinds of global connections. Technologies such as jet planes, computers, and satellite communications have helped to make all of these connections fast and easy.

Figure 17.2 Basketball tournament on Halifax Commons. The player at centre is William Njoku, who was born in Nigeria, raised in Halifax, chosen to play for Canada's National Basketball team, and drafted by the NBA's Indiana Pacers. What types of connections are illustrated by his story?

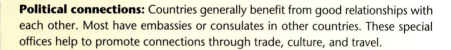

Some Global Connections

Political connections: Countries generally benefit from good relationships with each other. Most have embassies or consulates in other countries. These special offices help to promote connections through trade, culture, and travel.

Trade connections: Today, technologies such as computers and jet planes help make trade connections fast and easy. Computer parts made in Taiwan, chairs made in Sweden, and bauxite (for making aluminum) mined in Guyana are examples of the goods we import. Paper products, fish products, minerals, and artwork are examples of the goods we export.

Cultural connections: Atlantic Canadians have family and friends all over the world. They also enjoy music from many countries, read books by authors from many lands, and enjoy television shows from a variety of other countries.

Travel connections: Atlantic Canadians can travel to British Columbia on business, holiday in Bermuda, or visit family in Lebanon. They can play basketball against visiting teams from the United States, and enjoy a wide variety of other travel connections.

OUR VIEWS OF THE WORLD

The Global Village

How do our global connections influence us? Canadian communications theorist Marshall McLuhan pointed out the powerful effect of growing connections around the world. In the 1960s, he studied the effects of new communications and transportation technologies that were changing the world. Faster aircraft, telephones, television, and other technologies all meant humans could communicate much more quickly than ever before. McLuhan said such technologies were "reducing the distance" between the people of the world, giving them a sense of belonging to one large community or **global village**.

> "Society is moving from a print culture to a visual culture. Action and reaction occur almost at the same time. The medium is the message."
>
> Marshall McLuhan, 1967

Figure 17.3 Communications satellite. Advances in communications, transportation, and other technologies have made the world a "global village" in which people, products, and ideas move quickly and efficiently between distant places.

DID YOU KNOW...?

The world's first effective communications satellite, Telstar, was launched in 1962 from Cape Canaveral, Florida. Telstar orbited the Earth, receiving and sending telephone and TV signals. It was part of the age of high technology that emerged in the 1960s and continues to this day.

FOCUS ON FIGURE 17.4

1. In what way are images like this part of the global village?
2. What impact do they have on the viewer?
3. What actions or attitudes might result?
4. How might they affect our attitudes towards other parts of the world?

Figure 17.4 A woman and her child are turned away from a boat taking refugees from Albania, during civil unrest in 1997. Images such as this have an impact on us, travelling rapidly around the world and entering our homes on television and in newspapers.

EXPLORATIONS

APPLYING YOUR SKILLS

1. Find individuals in your class or school for whom the following statements are true. Make a list showing the name of each person and the country in each case.

    a) has travelled to another country
    b) has a pen pal in another country
    c) is learning a second language
    d) has a relative in another country
    e) has helped a visitor from another country
    f) owns a tape or CD of music from another country
    g) is wearing something that was made in another country
    h) has eaten food produced in another country
    i) can name a famous sports star from another country
    j) has talked to someone who has lived in another country
    k) lives in a home where more than one language is spoken
    l) saw a story about another country in the newspaper recently
    m) learned something about another country on TV recently
    n) owns a TV or other appliance made in another country
    o) has a parent or other relative who was born in another country.
    p) has received e-mail from another country

2. Do we seem to be more connected with some parts of the world than with others? If so, can you suggest why?

3. What would happen to our lives if all of these connections disappeared? Outline the way in which your day-to-day activities would change.

Source: G. Pike and D. Selby, Global Teacher, Global Learner *(London: Hodder and Stoughton, 1988), pp. 113–114.*

DEVELOPING A VIEW OF THE WORLD

Our sense that we now belong to a global village has changed the way we relate to the world around us — in other words, **it has changed our view of the world.** The way we see the world, however, does not begin with global connections. It often begins with many other factors that are closer to home.

Table 17.1 shows some of the factors that play an important part in the way our view of the world develops. These factors combine in different ways to influence the way we relate to the people and communities around us. They affect us all in different ways, so that the behaviour of individuals and groups often varies, based on differing views of the world. Try to decide how these factors have influenced your view of the world. How have they affected the way you relate to others around you?

Table 17.1 Some factors influencing the way we view the world

- Family values and traditions
- Religious beliefs
- Culture
- Interaction with other groups
- Economic circumstances
- Physical setting
- Attitude towards nature
- Education
- Political opinion
- Technology

Figure 17.5 What views of the world are evident in the pictures and extracts on these pages?

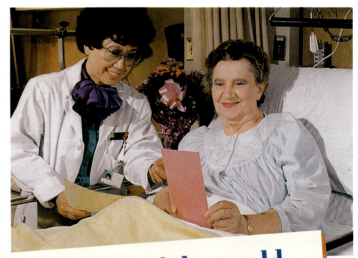

> "I think community is all-important. Ultimately, nothing will be solved, nothing will last, if we don't do it together, acknowledging our differences, but giving precedence to the benefits of cooperation, collaboration, and shared vision."
>
> *University of New Brunswick president and vice-chancellor Dr. Elizabeth Parr-Johnston*

A program to change your view of the world

Katimavik, a program for 17- to 21-year-olds, aims to build character, community, and national unity. How does it affect the participants' view of the world?

The pay is $3 a day, you have to be home by 10 p.m. on weekdays and there's precious little privacy when you're there.

Throw in volunteer work on evenings and weekends and it's a brutal schedule totally alien to most people. But the young people from across Canada here on the Katimavik program of community service say it's the best experience of their lives.

"It's changed my life. It's put me on the right track," says Dan Nadasdy, 18. He's one of nine participants from Ontario, Yukon, Saskatchewan, Quebec and New Brunswick on a federal program that lets them work in three different provinces for 10 weeks at a time....

Katimavik means "meeting place" in Inuktitut and the program's goal is to allow young people to experience their country, serve the community, and learn how to work together as a group. Participants are a cross-section of society from college graduates to the unemployed.

The program is no paid vacation. It's supposed to teach the participants about discipline, co-operation and community spirit.

In any case, the pay doesn't go far.

"If you can live on $21 a week, you can change the world," laughs Danika Gallan, 19, of Whitehorse.

The team gets an hour or two break when they get home from their day jobs before they're off on a team project or doing volunteer work. Weekends they've been helping out on such events as dog sled races.

The program is designed to challenge participants. The team has a weekly food budget of $300 on which they all have to agree, and they also have to make group decisions on a variety of subjects dictated by the program. There's nowhere to hide for young people who've never in their lives had to spend so much time so close to so many other people.

Figure 17.6 Madeleine Smith, Katimavik program coordinator for Edmonton, poses with some participants.

"If there's a problem, you have to talk about it and work it out, and that doesn't happen in a lot of families. Some adults could learn from that," says participant Danika Gallan.

Source: Dave Finlayson, "The time of their lives" (SouthamStar Network) March 18, 1997.

INTERDEPENDENCE

Students in Dalhousie and Bathurst, New Brunswick, clear up local wooded areas

> A people's view of the world is their understanding of how they fit into history, and how appropriate relationships between people and spiritual beings are formed and maintained. Their view of the world also includes the way in which the environment, history, and human relationships are valued.
>
> Source: Adapted from R. M. Leavitt, *Maliseet and Micmac: First Nations of the Maritimes* (Fredericton: New Ireland Press, 1995), p. 67.

EXPLORATIONS

ANALYZING AND REFLECTING

1. a) What do the following actions tell you about each student's view of the world?

   i) Brian volunteers at literacy classes at his local community centre. He helps newcomers to Canada and other teens who need to improve their reading and writing skills.

   ii) Peggy knows paint thinner is a toxin that can pollute the water supply but, once she has finished painting, she pours the thinner down the drain anyway.

   iii) Shona, with a group of other students, holds a car wash to raise money to sponsor children who live in less industrialized countries.

b) Write one statement for each of the five following themes to illustrate your own view of the world. Start each statement with the words "I believe…"

   i) physical environment
   ii) culture
   iii) economics
   iv) technology
   v) interdependence

c) Using Table 17.1 as a guide, identify the main influences on your view of the world as expressed in your statements.

CONNECTING AND EXTENDING

2. a) Would you like to participate in a Katimavik program? In what ways do you think you might benefit? How do you think it would affect your view of the world?

b) With a partner, write three questions you have about the program.

c) Do some research to find answers to your questions.

A Global World-View

Our view of the world often extends beyond our local communities to the world at large. In a community, people depend on each other in many different ways. One person may plow snow off the roads. Another may publish a community newspaper. Another may run a hardware store, or build sets for a community play. This kind of **interdependence** has been common in many places. In recent years, however, efforts have been made to cooperate on a global scale. Today, in our global village, people and countries depend on each other in many different ways. Let us take a closer look at some events and ideas that have created a **global world-view** — a view of the world that encourages cooperation between countries and a belief that countries have responsibilities outside their own boundaries.

Concern for People

Perhaps you have a relative who remembers the horrors of the Second World War. At the end of this war, people across the world hoped for an international arrangement that would prevent such terrible conflict from happening again. In April 1945, representatives from 51 nations including Canada met in San Francisco, California. Their aim was to form a new international organization, the United Nations. Among the UN's goals were:
- To keep world peace and prevent new wars from starting.
- To promote cooperation and an awareness of interdependence among peoples.
- To make sure all the world's people enjoy basic human rights.

Figure 17.7 The tied mules cannot eat while both think only of themselves. When they cooperate, however, they can share the food. How does this relate to the global world-view? Do you believe that everyone agrees with global cooperation? Why might some people have a different view of the world?

United Nations Declaration of the Rights of the Child, 1959

This declaration is one of many passed by the UN in its efforts to meet its main goals. As you read its ten statements, think about your own childhood. To what extent have you enjoyed the following rights? How might the situation be different in other parts of the world? What are our responsibilities stemming from this declaration?

1. The child shall enjoy rights without discrimination on account of race, colour, sex, language, religion, political or other opinion, national or social origin, property, or birth.
2. The child shall enjoy special protection, opportunities, and facilities to develop fully in a normal manner with freedom and dignity.
3. Every child is entitled to a name and nationality at birth.
4. As every child is entitled to grow in health, they and their mothers need special care — adequate nutrition, housing, recreation, and medical services.
5. A child who is physically, mentally, or socially handicapped shall be given the treatment needed.
6. The child has a right to grow up in the care and responsibility of parents in an atmosphere of affection and moral and material security.
7. The child has a right to an education as well as an opportunity for play and recreation.
8. In all circumstances, the child shall be the first to receive protection and relief.
9. The child is to be protected from neglect, cruelty, and exploitation. The child shall not be employed before an appropriate minimum age.
10. The child shall be brought up in a spirit of tolerance and friendship.

Figure 17.8 Although child labour is banned in many countries, it is still a global problem. At the age of 13, Canadian Craig Kielburger started the "Free the Children" organization to protest against child labour. He is shown here meeting with child workers in a market in India. Which UN Rights of the Child may have been denied to these young people? Research the steps Kielburger has taken to protect the rights of children around the world. What steps can you take to help?

Table 17.2 Some UN agencies. All member countries contribute to the UN's budget to help pay for the programs of agencies such as these. Most countries pay less than 1 percent of the total UN budget. Canada pays 3.1 percent of the budget.

United Nations Educational, Scientific, and Cultural Organization (UNESCO)
World Health Organization
UN Peacekeeping Operations
United Nations Conference on Trade and Development (UNCTAD)
United Nations Institute for Training and Research (UNITAR)
United Nations Children's Fund (UNICEF)
United Nations High Commission for Refugees (UNHCR)
Food and Agriculture Organization-World Food Program

Concern for the Environment

In the 1970s, many citizens of industrialized countries began to realize that the earth's resources were limited, and their lifestyles were causing many environmental problems. People who had never thought much about the environment before began turning back the heat in their homes to save energy. Some formed groups to help save endangered animals, and many began recycling cans and jars. A new environmental view of the world was emerging, based on principles that had been recognized for centuries by Aboriginal peoples around the world:

◆ Nature is not a machine but a living organism or system, in which all the parts are connected in a complex way. Damage to one part of the system will affect other parts as well.

◆ Humans are part of this global organism. Whatever affects nature affects humans too.

◆ Humans are part of nature. They should use nature only in ways that preserve the life of the whole global organism.

> "The land is my mother. Like a human mother, the land gives us protection and provides for our needs—economic, social, religious. We have a human relationship with the land: Mother-daughter, son. When the land is taken from us or destroyed, we feel hurt because we belong to the land and we are part of it."
>
> *Djiniyini Gondarra, member of Australian Aboriginal nation*

The Brundtland Report

In the 1980s, the United Nations set up a Commission on Environment and Development to consider the future of our planet. The commission's report was called *Our Common Future*, but it is often referred to as the "Brundtland Report," after the commission's chairperson. Its main recommendations were:

◆ The world should work towards getting rid of poverty. As long as some of the world's people are very poor, attempts at development and environmental protection will not succeed.

◆ The choices the world makes now, with regard to matters such as energy use, population control, and food production, will greatly affect its future.

◆ All future development should be **sustainable**. In other words, all development should meet the needs of the present without compromising the ability of future generations to meet theirs.

> "All nations will ultimately share the same destiny. Our environment and economies have become so intertwined that we may no longer choose to remain apart. The environment respects no national boundaries. We cannot act as if it did. Nations must [now focus on their] common future."
>
> *Gro Harlem Brundtland*

Figure 17.9 Gro Harlem Brundtland, Chair of the UN Commission on Environment and Development and former prime minister of Norway

CASE STUDY

THE PUGWASH CONFERENCES

Near the end of the Second World War, the United States dropped atomic bombs on the Japanese cities of Hiroshima and Nagasaki. People around the world were horrified at the devastating results of these nuclear weapons. A group of scientists decided to take a stand against the use of science for destruction. In 1955, scientist Albert Einstein and 10 other leading thinkers signed an international manifesto, or declaration, urging peaceful solutions to future problems.

"In view of the fact that in any future world war nuclear weapons will certainly be employed, and that such weapons threaten the continued existence of mankind, we urge the Governments of the world to realize, and to acknowledge publicly, that their purpose cannot be furthered by a world war, and we urge them, consequently, to find peaceful means for the settlement of all matters of dispute between them."

Anti-nuclear manifesto issued in London, England, July 9, 1955

DID YOU KNOW...?

Cyrus Eaton made his fortune in coal, steel, and railways. When a large part of Pugwash burned down, he agreed to rebuild it, establishing a beautiful park next to his white clapboard summer home, the site of the first Pugwash Conference.

Figure 17.10 Pugwash, Nova Scotia

At the same time, Cyrus Eaton — an industrialist born in Pugwash, Nova Scotia — was making interesting plans. He wanted to turn his birthplace into a place where scientists, philosophers, business people, and other thinkers could gather to discuss global problems. He invited the 11 people who had signed the 1955 Manifesto to his home. Over the course of the next two years, they held a few small meetings at Pugwash. Then, in 1957 came the first Pugwash Conference on Science and World Affairs. Leading thinkers attended from Canada, the United States, Europe, Australia, and the Soviet Union.

That 1957 conference was the first in a series. Some were held in other parts of the world, but they were all called Pugwash Conferences. Over the years the Pugwash Conferences continued to encourage the responsible use of science, encouraging nations to sign treaties limiting their use of weapons and to use science for the benefit of the environment. Today, Pugwash still hosts conferences, although they are on a smaller scale than those of the late 1950s and 1960s. The importance of these continuing efforts was recognized in 1995, when the Pugwash Conferences on Science and World Affairs were awarded the Nobel Peace Prize.

Figure 17.11 Dr. Joseph Rotblat, who received the Nobel Peace Prize on behalf of the Pugwash Conferences on Science and World Affairs.

CASE STUDY

A Place of Refuge

Refugees are people who leave their country because they fear for their safety. The United Nations, through the UN High Commission for Refugees (UNHCR), tries to help refugees by providing emergency food, water, shelter, and medical assistance. Many individual countries also provide help, by accepting refugees as new immigrants. Many of the world's refugees have hoped to make their home in Canada, where most people live in safety and comfort.

Meet a Refugee

Lina Garcia was a refugee. In 1982, when Lina was 18, civil war in her home country of Guatemala, in Latin America, threatened her family's safety. Today she lives in Charlottetown, Prince Edward Island. What does her experience reveal about the global world-view of Canadians? What does it reveal about her own view of the world, as a refugee?

Figure 17.12 Lina Garcia visited Guatemala in 1995. How might her view of the country have changed since 1982?

Q: What happened in your town in 1982?

A: The town hall was burned by rebels. People were killed — I don't know if by rebels or government soldiers. There were bombings, shootings, a lot of terror.

Q: What did you do?

A: My parents and brothers and sisters and I ran away. First we ran to another town in Guatemala, and then we fled to Mexico.

Q: How did the Mexican government treat refugees like yourselves?

A: They lent us land to grow food, but we had to struggle to survive. It was not a community — just people living in the jungle. The UNHCR gave us some help.

Q: Was this actually a refugee camp?

A: Yes. We weren't allowed to travel more than 80 km from the centre of our camp. If found, we would be forced back to Guatemala.

Q: How did the refugee camp affect you?

A: Ever since I was a child, I had dreamed of going to university… achieving something in life. In the camp I became depressed, sick. I felt as if I was in four walls with no view of the outside world. At last I met someone from the Mexican government, who arranged for me to move to Mexico City. There I found a job, but still no way of fulfilling my childhood dreams.

Q: Did you and your family ever try to move to another country?

A: In 1983 we approached the Canadian Embassy because we knew Canada accepted refugees. But the Canadian government refused us. They said we didn't have enough training, that we couldn't survive in Canada.

Q: But here you are in Charlottetown. How did that come about?

A: My sister met a Prince Edward Islander. He offered to

266 INTERDEPENDENCE

find us **sponsors** — people who would guarantee to support us if necessary. Within two weeks, three Charlottetown churches had agreed to sponsor us. Within five months, all the government papers were ready. Thirteen members of my family including my sister moved to Prince Edward Island. That was in 1986. I followed in 1987.

Q: What did you do when you arrived in Charlottetown?

A: I took an English course at Holland College for six months. Then I started working at the Prince Edward Hotel, first in the laundry and then in the restaurant, where I've worked ever since.

Q: Were you able to pursue your childhood dream of further education?

A: Yes, Canada gave me my second chance. I enrolled in a B.A. program at the University of PEI, studying political science and history. I go to school full-time and work part-time.

Q: How are your sisters and brothers getting along in Canada?

A: Fine. I have nieces and nephews, too. The children all go to school, and the adults all work.

Q: Have you been back to Guatemala?

A: I went back in 1995 to marry Roberto Ortiz, a man I had been corresponding with for about two years. Roberto had to wait 11 months for his papers before he could join me in Canada. Now he's taking courses to learn English.

Q: Do you have any advice for Atlantic Canadian high-school students?

A: There's so much out there! There's so much to learn about other cultures, people, and places. And school is like a window on the world. I'd say, "Stay in school, but not only to prepare for a job. Think first about all you can learn."

Explorations

REVIEWING THE IDEAS

1. Think of your neighbourhood or a similar community with which you are familiar. Make a chart to show ways in which the global village is similar to and different from this community. Follow the example, adding any other categories that seem appropriate.

	My community	The global village
Cooperative efforts Helping individuals Problem solving Communication		

APPLYING YOUR SKILLS

2. How have the events and ideas described in this chapter affected your view of the world? How have they affected the way you live your life?

   a) Prepare a diagram, cartoon, or short paragraph to show the influence of one of the following on your view of the world:

   i) communications technology

   ii) belief in rights of the child

   iii) awareness of the environment

   b) Make a class bulletin board display of your work.

ANALYZING AND REFLECTING

3. a) Work in a group. Discuss one of the three main points from the Brundtland Report. Suitable questions for discussion include:

   i) Why would the Commission's members think it important to make this point?

   ii) Do you agree with the point made? Why? Do you disagree in any way? Why?

iii) Are there aspects of the point you don't understand?

iv) What research could you do to understand the point better?

b) Share your ideas with at least two other groups that have focused on different points from the Report.

4. Describe what you think may have been the motives and views of the world of each of the following:

   a) the soldiers or rebels who burned the town hall in Lina's home town

   b) UNHCR field workers who helped Lina and other refugees in Mexico

   c) the Canadian government that refused entry to Lina's family in 1983

   d) members of the three Charlottetown churches that sponsored Lina's family

5. **a)** With a partner, discuss the following:

   i) Are the Pugwash Conferences less necessary today than they were in the past? How do general circumstances today differ from those after the Second World War? How are they the same? How do differing circumstances affect the goals of the conference?

   ii) Why is sustainable development especially important for young people?

   b) Imagine you have been asked to a Pugwash Conference, to represent the views of young people about the responsibilities of science with regard to world peace and the environment. Prepare either a written paragraph or a short speech giving your views.

6. Debate: Everyone should have a global worldview.

CONNECTING AND EXTENDING

7. Use the research model given in Figure 14.13 (page 221) to find out more about one of the following topics. You may wish to complete the activity as a jigsaw, by assigning different topics to different students and then combining the information you have collected in a single display.

   a) the 1951 Geneva Convention

   b) the work of the UNHCR

   c) refugee camps

   d) the current situation in Lina Garcia's home country, Guatemala

   e) Lina Garcia is Mayan, a member of one of Latin America's Aboriginal nations. Find out more about the Mayan culture. You could compare it with the culture of an Atlantic Canadian Aboriginal nation.

   f) the Mexican government's attitude towards, and treatment of, refugees

   g) the Canadian government's current policy on refugees

   h) refugees in your community or province

Becoming a Contributing Member of the Global Community

Many of us are actively involved in our local communities — through school activities or youth groups, perhaps. How can we become involved in the global community? How can we become effective, contributing global citizens? Here are some suggestions:

♦ Take an interest in other people. Individuals and communities can learn from each other.

♦ Learn about the world. Knowledge, understanding, and appreciation of other cultures will allow you to make sound judgements about global issues.

♦ Promote world peace. Start by helping resolve conflicts around you.

♦ Promote the rights of children (see page 263) and all other human rights.

♦ Protect the environment. Do what you can to reduce pollution and conserve natural resources.

- Prepare for your future. Keep global trends in mind while preparing for your own life's work.

- Choose your career carefully. Avoid work that promotes war, violates people's rights, or damages the environment.

- Make your opinions known. Write to newspapers; to your municipal, provincial, and federal government representatives; to corporations. When appropriate, join or organize a public meeting.

- Volunteer. Support charities and other organizations that work to improve the global community. You could volunteer your time, give money, or help to raise funds.

Figure 17.13 In India, hosts often go out of their way to make sure that visiting family members are made comfortable. For example, family members might give up their bedrooms to visiting relatives. How might knowing about these values affect your own attitudes?

EXPLORATIONS

CONNECTING AND EXTENDING

1. Review newspapers, magazines, and television for current global issues. Choose one of the suggestions above for becoming an effective contributing member of the global community that might help in one of the issues you have seen. Then do it!

SEEING THE BIG PICTURE

1. Make a diagram, illustration, collage, or cartoon to represent your view of the world.

2. Assume you were in charge of the world for a period of ten days. What would you do? Be sure to base your answer on the view of the world you have described in Activity 1 above.

3. You may not be in charge of the world, but you know you are in charge of your own actions. Individuals and small communities are the building blocks of the global community. What can you do to think globally and act locally? Try to focus on some of the goals you identified in Activity 2 above. For example, you might arrange for a used clothing drive, using a poster campaign or announcements in places of worship. Once you have made your list, choose the most practical suggestion from it. With your classmates, act on this suggestion.

OUR VIEWS OF THE WORLD

CHAPTER 18

Our Global Connections

Figure 18.1 *Above*: Bob Geldof sings at the Live Aid concert. His efforts convinced millions of people that they could be contributing global citizens.

> "When you look out and see Earth...something comes to life for you, an incredible emotion. You realize that it's a total planet.... You realize we need all the resources of every culture."
>
> Roberta Bondar, astronaut

In 1985, Irish rock star Bob Geldof took a step that changed the way millions of people related to the world. Geldof was horrified by images he saw on television of people dying from the effects of a serious famine in Ethiopia. Determined to help, he organized the "Live Aid" concert. Rock stars from many countries donated their time to perform in a massive concert that was held simultaneously in locations on either side of the Atlantic, and broadcast live around the world by satellite. Money raised by the concert and recordings of it went to help the victims of famine. Young people everywhere were drawn into the "Live Aid" effort; they watched the concert, they bought the recordings, they raised money for victims of famine in countless other ways. They confirmed Geldof's belief that we all have a responsibility to the people of the world; we all have a part to play.

- Since "Live Aid," other rock stars have helped people in need in similar ways. What other efforts do you know about? Why are rock stars in a powerful position to help?
- What is the role of Atlantic Canada in efforts like these?
- In what ways does our well-being involve cooperation with the national and global community?

A Vision of the Future

Bob Geldof was able to have such an impact partly because he had a vision of the future. He believed there were alternatives to the reality he saw. He had a vision of the way things could be — even of the way things *should* be.

In this chapter we will look at some developing trends in the way Atlantic Canadians relate to the world. As you read about our global connections in a number of important areas, think about the following questions:

◆ What is the *probable* future for Atlantic Canadians as global citizens?
How is our region likely to develop, in terms of physical environment, culture, economics, technology, and interdependence?

◆ What is the *preferable* future?
What would be the ideal, or best, way for our region to develop? If you could make a "wish list" for the future of the region, what developments would you include?

Source: Adapted from G. Pike and D. Selby, *Global Teacher, Global Learner* (London: Hodder and Stoughton, 1988), p. 13.

You will return to these questions through the chapter. Based on your answers, you will consider one other important question: What can we do to make our preferable future a reality?

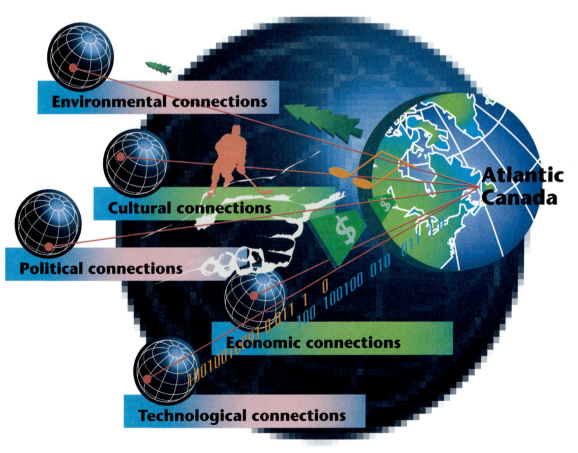

Figure 18.2 How is Atlantic Canada part of the global community? This diagram shows some of our connections. The future of our region lies in developing all of these connections.

OUR GLOBAL CONNECTIONS 271

OUR ENVIRONMENTAL CONNECTIONS

Astronauts who have circled the earth often marvel at its fragile beauty. From a distance, they are able to appreciate how earth's many distinct natural systems function within one whole interconnected system supporting life. Microorganisms, plants, and animals are all part of a solar-driven cycle of energy and nutrients provided by earth, air, and water. In spite of the natural ability of these systems to sustain themselves, the actions of humans often pose serious threats to the finely tuned set of checks and balances that exist within nature. Furthermore, environmental problems know no boundaries. Problems that originate in one country often affect others.

Table 18.1 Some global environmental problems

Acid rain
Destruction of forests
Production of greenhouse gases
Thinning of the ozone layer
Household, commercial, and industrial garbage
Pollution of land and water by industrial waste

Effects of acid rain

- Harmful to surface water and ground water
- Harmful to soil and plant life
- Harmful to animals, especially aquatic life
- Erodes buildings, monuments, and statues

Rock with high carbonate levels — such as limestone, dolomite, and marble — as well as fine-textured soils with high carbonate levels have the ability to neutralize acid rain. Rock with high concentrates of silica — such as granite, gneiss, sandstone, and quartzite — have the lowest capacity to neutralize acid.

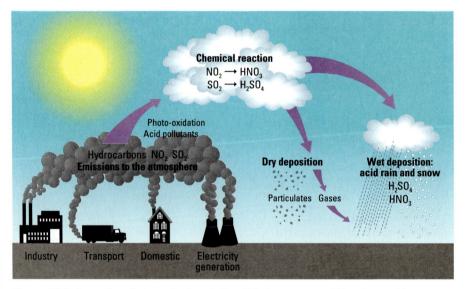

Figure 18.3 Formation of atmospheric pollution. Winds can carry acid-bearing moisture over large distances, so many areas suffer from acid rain produced by industrial activity elsewhere.

Addressing Environmental Issues

Individual efforts: Most Atlantic Canadians are aware of the "3 Rs": Reduce, Reuse, Recycle. In many places, blue box programs allow residents to separate recyclable garbage such as cans, bottles, and newspapers.

Education: Schools and environmental organizations have aimed to educate the public through school programs, media, and books.

Conservation: Through a well organized system of provincial and national parks, natural areas of particular value in the Atlantic provinces and other parts of Canada are protected. Many other countries protect their natural heritage in similar ways, and the UN encourages conservation through its World Heritage Site program.

Sustainable development: Industries in many parts of the world are encouraged to practise sustainable development.

NGOs: Organizations such as the Worldwatch Institute and Pollution Probe campaign for protection of the environment.

International efforts: International conferences to discuss the environment are held regularly, and aim to involve all of the world's countries.

CASE STUDY

RAISING THE IRVING WHALE

In September 1970, the *Irving Whale*, an oil barge, sank 60 km off West Point, Prince Edward Island. Government and the public were aware that oil was leaking from the wreck, but at the time, few Canadians realized the dangers posed by the PCBs (polychlorinated biphenyls) in the barge's heating system. These oily liquids were once widely used in industry as heat transfer fluids, wax extenders, and electrical insulating fluids.

In 1973, the international Organization for Economic Co-operation and Development (OECD) asked its members to restrict their use of PCBs. Researchers suspected that they caused many ill effects on mammals, fish, and birds. In 1977, 1980, and 1985, the Canadian government passed a series of laws severely limiting the use of PCBs. All this time, the *Irving Whale* was lurking on the seabed like an environmental time bomb.

It was only after plans were under way to raise the *Irving Whale* that the public became aware of the PCBs on board. That was in July 1995. Though the process of raising the barge would itself be hazardous, the government decided to go ahead. Fisheries and Oceans minister Brian Tobin announced, "The presence of PCBs in the barge's heating system underlines the importance of proceeding with the project and removing this threat to the Gulf of St. Lawrence and its resources."

"Pollution — including PCBs — touches us indirectly by affecting the health and survival of our resources, posing both ecological and economic risks. In addition, because contaminants can accumulate in our foods, we can be directly affected. Chemicals that cause ill effects on sea creatures can, in the same way, affect our health."

Dr. Usha Varanasi, Dalhousie University, Halifax, Nova Scotia.

Figure 18.4 Raising the *Irving Whale*

Weather kept the project from proceeding in 1995, but in July 1996, the *Irving Whale* was finally raised. Several months later it was reported that about 80 percent of the *Irving Whale's* PCBs had leaked out before the lift. Probably they escaped into the ocean in 1970, when the barge sank. This was bad news.

PCBs from the *Irving Whale* are only part of a much bigger problem. The North Atlantic Ocean is a major PCB "sink," holding 50 to 80 percent of the world's total. Although Canada and other North Atlantic nations began severely limiting PCB use in the 1970s, less industrialized nations keep using them. And PCBs know no boundaries. Those used in warmer, southern countries tend to disperse into the air and condense over colder, northern waters. As a result, the countries of the world are looking at ways of cooperating to manage the use and storage of such chemicals. In a variety of efforts, partly sponsored by the United Nations, industrialized and less industrialized countries are beginning to work together on environmental issues.

Explorations

REVIEWING THE IDEAS

1. Make a web diagram entitled "Atlantic Canada's connections with the world." On a large piece of paper, use about a quarter of the area to show common environmental concerns around the world. Include information from this chapter, from the rest of this book, and from general knowledge. You will be asked to add to this diagram through the chapter.

APPLYING YOUR SKILLS

2. Start a "What if" chart similar to the one below to think about some future possibilities for Atlantic Canada in the global community.

What if…	How Atlantic Canada might be different

In your chart, list some possible consequences of the following scenarios. Add some of your own "what if" scenarios based on the themes of this chapter.

What if…

a) All Atlantic Canadians practised the "3 Rs"?

b) Countries of the world agreed to drastically reduce their output of carbon dioxide and other atmospheric pollutants?

c) Emissions of atmospheric pollutants increase?

d) Forests around the world continue to be cut at the present rate?

ANALYZING AND REFLECTING

3. Clearing of the rainforest has caused much heated debate among industrialized and less industrialized countries. Environmentalists argue that governments in countries that have tropical rainforests should limit the destruction. Others argue that these countries have the right to develop their resources and improve their standard of living. Give opinions of the issue from the viewpoint of the following:

a) An importer of rainforest wood in an industrialized country

b) An official from a Canadian forestry company

c) A minister of industry and development from a country that has tropical rainforests

d) A manufacturer of medical products that require rainforest plants or animals

e) A representative of an environmental organization

CONNECTING AND EXTENDING

4. a) Research the effects of an environmental problem in your province. What is the source of the problem? What is the impact of the problem on the land, water, or built environment? What is the global impact? What solutions have been suggested?

b) Prepare a report or display of your findings.

Our Cultural Connections

As Atlantic Canadians increase their interaction with other people around the world, they have opportunities to learn from other cultures and to share their own culture with the people they meet. Cultural connections can have an impact on social life, values and beliefs, the economy, politics, education, and more. As you read some examples of cultural connections, think about the benefits they bring.

Heritage and Tradition

Figure 18.5 Greek Orthodox Church in Halifax. Heritage connects many Atlantic Canadians with other parts of the world, and influences their religion, traditions, and values.

Sports

Figure 18.6 Team Canada at the Special Olympics for athletes with disabilities. Many Atlantic athletes hope to compete in international events, including world championships, the Commonwealth Games, and the Olympics.

Arts and Entertainment

Jazz festival draws talent from Africa

Exhibition of Egyptian artifacts to open

France's cultural ministry honours five Canadian authors

Beijing Opera on Tour

Figure 18.7 The Riverdance troupe, from Ireland and the United States, won enthusiastic acclaim for their presentations of Celtic music and dance. Atlantic fiddlers and other musicians have been part of a revival of Celtic music and dance in many parts of the world.

Travel

Figure 18.8 Charlottetown, Prince Edward Island. Atlantic Canada has always been a popular destination for vacationers from other parts of Canada. In recent years, it has also attracted visitors from many other countries. In addition, Atlantic Canadians are travelling much more than ever before, for business, family contacts, and leisure. What evidence do you see of the impact of travel and tourism in your province? What plans do you have for future travel?

Education

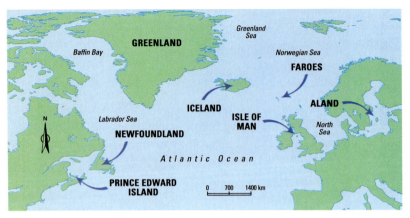

Figure 18.9 Students at the Institute of Island Studies at Prince Edward Island University can now study in a North Atlantic Islands Program, run in conjunction with an educational institution in Stockholm, Sweden. Students focus on the islands shown here, to study ways of encouraging positive development in public policy and business in the seven islands.

DID YOU KNOW…?

Many Atlantic educators are involved in international student programs that encourage students from other parts of the world to study in schools in the region. In some cases, students arrive on exchange programs that also allow Atlantic Canadians to study abroad.

EXPLORATIONS

REVIEWING THE IDEAS

1. Add to your web diagram of "Atlantic Canada's connections with the world," showing cultural connections. Include information from this chapter, from the rest of this book, and from general knowledge.

APPLYING YOUR SKILLS

2. Continue your "What if" chart on future possibilities for Atlantic Canada in the global community. List possible consequences of the scenarios below. Add some of your own "what if" scenarios based on our cultural connections.

   What if…

   a) Atlantic Canada was able to attract more immigrants?

   b) Atlantic Canada becomes an important centre for the music industry?

   c) Atlantic Canada continues to attract many more visitors?

   d) International student exchange programs became much more common?

ANALYZING AND REFLECTING

3. What role does travel play in promoting cultural understanding? Work in a group. Give some opinions from the viewpoints of the following people:

   a) an international student completing his or her studies in Atlantic Canada

   b) an Atlantic Canadian student participating in an international event

   c) a business person who travels extensively

   d) a politician or embassy official who deals with foreign affairs

CONNECTING AND EXTENDING

4. **a)** List ten jobs in your community that are related to the travel industry.

   b) If you wanted to encourage someone to visit your community, what attractions or activities would you mention?

   c) Choose a place anywhere in the world you would like to visit. Briefly describe the attractions of this destination, how you would get there, and what the cost would be. Outline an itinerary for the trip. If possible, use the Internet to find suitable locations.

Our Political Connections

Canada is known around the world for its efforts to promote world peace and understanding among nations. The information that follows shows just some of the political connections that connect us with the countries of the world.

Foreign Aid

Like many other industrialized countries, Canada assists less industrialized nations. **Short-term aid** is given to countries during natural disasters such as earthquakes, droughts, or famines. **Long-term aid** helps countries develop their economies.

Canada benefits from aid programs, too. Aid programs help to ensure world peace. In addition, when conditions improve, less industrialized countries can provide a source of materials for Canadian manufacturers, a market for finished products, and opportunities for investment.

Figure 18.10 Canadian armed forces leave from Halifax. Canadian peacekeepers have participated widely in UN operations. Bases in Atlantic Canada often serve as staging points for contingents heading overseas.

Table 18.2 This list shows some of the international organizations of which Canada is a member.

The United Nations
The Commonwealth
La francophonie
North Atlantic Treaty Organization (NATO)
North American Air Defence (NORAD)
Group of Seven (G-7)
The World Trade Organization (WTO; formerly GATT)
North American Free Trade Agreement (NAFTA)
Organization of American States (OAS)
Organization for Asia-Pacific Economic Cooperation (APEC)

Figure 18.11 Trade talks can sometimes be used as an opportunity to press for human rights in countries where abuses are known to have occurred. This cartoon shows Canada's Minister for External Affairs Lloyd Axworthy during trade talks with China, with a "hidden agenda" of human rights. Why might this approach be more effective than introducing human rights as the main agenda?

Table 18.3 The Canadian International Development Agency (CIDA) was set up by the federal government to coordinate all Canadian aid projects. CIDA provides aid according to the criteria shown here.

- The main object of CIDA is to encourage economic development.
- Aid is to be granted to the countries that need it most.
- Aid should help people acquire the skills they need to solve development problems for themselves.

Human Rights

Many Canadians believe it is important to take a stand on human rights. In some cases, trade can be a powerful tool. For example, the Canadian government lobbied other countries to impose sanctions on South Africa, contributing to the dismantling of the apartheid system in that country. What is Canada's track record on human rights? How might we improve our record?

CASE STUDY

THE COADY INTERNATIONAL INSTITUTE

The Coady International Institute is an NGO based at St. Francis Xavier University in Antigonish, Nova Scotia. It began in the 1930s, when several priest-professors including Dr. M.M. Coady and Dr. Jimmy Tompkins helped Maritimers organize themselves through cooperatives in areas such as fishing, agriculture, housing, and savings and credit. The movement soon attracted attention from other countries, and in 1959, the Coady International Institute was founded to provide people in less industrialized countries with the knowledge and skills to help themselves improve their living conditions. Today, the institute trains government officials, community organizers, and educators from around the world. The article below describes just one of the projects in which it has been involved.

Table 18.4 Some programs run by Coady Institute graduates

- Sri Lanka: Evaluating a special project to help fishers develop a sustainable fishery
- Dominica: Helping the Aboriginal Carib community develop a model for self-government
- India: Helping women earn incomes through small enterprises
- Kenya: Helping nomadic tribes improve their standard of living without giving up their traditional lifestyle
- Ghana: Teaching farmers how to store maize and new techniques in sheep rearing, poultry raising, and bee keeping, so that they have enough food for their needs as well as surplus to sell at local markets

The Coady Institute and community health

In recent years, the less industrialized countries have cut their infant mortality rate and raised life expectancy dramatically. This achievement is largely due to community projects that have improved water and sanitation, provided immunization, and promoted better nutrition. Yet there are still many areas where health care services and education are urgently needed. The Coady Institute and partner organizations throughout Asia, Africa, Latin America, and the Caribbean have been bringing people together to provide for their own health care needs.

In Kenya, for example, women in rural areas are promoting the health of their communities. Sister Imelda Akongo, a graduate of the Coady Institute, works with women leaders of small communities to develop an awareness of good nutrition and sanitation practices.

Sister Imelda works in an area that has the highest infant mortality rate in the country. A clinic to educate mothers of malnourished children has been set up in one town, but many rural mothers do not have access to transportation, so they cannot reach it.

Through workshops, however, women leaders from surrounding villages are learning how to grow small vegetable gardens at home to improve their family's diet, and how to motivate their neighbours to do the same.

Figure 18.12 Sister Imelda Akongo (left) encourages people in rural areas to take more responsibility for their own medical needs by learning how to practise preventive health care.

EXPLORATIONS

REVIEWING THE IDEAS

1. Add to your web diagram of "Atlantic Canada's connections with the world," showing political connections. Once again, include information from this chapter, from the rest of this book, and from general knowledge.

APPLYING YOUR SKILLS

2. Continue your "What if" chart on future possibilities for Atlantic Canada in the global community. List possible consequences of the scenarios below. Add some of your own "what if" scenarios based on our political connections.

   What if...

   a) A Canadian was chosen to be Secretary-General (the chief official) of the United Nations?

   b) Canada establishes closer political and economic ties with countries of the Commonwealth?

   c) Canada increases foreign aid?

   d) Several Asian countries open consuls, trade missions, or tourist offices in the Atlantic region?

ANALYZING AND REFLECTING

3. In recent years there has been much debate about whether or not Canada should reduce or increase its foreign aid. Research and debate the issue.

CONNECTING AND EXTENDING

4. a) Research the purpose and some of the activities of one of the organizations shown in Table 18.2.

   b) Prepare a report or display of your findings.

OUR ECONOMIC CONNECTIONS

Today's global economy is bringing many exciting opportunities for individuals and businesses. Economic connections have become important for a number of reasons:

- **Regional specialization.** Regions export their goods and services to locations where those goods and services are not produced. At the same time, they import goods they do not produce at home. Atlantic Canada, for example, exports fish products that are in demand elsewhere. At the same time, we import fruits such as kiwi, grapes, pineapples, and oranges that do not grow here.
- **Location.** Neighbouring countries or regions often trade heavily with each other. Relatively short distances between neighbours help reduce transportation costs.
- **Competitiveness.** Countries compete to gain a share of the global market. To produce reasonably priced goods and services, regions try to make the best of their assets, be they natural resources, a skilled work force, or high-tech services.

Industry	Percent of total imports
Non-conventional crude oil	29.46
Motor vehicles and parts	11.97
Machinery and equipment	8.64
Conventional crude oil and natural gas	4.58
Fish products	3.46
Construction, mining, and materials handling equipment	2.78
Primary smelting and refining equipment	2.63
Refined petroleum products (except lubricating oil and grease)	2.63
Electrical industrial equipment	2.37
Industrial organic chemicals	1.84

Table 18.5 Atlantic Canada: Top ten imports, by industry, 1995. Compare these imports with Atlantic Canada's top exports, as shown in Table 12.3 on page 188. What can you tell about regional specialization?

Figure 18.13 Atlantic Canada: Selected major imports and exports, percentage share for top eight countries, 1995

FOCUS ON FIGURE 18.13
1. What evidence is there that Atlantic Canada imports raw materials and then processes them for export?
2. What evidence is there of regional specialization in Atlantic Canada?

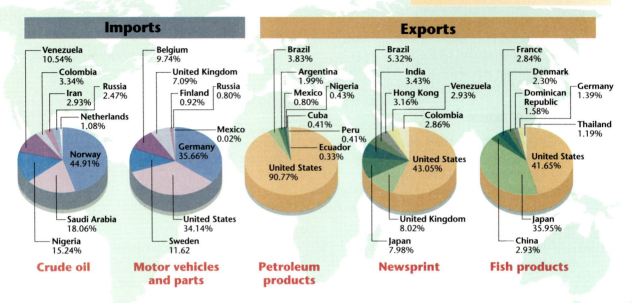

Imports

Crude oil
- Venezuela 10.54%
- Colombia 3.34%
- Iran 2.93%
- Russia 2.47%
- Netherlands 1.08%
- Norway 44.91%
- Saudi Arabia 18.06%
- Nigeria 15.24%

Motor vehicles and parts
- Belgium 9.74%
- United Kingdom 7.09%
- Finland 0.92%
- Russia 0.80%
- Mexico 0.02%
- Germany 35.66%
- United States 34.14%
- Sweden 11.62

Exports

Petroleum products
- Brazil 3.83%
- Argentina 1.99%
- Mexico 0.80%
- Nigeria 0.43%
- Cuba 0.41%
- Peru 0.41%
- Ecuador 0.33%
- United States 90.77%

Newsprint
- Brazil 5.32%
- India 3.43%
- Hong Kong 3.16%
- Venezuela 2.93%
- Colombia 2.86%
- United States 43.05%
- United Kingdom 8.02%
- Japan 7.98%

Fish products
- France 2.84%
- Denmark 2.30%
- Germany 1.39%
- Dominican Republic 1.58%
- Thailand 1.19%
- United States 41.65%
- Japan 35.95%
- China 2.93%

FOCUS ON TABLE 18.6
1. Which Canadian products are used around the world?
2. What do you think draws companies to set up branch plants in Canada?
3. How can foreign investment benefit Atlantic Canada?

Table 18.6 Multinationals are corporations that operate in more than one country. In nearly all cases, head offices are located in industrialized countries, and branch plants are located in a wide variety of other locations. This table shows some multinational companies operating in Canada.

Company	Products	Location of Parent Company
Bombardier	snowmobiles, sea-doos, aerospace and other transportation equipment	Canada
Canada Safeway	groceries	United States
DeBeers	diamond mining	South Africa
General Motors of Canada	automobiles	United States
Husky Oil	petroleum	Japan
IBM Canada	computers	United States
Irving Group	oil and lumber products	Canada
McCain Foods	frozen foods	Canada
Michelin	tires, travel guides	France
Nestle Canada	groceries and confectioneries	Switzerland
Philips Electronics	electronics	Netherlands
Royal Insurance Group of Canada	insurance	United Kingdom
Siemens Group	telecommunications	Germany
Suzuki Canada	motorcycles, automobiles, boat motors, all-terrain vehicles	Japan
Toshiba	computers and other electronics	Japan
Twinpak	manufacturing equipment	Australia

INTERDEPENDENCE

Table 18.7 Some global careers. The global economy offers many new and exciting job opportunities. What kinds of skills and attitudes are required in these jobs?

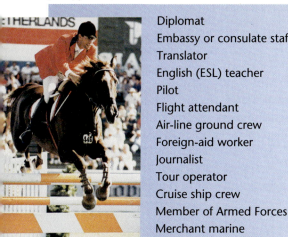

Diplomat
Embassy or consulate staff
Translator
English (ESL) teacher
Pilot
Flight attendant
Air-line ground crew
Foreign-aid worker
Journalist
Tour operator
Cruise ship crew
Member of Armed Forces
Merchant marine
Professional sports player
Sales representative for a Canadian company
Buyer for a Canadian company
Import/export agent
Engineer for companies that fill contracts abroad
Geologist for companies that fill contracts abroad

Old Ties Mean New Business

It's an historic homecoming with a tourism and business kick that's expected to boost the economies of Nova Scotia and Louisiana. Almost 250 years after their tragic deportation from Nova Scotia, Acadians from Louisiana will return to their ancestors' homeland this week, when a Cajun trade group starts a six-day trade mission.

"We're looking forward to welcoming the group. These people don't just share a common heritage, they share a desire to do business globally. Nova Scotia Acadians and Louisiana Cajuns have a tremendous chance to strengthen their cultural ties and use them as a springboard for increased trade," says Economic Renewal Minister, Richard Mann.

Source: Halifax Chronicle-Herald, September 12, 1996.

Figure 18.14 Many fast-food restaurants are American multinationals.

OUR GLOBAL CONNECTIONS

Explorations

REVIEWING THE IDEAS

1. Add to your web diagram of "Atlantic Canada's connections with the world," showing economic connections. Once again, include information from this chapter, from the rest of this book, and from general knowledge.

APPLYING YOUR SKILLS

2. Continue your "What if" chart on future possibilities for Atlantic Canada in the global community. List possible consequences of the scenarios below. Add some of your own "what if" scenarios based on our economic connections.

    What if...

    a) NAFTA (see Chapter 12) were extended to include all the countries of South America?

    b) Atlantic Canadians built more economic connections based on their cultural origins?

    c) More Atlantic Canadian businesses made partnerships with companies abroad?

ANALYZING AND REFLECTING

3. There has often been debate about the value of multinational corporations. Critics claim that multinationals take advantage of low wages and large markets in less industrialized countries and then funnel their profits back to their home bases in the industrialized world. Supporters point out that they create millions of jobs and invest in the economies of less industrialized countries. Work in a group. Assume a Canadian frozen food manufacturer wants to open a plant in a tropical country to process fruits and fruit juices. Give opinions of the issue from the viewpoint of the following:

    a) An executive of the Canadian company

    b) A worker in the Canadian company

    c) A local manufacturer who wants to open his or her own plant in the country

    d) The minister for industry and development in the tropical country

    e) A worker in the tropical country

CONNECTING AND EXTENDING

4. Choose one of the careers shown in Table 18.7 or any other "global career" that appeals to you. Find out the following:

    a) What opportunities exist in that field?

    b) What skills and qualifications are required?

    c) How can you obtain the necessary skills and qualifications?

    d) What can you do now to prepare yourself for this career?

Our Technological Connections

Atlantic Canada is basing many of its plans for the future on technology. Technology will have a role to play in the economy, in communication, in education, in health care, and in many other aspects of everyday life.

Figure 18.15 Diagnostic Chemicals Limited in Prince Edward Island supplies products such as enzymes for biological research, diagnostics, and environmental testing worldwide.

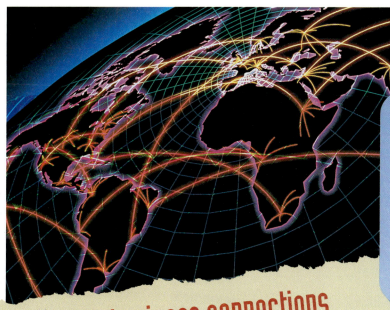

> **DID YOU KNOW...?**
>
> Canada's first Direct-To-Home (DTH) satellite service was approved in 1997. The DTH system beams television programs directly from satellites into your home. It can carry far more than any cable, opening the possibility of receiving up to 500 channels beamed from countries around the world! The system uses digital signals to produce top quality pictures and sound.

High-tech business connections

Networking. It's a business practice as old as business itself. And more and more it's being done on a global scale.

Take Hermes Electronics, for instance. At its large, modern factory in Dartmouth, Hermes specializes in technically complex electromechanical products, mostly for the defence industry. And in a market where even many of the big multinationals can't survive, Hermes does it very well. It's one of only six companies to build sonobuoys for the world's navies.

Of those six, Hermes has forged production partnerships with two: Ultra Maritime in the United Kingdom and Thompson Sintra in France.

"We're partnering with companies that need complicated products built at a reasonable price," says Paul Adlakha, Director of Business Development. "That could be anything from mobile satellite antennae to power supplies for aircraft entertainment systems. We can meet their requirements because we've got the sophisticated manufacturing facilities, the technical expertise, and the skilled labour, all at relatively low cost."

Operating out of Nova Scotia has other advantages as well. The location is a real selling point to international partners looking for an entry to the North American market opened up by the NAFTA. The world-class ports make shipping cargo easy and inexpensive. And the time zone allows telephone contact with both Los Angeles and London, England, on the same working day.

Source: *The Nova Scotia Advantage: The International Partner.*

Figure 18.16 Participants in Ottawa watch as Aline Chrétien, wife of Canada's prime minister, and Hilary Rodham Clinton, wife of the US president, visit a school in Washington, DC, to take part in an Internet session between students at that school and students at a school in Ottawa. Computers were loaned to the students in Washington especially for the visit, but Canadian telecommunications giant Northern Telecom later donated computers to the school, after hearing of its lack of equipment.

Injured Internet man saved by NB woman

John Elliott, 24, who has cerebral palsy, was at home in Didcot, in central England, playing Scrabble with a friend in New Brunswick on the Internet when he suffered a spasm. He fell off his chair, dragging the computer keyboard to the floor with him.

"All of a sudden I lost him," said Carla MacInnis Rockwell, his cyberspace Scrabble partner 5000 km away in Stanley, New Brunswick. "Then he came back on channel and said he fell out of his wheelchair. I asked him if he was hurt, and he was able to indicate that he was with a Y."

MacInnis Rockwell phoned the local RCMP and explained that her friend in England needed help. An officer contacted an Interpol officer at RCMP headquarters in Ottawa, who notified the Interpol office in London.

They launched an eight-hour search for Elliott, involving emergency services in the United States, Canada, and Britain. Calls were also made to police in the Isle of Man to find Elliott's Internet provider. Eventually they traced him through a journalist in his home town, and were able to come to his aid.

Source: Canadian Press, April 11, 1997.

Figure 18.17 Students on a field trip in the Seychelles, a group of islands off the east coast of Africa. A Newfoundland company, Softwaves Educational Software Inc., has developed a multimedia CD-ROM for use in the Seychelles. The program educates students about the environment and sustainable development in the area.

Figure 18.18 A student in Dalhousie, New Brunswick, works in the Family Treasures Project, which allows students to explore their family heritage and share it electronically with students in other provinces.

EXPLORATIONS

REVIEWING THE IDEAS

1. Add to your web diagram of "Atlantic Canada's connections with the world," showing technological connections. Once again, include information from this chapter, from the rest of this book, and from general knowledge.

APPLYING YOUR SKILLS

2. Continue your "What if" chart on future possibilities for Atlantic Canada in the global community. List possible consequences of the scenarios below. Add some of your own "what if" scenarios based on our technological connections.

    What if…
    - Every home in the Atlantic provinces had a computer with an Internet connection?
    - Atlantic Canada, as a region, began to specialize in communications technology?
    - Educational materials produced in Atlantic Canada were used all over the world?
    - Most Atlantic Canadian homes received 500 television channels from around the world?

ANALYZING AND REFLECTING

3. While information technology has become a part of everyday life, it has also raised several important issues. Research and discuss one of the following topics or any other relevant issue. Try to propose solutions to the problems you identify.

    a) Communications technology is posing a threat to privacy.

    b) The Internet is a powerful vehicle for hate messages and pornography.

    c) Computers are expensive. People who cannot afford to buy them do not have equal access to information.

Conclusion: A Personal Vision

In 1996, the choir from Holy Heart of Mary School from Newfoundland travelled to Vienna, Austria, to give a series of concerts and participate in an international music competition. The choir won a prestigious award for their performance, but many choir members felt they gained more than a prize. Andrea Boone, a Grade 12 student, was a member of the choir. Here is her account of the experience and what she learned from broadening her horizons.

Figure 18.19 Andrea Boone went on to study music at Memorial University in St. John's, Newfoundland.

As a member of the choir, this trip meant a great deal to me, as it did to all choir members. It took a lot of hard work and dedication on the part of everyone involved.

We were all very excited about visiting Europe. For most of us it was our first time there; for some, the first time on an airplane. We were filled with wonderful expectations. We knew how beautiful the countryside would be, and how sacred and spectacular the old Gothic cathedrals would seem. We knew we would experience a world completely different from our own.

Our first concert was in a tiny chapel in a countryside community. We performed many pieces that night, a lot of them Newfoundland folk songs. A most unusual thing happened during one song "Ah, the Sea." In this music you can almost hear the sounds of nature, the running waves of the ocean crashing against the shore. While we were singing the song, the lights flickered, the shutters and the front door slammed back and forth in a sudden gust of wind, and a violent rain shower fell. At the end of the song everything was silent — the audience and the choir, and the rain had stopped just as quickly as it had started. We all knew at that moment we had just shared a very important part of our culture with the audience. Even though they did not understand our language, we had communicated through our music.

As a group and individually, we all learned a lot — not only from the trip, but from the entire year of working together. When we competed in Vienna, nobody cared about the trophy or being dubbed "the best in the world," for we knew there is no such thing as "the best in the world." We cared only about giving the best performance we had ever given. We learned that goals and dreams are attainable, no matter how big they are, as long as you are forever willing to be a student — to open your mind to new ideas and possibilities and to work hard for your aspirations.

SEEING THE BIG PICTURE

1. a) Divide your class into five groups. Focus on one of the five themes of this chapter, which are based on the main topics of this text. Return to the questions you considered near the start of the chapter. Complete a chart similar to the one below, for your group's theme.

b) Combine the ideas of the five groups into one large chart.

	Probable future	**Preferable future**
Physical setting/environment		
Culture		
Economics		
Technology		
Interdependence		

2. Choose a preferable scenario for your theme. Explain what you can do to make this scenario a reality. Consider at least one step to take in each of the following roles:
   a) as a member of your local community
   b) as a Newfoundlander/Labradorian/Prince Edward Islander/Nova Scotian/New Brunswicker
   c) as an Atlantic Canadian
   d) as a Canadian
   e) as a citizen of the global community

3. Choose just one step from the list you have made. Do it: you can make a difference! Here are some possibilities:
   - Volunteer in your community: Work with children, people learning English as a second language, or seniors.
   - Volunteer at a food bank or hospital.
   - Volunteer to help an NGO.
   - Raise money to help people in need in other parts of the world.
   - Join the youth wing of a political party.
   - Get involved in a public health-awareness program.
   - Get involved in an anti-racist program.
   - Establish connections with people in other places — within Atlantic Canada, in other parts of Canada, or in other parts of the world.
   - Get involved in protecting the environment: plant trees, promote conservation and the "3 Rs," find out what you can do to help endangered species.
   - Volunteer to help in local businesses where you might learn about other connections with the world.

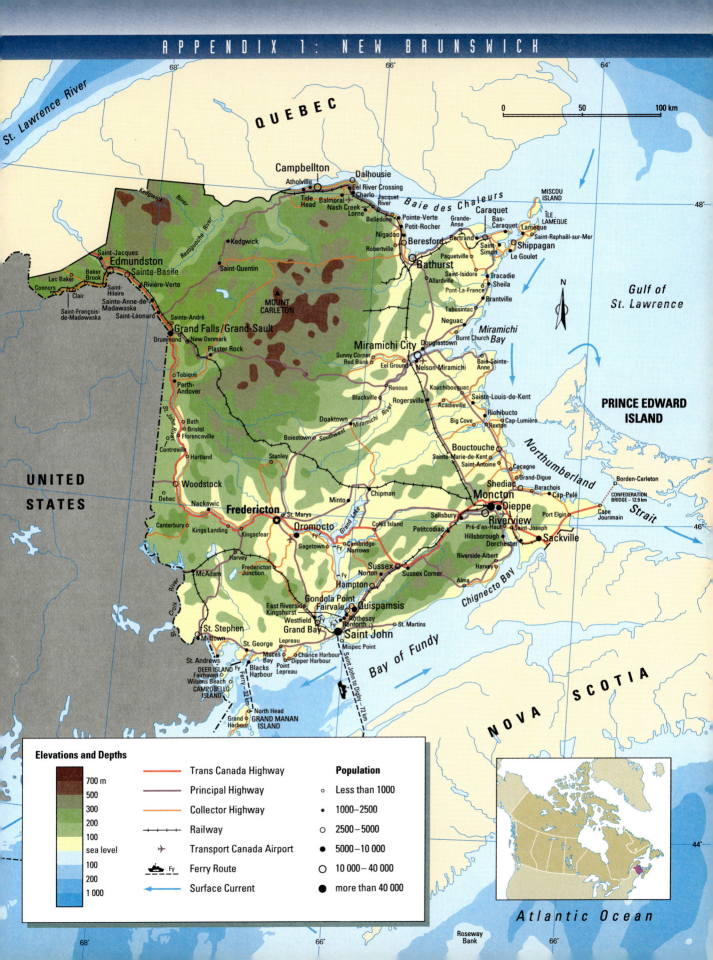

APPENDIX 2: NOVA SCOTIA

APPENDIX 3: PRINCE EDWARD ISLAND

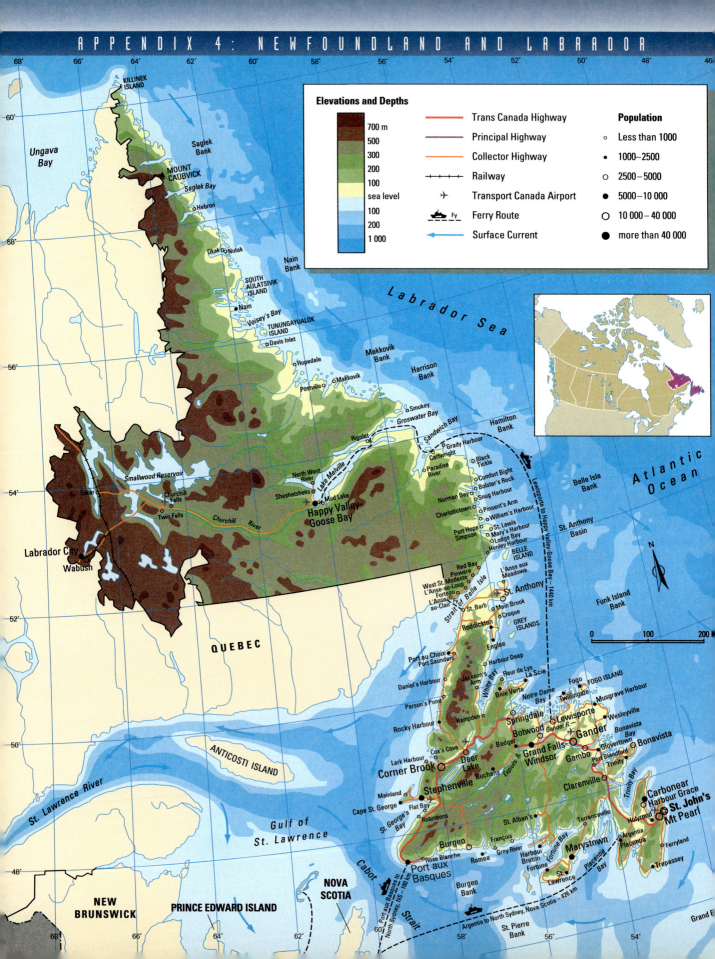

Glossary

absolute location the exact location of a point on the earth's surface identified by coordinates

Acts laws passed by government

air masses large volumes of air with similar temperature and moisture conditions throughout

allowable annual cut the limited amount of timber that can be cut in a province each year

anthropologists social scientists who study human cultural characteristics

aquaculture the raising and harvesting of aquatic fish and/or plants in a controlled environment; sometimes called "fish farming"

assimilate become absorbed into the mainstream culture

baby boom the sharp increase in birth rate in Canada after World War II; people born in this period are known as **baby-boomers**

bay a partially enclosed body of water with an opening to the sea

bills proposals for new laws

bogs wetlands composed mainly of peat, featuring mosses, low shrubs, and sparse black spruce or tamarack

brain drain migration of highly educated individuals away from an area

branch plant a plant or factory owned by a company based elsewhere

cabinet selected members of parliament from the governing party responsible for most major decisions; members of the cabinet, called "ministers," must have the support of the majority of the elected representatives in order to govern

candidates individuals who run in an election, hoping to become the elected representative for the riding

caucus the members of parliament or assembly in the same party

climate average conditions of temperature, precipitation, humidity, air pressure, and wind

collective bargaining process of negotiation whereby a union bargains on behalf of workers with employers on issues that affect them

commodity article or raw (unprocessed) material that can be bought or sold

competition in economic terms, providing goods or services at a lower price or providing better value than other producers

compound interest interest added to the original invested or borrowed sum, so that further interest is calculated on the original amount plus interest already earned

computer automation the use of computers to control tasks done automatically by machine

computer integrated manufacturing (CIM) a system that links various machines so that production is automatically controlled to match output at each stage of the process

computer-aided design (CAD) a system of developing and testing designs on a computer screen

condensation the process by which moisture in the air changes to liquid or solid form (e.g., rain, clouds, snowflakes); see also **orographic, convectional,** and **frontal condensation**

constituents people who live in a riding or constituency

consumers customers or people who will buy an economic good or service

Continental Arctic air a cold, dry air mass originating in northern Canada

contour plowing plowing along slopes instead of up and down, to prevent soil run-off in heavy rains

contributing cultures cultures of groups within a society that are distinct from the mainstream but contribute to and enrich the mainstream

convectional condensation condensation formed by air rising when warmed from below

coordinates the points at which lines of latitude and lines of longitude intersect; coordinates are used to indicate the absolute location of a point on the earth's surface

crop rotation growing one crop on land where another, different crop was grown previously

cultural diversity variety and differences among cultures

cultural features features on the earth's surface caused by human activity

cultural group a group of people who share a common culture

demand the quantities of an economic good or service that consumers will be willing and able to buy at certain prices

discriminate treat a particular group, or member of a particular group differently or unfairly

disparity inequality or gap in wealth or quality of life

distance education teaching students who are at distant locations; distance education courses may rely on mailing materials, televised classes, or on-line communication

diversify become more varied; used especially in connection with the economy; **diversification** is the process of making the economy more varied

downsizing reducing the staff and services of a business

economics the study of our efforts to satisfy our unlimited wants through the use of limited resources

election the process of voting for representatives, open in Canada to all citizens 18 years of age or older

emotional needs human needs for conditions such as friendship, love, a sense of belonging, and self-expression

entrepreneurs people who turn ideas into businesses

ethnic group a group of people who share racial background, which can include country of origin; there can be different ethnic groups within a racial group

ethnocentrism belief that one's own culture is better than other cultures

factory-freezer trawler large vessels equipped to catch, process, package, and freeze fish on board

farming a set of activities devoted to producing food and other products from arable land

federal government national government dealing with concerns of the nation as a whole

fens wetlands composed mainly of peat, and fed by streams, so that the water table is at or above the surface of the peatland

fiord a long, narrow inlet of the sea, bordered by steep mountain slopes

first-stage manufacturing initial processing of raw materials

folding a bending of the earth's crust to form physical features such as mountains

folk art paintings and other artistic work done by untrained artists, usually depicting everyday life in a simple, direct style

formal groups organized groups that contribute to a culture

free trade the elimination of tariffs, quotas, and restrictions on imported goods

front the leading edge of an air mass, bringing characteristics of the air mass that drives it and often sudden changes of temperature

frontal condensation condensation formed when warm, moist air rises over cold air

genetic engineering a form of science in which the basic characteristics of a plant or animal are changed by removing, splicing, and altering genes

Global Positioning System (GPS) a type of technology that uses satellites to give the precise location of any place on the earth's surface

global village term coined by Marshall McLuhan to describe the impact of communication and transportation technologies, which have reduced the distance between different parts of the world

global world-view a view of the world that encourages cooperation and the development of common interests between countries

goods commodities or products such as sugar, lumber, or computer chips; an **economic good** is an item scarce enough to command a price

Gross Domestic Product (GDP) the total value of goods and services produced within a given area in a given year; **GDP per person** or **per capita** is the average GDP, or the total GDP divided by the number of people who live in the area

Gulf Stream an Atlantic Ocean current from the south, bringing warmth to the southeastern waters of the Atlantic provinces

gulf a very large area of the sea partially enclosed by land

hidden market potential customers, not being served by existing goods and services

high pressure an atmospheric condition caused by the sinking of cool air

impulse buying making a purchase without weighing the opportunity cost

informal groups groups of people who meet casually for a common purpose

Information Age term used to refer to the modern era with its sophisticated communications systems

institutions organizations with social, educational, and religious purposes

interdependence the interconnection of all people and all living things

interest money paid for the use of money lent

judicial system the legal or court system that allows people to challenge actions that threaten their rights

Labrador Current an ocean current from the north, bringing cold waters to much of the Atlantic coast

lake a large body of water surrounded by land

large-scale map map showing a large amount of detail

life-long learning constant training and upgrading of skills

lifestyle the way people live within their culture

lines of latitude imaginary lines on the surface of the earth, drawn east-west to show distances north or south of the equator

lines of longitude imaginary lines on the surface of the earth, drawn north-south from pole to pole to show distances east or west of the Prime Meridian

linguistic group a group of people who share a common language

lobbying trying to persuade politicians to support a cause, usually by supplying them with information; lobbying can be done by individual **lobbyists** or by **lobby groups**

long-term aid aid intended to help countries develop their economies

low pressure an atmospheric condition caused by the rising of warm air

mainstream culture the general culture of the majority of the people

Maritime Polar air a cool, moist air mass originating in the Atlantic, east of Newfoundland

Maritime Tropical air a warm, moist air mass originating in the Caribbean

marketing selling an idea, product, or service

marshes wetlands either seasonally or permanently covered by water; stands of sedges, grasses, and rushes are divided by channels that carry off water very slowly

material culture the physical objects produced and/or used by a society

media means of communication, including newspapers, magazines, television, and radio

meteorologists weather experts who study conditions in the atmosphere, often for the purpose of making weather forecasts

ministers members of parliament/assembly selected to be part of the cabinet

modern legends stories about ordinary people, often in urban settings, describing events that are unusual, but could — in theory — happen

mountain a mass of land that is significantly higher than the surrounding area

multicultural encouraging contributing cultures to maintain their identities while still participating in the economic, political, and social life of the society

multinationals corporations that operate in more than one country, usually with head offices located in industrialized countries and branch plants in a wide variety of other locations

municipal government a form of local council, concerned with looking after local matters under the direction of the provincial government

natural resources naturally occurring substances such as water, soil, forests, fish, and minerals that are useful to people

Non-Governmental Organizations (NGOs) organizations not controlled by government that work to improve social, environmental, or economic conditions

non-material culture elements of culture that are not physical, including spoken language, religious beliefs, and ways of behaving

non-renewable natural resources non-living things; once a non-renewable resource is used up, it cannot be replenished except over an extremely long period of time

North American Free Trade Agreement (NAFTA) free trade agreement including Canada, the United States, and Mexico

ocean a very large body of salt water; the world's oceans include the Atlantic, the Pacific, the Indian, and the Arctic.

ocean currents the movement of water in the world's oceans

offshore outsourcing producing goods in another country and then transporting them back to be sold

opportunity cost something given up in order to obtain something else

Opposition members of parliament who do not belong to the governing party

oral tradition the use of storytelling to pass history, morals, and lessons learned over time from one generation to the next

orographic condensation condensation formed when air cools as it rises over high ground

outmigration movement away from an area

outsourcing hiring part-time, temporary, and contract workers to supply goods or services to a business if and when they are needed

physical distance the measured distance between two points

physical features features on the earth's surface caused by natural forces, e.g., river valleys

physical needs human needs for items and conditions that sustain life, such as food, water, clothing, shelter, and safety

political activists individuals who use direct action to draw attention to and promote a cause

political party an organized group formed by individuals who have similar views on public issues

pond a fairly small body of still water

popular culture culture shared by many groups in Western society and, increasingly, around the world; includes popular music, television shows, brand-name clothing and foods, etc.

population density a measurement of the number of people living on a given area of land, found by dividing the population of a given region by the area of that region

population distribution patterns of settlement, including compact, clustered, loose-knit, and linear

project teams teams of workers with specialized skills and knowledge who work on specific projects

precipitation rain, snow, and any other forms of water particles that fall from the atmosphere

prejudice a view based on previously held ideas, rather than on knowledge or experience

premier leader of the largest party in the assembly, which forms the provincial government

primary industry economic activities in which people use, extract, or harvest natural resources

prime minister leader of the largest party in the House of Commons, which forms the federal government

principal a sum of money invested or borrowed, not including additional interest payments

producers sellers or people who produce an economic good or service

provincial government government dealing with the concerns of the province

quality of life standard of living based on criteria such as GDP per person, birth rate, life expectancy, literacy, and equality

quaternary industry economic activities that involve specialized technology and information

racism mistreatment of people on the basis of race, place of origin, or ancestry; belief that one group of people is inferior or superior to another

radiosonde a piece of equipment carried into the atmosphere by a small balloon in order to collect information about the upper atmosphere

rapid prototyping (RP) the use of computers to make models of objects designed on screen

rate of interest amount of interest paid on a borrowed or invested sum expressed as a percentage

rationed limited, given in fixed allowances

refugees people who have had to flee their homes because they are in danger as a result of their race, religion, or political beliefs or as a result of natural disaster

region an area sharing common physical or cultural features that make it different from other areas

regional disparity wealth gap among provinces or regions of the country

relative location the general location of a place described in terms of distance or direction from another place

religious group a group of people who share a common religion

remote sensing technology sensors that allow people to collect information from a distance

renewable natural resources natural resources that have the ability to replace themselves

representative democracy form of government in which individuals are chosen to represent a riding, constituency, or group

representatives individuals elected by voters to represent a geographic area in government

resources available stocks or supplies on which we can draw to meet our needs and wants

riding a constituency or area that is represented in parliament

rites ceremonies that are part of a traditional culture

river a long, narrow body of water that flows in a channel from high to low land and empties into a body of water such as an ocean or a lake

rural areas sparsely settled areas in the countryside

rural pull conditions in rural areas that attract people from urban areas

rural push conditions in rural areas that encourage people to leave

scale a measurement that relates distance on a map to actual distance on the ground

scarcity shortage; in economic terms, something is scare (or in short supply) when someone will buy it for a price

seasonal employment employment for only part of the year in industries tied closely to weather and seasons

second-stage manufacturing use of processed materials to make finished products

secondary industry economic activities that process raw material into finished goods

Senate the upper house of the federal legislature; members are appointed, not elected

services work done for other people; for example, barbers, musicians, or architects provide services; an **economic service** is a service scarce enough to demand a price

short-term aid aid given to countries in response to specific disasters such as earthquakes, droughts, famine, or political unrest

small-scale map map showing a small amount of detail

social unrest angry discontent and disturbance in an area, verging on revolt

socialization the process of learning behaviour that is considered suitable in your culture

stereotype an image that represents all members of a group as being the same

strategic alliance a partnership formed to help companies develop by working together to produce goods or services that neither company could produce alone

substitution effect tendency of customers to buy cheaper substitutes for expensive products

supply the quantities of an economic good or service that producers will be willing and able to supply at certain prices

sustainable development the use of resources to meet our present needs without reducing the ability of future generations to meet theirs

swamps wetlands occurring where water collects in pools, and containing mature trees such as black spruce

tariffs taxes paid on imported goods

technology the application of knowledge and skills to make goods or to provide services; technology refers to both **products** (the tools and machines that people use to convert natural resources into items they need) and **process** (the methods people use)

telemedicine the use of computer systems that help medical staff see, diagnose, and treat patients from a distance

telework activities of people who use computers to connect with other computers in order to do their work

tertiary industry economic activities that provide services rather than goods

time distance the time it takes to get between given points

time zone a band, roughly 15 degrees of longitude in width, in which all clock time is the same

topographic map a detailed map showing physical and cultural features and the elevation, or height, of the land

trading bloc an organization that encourages trade among member nations, especially by free trade

traditional culture culture passed down from one generation to the next

traditions customs, beliefs, opinions, and stories passed down from one generation to another

transfer payments federal government program to transfer some of the taxes collected in provinces with the highest GDPs to provinces with lower GDPs

urban centre a settlement that has at least 1000 people and a population density of 400 or more persons per square kilometre

urban pull conditions in urban areas that attract people from the countryside

urban push conditions in urban areas that encourage people to leave

values ideas, beliefs, and ways of behaving that are valuable or important to people of a particular culture

weather conditions of the atmosphere over a short period

weather radar stations locations where radar is used to analyze conditions in the atmosphere

wetlands waterlogged areas that are neither solid ground nor open water, including bogs, fens, swamps, and marshes

INDEX

A
Aboriginal peoples, 55, 56
Absolute location, 3
Acadian culture, 105
Acadian World Conference, 106
Acadians, 58
Acid rain, 272
Acts of Parliament, 128
Adams, Wayne, 130, 131
ADI Limited, 213
Aerospace Industry Association (AIANS), 193
African-Canadian communities, 61
Africville, 62
Agents of socialization, 74, 75
Air masses, 38, 39
Algonquian nations, 56
Allowable annual cut, 162
Anne of Green Gables, 100, 101
Anthropologists, 68
Aqua Bounty Farms, 210
Aquaculture, 161, 229
Assimilation, 83
Atlantic-Allstar Genetics, 190
Atlantic Canada Opportunities Agency (ACOA), 187
Automobiles, 215

B
Baby boom, 186
Backbenchers, 129
Ballot, 127
Bar/bat mitzvah, 72
Bargain in good faith, 136
Bay, 27
Bell, Alexander Graham, 196, 197
Beothuk, 56
Bills (in Parliament), 128
Black Cultural Centre for Nova Scotia, 91
Bogs, 26
Borrowing money, 150, 151
Brain drain, 186
Branch plant, 180
Breathing Wall, 243
Brig, 204
Brundtland Report, 264
Budget, 148, 149

C
Cabinet, 129
Canadian International Development Agency (CIDA), 184, 277
Candidates, 127
Canoe, 202, 203
Careers, 178, 248, 249, 281
    coast guard captain, 6, 7
    entrepreneur, 176, 177
    ESL teacher, 84
    journalist, 137
    meteorological technician, 45
    owner of high-tech company, 244, 245
Caucus, 129
Celtic culture, 71
City road map, 12
Clear cutting, 234, 235
Climate, 37
Coady International Institute, 278
Cod fishery, 227
Collective bargaining, 136
Communications technology, 218, 219
Compact disks (CDs), 252
Competition, 159
Computer-aided design (CAD), 250
Computer automation, 251
Computer chip, 198
Computer integrated manufacturing (CIM), 250, 251
Condensation, 34
Confederation Bridge, 216, 217
Confirmation, 72
Conners, Janet, 135
Constituencies, 125
Constituents, 125
Consumer credit, 150
Consumers, 144
Continental Arctic air, 38
Contour plowing, 167
Contributing cultures, 78
Coordinates, 3
Court system, 134
Cultural changes, 81
Cultural diversity, 68, 82
Cultural features, 8
Cultural group, 82
Culture, 67

D
Dairy farmers, 237, 238
David, 204
Daylight saving, 23
Demand, 144
Dialogue, 77
Diamond Fields Resources, 164, 165
Direct-To-Home (DTH) satellite services, 283
Discovery Hill, 164
Discrimination, 87
Disparity, 183
Distance education programs, 223, 224
Diversification, 119, 170, 187
Downsizing, 241

E
East Coast Music Awards (ECMA), 93–95
Economic good or service, 144
Economics, 141
Ecotourists, 113, 114
Elections, 127
Enterprising skills, 249
Entrepreneurs, 176
Equator, 3
Ethnic group, 82
Ethnocentrism, 56
European settlement, 57–60
Exports, 188

F
Factory-freezer trawler, 228, 229
Fairy tales, 96, 97
Farming, 163, 237, 238
Fashion, 104
Federal government, 124, 126
Fens, 26

Fiord, 25
First-stage manufacturing, 169
Fish farming, 161, 229
Fisheries, 227–229
Fixed link, 216, 217
Fog, 38
Folding, 24
Folk art, 97
Folk tales, 97, 98
Food Technology Centre (FTC), 173
Foreign aid, 277
Forests, 162, 234–236
Formal groups, 76
Free trade, 189
French fries, 170, 171
Front, 38

G
GDP, 158
Generic skills, 248
Genetic engineering, 210, 211
Ghiz, Joe, 83, 117
Global careers, 281
Global economy, 279
Global environmental problems, 272
Global positioning system (GPS), 5
Global village, 258
Global world-view, 262
Glooscap, 30
Goods, 141
Gravity Base Structure (GBS), 188
Greenhouse effect, 41
Gross domestic product (GDP), 158
Gulf, 27
Gulf Stream, 38

H
Health in the workplace, 243
Hermes Electronics, 283
Hibernia, 188
Hidden market, 146
High pressure area, 36
High-tech revolution, 198
HMCS Halifax, 206, 207
Human rights, 277

I
Immigration, 63, 87, 88
IMP Aerospace, 193

Impulse buying, 143
Industrialized countries, 183, 184
Informal groups, 76
Information Age, 220
Innu, 56
Instrumar Limited, 192
Interdependence, 262
Interest, 150, 151
Internet, 220, 221. *See also* World Wide Web (WWW)
Inuit, 56, 112–114
Inuit art, 114
Investment credit, 150
Irish Festival, 83
Irving Whale, 273

J
Joe, Rita, 90
Judicial system, 134

K
Katimavik, 260
Knowledge-based economy, 174, 175

L
Labour unions, 136
Labrador Current, 38
Labrador Inuit, 112–114
Lake, 26
Large-scale map, 12
Latitude, 3
Law of supply and demand, 144
Lebanese immigrants, 115
LeBlanc, Roméo, 105
Less industrialized countries, 183, 184
Life-long learning, 248
Lifestyle, 110
Line scale, 20, 21
Lines of latitude, 3
Lines of longitude, 3
Linguistic group, 82
Live Aid concert, 270
Lobby groups, 133
Lobbying, 133
Lobbyists, 133
Lockout, 136
Long-term aid, 277
Longitude, 3
Low pressure area, 36
Loyalists, 59, 61
Lunenburg, 118–121

Lunenburg Bump, 120
Lunenburg cure, 119

M
Maillet, Antonine, 105
Mainstream culture, 78
Manufacturing, 169
Manufacturing Technology Centre, 251
Maps, 10–12
Maritime Polar air, 38
Maritime Tropical air, 38
Marketing, 251
Marshes, 26
Maslow, Abraham, 109
Material culture, 71
McCain Foods, 170, 171
Mechanical tree harvesting, 236
Media, 133
Mediation, 77
Members of Parliament (MPs), 125
Members of the House of Assembly (MHAs), 125
Members of the Legislative Assembly (MLAs), 125
Meteorologists, 43
Milking cows, 237, 238
Mining, 162, 164, 232
Ministers, 129
Modern legends, 99
Montgomery, Lucy Maud, 100
Mountain, 24
Multiculturalism, 83
Multinationals, 280
Municipal governments, 124
Music CDs, 252
Mussels, 191

N
Natural resources, 159
Networking, 283
New economy, 174, 175
Night work, 110
Non-governmental organizations (NGOs), 134
Non-material culture, 71
Non-renewable natural resources, 230
North American Free Trade Agreement (NAFTA), 189
North, countries of the, 184
Northern cod, 227

O

Occupations, 109–111, 246–248, 281
Ocean currents, 38, 39
Offshore outsourcing, 242
On-line services, 222
Opportunity cost, 142, 143
Opposition, 128
Oral tradition, 96
Outmigration, 52, 186
Outsourcing, 241, 242

P

Personal finances, 147–149
Physical distance, 21
Physical features, 8
Plain, 25
Political activists, 133
Political party, 128
Politics, 124
Pond, 26
Popular culture, 72
Population density, 50
Population distribution, 50
Potato farming, 166–168
Precipitation, 37
Prejudice, 87
Premier, 129
Primary industry, 157, 159
Prime Meridian, 3
Principal, 150
Problem solving, 77
Producers, 144
Provincial government, 124
Provincial road map, 12
Pugwash Conferences, 265

Q

Quality of life, 183, 184
Quaternary industries, 157, 172

R

Racism, 86–90
Radiosonde, 46, 47
Rainforests, 235
Rapid prototyping (RP), 250
Rate of interest, 150
Rationing, 142
Red Crane Enterprises, 104
Refugees, 63, 88, 266
Region, 19
Regional disparity, 185
Relative location, 3
Religious group, 82
Remote sensing technology, 237
Renewable natural resources, 230
Representative democracy, 125
Representatives, 125
Resonant vibration, 200
Resources, 141
Ridings, 125
Rites, 72
River, 26
Robotics, 233
Rule of 72, 150
Rural areas, 51
Rural push, 51

S

Sabian Cymbals, 180–182
Saint John Shipbuilding Company Ltd. (SJSL), 206, 207
Satellite technology, 8
Satire, 87
Scale, 20
Scarcity, 141
School culture, 76
Seasonal employment, 185
Second-stage manufacturing, 169
Secondary industries, 157, 169
Service industries, 121
Services, 141
Ship building, 205–207
Short-term aid, 277
Sick-building syndrome, 243
Site, 53
Small-scale map, 12
Snow, 34, 35, 204
Sobey, Gordon, 166–168
Socialization, 74
South, countries of the, 184
Speaker, 129
Squires, Gerald, 102, 103
St. John River Society, 31
Stereotype, 86
Storytelling, 96–99
Strategic alliances, 187, 192, 242
Street maps, 12
Strike, 136
Substitution effect, 146
Sunshine, 38
Supply, 144
Sustainable development, 230
Swamps, 26
Syliboy, Alan, 104

T

Tariffs, 189
Technological time line, 199
Technology, 197
TecKnowledge Health Care Systems, 222
Telemedicine, 222
Telemedicine and Educational Resources Agency (TETRA), 224
Telework, 242
Tertiary industries, 157, 172
Time distance, 22
Time zones, 22, 23
Titanic, 14–16
Topographic map, 10, 11, 28
Trade, 188
Trading blocs, 189
Traditional culture, 72
Traditional stories, 97
Traditions, 72
Transfer payments, 187
Twin cities program, 54

U

Unions, 136
United Nations, 262, 263, 266
Urban centres, 51
Urban pull, 51
Value added, 157
Values, 71
Voisey's Bay, 164, 165
Voting, 127

W

War brides, 63
Water transportation, 202, 203
Weather, 37
Weather radar stations, 43
Wetlands, 26, 27
Whip, 129
Wilson House, 120
Wind, 36
Work, 109–111, 243, 246–248, 281
World peace, 262
World Wide Web (WWW), 251. *See also* Internet

CREDITS

Every reasonable effort has been made to trace the ownership of material reprinted in this book and to make full acknowledgement for its use. The publisher would be grateful to know of any errors or omissions so they may be rectified in subsequent editions.

Literary material

Page 14: "The Titanic": From E.J. Pratt, *Complete Poems*, edited by Sandra Djiva and B.G. Moyles, University of Toronto Press, 1989. Page 33: "Storm Closes School": Damon Clarke: *The Northern Pen*, March 25, 1987, p. A3. Page 34: "Canadian January Night": Reprinted with the permission of Stoddart Publishing Co. Limited, Don Mills, ON. Page 62: "The Spirit of Africville" by Terry Dixon, Formac Publishing Company Limited, 1992. Page 71: "Celtic culture in Cape Breton": © Silver Donald Cameron, 1996. Reprinted by permission. Page 90: "I lost my talk": Used with permission of Ragweed Press, Charlottetown, PEI, from *Song of Rita Joe: Autobiography of a Mi'kmaq Poet*, 1966. Page 116: "As Birds Bring Forth the Sun" by Alistair MacLeod. Used by permission, McClelland & Stewart, Inc. *The Canadian Publishers*. Page 140: "If I had \$1 000 000": Written by Step Page/Ed Robertson. Copyright Treat Baker Music/WB Music Corp. Used by permission. Page 174: "Atlantic Canada moving toward knowledge-based economy": courtesy *The Evening Telegram*.

Statistics Canada information is used with the permission of the Minister of Industry, as Minister responsible for Statistics Canada. Information on the availability of the wide range of data from Statistics Canada can be obtained from Statistics Canada's Regional Offices, its World Wide Web site at http:/www.statcan.ca, and its toll-free access number 1-800-263-1136.

Visuals

Chapter 1 1.2: Top: G. Motil/First Light. Bottom: Canapress. 1.4: © Barrett & MacKay Photo. 1.5: City of Fredericton, Tourism. 1.6: Tourism Nova Scotia. 1.7: D. Minty. 1.10: Courtesy of Capt. R. Lundrigan. 1.12: Canada Centre for Remote Sensing. 1.13: V. Last/Geographical Visual Aids 1.14: This map is based on information taken from the National Topographic System map 11L/06 and 11L/11©1991, 5th.ed. Her Majesty the Queen in Right of Canada with permission of Natural Resources Canada. 1.15: J. Sylvester/Tourism PEI. 1.16: City of Fredericton, Tourism. 1.17: City of Fredericton, Tourism. 1.18, 1.21, and 1.22: IMAX Corporation/Undersea Imaging International Ltd. & TMP (1991) Limited Partnership.

Chapter 2 2.1: Top: © Barrett & MacKay Photo. Bottom: "Maritime Provinces Aerial Slides and Guide." © Atlantic (Maritime) Provinces Education Foundation. Reprinted with permission. 2.3: This data is based on information taken from the GeoAccess Division © 1996. Her Majesty the Queen in Right of Canada with permission of Natural Resources Canada. 2.5: Hutchison House/Peterborough Historical Society. 2.7 and 2.8: D. Minty. 2.10: "Maritime Provinces Aerial Slides and Guide." © Atlantic (Maritime) Provinces Education Foundation. Reprinted with permission. 2.11: Tourism New Brunswick. 2.12: Centre for Topographic Information/Natural Resources Canada. 2.13: Tourism New Brunswick. 2.14: "Maritime Provinces Aerial Slides and Guide." © Atlantic (Maritime) Provinces Education Foundation. Reprinted with permission. 2.15: © Barrett & MacKay Photo. 2.17: Wesleyville: Night Passage Bennets High Island, 20" x 32", 1981, original etching by David Blackwood.

Chapter 3 3.1: D. Clarke, *The Northern Pen*. 3.5: Communications New Brunswick. Page 36: Atlantic Wind Test Site. 3.11: J. Sylvester/Tourism PEI. Page 40: City of St. John's. 3.16: R. Kenyon. 3.17 and 3.18: Environment Canada. 3.20 and 3.21: C. Kennedy/CFB Gagetown.

Chapter 4 4.1: Top: Tourism Nova Scotia. Bottom: J. Sylvester/Tourism PEI. Tab. 4.1: Reproduced by authority of the Minister of Industry, 1997, Statistics Canada, Population Density of the Atlantic Provinces *adapted* from Urban Areas, Catalogue No. 93-305, 1991. 4.3: Courtesy Provincial Archives of Newfoundland and Labrador (NA 2298). 4.4: The Carleton University History Collaborative, Canadian Museum of Civilization, Mercury Series, History no.44, 1993, page 41, figure I13. Tab. 4.2: Reproduced by authority of the Minister of Industry, 1997, Statistics Canada, Urban-rural Population in Atlantic Canada *adapted* from Urban Areas, Catalogue No. 93-305, 1991. Tab. 4.3: Reproduced by authority of the Minister of Industry, 1997, Statistics Canada, CANSIM database, Matrix No. 6365. 4.5: Fredericton Tourism. 4.8: National Archives of Canada. 4.11: Artist: Lewis Parker; commissioned by Canadian Heritage (Parks Canada), Atlantic Region. 4.12: Clyde Rose. 4.14: New Brunswick Museum, Saint John, N.B. 4.18: "The Spirit of Africville" by Terry Dixon, Formac Publishing Company Limited. 4.19: Canadian Army Photo; Courtesy of Public Archives of Nova Scotia G1066. 4.21: R. Hemingway. Unit 2 Page 65: Top right: First Light. Centre left: © D. Callis. Centre right: J. MacGregor/Federation Acadienne de la Nouvelle-Ecosse. Centre left: M5 Communications. Bottom right: Canapress.

Chapter 5 5.1: Left: New Brunswick Telegraph Journal. Right: B. Nielsen. 5.2: Adapted from Exploring World Cultures by R.Neering, S. Udukawa, and R. Kudicek, copyright © 1988. Reprinted with permission of ITP Nelson Canada. 5.3: LE ROCK STUDIO 5.4: Left: © Barrett & MacKay Photo. Top: Saudi Aramco Photo. Bottom: Patricio Baeza/International Development Photo Library. 5.6: Fredericton Tourism. 5.7: David Young-Wolff/Tony Stone Images. 5.8: © D. Callis. 5.9: K. Bruce Lane, Spectrum Corporation. 5.11: Courtesy Gabrielle Abrahams. 5.12: Bob Semple/New Media Services. Page 76: Comstock. 5.13: Earlscourt Child and Family Centre.

Chapter 6 6.1: Centre: S. Isleitson. Left and right: First Light/Steve Smith (left); Ken Straiton (right). 6.2: Top: First Light/Lee White. Bottom: Photo by L. Jenkins. 6.3: Courtesy of government of PEI/Brian Simpson. 6.4: Left: Multicultural Association of Nova Scotia — Annual Multicultural Festival. Right: © D. Callis. 6.5: Courtesy A. Foley Keats. 6.7: Salter Street Films Limited/22 Minutes Incorporated. 6.8: Vonnie Barron. 6.10 and 6.11: Used with permission of Ragweed Press, Charlottetown, PEI, from *Song of Rita Joe: Autobiography of a Mi'kmaq Poet*. 1996, p. 96. 6.12 and 6.13: Black Cultural Centre of Nova Scotia.

Chapter 7 7.1 Bottom & Top: G. Landry. 7.2 Top: Breakwater Books. Bottom: G. Landry. 7.3: Tony Caldwell. 7.4: Art Gallery of Nova Scotia. 7.5: L.M. Montgomery is a trademark of the Heirs of L.M. Montgomery INC., and is used with their permission. 7.6: © Barrett & MacKay Photo. 7.7: Bob Brammner/Prince Edward Island Tours. 7.8: M. Lyons/Gerald and Esther Squires with painting in progress. 7.9: *Resettlement*, Gerald Squires. 7.10: B. Berry. 7.11: M. France Coallier/The Montreal Gazette. 7.13: J. MacGregor/Federation Acadienne de la Nouvelle-Ecosse.

Chapter 8 8.1: Left: Marine Institute. Centre: A. Murchison. 8.3: Parks Canada. 8.6: B. Carter/National Geographic Society. 8.8: The Peary-Macmillan Arctic Museum, Bowdoin College. 8.9: M5 Communications. 8.10: NWT Archives/GNWT/G-1995-0C1: 3571. 8.12: David Weale Collection. 8.13: © P. J. Burden. 8.14: "Little Joe Ghiz and his Aunt" from the collection of Rose Ellen Ghiz. 8.15: "Bird's Eye View of Lunenburg", 1890. Public Archives of Nova Scotia, PANS Neg. no. OSPANS N-8573. 8.16: Fisheries Museum of the Atlantic, Lunenburg, NS. 8.17: Knickle's Studio and Gallery. 8.18: Terry James. 8.19: Sky-Shots Aerial Photography Inc. 8.20: Bill Plaskett.

Chapter 9 9.1: Left: M. Shark. Right: Bob Semple/New Media Services. Page 124: Left: CFB Halifax, photo by Cpl. R. Duguay. Centre: M. Shark. Right: City of St. John's. 9.2: Statistics Canada, "Population Statistics", Catalogue No. 91-002, Volume 10, Number 1, 1996. 9.3: Reprinted with permission from The Chronicle-Herald and the Mail Star. 9.4: Agora Excavation © American School of Classical Studies at Athens. 9.7: House of Commons. 9.8: Canapress/D. Ives. 9.9: Courtesy Wayne Adams. 9.10: Courtesy Shirley Bear. 9.11: Canapress/J. Young. 9.12: Reprinted with permission from The Chronicle-Herald and the Mail Star. 9.14: Courtesy Ian Hanomansing. Unit 3 Page 139: Top left: Richard Flynn. Top right: © Barrett & MacKay Photo. Bottom: NASA.

Chapter 10 10.1: R. Hemingway. 10.2: Richard Flynn. 10.3: Toronto Star. 10.5: Janet Gill/Tony Stone Images. 10.6: Gordon Beck/The Montreal Gazette. 10.11: Reprinted with permission — The Toronto Star Syndicate. Copyright: King Features Syndicate.

Chapter 11 11.1. Centre: R. Hemingway. Page 157: Top left and to right: © Barrett & MacKay Photo. Bottom left: Multicultural Health Education Program, Vancouver Health Department. Bottom right: Dept. of Industry Trade and Technology/Government of Newfoundland and Labrador. 11.2: © Barrett & MacKay Photo. 11.6: V. Last/Geographical Visual Aids. Page 163: © Barrett & MacKay Photo. 11.8: Voisey's Bay Nickel Company. 11.9 and 11.10: Courtesy Gordon Sobey. 11.15: Courtesy McCain Foods. Page 170: Comstock 11.17: Atlantic Provinces Economic Council 11.18: © Barrett & MacKay Photo. 11.19: First Light. 11.20: Courtesy Adeline Misener.

Chapter 12 12.1: Left: Robert Kenyon. Right: Courtesy Sabian Ltd. 12.3–12.9: Courtesy Sabian Ltd. 12.10: Robert Kenyon. 12.12: Roger Lemoyne/International Development Photo Library. 12.14: © Barrett & MacKay Photo. 12.15: Statistics Canada, "Changing Age Structure in Atlantic Provinces", from "Annual Demographic Statistics, 1995", Catalogue No. 91-213. 12.16: Greg Locke. Tab. 12.3: Statistics Canada, "Atlantic Exports, \$ Thousands, 1995" from "Exports by Country", Catalogue No. 65-003. 12.17: Canapress/T. Hanson. 12.19: Rod Stears/Port of Saint John. 12.21: Dept. of Industry Trade and Technology/Government of Newfoundland and Labrador. 12.22: R. Ritchi/Canadian Airlines. 12.23: Photo compliments of Spar Aerospace Limited. 12.24: NASA. Unit 3 Page 195: Top right: R. Watson/Tony Stone Images. Centre left and centre right: © Barrett & MacKay Photo. Bottom left: First Light.

Chapter 13 13.1: Top and bottom: Archival Collection, A.G.Bell N.H. Site, Baddeck, N.S. Centre: First Light/William Taufic. 13.2: Archival Collection, A.G.Bell N.H. Site, Baddeck N.S. 13.1: Top left: The Granger Collection, New York. Top right: Automobile Quarterly. Bottom: Reg Watson/Tony Stone Images. Page 199: Top left: The Granger Collection, New York. Bottom right: Archive Photos. 13.4: Left: Provincial Archives of New Brunswick, P5-243 PAN B (Taylor Collection). 13.5: Left: Jandec Inc. Right: Brian McFarlane Collection. 13.6: V. Last/Geographical Visual Aids. 13.7: Left: First Light/J. L. Pelaez. Right: Archive Photos. 13.8: Left: Chuck Kekler/Tony Stone Images. Right: Archive Photos. 13.9 and 13.11: The Mariner's Museum, Newport News, VA. 13.12: Courtesy of the Geological Survey of Canada. 13.13: The New Brunswick Museum. 13.14: R. McLean. 13.16: The New Brunswick Museum. 13.17: Maritime Museum of the Atlantic. 13.18–13.23: Saint John Shipbuilding. 13.24. Top left: First Light/Yoav Levy/Phototake NYC. Top right: World Perspectives/Tony Stone Images. Bottom: D. Minty. 13.25: A/F Protein Canada Inc. & Aqua Bounty Farms. 13.26: Archive Photos. 13.27: Reprinted with permission: Toronto Star Syndicate. Copyright 1997 Tribute Media Services.

Chapter 14 14.1 and 14.2: ADI Group Inc. 14.3: Top: British Airways. Bottom: Oceanex. Page 214: Photo courtesy Provincial Archives of Newfoundland and Labrador (N.A. 2298). 14.4: © Saturn Corporation, used with permission. 14.6: Photo by Boily. 14.7 and 14.8: © Barrett & MacKay Photo. 14.9: ©MAX. 14.10: Andrew Brookes/Tony Stone Images. 14.11: Canapress/A. Vaughan. 14.15 and 14.16: W. Butt.

Chapter 15 15.1: Left: Gord King. Right: D. Minty. 15.2: D. Minty. 15.3: G. King. 15.5: C. Bruce Morser/National Geographic Image Collection. 15.6: Dennis Minty. 15.10: M. H. Knox. 15.11: Canapress. 15.12: Nova Scotia Department of Natural Resources. 15.14: Temagami Wilderness Society. 15.16: D. Minty. 15.17: Right: Robert Ward. 15.18: Dan Murphy.

Chapter 16 Fig.16.3: Purolater Courier Ltd. 16.7: Rebecca Rose. 16.9: Courtesy Mona El-Tahan. 16.12: LE ROCK STUDIO 16.13: LE ROCK STUDIO 16.14: Dept. of Industry Trade and Technology/Government of Newfoundland and Labrador. 16.15 and 16.16: R. Hemingway. 16.19: Courtesy Manufacturing Technology Centre. 16.20: Copyright 1996 Netscape Communications Corp. All rights reserved.

Chapter 17 Page 256: Top: Brian Gauriloff/The Edmonton Journal. Cèntre: Joan Marcus. Bottom: Bill Frymire/Masterfile. 17.1: Top: First Light/J. Feingersh. Centre: First Light/K. Aitken. Bottom left: Erik Svenson/Tony Stone Images. Bottom centre: First Light/H. Studios. Bottom right: First Light/B. Peterson. 17.2: Bob Semple/New Media Services 17.3: Communications Canada. 17.4: Archive Photos. 17.5: Multicultural Health Education Program, Vancouver Health Department. 17.6: Brain Gauriloff/The Edmonton Journal. Page 261 Left: M. Shark. Right: Courtesy Avis Fitton. 17.7: Drawn by Tom Leimdorfer, Once Upon a Conflict, Education Advisory Program of Quaker Peace and Service, 1992. 17.8: Canapress/T. Hanson. 17.9: Archive Photo. 17.10: Tourism Nova Scotia. 17.11: Canapress/A. Grant. 17.12: Courtesy Lina Garcia. 17.13: Jagdish Agarwal.

Chapter 18 18.1: Left: Canapress. Right: D. Minty. 18.4: Environment Canada. 18.5: Bob Semple/New Media Services 18.6: Courtesy Special Olympics (Newfoundland) 18.7: Joan Marcus. 18.8: Brian McInnis/Tourism PEI. 18.10: Canadian Forces Photo. Fig .18.11: Reprinted with permission, Toronto Star Syndicate. 18.12: Coady International Institute. Page 281: Top left: Jayne Huddleston Photo. Centre: Air Canada. Top right: Canadian Forces Photo. Bottom left: City TV. Bottom right: Kathy Sperberg/International Development Photo Library. 18.14: Comstock/M. Roessler/H. Armstrong Roberts. 18.15: ©Barrett & MacKay Photo. Page 283 top: Bill Frymire/Masterfile. 18.16: Canapress/D. Lucasa. 18.17: D. Minty. 18.18: Courtesy Avis Fitton. 18.19: Courtesy Andrea Boone.

HRSB
Dartmouth Teachers'
Centre